This book will enable you to increase the perceptions of your present personality and so impress your subconscious mind by the attitude of your creative will that the subconscious will do for you what it is powerless to do except at second hand—change your body.

In its striking, in-depth interpretation of the symbology of the 22 Major Arcana cards, *The Rabbi's Tarot* will lead you to profound depths of self-development and spirituality.

You will learn how the practical occultist develops the Pineal and Pituitary glands by energized currents coming through the seven chakras, which are referred to in mystical Christianity as the seven golden candlesticks and the seven churches of Asia. When the Pineal gland is energized by the transmuted sex force, the result is the White Light, as depicted by the seven White Stars in the Tarot card The Star. This occult magic can be worked in your body and outside your body. It is also referred to as Cosmic Consciousness, Illumination, or Enlightenment.

The object of this book is not merely to show you the Laws of the Universe, but how these Laws work out in you. The teaching of the book is that the self-conscious, by assiduous endeavor, may bring into your body more and more of the superconscious in the form of the Cosmic Mind-Stuff. The symbols of the Major Arcana suggest how you set about realizing your own perfection. They show that we evolve only by desire, and that no matter what desire we cherish, it is but a stepping-stone to a higher one.

The Rabbi's Tarot is one of the most intense studies of the Major Arcana ever published. It is a must for all who work with the Tarot and for all who want to develop themselves to the utmost.

About Daphna Moore

Daphna Moore, co-author of *The Rabbi's Tarot*, has maintained a busy counseling practice in Lakewood, Colorado since 1980. Experienced in many methods of therapy, she is currently doing numerology readings throughout the world. Daphna has taught Personal Growth Workshops and Metaphysical Bible Interpretive classes, and she has studied massage therapy, polarity, aura balancing, and hypnosis. From 1972–1977 she was instructed (for her own personal growth) through automatic writing. Daphna enjoys conducting Question and Answer Open Forum Workshops, as she feels everything we do in life is a teaching/learning, learning/teaching experience. She is a member of the American Massage Therapy Association, American Hypnotherapy Association and is currently living in Lakewood, Colorado.

To Write to the Author

We cannot guarantee that every letter written to the author can be answered, but all will be forwarded. Both the author and the publisher appreciate hearing from readers, learning of your enjoyment and benefit from this book. Llewellyn also publishes a bi-monthly news magazine with news and reviews of practical esoteric studies and articles helpful to the student, and some readers' questions and comments to the author may be answered through this magazine's columns if permission to do so is included in the original letter. The author sometimes participates in seminars and workshops, and dates and places are announced in *The Llewellyn New Times*. To write to the author, or to ask a question, write to:

Daphna Moore
c/o THE LLEWELLYN NEW TIMES
P.O. Box 64383-572, St. Paul, MN 55164-0383, U.S.A.
Please enclose a self-addressed, stamped envelope for reply, or $1.00 to cover costs.

Llewellyn's New Age Tarot Series

THE
RABBI'S
TAROT

Daphna Moore

1992
Llewellyn Publications
St. Paul, Minnesota 55164-0383, U.S.A.

Cover Painting: Lissanne Lake

First Edition, 1989
Second Printing, 1992

Library of Congress Cataloging-in-Publication Data
Moore, Daphna, 1937–
    The rabbi's tarot: spiritual secrets of the tarot / by Daphna
Moore.
    p.   cm. - (Llewellyn's new age tarot series)
    ISBN 0-87542-572-o : $12.95
    1. Tarot.   I. Title.   II. Series.
BF1879.T2M655 1989
133.3'2424—dc19   89-2489
ISBN 0-87542-197-0

Llewellyn Publications
A Division of Llewellyn Worldwide, Ltd.
P.O. Box 64383, St. Paul, MN 55164-0383

With my love this book is dedicated to

Michael W.

Acknowledgements

I would like to give a very special thanks to Kay Woodburn. Also I would like to thank Mary Cassell, Ilsa Mitchell, W. Reed McIntyre, Kathy McIntyre, Shirley Monharis, Uri Neal, Lizabeth A. Moore, Robert Morris Williams, Jr., Todd Steiner, Gina, Alice, Jay, George Grindol, James Connley, Norv Morgan, and all of my clients who are too numerous to list. Each one of them together constitutes the channel through which this book is brought into being.

Contents

TRANSFORMATION

In the deep, deep caverns of your mind
You search endlessly for eternity,
Your hour of possession has come.
We, the spirits, go slowly,
Glad to emerge out of your way.
There, you had bound us with your will,
Fixed on cerebral, intellectual play.

On the waves that you rode giving all of your commands
To the unknown forces that you didn't understand,
They washed you away with one final sweep,
Taking your soul, seeming forever to keep.
Beyond perception more of you dies.
Spirit to spirit I speak to you beyond words I can't convey.

From antiquity I have been bound to you and you to me.
We've faced each other on the field of battle
And come to terrible blows.
We've ended up with a stalemate love,
Reserved only for formidable foes.
Looking now with wisdom you suddenly recall,
The subtle fascination and the ecstasy of it all.

After awhile a sudden calmness overwhelms your mind.
Could it be that your hour has come?
There is no more flood, nor rain, nor sorrow,
Only a soothing, calming, joy burns this rock to clay.
Who is it that lives in fear?
It is the soul who is afraid to go beyond that
Which his hands are touching and his thoughts attached to.

—Daphna Ruth Moore
1977

INTRODUCTION

The Tarot has survived for hundreds, perhaps thousands, of years under two guises. The first is as a gaming tool. There are numerous games possible with the Tarot, even though they are rarely used today. Of course the Minor Arcana, with one less face or court card per suit, still functions as a deck of playing cards. The only remaining sign of the Major Arcana in bridge decks or poker decks is the joker, a card obviously derived from the Fool.

The Tarot's second guise has been as a deck for divination. This statement may be surprising to many of the people reading this book, but read on. The Tarot has found a niche in the New Age as a tool for divination because it works so well in that function. In the past two decades literally hundreds of Tarot decks, and decks similar to the Tarot, have been published. The Tarot in its many forms is still increasing in popularity. Although there is some interest in collectability (for several decks are remarkable works of art), the main interest is in divination.

Divination is a noun that literally means "to make godlike." The symbols on the Tarot cards, and especially those on the 22 cards known as the Major Arcana, are far more than just drawings—they are truly archetypal images from what Carl Jung called our Collective Unconscious. Looking at these evocative images allows us to tap into the Collective Unconscious, which some people have equated with the *Akashic Records,* the mystical record of all events that ever were and ever will be. It is no wonder that as a divinatory tool the Tarot is so effective.

Although the Tarot has been around for an unknown length of time, its real surge in popularity began in 1910. Up until that time there had been some books about the Tarot published, as had been several decks. But there was no connection. In the year mentioned, Rider publications released a Tarot deck *and* book by the prolific writer, occultist, and member of the famous Hermetic Order of the Golden Dawn, A.E. Waite. This new deck, drawn in a popular and clear style by Pamela Coleman Smith and known as the Rider-Waite deck, is currently the most popular one available.

The deck was a departure from previous decks in that the cards of the Minor Arcana, previously strictly numerical, were each given a symbolic image after the fashion of the Major Arcana cards. This made them far easier to read for the beginner.

But in the world of occultism and metaphysics there are many methods of divination open to the student and practitioner. We should ask ourselves why the Tarot has received such popularity among serious students of the secrets of life and the multiverse instead of other divinatory systems, such as looking in a crystal ball, interpreting tea leaves, or reading the patterns of birds in flight.

The answer can be found in the book by Waite from 1910. In *The Pictorial Key to the Tarot* Waite uses the subtitle "Being Fragments of a Secret Tradition under the Veil of Divination." This was a little-noticed but important bit of information. As it turns out, the Tarot can be used for divination, but it can also be used for much more. I like to say that using the Tarot only for divination is like using a car only to store gasoline. Sure, both can be used for those purposes, but they can also be used for so much more.

The "Secret Tradition" Waite was talking about was the tradition of the Golden Dawn. That order, which originally flourished in the late 1800s and early 1900s, directly or indirectly influenced virtually every Western-oriented book on metaphysics and occultism over the last century. So what was this Secret Tradition?

Simply put, the Tarot, and especially the Major Arcana, can be seen as part of a map to the universe. And by following the Hermetic axiom, "As above, so below," that means the Tarot can be used to understand the physical and nonphysical universe as well as the psychology and psychic makeup of every person within it. Thus, the Tarot can function as a means of divination, a tool for understanding human action and psychology, a way to understand the physical world, and a method for understanding the astral, etheric, and higher planes of existence. No wonder the Tarot is still held in high regard by so many individuals and groups around the world today. It can be used for divination and much more.

Perhaps the first law of occultism is to "know yourself." It is said that this was written over the entrances to the mystery temples of Egypt and Greece. In a very real sense, that's what *The Rabbi's Tarot* is all about. As the text states, Tarot is a vehicle for "increasing the perceptions of your present personality and for developing a higher personality even of the same type. It is a vehicle for so impressing your subconscious by the attitude of your creative will . . . [to] change your body." This book reveals how you can develop the pineal and pituitary glands by energized currents coming through the body's power centers, known in the East as *Chakras.* This leads to the experience called Cosmic Consciousness, Illumination, or Enlightenment. Amazingly, what has been described just scratches the surface of what you will find in this marvelous book.

Daphna Moore gives the story that the original work on this book was done by a rabbi, hence the title of this book. This was then given to an ex-Jesuit priest who spent 40 years working on it. Finally, she received it, and is passing it on in as pure a form as possible. Is this a true story or a myth? Frankly, I don't know. Perhaps the 40 years is a clue of Biblical proportions. Note that the Israelites wandered the desert for 40 years. Note also that the deluge lasted for 40 days and 40 nights (an unusual way to describe it since in Judaism a day starts at sunset). Perhaps all of those numbers are symbolic. Certainly several Biblical scholars have suggested as much in regard to the Old Testament.

Actually, the astute Tarot student will see many similarities with expansions on the work of Paul Foster Case, founder of the Builders of the Adytum and onetime member of the Golden Dawn. The question we must ask is, is this only an expansion of Case's work, or is it that the authors (whoever they may be) tapped into the same sources as Case tapped into?

In the final analysis, it doesn't matter. What does matter is that this work is being made available to the student of psychology, Tarot, spirituality, and metaphysics. This book will bring new and/or deeper insights to these students and to all those who seek to attain the highest levels of consciousness.

To some, this book will be scary and dangerous. This is because learning from this book will cause actual changes in your life. Letting go of what is secure and safe, even though obsolete, is difficult for many people to do.

By studying this book you will become an explorer—of self and of the multiple planes of the universe. It requires the same strength and determination of will manifested by all the explorers of the past, present, and future. But instead of conquering Mt. Everest, the North Pole, or the depths of outer space, you will be conquering the disagreeable aspect of self, resulting in a happier, more knowledgeable, more successful you. I think it's worth it!

—Donald Michael Kraig
1988

THE FOOL.

" It is imagination which is required to step off " The known into the unknown "

1st Hebrew Letter	*ALEPH*
Symbol For	*Breath of Life*
Element Attributed to	*Air*
Color	*Bright Pale Yellow*
Numerical Value	*1*
Syllables	*ALP*
Sound	*E-Natural*
Planet	*Uranus*
Translation	*Ox or Bull*
Sign in Zodiac	*Taurus*

1

NOTES

THE FOOL

In order to recognize and utilize the information imparted by the Hebrew letter you must become familiar not only with the outline but also with the attributions assigned to them. This list of attributes you must memorize. The attributes of the first Hebrew letter are as follows:

 ALEPH (pronounced AW-lef) spelled in Hebrew ALP, meaning OX. It is called a MOTHER LETTER, of which there are three in Hebrew: one for FIRE, one for WATER, and one for AIR. The Hebrew wisdom considers Earth but a condensation of Fire, Water and Air. Hence there is no Mother Letter for the element of Earth. ALEPH is the sign or symbol for the LIFE BREATH, called in Hebrew RUACH. All languages designate the Spirit by a word meaning the air which we breathe. "Spirit" comes from the Latin root meaning "to breathe," as does the symbol for the Life Breath. Aleph stands for the element Air, the FIERY INTELLIGENCE, the planet URANUS, the color LIGHT YELLOW, and the note E-NATURAL. Its numerical value is 1. All the Hebrew letters have an outer value and a secret value. They communicate their mystic message by their shape and relation to other shapes, by the object they stand for, and by numerical values.

The letter ALEPH is a synthesis of the entire Hebrew alphabet, and the card it goes with, THE FOOL, is a synthesis of the entire Tarot Tableau, or set of trumps. The slanting parellelogram, slanting downward, represents the physical plane or the threefold personality. Into this streams downward the superconscious and upwards the subconscious. The two are really the same thing, differentiated only by the point of the self-conscious in the same way a curve is concave or convex merely from the direction you look at it. Our bodies are submerged in a sea of subconscious mind-stuff. The mystic raises his vibration or has it raised and ascends into the superconscious; the occultist deliberately raises his vibration and descends into the superconscious by way of the subconscious, just as two travelers (one going East and the other going West) must meet each other if they girdle the globe.

What we call the self-conscious is merely that in us which is aware and wills (by Will, we mean the right of choice). The Intellect is not the Will but merely the agent through which the Will becomes

3

aware of what is going on in the body and in the outside world. Hence, the Intellect is what determines the Will, or choice, upon its course.

The numeration of the letter Aleph is 1. It is THE ONE, the I AM, the ABSOLUTE, THE CONCEALED, the one muffled in mystery, who descends into the subconscious to discover the laws of being and becoming, and with this knowledge He may throw off the bonds of matter and rise again to His own plane. The figure 1 and letter 1 have the same meaning: the I AM who is manifest on the Heaven plane or upon the Earth plane as the personality of yourself, the potential I AM.

In the card THE FOOL you have a picture of the I AM descending into matter and the equipment He brings with Him to ascend again out of it. This type of Intelligence is called the CULTURAL INTELLIGENCE. He who descended into matter ascends again out of it by self-cultivation.

First, through the cultivation he receives by the education of nature;

Second, by the advanced cultivation he receives through group living, by what we call civilization and all its instrumentalities—government, philosophy, art, religion; and

Third, by taking himself in hand when he has reached the point in evolution where he feels the compelling urge to do so, he speeds up his evolution by intensive work upon his organism as a practical occultist or mystic. Always from the beginning we feel the urge in us for self-cultivation which, in the end, takes us back to our source. Why do we feel it? *Because THE FOOL brings his vision down with him.*

All the pioneers of the world—the teachers, the artists, the doers—have been those whom their sensible neighbors called "fools." Why? Because these fools were unaccountably willing to put aside acquisitions of pleasure for the sake of a vision as yet unrealized. When it became realized at last, their neighbors hastened to say how wise they were, and that they had always known they had something in them which would at last work out. To be working and sacrificing for what does not as yet exist sounds foolish to most people. It is not until the inventor can make a physical plane invention that works, until the business man or the promoter can objectify his scheme, that people are willing to call him practical; before that he was a visionary.

It is claimed that the Tarot, if properly applied, will help you to objectify your dreams. The wisdom of practical men concerns itself entirely with the sensory level—with things.

There is an occult proverb which says that unless Wisdom gets beyond this level, it is not Wisdom at all. "The Wisdom of men," says the proverb, "is foolishness to the gods." What the gods call Wisdom is the manner of thinking employed by THE FOOL in this picture, the Higher Self. Whatever helps the personality towards the final accomplishment of THE FOOL, his vision is Wisdom; whatever does not, is foolishness. If a man would be wise, in the GOD sense, he must reach up and tap the subjective level of consciousness. That subjective level is represented by THE FOOL in this card, descending into matter with his eye on his distant vision and with the confident expectation of realizing it in the end. The symbols in this card suggest to you what that vision is and tell you definitely how you can set about realizing it; *and that you have in yourself all the power to do this.*

You are composed of innumerable subconscious elements; each cell and group of cells in your body performs its specialized work in the whole organism. There is nothing to direct, to make the whole organism work as one except you, the Creative Will, the self-conscious. Although it can perform all the marvelous processes of your body, the subconscious has not the least idea how to direct your life. Only the Creative Will can do that, with the Intellect as its agent. It is a reluctant, hostile agent at first because it prefers the satisfactions of the present and objects to sacrificing them for the future.

Tarot is a vehicle for widening your channel, for increasing the perceptions of your present personality, for developing a higher personality even of the same type. It is a vehicle for so impressing your subconscious by the attitude of your Creative Will that she, the subconscious, will do for you what it is powerless to do itself except at second hand—change your body. But you yourself *must* start this process and keep it going, and unless you start it, it is never started. You start it and keep it going by *constantly looking within* at your vision.

SYMBOLISM

It is necessary to formulate your vision. What is it that you want most in the world? First let us see what is the vision of THE FOOL. It is out of sight, but in two other cards we see what occupies that upper corner: The Angel, the Perfected Man—not present-day man, but man when he shall have become perfected—what the mystics and occultists call the superman, which the religions and Scripture call the Angel. How does man become perfected? Man becomes perfected only by perfecting himself. The ROSE, in the other hand of THE FOOL, tells you how he perfects himself. The Rose with all people, even the most primitive, has always been the symbol of desire. This is a WHITE Rose, the symbol of purified desire. How do you purify desire? We purify desire by the balanced action of the conscious and the subconscious. This is pictured by the TWO LEAVES out of which the White Rose springs. The leaves are threefold. THREE is the creative number symbolizing the Father, Mother, and Child. Three is also the number of man's bodies, in each of which he must purify Desire, Appetite, and Emotion: the first for the Physical Body, the second for the Astral Body, and the third for the Mental Body.

The whole object of Tarot is to tell you the mechanics of purifying desire and of securing the balanced reciprocal creation of the self-conscious and the subconscious. The Higher Self thinks that a desire which approximates His is a wise desire: A desire which is dictated by appetite, emotion, and ambition alone is a foolish desire.

You are like a plant, a germinating seed, which finds in the earth in which it is placed the juices that will enable it to grow according to its pattern. It selects those juices and those only. *Exercise the entire intensity of your mind in building your image, an image of yourself in action doing your chosen work.* If the highest image you can make yourself want to construct is to have and to get something, then go ahead. *We can evolve only by desire,* be that desire what it will. No matter what desire we cherish, it is but a stepping-stone to a higher one; meanwhile we must step up on the thing we are keyed to at the time. Think carefully whether the acquisition you think you must have is really the inmost craving of your heart. For though you grow by it, whatever it is, remember that you may come to your growth only by pain and suffering because you have gotten what you wanted. Recall that most of the folklore tales (which are simply little dramatizations put forth by teachers of the race of the Ageless Wisdom) are about bad wishes gratified when the wisher had a chance to make better ones. In the fairy tales, it was the fairy godmother who granted wishes. Your subconscious is your fairy godmother who will bring about your wish if you are wholeheartedly centered upon it and bend your mind to it. If you choose badly it will mean, for the time, a frustration of the higher things, but in the economy of the Higher Self, low desires have their place as well as higher ones. It was necessary for you to go through the lower in order to get to the higher. The highest wish man is capable of making is stated in general terms in the Lord's Prayer. In His personal aspect, the God to whom we pray is the Higher Self of the mystic and the occultist. We pray to the Higher Self that His Kingdom may come, His will be done in earth as it is in heaven. Earth means the physical body, the seat of our personality. May we permit him to do His will in us, on our plane as it is done on His own plane, which the religionist calls "Heaven." His plane is the Golden Plane.

TAROT and the Secret Wisdom of the Hebrews condense the seven planes of the Hindu teaching into three. These three planes are subdivided so as to include the seven planes of the Hindu. There is the first and highest, the *Great Spiritual Plane,* the *Great Mental Plane,* and the *Great Physical Plane.*

The WHITE SUN symbolizes the Spiritual, or White, Plane from which THE FOOL of God is sent forth down into the Mental, or Golden, Plane. He is leaving the Golden Plane and is about to descend as the personality into the Great Physical Plane. Stretching up beyond the Physical Plane into the Mental are the heights of abstract thought. These are the last thing THE FOOL leaves behind him on his way into the lowest grade of matter. Also as the human personality ascends out of the lowest grade of matter, in self-identification with Him, these peaks of abstract thought are the first things it encounters on its heavenward journey.

The PEAKS are WHITE because abstract thought is characteristic of the White Plane of Spirit. It is the Golden Plane of Mind in which abstract thought becomes concrete—that subjective thought becomes objective. *Whenever you see WHITE in these cards, it means belonging to abstract thought, or to the Spiritual Plane.* Our business is to bring the Spiritual plane down to our personality. In the next card you will see THE MAGICIAN doing this.

Below the shelf on which THE FOOL is standing, just about to step off into the denser physical plane, is a BLUE MIDDLE REGION with TWO MOUNTAIN PEAKS. This Blue Region pictures the information which we receive in our sleep, whose source is the Cosmic Memory. This is depicted by the card called the HIGH PRIESTESS, the card following THE MAGICIAN. The TWIN PEAKS are "Wisdom" and "Understanding." These two words are synonymous in English, but in Hebrew they are differentiated. The text in Proverbs says: "Get Wisdom and with all thy getting, get Understanding." We shall go into the precise difference later. At present it is sufficient to say that Wisdom refers to the Cosmic Memory, and Understanding refers to the Imagination.

The SHELF on which THE FOOL is standing, about to step off, is made in the shape of a crescent. Whenever you see a crescent in these cards it designates the subconscious. Matter is really the subconscious, but the only way the card can deliver its message to you is to represent THE FOOL as doing what he is about to do. Note the peculiar color and formation of this shelf. It is largely reddish shading into yellow into gray and the shelf is of a flaky formation. The colors in these cards are vital to their meaning. YELLOW is the color of the mind. GRAY is the color of the mineral and stands for stone (or the physical world). RED stands for desire and action. *All action is prompted by desire and if there was no desire we would never act.* The color symbolism of the Shelf means that we can flake off our subconscious or make the matter which composes it less and less dense by desire and action, instigated by the self-conscious which is the mind. This process is called Alchemy, and Alchemy is the object of Tarot exercises. The object of any system is to replace the grosser matter in our bodies with matter more and more refined. By doing this you bring in more and more of the WHITE and the BLUE in this picture, or in theological terms, more and more of the spirit and the Holy Ghost.

You note that the BOOTS of THE FOOL, as he plunges down into matter, are YELLOW. The symbolism here is that the mind is the guide of our feet, telling where to plant our next step. As THE FOOL descends into matter his gaze is fixed on his vision, his vision of perfected man, which he knows nothing can frustrate. That is why his attitude shows buoyant confidence. Begin your impersonation of THE FOOL by impersonating his attitude. *In order to make contact with your real and limitless resources you must first of all believe that they are accessible and that you can learn how to use them.* You must have a definite objective, a vision of something beyond your present place in life. This requires IMAGINATION. Do you see now what the Bible means when it says: "Get Wisdom, and with all your Wisdom get Understanding?" Understanding concerns the imagination. *Get a vision.*

The little DOG represents the Purified Intellect, the intellect that has abandoned all its earthly estimates of success and substituted instead THE FOOL'S idea of success. Note that he is halfway over the abyss and does not know it, for his adoring eyes are solely upon his master, just as his master's eyes are solely upon his vision. The real man is above the Intellect and the Intellect should only be his agent. When the Intellect is in its proper place it is devoted to its master; otherwise it thinks IT is the master. Neither sees the abyss yawning at their feet, and as long as they keep their eyes where they belong they will never see it, and will never reach it.

The Life Power is coming down into the flesh. To do that, He must put on the ROBE OF IGNORANCE. BLACK in these cards represents ignorance at its lower level, and at its higher level the superconscious perception that comes from occult practices is the result. The inner lining of the Robe is RED, signifying desire and action that springs from that desire. Desire is the sole reason of evolution and only by renewing desire can we evolve. His innermost GARMENT is the WHITE of the Spirit. This symbolism is very significant. No matter how unevolved or how sunk in materiality we are, there is always something in our heart of hearts that tells us of our origin and urges us forward to our ultimate destiny, which is to be One with the Father. Whether we are in ignorance of it or whether we know it by mystic perception, we live in consequence of the laws of the Life Power and by our use of these laws. These laws are indicated by the figures on his robe.

There are EIGHT 8-SPOKED WHEELS, each surrounded by SEVEN TREFOILS. The "yellow Wheels" are the radiant Solar Energy, the fundamental characteristic of which is rotary motion; the WHEEL is YELLOW to represent the physical Sun. The RED SPOKES are the eight forms of energy. Light in action, therefore, is the meaning of the Wheel, or conscious energy. There are eight Wheels and in addition, two RED and YELLOW figures. The Hebrew Wisdom teaches that for creation there were ten instantaneous emanations of the Life Power. They correspond to the great laws of Nature working on all planes and exhibiting in forms appropriate to each plane. The philosophical terms for these are expressed as follows:

(1) Will—The Life Power is, in itself, both unmanifest and manifest, the only WILL; when manifested, it produces the universe.

(2) Wisdom—It is the unfailing WISDOM which knows every principle of reality.

(3) Understanding—It is the Perfect UNDERSTANDING of every condition and situation.

(4) Substance—It is the limitless SUBSTANCE from which all forms are built.

(5) Law—It is the absolute LAW which operates without deviation.

(6) Beauty—It is always working toward BEAUTY, though through

stages of temporary ugliness.

(7) Victory—It is a power which cannot fail in *VICTORY*.

(8) Glory or Splendor—It is that whose self-expression is *GLORY or SPLENDOR*.

(9) Foundation or Basis—It is the *BASIS or FOUNDATION* of all human, subhuman, and superhuman expression of activity.

(10) Kingdom—And it is that which manifests itself in perfect order or *KINGDOM*.

Around the eight Wheels of Solar Energy which ornament the Robe of THE FOOL, are SEVEN TREFOILS for each wheel. These represent the seven great phases of the Life Power's activity, and they correspond to the seven centers of the body. The object of studying Tarot, and of any form of occult concentration and meditation, is to make these centers work properly. This is one of the most important occult secrets and endeavors. Thus the Wheels on the Robe indicate eight aspects of the Life Power, each manifesting in eight different forms and through seven phases of activity.

There are TWO FIGURES on his Robe quite different from the Wheels. One is on the chest and the other is on the thigh. These two Figures represent two great changes in the body which accompany a third great change in the head; the three being the object of the practical occultist and the final goal of his work upon his own organism—the work of Alchemy. All these changes are worked automatically by the subconscious. They are all accomplished by that balancing of the conscious and the subconscious portrayed by the two balanced LEAVES of the White Rose in THE FOOL'S hand. They come along with or as a consequence of what the mystic or occultist calls "lifting the sex force to the head."

This is typified in the picture by the RED FEATHER waving from THE FOOL'S head. It is the wing feather of an EAGLE. The feather is RED to represent action and desire, for this perception is not static but active and productive. One of the things it does is to open the Wallet of the Cosmic Subconscious. This is depicted by the eagle-shaped BAG at the end of the WAND which THE FOOL carries on his shoulder.

The OPEN EYE on the flap of the Wallet also has many deep mystic meanings. The one that concerns us here is VISION, the eye of imagination that unlocks the treasure house, or the wallet, of subconscious.

The WAND, by which THE FOOL carries the Wallet, is BLACK tipped with RED. This means that the Wallet is opened by practical occultism, by occult practice and the making of images.

The HEADDRESS out of which waves the Red Feather tells the same story. The headdress is a WREATH OF PLAITED GREEN LEAVES, and GREEN in color symbology of the Tarot stands for the Creative Imagination. The image is made by the self-conscious mind. It is carried out and created in matter by the subconscious mind.

If you will look carefully, you will detect that the plaiting of the Leaves forms two vertical figure 8's. These figures designate the transformed self-conscious and the transformed subconscious. The subconscious thus transforms him after he has equipped her with the power to do so. As a result of the double transformation comes the mingling of the two streams of consciousness depicted in card 14. This mingling is performed by the Higher Self in the thighs. The second result is that the heart is changed from an involuntary, or feminine, organ into a volitional, or masculine, organ. You will see this latter result quaintly depicted in many sculptures in the cathedrals of Europe, where a saint carries his head in his hand over his heart. It means, in exact terms, that the head now has become the heart and the heart has become the head; that is, the head no longer takes the initiative but carries out the instructions of the heart. To allow it to do so before both have been transformed is lunacy.

Finally, around the waist of THE FOOL is the BELT OF THE ZODIAC. This typifies Time and Space. The Divine Spark must necessarily limit itself in order to manifest. Nothing can be manifested without a body, and a body means limitation.

The White Sun has 14 rays. Fourteen is the concealed value of HEH and the value of the Hebrew name for God, ID, the Almighty Hand. Another divine name is AL, meaning strength, and its value is 31. Fourteen times 31 = 434, or the value of the letter-name DALETH, the process whereby the Life Power manifests in images. Fourteen is also the number of cards that make up each suit of the Tarot. Thus each suit of the Tarot tells how the Almighty Hand reached down to manifest Itself, Its potency, on each one of the four planes which designated the passing down of the Archetype image through the Creative and Formative Worlds into the Physical world. "Creation began with the Letter HEH" is the mystic statement whose (HEH's) value is 14.

There are eight forms of energy, and each form of energy goes through seven phases corresponding to the seven Centers.

Make a little picture of THE FOOL as you study this card. Get into the habit of making mental pictures of these cards. Try to recall them when you are in a relaxed state. Try to recall everything that is in the card until the card has impressed itself truly in your memory.

Tarot is like every other form of education. It returns to you precisely in proportion what you give it. The study of the roots of words is very fascinating and very astounding. How do words come to have the roots they have—roots which often seem entirely disconnected from the present meaning? Philologists explain this disconnection by saying that the connecting links have dropped out and the words have, by usage, come to have other meanings than those originally intended. In general that is true, but not always. The truth is that all languages, in their fundamental meanings, were invented by occultists. We have many words that have secret meanings, meanings which lie under their surface meaning and are understood only by the mystics and occultists. Let's take for example the word *religion.* It is very apparent that "religion" is a word made by mystics and occultists. "Religion" means to "bind back."

"Fool" is one of the words that was made by occultists. It has the strangest derivation possible. It came from the Latin *follis,* which means "a bellows." A bellows has no usefulness until it is filled with air, which it intensifies and directs. Now this is the entire occult idea in a nutshell. The air to which we owe our life, the occultist learns how to control, to intensify, to direct. This is not a spectacular statement, nor do you need to know anything of occult doctrines to be persuaded that it is true. All you need to know is the root meanings of words.

In every scripture the "breath" is used to designate the Divine Working Power. This power is limitless and means life. This power is called "breath" in every civilized language. We use the word "spirit." "Spirit" comes from the Latin, meaning "breath." We have two Greek words for Spirit that mean breath: *pneuma,* which is the root we use, as in "pneumatic" tires, and *nous.* Both of these words mean "spirit." The Hindu word *prana* means "breath." The Hebrew word for the Spirit, "RUACH," means BREATH. You may have heard the expression "The Fool in Christ." This is the man who identifies himself with the Higher Self, and is one who can draw the Life Breath.

The letter we had the last time, Aleph, the first letter of the Hebrew alphabet, means the same thing as RUACH, RVCh as it is spelled in Hebrew. It concerns the use of the power we all possess, but which most of us do not govern. When we govern it as the Higher Self would have us govern it, then we become "The Fool in Christ" (the man who has estimates of things different from so-called practical and sensible people). He is called THE FOOL by his neighbors because he refuses to accept their opinions and estimates that are desirable and important. He is the man who directs the Life Breath.

"The wisdom of man is foolishness to the Gods," states the occult proverb. The people who estimate life according to acquisition and possession, the Gods call "fools," and you will find that often happens in your dreams. For instance, someone in your dream tells another that you are a fool. It is because you, having worldly estimates of things, send the dream to yourself by your Higher Self. In our popular speech we find many examples of the use of the root for "fool" meaning "bellows." The fool who talks a great deal is called a "windbag"; thus the bellows is the kind of windbag that can control and direct the wind. The "windbag" is a person who does not direct or control the air he produces and instead lets it direct him.

Now, substitute for the word "bellows" the word "body." Are you letting your body direct your use of air you breathe or are you directing it yourself? Perhaps that sounds a little figurative just now. Let us make that more literal. Are you governing the Life that passes through you or are you letting your body govern it? The appetites come from the physical body, the desires from the mental body, and the emotions from the emotional body. The occult and mystic teachings group these three together as representing your personality, which the occultists call your subconscious. Query: Are you directing these three components or are they directing you?

Let us see what story is indicated by the word RUACH, spelled in Hebrew RVCh:

R   stands for the head, or the Sun. The occult teaching being that Solar energy expeses itself through the head.

Ch   stands for the Moon. The occult teaching being that the energy of the Moon expresses itself through the body of the subconscious.

V   Note that between these two (R and Ch) is the letter V. V means "nail or link," that which joins two things together. It can, however, designate several things or several kinds of joinings.

THAT WHICH LINKS THE BODY TO THE SPIRIT IS THE SOUL—THE HIGHER SELF. THAT WHICH LINKS THE SUN AND THE MOON ON THE PHYSICAL PLANE IS OUR FLESH—THE EARTH.

There are two specific kinds of light vibration: direct light and reflected light. Sunlight includes the light of all the light-giving bodies, all the bodies that give out light. Such bodies we call true stars, and our Sun is a Star. The Bible very beautifully calls it "The Day Star." Our Sun is a Star and perhaps the smallest of all the stars.

Reflected light is the light which is reflected from all the moons and planets. They don't give out light of their own but reflect the light of the Sun. Sunlight and moonlight mixed in the earth's atmosphere constitute our air, the thing that we breathe and by means of which we live. It is the air which gives us light. The physical side of this energy gives us our life; the Spiritual side, the immaterial side, gives us con-sciousness. Self-consciousness and subconsciousness are the spiritual side of the sunlight and moonlight, thus they are mingled in these bodies of ours which are made from the dust of the earth.

In Alchemy, these two, the self-consciousness and subconscious-ness, are called the "subtle" and the "gross." There is an alchemical maxim, or precept, which reads: "You must learn to separate the subtle from the gross, and separate it smoothly and gently." This notion shows us at once what the mystic and occultist deems the major obstacles to understanding within the Church. The Church told you to despise the body, to be severe with it, to belabor it. The body is to be loved and disciplined. Not loved without discipline, and not disciplined without love. It is to be treated as the wise person treats a pet, a dog. Above all, the body is to be kept in its place. *When the mind controls the body, the body is in its proper place. When the body controls the mind, it is out of its proper place.* This latter, the body, controlling the mind, is what it does in all of us until we take our evolution in hand. When we do that we begin to separate them. Hence we must learn to separate them and not mix the two up.

THE MAGICIAN.

The Magician plants the images of desire in the Subconscious (the Empress)--- It is the attention of the self conscious mind which dictates what your desires will be --- The desire to change physical energy into mental energy or Nerve energy

2nd Hebrew Letter	*BETH*
Symbol For	*Pair of Opposites– Life and Death*
Color	*Yellow*
Numerical Value	*2*
Syllables	*BITh*
Sound	*E-Natural*
Planet	*Mercury*
Translation	*House*

NOTES

THE MAGICIAN

ב **BETH**, spelled in Hebrew BITh, means HOUSE. It is the second Hebrew letter and the first DOUBLE LETTER. It is the sign and symbol for the pair of opposites, LIFE AND DEATH. It stands for the direction ABOVE and for the TRANSPARENT INTELLIGENCE, the planet MERCURY, the color YELLOW, and the note E-NATURAL. Its numerical value is 2. In Roman characters it is written "B."

The type of Intelligence assigned to this card is the TRANS-PARENT INTELLIGENCE. The idea is that the Solar force, which we bring down from heaven and which we later learn to bring down abundantly, should flow through us unobstructed, just as light comes through a windowpane. There are, of course, certain constituents in light, certain rays that cannot go through the glass. *Not only should this light flow into the body but through the body and out again.* It is intended that it be transformed in its passage by your thought, by that particular combination which is YOU, your personality, a combination which never occurred before and which can never occur again. You cannot get the influence of that combination until you become transparent to the light. What we have to do is to improve our self-conscious and refine our subconscious so that the Light can go through it and then through our body without obstruction.

Let us look at the alphabet and at the formation of the letter BETH. At the bottom of Beth is a parallelogram which represents the physical body. Into that parallelogram comes down a letter which you will have at the bottom of this row. This letter is RESH and means the Solar Energy. So the letter Beth is a picture of the Solar Energy entering the physical body through the head.

This letter is a Double Letter. ALEPH is a Mother Letter. There are three Mother Letters in the Hebrew alphabet, and they are assigned to the elements Air, Water, and Fire. Aleph is the sign for Air. Air, Water, and Fire are names given to three things in your organism. On the other hand, the ancients held that out of the four elements (Air, Water, Fire, and Earth) all things were made. Hebrew wisdom says that Earth is only a condensation of the other three elements. Consequently, that is why there is no Mother Letter for Earth. The element Earth is assigned to one of the other letters. You will find in Genesis, first chapter, that the Earth came out of the Water. So these three Mother Letters in Hebrew represent the three root aspects of the Life activity, or Light.

Hebrew represent the three root aspects of the Life activity, or Light.

BETH is called a Double Letter. In its exoteric sense—that is, in its direct meaning—a Double Letter is one that can be pronounced hard or soft. In English, "S" is a Double Letter; it can be pronounced like a soft "C" or it can be pronounced like "Z."

Now the esoteric significance of a Double Letter is very different. It means that the letter stands for a pair of opposites and the opposites in this case are Life and Death. There are seven Double Letters, and they correspond to the seven centers of the body (called Chakras in Kundalini Yoga and the Seven Golden Candlesticks in orthodox religion). These are the centers whose vibrations we need to become conscious of in our color and sound exercises. When these centers are working properly we are healthy. When they're working inadequately the result is imbalance or illness.

The letter BETH means HOUSE. The physical body is your house, but who are you that lives in it? Who are you that lives in your house? *You are Mind, and the Essence of Mind is Will.* The body is the house of the Mind, but the Mind is the house of the Will. There is always a stream of consciousness flowing though our minds.

THE MAGICIAN stands for that in you which is acutely aware, which WILLS. You are not your body and you are not the stream of consciousness which flows through your mind. *You are the awareness which looks at your stream of consciousness, which flows through your mind and selects from it for your own purpose.* The awareness which wills is what you are; AS ABOVE, SO BELOW. This universe is the house of the Eternal Light, or Life, the Energy which we call God. This Prime Energy is the AWARENESS, the alert spectator, the actor in its house, the universe, just as we should be an alert spectator or actor in our house, the body; but God's house, if we could see it with His eyes and know its purpose, is perfect. *He and His House are One.*

Due to the misuse of our body in our previous lives, we cannot identify ourselves with it until we make it over, but the ONE LIFE which we call GOD naturally can and does identify itself with ITS body, the Universe. There was nothing out of which it could make the Universe but Itself. For the purpose of manifestation, the One Energy divided Itself into Two (the masculine principle and the feminine principle). These two are called the superior and the inferior natures, though they are really equal. The superior nature is the Will, and by working upon another part of itself, the inferior nature (the substance), it produced all the things which go to make up the Universe. The Will supplied the ideas, the images. The inferior nature supplied the substance out of which those images took shape and gave them the shape which the Will instructed it to take. √

The receptor in our minds which perceives, which discriminates, and which recognizes the relationships, is identical with the superior nature of this One Energy which we call God. It is in this sense that we are made in the image of God. Our awareness which wills our Will is identical with His. This awareness we call the "Self-conscious." We possess the power of ATTENTION, the power of seeing how things are related in cause and effect, only because that Energy possesses the same. If He did not possess it, we could not. It is this Energy which is aware of what is going on, which wills, and which selects. We call that the self-conscious (the consciousness of Self).

In the Bible, in the terminology of theology, the self-consciousness is often called Adam. An ancient and occult proverb says that Adam was set in the Garden of Eden to grow roses. The Garden of Eden is an allegory for the human body, though most unfortunately you are not told this by the orthodox churches. And what is the consequence? Most people think this is one of the quaintest stories ever written, this story of the Garden of Eden. Being so full of contradictions people think it is merely a whimsical superstition trying to explain something that is not explainable. There is a theological phrase which we meet often in the Scriptures, "the Old Adam." The Old Adam is the "natural man."

THE MAGICIAN in this card is the SPIRITUAL MAN. Spiritual man has made himself out of the natural man by working on himself. In this card you see him cultivating his roses, making himself spiritual; *the garden is his own body.* Stripped of this little allegory it means that the self-conscious was set in the body to refine the desire of the body—to civilize it, as we say. Our body is the first medium of our activity, and all our activity of expression must be manifested by means of our body on this physical plane. It is the mechanism of our expression.

If the Garden of Eden is our body, and Adam is the self-conscious mind, then *who is Eve?* Eve is the ruling mentality in the subconscious, the Collective Subconscious. We have two different consciousnesses in our body: the self-conscious, or Adam, and the subconscious, or Eve. The work of all practical occultism is to teach us to balance them. Tarot calls Eve THE EMPRESS (card III), or Venus. At present your subconscious vastly outweighs your self-conscious, though you think it is just the other way around. You think your self-conscious is a slave to you, but your subconscious is a slave to your sub-conscious at present. Let's look at that more closely.

The Center, BETH, stands for the thinking lobe of the brain and that part of it which is greatest, the PINEAL GLAND. The Pineal Gland is shaped like a pine cone, which is why it is called pineal. In dreams and in myths the pine tree is constantly used as a symbol of intuition for the same reason. *Intuition comes from the Pineal Gland.* The PITUITARY GLAND is sometimes called the "master gland," and the glands it controls are called "target glands." The Pituitary was once believed to be of little or no importance. It is now known to be extremely important in releasing hormones, and some of these control the activity of the other endocrine glands. It was to these glands that the Master Jesus made reference when He said, "Blessed are the eyes that see." As its name signifies, the Pineal Gland is the sacred pine cone in man—the eye single, which cannot be opened until the Spirit Fire is raised through the sacred seals which are called in orthodox religion the Seven churches in Asia, the Seven Golden Candlesticks, and which are called in Eastern teachings, Chakras.

The Pineal Gland is about the size of a pea and it is located in the top part of the center of the brain. It possesses a very peculiar body, almost like a hive. It is full of little pigeonholes filled with a granular substance which is called "brain sand." When you read in Scripture that a person goes up to the Mount to pray, it means he sends his consciousness into his Pineal Gland. You might recall that Moses went to Mt. Sinai to receive the Law and that Jesus was always going up onto the Mount to pray. Why did they not receive the Law and pray on the plain? That is what is meant by these sayings. Prayer, then, is for "High Places" in the occult reading of the Scriptures.

BLACK in the cards has two meanings: a lower meaning and a higher one. The lower is IGNORANCE and the higher is MYSTICAL KNOWLEDGE. STONE and STONE COLOR in all the cards have two meanings. The lower meaning of Stone signifies the NATURAL BODY, the physical body, which the Bible says is made out of the dust, a mineral. Remember that dirt is powdered stone. The higher meaning signifies the UNION OF THE SON (dust) WITH THE FATHER (stone). That is to say, the union of the personality with the Higher Self. This union is brought about when the *brain sand,* in the Pineal Gland, is fused into the crystal stone. When it is fused we become, in the occult use of the word, *ALIVE.* Hence the pair of for, and this is precisely the use of the two words, the *quick* and the *dead*, in the Gospel narrative. Whenever Jesus speaks of the quick and the dead, the *quick* means those people whose Pineal Gland is functioning. By the *dead* he means ordinary people.

It should be quite apparent to any careful reader that many expressions in the Scriptures have a double meaning very different from their ordinary meaning: words such as faith, death, birth, blindness, and poverty. Let us take one of these beatitudes: "Blessed are the poor in spirit." What a strange expression. Why should the poor in spirit be blessed? It certainly does not mean being spiritless and not standing for your rights. It must have some ethical meaning. The ethical meaning is non-attachment to THINGS. Blessed are they whose life is not in things, in possessions, or in acquisitions.

One of the central ideas of Jesus was that the multitude should be taught in parables, and that the hidden things should be revealed only to those who are ready for them. It is constantly forgotten by the orthodox churches (if it was ever known) that much of what Jesus said was intended only for his disciples. "I teach you," he said, "the real mystery of the things of the Kingdom of Heaven. I teach the multitude in parables." He cautioned them against "casting their pearls before swine." The things that were meant for the *quick* should never be cast before the *dead*. The churches have never made any satisfactory explanation of these statements. Surely the teachings of Jesus would have no point unless they were meant for everybody, unless there is a hidden meaning in them. What did Jesus mean by saying, "Don't cast your pearls before swine?" He told his disciples he would reveal to them the mystery of the Kingdom of Heaven. The principal idea in the Ancient Mysteries was that man, by his own work upon himself, died and was born again into a higher type of man. The Old Adam, the natural man, died and was born into the spiritual man. The ordinary, unawakened person Jesus referred to as the *blind* and the *deaf* by the words, "Those who have eyes to see, let them see, and those who have ears to hear, let them hear." Those who were in the graves did not mean the dead people, but those who had not awakened their Pineal Gland—those people subscribing to orthodox knowledge. The word *dead* ordinarily means those who are in their graves. He said that He came to teach both the *quick* and the *dead*. To the *quick* He taught the mysteries of the coming of Heaven. To the *dead* He talked in instructive parables. The *quick*, or *alive*, were those who had reconstructed their bodies, who had made the spiritual mán out of the natural man.

The chief index of this reconstruction is the awakened Pineal Gland. The highest function of Mercury, the mind, is to awaken the Pineal Gland and, by its use, bring down the White Light from the White Plane into our physical bodies.

This card shows THE MAGICIAN, and of course a magician is a man who works magic. The modern magician is not a magician at all, he is only a sleight-of-hand man. He does things so quickly that he deceives the eye, and he knows how to distract the eye while he does it, so that the eye does not perceive when he does it. He performs tricks with his hands which deceive our eyes. A magician, in our modern association, means a man who presents an illusion to make you believe it.

This card shows THE MAGICIAN bringing down the WHITE LIGHT, the Force from above to transfuse and transform his house (his body). Not only can he transform his body, but by passing the White Light through his transformed body, he can transform his more distant environment. All Nature has the same composites as the subconscious, and the subconscious is what is transformed. Our environment begins with our house, our body. *The Body is the House of the Mind. The Mind is the House of the Will.* So your first house is your mind, your second house is your physical body, and your third house is outside your physical body. When you affect the animal, plant, and mineral bodies that surround you, it is called a miracle—but a miracle only means a change that is worked by an unknown force. If we use this force to control other human bodies or to get anything for ourselves, it is called Black Magic, as distinct from White Magic. The same force is used and the same force is brought down. When it is used with guilty design or to enslave other human beings to our Will, or to fetter their Wills in the least way, it is employed for evil and not for good purposes. So you see the motive of its employment is what constitutes the difference between White Magic and Black Magic; the force is the same. There is no moral quality in a force. The moral quality is, instead, in the motive.

In THE FOOL'S hand is a WHITE ROSE and the meaning of this is PURIFIED DESIRE. The Five Roses in THE MAGICIAN'S garden are not WHITE but RED. Remember, Black Magic is just as much a magic as White Magic. *You don't have to have purified desire in order to be a magician.*

Now, what does THE MAGICIAN do to bring down the White Light? The basis of all occult magic is the use of the sex force. It is a sex force at its mental level, not at its physical level. That is to say, it is sex force transmuted, sex force lifted to the mental plane where it functions as a powerful nerve force, a force which has nothing primarily to do with the biological function of reproduction.

By lifting the sex force to the head and transmuting it into mental sex force, THE MAGICIAN establishes definite contact with the superconscious. That is what the sex symbols in the Church mean.

This MAGICAN has established definite contact with the super-conscious by lifting the sex force to the head, transmuting something which was a physical force into a mental force. The whole teaching of the mystic about sex differs very much from that of the Church. The occultist or mystic very much regrets the tragic mistakes of the churches in having the idea that there is anything evil in the conception and the use of sex. The churches teach that it is better to get along without the employment of physical sex and that it is evil to use sex under any conditions other than ceremony—and only then it is officially condoned to use sex. The churches do not inquire of two people who have joined in wedlock how they live. It was thought that what evil there was in sex was avoided if they were married by the Church. The mystic teaching about sex is very different from this. This teaching is that the physical use of sex *must always be accompanied by love.* Any use of sex without love is blasphemy—blasphemy against the Life Force, whether the two have been married or not. The occultist and mystic teach that if unmarried people love and are not encroaching upon the rights of others, there is no essential evil in their physical use of sex.

These cards present the highest objective possible in the particular state of consciousness that each one depicts. In this card the highest use of the Mind is to bring down White Light by the agency of the mental sex force. *There is no reason whatever for a person to seek to transmute his sex force unless he feels the inner urge to do so!* In the preliminary stages you cannot complete the process and engage in the physical use of sex at the same time. This is exceedingly dangerous in itself, as it prevents completion of the process. The reason is a practical one. To complete the process it is necessary for you to make certain new cells in your brain. The construction of these new cells demands certain chemicals which, at the present time, Nature is using for the physical sex force. To raise the sex force to the head compels the temporary suspension of the physical use of sex. When the process is completed, the physical use will be resumed without impairing the function of the mental. It is from the aforementioned fact that the very regrettable attitude of the churches toward sex arose, thus appearing to condemn sex. The mystic or the occultist advises no one in this personal matter whether it is time for you to try to raise the sex force. The time to attempt it is when you feel that it is time. In the same way the occultist says that it is a perfectly personal matter when you think you should give up other things. No one else knows enough about you to insist you should undertake this process.

The organ that the practical occultist develops is the Pineal Gland. This makes new brain cells in the Reasoning, or left lobe, of the brain. Unless the Pineal Gland is energized by currents coming from the sex ganglia, the gland remains as is. When the Pineal Gland is energized by the transmuted sex force, the sex force then is turned into nerve force and then into the White Light. The occult magic, as it is called, can be worked in your body and outside your body. The process is completed when an Adept comes into being—a person who can accomplish to perfection all magical works. If a man is a White Adept, he never uses his personal Will, he uses the Will of his Higher Self. He does not make the kind of magic satisfying personal desire. He carefully avoids this choice.

Now we come to the examination of Reason. We all base our mental patterns or thoughts upon our observations. Observation is what comes to us through our five senses and our interpretation of what we get from them. "This is bad," we say, because we found it to work out badly. "This is good," because we have found it to work out justly. We say a man reasons badly because there is a gap in his mental process. His mental patterns don't mesh well, nor do his ideas of cause and effect. The accuracy of our mental patterns is entirely determined by the alertness with which we pay attention to what is going on around us and by the alertness with which we observe what happens in these processes. Almost no one pays close, continuous attention. It is something we have to learn. Unfortunately, it is not taught in the schools.

To pay attention involves three steps:

(1)   The first step is to see the object plainly, definitely, and functionally.

(2)   The second step is to see in what class of objects it comes, what it is like.

(3)   The third step is to see how it is different from others of its class.

These three things are involved in the act of adequate attention, in seeing anything distinctly. Do you wonder that everybody is deficient in the ability to pay attention? It is more necessary to cultivate attention than anything else in the world, more necessary than the ordinary business of living. *It is especially necessary for the occultist.*

There are several ways to cultivate alertness of attention. All of them are good. If you read the biography of any of the modern magicians, those sleight-of-hand men, you will find that from infancy their power of attention was cultivated by artificial processes. From early childhood they began to cultivate their attention. The way which covers the widest field is to learn to read accurately.

In the same way you must cultivate an instrument which will make you transparent to your Higher Self. The instrument for recording sense impressions is the brain. The instrument for receiving the instruction of the Higher Self, which we call intuition, is the Pineal Gland. As a general rule your senses work and work accurately, your brain senses work and work accurately, and your brain records what your senses receive, but you are not present at the switchboard to get the message. *You are not paying attention.* The instrument for recording sense impression is the brain, and the instrument for receiving the instruction of the Higher Self is the intuition, which comes from the Pineal Gland.

In the first card of the Tarot, THE FOOL, you have the Life Power depicted. You see on his Robe the ten figures of the Ten Emanations. In the second card of the Tarot (the one you are studying now) you see this Power being directed by a human being who has learned how to use it. THE MAGICIAN'S pose is intended to be very significant. It presents a studied effort without any strain whatever. If you look at him carefully, you will see that one hand is putting forth strenuous effort, and the other is relaxed and takes up and distributes the strain. This seems very complex to put into words, but it is the only way you can accomplish skill in anything. You are thoroughly familiar with this experience already. You learn how to do a thing with effort and then you exercise the effort without strain. It is true that you cannot do it competently until you can do it without strain. How could you drive an automobile if you gripped the wheel with intensity, as you did at first?

SYMBOLISM

You see the artist has very well suggested that one half of THE

MAGICIAN is rigid and the other half is loose. You can see that in his hands. He is holding up his right hand very rigidly while the other hand has no tension at all, so that the force comes down and just drips off his fingers. That is the experience which you will have if part of you is loose. As you approach it you will note how it follows of itself. This is the body attitude to try for. I do not know of any way to further describe it. His pose appears to be a steady effort without any strain whatever. That statement sounds contradictory on the face of it, "Steady effort without any strain." One half of him is putting forth strenuous effort. The other half of him is relaxed so that he takes up the strain, or absorbs the strain. In taking things with ease, THE MAGICIAN conversely shows his mastery of them.

THE MAGICIAN'S pose shows the technique of concentration. The general impression is that concentration is difficult. It is difficult in that it takes a great deal of experimenting. When you have learned it you wonder why you were so long experimenting with it, it is so simple. I don't know that anyone will be able to tell you how to go about it, or how to learn it. Continuous practice, with awareness, will surely yield results.

If you take THE MAGICIAN'S attitude—part of you very tense and part of you very loose—you will find yourself concentrating before you know it. It is your *self-conscious that you hold rigid* and it is your *subconscious that you relax.* The only effort you are putting forth should be in the mind, and you balance that effort through an entire lack of tension in the body. An entire lack of tension is called relaxation. Relaxation is just the opposite of concentration. This must be learned, otherwise you would be devitalized in order to relax. You will learn that, too, with effort. Where effort is not present you are not relaxing; suddenly, without making effort, you find that you have achieved it.

Upon what have you concentrated? Not your mental force, you do not concentrate upon that. *You concentrate upon the Light (White) that comes down from THE FOOL, as it passes through your brain.* You keep that effort going while you look at it as long as you please. If you can hold that in your mind, you automatically put yourself in touch with the boundless resources of the subconscious.

On the next card, THE HIGH PRIESTESS, the subconscious is infinitely more vast than you, the awakened consciousness. Someone has said that the subconscious is a sea on which you, your consciousness, is only a wave—a wave on the surface. How do we find the subconscious? THE SUBCONSCIOUS IS ALL YOUR PAST. The awakening consciousness is only your awareness of the present, only that part of your awareness (not awareness without attribute) which is centered in the brain.

We have a highly developed mechanism for using the subconsciousness of the past. It is the body. We have an excellent mechanism for using the awareness of the present. It is the brain. The brain is unsatisfactory only because we have not yet learned to use it properly. We haven't achieved alertness of attention, but generally speaking the mechanism of the brain is all right. If we could train it to pay attention adequately, we should have very little to complain about. We have a very rudimentary and imperfect mechanism for receiving superconscious impressions. That mechanism is the Pineal Gland, for it is only vestigial in most of us at present. The business of the mystic and the occultist is to develop the Pineal Gland so that instead of having intermittent flashes (as perhaps most people do) we can establish continuous contact with the superconscious.

The Tarot is said to be the best means and the safest means of establishing continuous contact with the superconscious. If you are going to use the Tarot successfully you must never be mechanical about it. That is to say, you must never for a moment cease to pay attention. These are very simple exercises, and we are told there is no limit to what they can do for us if we bring our mind fresh to them each time.

The horizontal Figure 8 over THE MAGICIAN'S head is the index of his transformation by the subconscious after he has transformed her. It is the symbol of his transformation by the subconscious. She cannot transform him until he has transformed her. Now you see him in the act of transforming her by the White Light that has been brought down through his wand. As you can see, the self-conscious is rigid and the subconscious is relaxed.

What we call the Tarot Tableau are these 21 cards arranged in rows of seven cards each. Directly under THE MAGICIAN comes card number 8, demonstrating STRENGTH. You will also see a figure 8 over her head. That indicates that he has transformed her. In this card she (the subconscious) is transforming him. These two figure 8's you have already seen in the green headdress of THE FOOL. The figure 8 gives the perfect description of the continual interplay of the two forces, the self-conscious and the subconscious, or the Sun and the Moon (the direct light and the reflected light). Trace a horizontal figure 8 in the air with your finger. You see that it is a perfect sign of *as above, so below,* and conversely *as below, so above.*

The WAND here has two points. Each end is shaped like a pine cone or penis to indicate the uplifted sexual force.

THE MAGICIAN has BLACK HAIR to indicate that his present work is an occult work—that he has mystic perception. Hair in the symbolism of the Tarot, in dreams, and in the Bible means MENTAL EMANATION. You will recall that Samson's strength lay in his hair— that is to say, it was his Spiritual Strength. THE MAGICIAN'S black hair is banded with the Spirit and his body is the robe of the Spirit; over it he has thrown the voluminous RED ROBE of desire, whose innermost RED is the Red of Spirit. His desire is to make his body more capable of receiving the superconscious vibrations. He is bring- ing them down and wants to make his body more capable—replacing denser matter with finer matter.

What is his desire? His desire is to make his body more capable of receiving the superconscious vibration. He is bringing down into his self-conscious a subtler matter that is far more capable of receiving the superconscious vibration than the denser matter, the gross matter of the body. He is trying to make his body correspond to his mind, and the way to do that is to get rid of the grosser matter in his body and replace it with the finer matter. That is why the shelf in the card of THE FOOL has a flaky formation. You can flake it off as the rock formation you saw, which is red and yellow. You can also flake it off by action prescribed by the mind. RED means ACTION and YELLOW means MIND.

This process of refining the body is fully dramatized by the GAR- DEN. The Garden is really THE MAGICIAN'S own body, but you would not see what was being done if you had only his body to look at. You are further informed by the Garden that the FIVE RED ROSES are the SENSES, and the Senses are the source of ALL desire. They are cultivated Roses because he is refining his desire. The rose of Nature has only five petals. These are very cultivated roses. They have hun- dreds of petals. They were all improved by cultivation.

The FOUR LILIES with the BLUE and GREEN foliage indicate ABSTRACT THOUGHT. He is making his mind capable of Abstract Thought. The Intellect is capable only of concrete thought. They are four because there are four planes, or departments, of Energy. These departments are symbolized by IHVH, Jehovah: mental, emotional, etheric, and physical.

The TABLE is called the "FIELD OF ATTENTION."

The FOUR IMPLEMENTS upon the TABLE symbolize a great many things, but among them are these four aspects of IHVH. The Four Implements on the Table also represent the four essentials of life, which are Light, Water, Air, and Food.

(1) The WAND stands for LIGHT.

(2) The SWORD stands for AIR.

(3) The CUP stands for WATER.

(4) The PENTACLE stands for FOOD.

Why does the Sword stand for Air? Because Air cuts without resistance. They also represent the FOUR ANCIENT ELEMENTS which are not literally elements, but the elements used figuratively (Fire, Water, Air, and Earth). They have all these meanings, but the meaning most pertinent to magical creation is the four stages of an Idea on its way down through the physical plane as described in the above four.

The name IHVH, which symbolizes these four, is very clumsily printed on his arm. His uplifted arm usually bears the letters IHVH. He is bringing down from the Abstract Plane the White Light in order to make it a concrete thing on the physical plane.

You will note that all these implements are yellow except the Sword, which is blue. YELLOW is the color of the SELF-CONSCIOUS. BLUE is the color of the SUBCONSCIOUS.

If your creation is external you bring your creation down by the forces of Nature, which is the cosmic subconscious. The cosmic subconscious is the Sword which carves it out. The forces of Nature constitute the Sword which carves out your *abstract ideas,* which become concrete and are diverted into the physical plane. If your creation is to be internal and has to do with your personality, then your personal subconscious is the Sword which carves it out for you. *Everything that is done in your body is done by your subconscious at the instigation of the conscious.* The instigation of the conscious is the picture which you make in your mind, particularly every emotional picture attended with emotion.

Every picture that you make in your mind, particularly when attended with emotion, has got to work out. One must work it out in action, either in external action or internal action. If you inhibit it from working out in external action you will develop some mental, emotional, or physical disturbance in your body. *Beware of making pictures that you don't want to carry out in external actions.* When the expression "image" is used, that is what is meant. This means the picture of something attended by emotion.

A man in prison who was very addicted to alcohol was determined that he would never drink again when he came out. When he did come out, he immediately began to drink. Why was that? Because he was always imaging pictures of a drink while he was in prison. He externalized the thing he was mentally imaging all the time of his imprisonment. Had he not externalized it, these pictures would have hurt him—they would have worked out in some neurosis in his body. Every picture that you make has to be worked out in action. If you don't let it work out in external action, it works out in some mental, nervous, or emotional disharmony in your body (producing neurosis).

People make pictures of a wrong kind because of their inaccurate attention. The man mentioned above always thought of a drink, and the mental image was the preliminary cause of the physically manifested drinks.

Most people think that possessions and acquisitions are what makes happiness, so they picture themselves having these possessions and acquisitions. If they had paid attention they would have seen that the acquisitions, possessions and sensations, in themselves, cannot possibly make them happy. The more you want the more you get, and the more you get the more dissatisfied you are with what you have. As for sensation, it constantly diminishes to the vanishing point. It is like opium. The more opium you take, the more you have to take in order to get the same effect you got in the first dose.

The TABLE in the picture is called the FIELD OF ATTENTION, or the TRESTLEBOARD.

This card pictures the highest achievement of the self-conscious mind—THE MAGICIAN brings down the White Light from above. This is a very occult process; hence, this Table has BLACK LEGS.

The Channel for Communication between

The message sender – liaison
The subjective Mind – The Laws of Nature

THE HIGH PRIESTESS

your
Attention

Deductive?
Reasoning?
Mental Analysis

The Intellect

Subconscious

Conscious

The Spirit

Union of Intellect and Spirit

The Lunar (MOON) Consciousness
Controlled by the laws of Nature
Manage the Lunar Cycle through the 7 body System
to gain control of her powers -- How to make the laws of
Nature work for the individual.

3rd Hebrew Letter	GIMEL
Symbol for	Pair of Opposites— (Peace and Strife)
Color	Blue
Numerical Value	3
Syllables	GML
Sound	G-Sharp
Planet	Moon
Translation	Camel

How to manage the physical body to contain/retain

Universal or Cosmic Energy

31

NOTES

THE HIGH PRIESTESS

GIMEL, spelled in Hebrew GML, is the third Hebrew letter and the second of the seven double letters. It means CAMEL. It stands for the pair of opposites PEACE AND STRIFE; for the UNITING INTELLIGENCE; for the planet the MOON; for the color BLUE; the note G-SHARP; and for the direction BELOW. (In the card THE MAGICIAN, the direction was ABOVE. Above is superior consciousness and Below is inferior consciousness.) The numerical value is 3 and in Roman characters it is written G.

The shape of the Hebrew letter ALEPH is a slanting parallelogram with a Yod entering from the top and one entering from the bottom. The parallelogram represents the physical body with the superconscious entering it from above and the subconsciousness entering it from below. The superconscious flows into the body through three ports of entry—through the PINEAL GLAND, the PITUITARY GLAND and the TRANSFORMED HEART.

As entrance for the superconscious, all these channels a man has to make himself. You can get that in one of the sentences of the Gospel story: "Let us make three Temples"—The Pineal Gland, the Pituitary Gland, and the Transformed Heart. The physical organ in each case is there, but you have to make the superconscious (the spiritual) function yourself. Science, of course, is perfectly familiar with the physical function of the heart, and has discovered several of the physical functions of the Pituitary; but science has not yet discovered all the physical functions of the Pineal Gland, and as yet knows nothing about the superconscious function of any of these three.

In addition to the conscious and the subconscious, there is something called the *subjective* mind—not only the subconscious mind but the subjective mind—something above the subconscious. Inner Teachings of religions and mythologies have not only insisted on the self-conscious and the subconscious, but they insist on a peculiar influence which the subconscious and the subjective have on the objective mind and the self-conscious mind. So, the subjective mind the mythologies and the Inner Teachings of religions tell us about, the subjective mind and the subconscious, are entirely at the mercy of the self-conscious mind, yet at the same time they control it.

The subjective mind cannot of itself begin its superconscious functioning. It depends upon the self-conscious mind to begin it, to

33

start it. As for the subconscious mind, it can be very debased or exalted by the images of the self-conscious mind. At the same time, it is willing to execute the messages of the self-conscious mind. Yet both the subjective mind and the subconscious mind are stronger than the self-conscious mind (the intellect) which molds it.

In symbology the subconscious is called the Moon because it shines by reflected light of the Sun (the self-conscious). In Nature, the subconscious reflects the Laws of the Universe, which are the images imposed upon it by the Will of the Creator. The subconscious reflects the images imposed on us by the self-conscious in all matters and functions when that image can be imposed. It cannot generally be imposed on what we call the life process of the body. Doctors tell us that if the self-conscious has not the will to live, the body rarely recovers from the disease; and of course we know of people who have learned to control their pulse and their heartbeat and the circulation of their blood. In general, the self-conscious does not issue any commands about the life processes of the body. It does not attend to them and does not know how to do so. It has no knowledge of how they are carried on, to say nothing of being able to superintend them—but in all functions within the control and direction of the self-conscious, to let the subconscious control is lunacy. This is the root meaning of that strange word *lunacy*—strange to those who do not understand symbology. Lunacy is madness. It means to allow one's self to be governed by the Moon, or by one's subconscious.

The body can be compared to an orchestra—the self conscious, to the director of the orchestra. If you let the orchestra run itself, the result would be discord. Some higher authority, with an ear to the whole, must keep all the various parts in their place. Yet the director, who does not know how to manage each separate instrument, directs. As for each person in the orchestra, he/she knows when the piece is not being well-conducted. He/she knows when the things are wrong, though he/she cannot set them right and play their part at the same time. Our dreams are protests from various parts of our bodies that the conductor is not managing the orchestra well.

The preceding card, Mercury, represented the thinking lobe of the brain. In the same way, this card, THE HIGH PRIESTESS, represents both the normal and subnormal functions of the Pituitary.

The physical function of the Pituitary which concerns us here is:

1) She is the channel of communication between the self-conscious and the subconscious of the body, and

The channel between the Self. Conscious and
the Subconscious minds.

Memory - messages to the Subconscious

The High Priestess   35

2)   She is the principal seat of memory in the body, every cell of
     which also remembers.

The organ of communication between the self-conscious and the
subconscious (the Moon Center) is now the link between the cell
community of the front lobe of your brain, which is the distinctly
human part of you, and the other cell groups in your body which
perform all the complicated acts in the internal routine of your daily
existence. The message of the thinking cells are transferred by the
Moon Center to the cells whose function it is to carry them out. You
wish to raise a finger, for instance, and the message is instantly sent
down by the Moon Center by means of several relays to the muscles of
your finger. When you decide to do a thing, you impress it on the
Moon Center as a command: *Tora,* which is the Hebrew word for
"Law." She does not carry it out, but she sends it to that part of the
body which it concerns. *She herself carries out only the commands of the
Higher Self.*

Your body knows how to perform all sorts of intricate com-
plications you know nothing about, both mechanically and chemically.
Its various centers superintend all the operations that come within
their province without any interference from you; but when you wish
to issue commands to them, they must carry them out as far as they
can do so. The Moon Center is your channel of communication with
them. Remember, however, she merely sends them on, she exercises
no selective faculty. *She passes on messages without regard to whether they
are wise or foolish, constructive or destructive, and the cell workers at the other
end of the message eventually get the orders and carry them out—however
much they may grumble!* If you do not send wise or clear orders, you
experience discord as the immediate consequence of the Moon sending along these messages.

Thus you see the bearing of the name *camel,* which goes with the
letter GIMEL. Among the Eastern tribes where the Hebrew language
was invented, the camel is the vehicle of either peaceful commerce or
war. The name *camel* also applies to our second physical function,
memory. Existing in her are memories not only of this life but of all the
previous ones. They are there not in a concrete form, but they exist as
vibrations which can be stirred into response by upward stimuli.
From her come all the unexplained antipathies and attractions we feel
to people and to places we have never (as we think) encountered
before. This apparently causeless attraction or repulsion is one of the
outstanding facts of our lives. We have all felt it very often, and we are

constantly swept with a vague memory of something pleasant or unpleasant in a previous life.

These two, then, are the functions of the Pituitary Gland, and serve as the channel of communication between the self-conscious, the thinking lobe of the brain, and the body it directs.

In Tarot, the subjective mind is represented by THE HIGH PRIESTESS. The subconscious is represented by THE EMPRESS. It is impossible to talk of one without talking of the other. THE HIGH PRIESTESS is really the representative of Nature, the laws of Nature. THE EMPRESS is a representative of that part of Nature which functions in you and which you have exalted or debased during your long procession of incarnations. Nature is herself perfectly pure, but you in your long series of reincarnations have sullied Nature because you have bound her to your own appetites and passions.

THE HIGH PRIESTESS also represents what the Christians call the Holy Ghost. The Holy Ghost and Nature of the scientist are the same. The subconscious mind is represented as a wife who is as her husband makes her. She is associated with Venus, and in all mythologies there is a good Venus who uplifts man and a bad Venus who drags man down. That is to say, these personal consciousnesses can drag you down or uplift you, and she is what you have made her. The Venus in you, whether good or bad, is subservient to your Will. THE HIGH PRIESTESS in you is not subservient to your Will, THE HIGH PRIESTESS is subservient to the laws of Nature—that is, to the Will of the Creator—but you bring Her more and more into your body. As Jesus said, "I am come that you may have life and have it more abundantly."

THE HIGH PRIESTESS of the Tarot is the Holy Ghost (matter reflecting the designs of the Father). She anthropomorphizes the Cosmic Mind-Stuff—the Virgin Mind-Stuff out of which the Universe took form as a result of the images implanted in it by the Creator. *Remember, the object of the Tarot is not merely to show you the Laws of the Universe, but how these laws work out in you.* What, then, does THE HIGH PRIESTESS, the Virgin Mind-Stuff, do in Tarot, whose object is to depict the relation to your personality of the superconscious, the self-conscious and the subconscious? The teaching of Tarot and the esoteric teaching of Scripture narrative is that the self-conscious, by assiduous endeavor, may bring into your body (and your body is your self-conscious) more and more of the superconscious in the form of Cosmic Mind-Stuff.

There are three forms of the superconscious that you may bring into your body. The first we had in the previous card, BETH, THE MAGICIAN. You may bring in the White Light of the Spirit. The second we have in the card GIMEL, THE HIGH PRIESTESS. You may bring in the untainted Mind-Stuff out of which the Universe was made. The third we have in the card TETH, STRENGTH. You may bring into your body, through the Transformed Heart, the Stellar sex force and manipulate it by means of the White Light, the Cosmic Mind-Stuff which you bring into your body to perfect your body. By means of the Stellar sex force which you bring into your body through the Transformed Heart, you can help to perfect everything outside your body—everything which lies within your sphere of influence.

The Cosmic Mind-Stuff you bring into your body is not subservient to your Will. She does not take the impress of your images. She is subservient only to the Will of the Higher Self. She takes only the impress of His images.

THE HIGH PRIESTESS is this Holy Ghost of the Christian theology in that aspect of her which is not responsive to the Will of the personality, but which nevertheless can be regained by the personality and can be brought into the body through the Pituitary Gland. There is a part of the Cosmic Mind-Stuff which you bring into your body to perfect your body. The Cosmic Mind-Stuff is as yet unspoiled, because when the Creator has worked upon it He has not debased it as you and I have debased our subconscious, which in the beginning, when it first came to use, was not debased. The occultist says that the subjective mind manifests itself in all things and forces as the Laws which govern matter. Madame Blavatsky expressed it perfectly when she said that *matter is Spirit as its lowest vibration.*

So here you have Spirit as its lowest vibration—Spirit at one side and matter at the other. Now between the two modes of the pole are all the myriad rates of vibration. All forms from the atom to the solar system are vibrating, and they consist of two parts—the body of denser matter and the Soul by a nucleus of matter less dense; and the nucleus matter less dense we may speak of relatively as Mind. *All forms consist of Mind and the outer form of matter.* Every atom consists of a central nucleus with a space of energy around it, and that central energy and space bind these particles in such a way as to make one kind of material different from another kind of material; that is to say, each little center of energy is different. They are spaced differently.

This center of energy the occultist calls Mind. It says there is Mind in everything. The mind of the atom has this central energy and it determines or dictates the rest of it, the outer body, just as your mind determines or dictates your outer body. We come up in the scale of Nature from the mineral to plant to animal to man to superman, and as we do, we get bodies capable of manifesting more and more Mind, and hence these bodies are more and more complex; but always they exist in conformity to the central energy, the Mind. As bodies become more and more complex, that is, as they ascend the scale of Nature, the Laws affecting these bodies grow wider and wider in scope. Plants and animals, roughly speaking, follow these Laws of their nature by what we call instinct.

These mineral, plant, and animal natures coexist in man. Man moves by instinct as do plants and animals; i.e., inert man is humanly inert as is the mineral. The acquiring of Wisdom and Understanding evolves man to the state originally intended by the Creator. When this is achieved, by the right use of Mind, man then has dominion over all the lower forms of Nature inside and outside his body.

Even plants and animals can be willful; and, on an extended time scale even minerals can be willful. As in man, some animals and minerals are more subservient to their instinct than others. This can be observed in the animal kingdom as you watch the process we call *domestication* in animals. The consciousness the animal exhibits when it is domesticated corresponds with what we call self-consciousness in human beings. The consciousness of domesticated animals usually is very frail. Consequently, these more remote animal notions, when compared to the self-consciousness of a human being, are activated only when man steps upon the stage of Nature or evolution. The self-consciousness becomes marked, and with it the phenomenon of man arrives at what we call the thinking cells of the brain. This is distinct from the recording cells of the brain. We share recording cells of the brain with the animals; however, ours are more complex.

The recording cells of the brain are in the back lobe of the brain and they record what our senses bring to us. The thinking cells of the brain are in the front lobe and they exist *only* in man. They are distinctly human.

So you see, self-consciousness did not come into manifestation until very long after subconsciousness, and just as we could expect we find the subconscious mind very much more perfect in its working than the self-conscious mind. That is the reason why it is so powerful in us, why it conditions every state of the self-conscious mind, while, at the same time, the self-conscious mind conditions it. Your self-conscious mind is a product of your consciousness of the past; however, at the same time it can change your subconscious in the future if you change the things that you think about.

As you can see, this condition, in itself, points to the old controversy between free will and determinant will. There is no such thing as free will; also there is no such thing as determinant will. We are partly determinant and we have partly free will, free will insofar as we have the capacity to choose. We are the inescapable product of our past; however, *we can change our future!* You have got to act on the subconscious that you have at present before you can change your subconscious for the future.

In Nature the subconscious reflects the Laws of the Universe, which are the Will of the Creator, with images imposed upon the Mind-Stuff by the Creator. Hence, our subconscious reflects images imposed upon her by her self-conscious. We cannot impose images over all our subconscious because there are a lot of things we don't know anything about in our bodies. These unknowns are called the *life processes.* You and I don't know how they are carried on. We cannot impose images upon our subconscious as far as that goes, and we cannot interfere with our life processes by imposing images on our subconscious as to things we know nothing about. So the subconscious must follow her methods in all those things where we cannot exert our authority.

This invites the fact that hardly any of us can be said to have any mind at all, because we exert full capacity of the mind ever so little. What does that come from? It comes from your attention. It is our business as self-conscious beings to keep alert and to keep awake and never be mechanical. We need to pay attention to what is going on outside ourselves and inside our minds. We have not learned to pay adequate attention! Unfortunately, education, either social education or intellectual education, seems to decrease our ability to pay attention rather than to increase it! PRACTICE AWARENESS CONSTANTLY.

The animal pays attention or it could not survive. People who live close to Nature (the farmer, the hunter, and the sailor) must pay attention or they cannot survive. When we come to the field of business in civilized life we must compete or drop out. Unless we learn to pay attention we must confine our efforts to a very narrow field. In school most of our so-called education is mostly memory work. Consequently in educated society we become conventionalized. What is the consequence of this? Most people see things in a blur and they do not pay attention." They do not make clear outlines of the thing they are concerned with at the moment, whether it is physical, emotional, or mental." One should know just as much about what is going on inside himself as what is going on outside of the eyes. That is to say, we should be able to analyze our thoughts and emotions. Most important of all, we should be able to perceive our motives. Instead of that, what happens? We all make mistakes about our motives. We parade before ourselves motives we do not possess. Compare the mind of the self-conscious with the subconscious. SHE IS NEVER, FOR ONE INSTANT, DEFICIENT IN ATTENTION. She never for one instant either consciously or unconsciously forgets herself, she knows precisely what her motive is. She attends to her business perfectly.

What is her business? *It is all things that concern memory, life processes, analysis and deductive reasoning.* Incidentally, the other word for analysis is deductive reasoning. This process is mostly self-evident at the outset. The subconscious builds all the living bodies and maintains their processes. Self-consciousness does not furnish that; the subconsciousness does. In order to do this she must have a perfect memory of all bodies heretofore constructed. She must have memories of all the natural laws of Nature. There must be in the subconscious a record of all past manifestations of life, however distasteful. The subconscious includes all phases of physical brain at this present moment and in this present incarnation. She comprehends, then scans, all phases of life and all things that you need memory for.

The highest vibration is what we call "decay." It is really the process of combustion. The very moment the body dies the self-conscious has left it and the subconscious no longer has a central control of it. Each cell proceeds to burn itself up. That process we call "rotting" or "decay" is simply combustion. In life these cells are kept in order by a "police squad," and these squads are sent out by your central subconscious acting under the authority of your self-conscious.

The above then is the highest authority of keeping your body in order, keeping the cells of your threefold body on the job. This state is symbolized by the next card, THE EMPRESS, the intellectual subconscious. This component is responsive to the commands of your intellect in the same way that the Cosmic Subconscious, in you, is responsive to the commands of the Higher Self.

The self-conscious and the subconscious have four aspects, just as your body has four aspects (physical, mental, emotional, and spiritual). The Higher Self and subconsciousness are identified as the Intuitive.

That part of you which takes instruction from your Higher Self is called Intuition and that part of your subconscious which takes instruction from the Holy Ghost is also called Intuition. The next aspect is the Intellectual. That part of your subconscious which controls the Intellect is known as the Emotional or Passional. The fourth is the Physical. Your subconscious and/or self-conscious have these four aspects: INTUITIVE, INTELLECTUAL, PASSIONAL or EMOTIONAL, and PHYSICAL. These are symbolized by four animals: The Eagle (Intuition), the Man (Intellect), the Lion (Emotion), and the Bull (Appetite).

The Physical aspect is the lowest and it controls everything within its sphere. It is controlled by the aspect above it, the Emotional. The civilized man is supposed to submit his appetites to emotions. He'll want some cake, and then he'll want to eat more cake. You say, "No, if I eat more I shall have a pain." So if you are wise you do not eat more cake, you sacrifice your appetite to your emotion. Civilized man is then supposed to sacrifice his emotion to his ambition, i.e., "I should like to run away with your lover, but if I do I forfeit my career."

Then above the *third*, the *Intellectual*, stands the *Intuitive*, the *fourth*. The self-conscious Intuition (The Fool) supplies that intuition. The Intuitive subconscious in you is symbolized by THE HIGH PRIESTESS, the third card. That function of the subconscious has to do with analysis or deductive reasoning. The subconscious has no power whatsoever of inductive reasoning. That belongs to the self-conscious alone. She, THE HIGH PRIESTESS, possesses perfect analysis. That is to say, if the self-conscious tells her to do a thing, she analyzes it and finds out how to do it best. She elaborates upon everything given her by the conscious through analysis. She represents what might be called the Ways and Means Committee. She does not criticize, react, or issue any judgment upon the command given her by the conscious mind. She proceeds at once to gather together the essentials to carry out these commands. She grows what you plant. She, the subconscious, knows how to do, you do not.

Inductive reasoning belongs alone to the masculine principle and its awareness. This was symbolized in the previous card as THE MAGICIAN. This power of deductive reasoning, or mental analysis, is the *fourth power* which the Cosmic and personal subconscious have in common. Each grows what its lord plants. Here a great shift occurs. There enters the lord of the Cosmic images. The lord of the intellectual subconscious has been, from the very beginning of humanity, planting unwise images. The intellectual subconscious has executed these images with as much wisdom as if they had been wise ones—with the same adaptation of means to ends, with the same analytic and deductive reasoning. Since they were unwise images, the process of bringing them to birth has corrupted and thus tainted her. To free her of these taints is the object of the alchemy of Tarot and of all mystical practices. That is of the mental side of religion. It is also the aim of all the devotional side of religion—hymn, prayer, and ritual.

You will see in the symbolism of this card how this self-conscious attempt to free the subconscious from the taints that he has imposed upon her (the Cosmic subconscious) takes a hand. Her cooperation is entirely dependent upon the self-conscious. She cannot set about her cleansing work until he has enabled her to do so; nor can the personal subconscious avail herself of her Mother's ministrations until he implants in her the images which will set her free.

That is where the vital necessity comes in of your giving her, the subconscious, good commands and good images. Good images can arise only from good attention. That is all her task, and beyond that we cannot interfere. This is dictated by the images that we furnish her. One cannot get her to change her habits until we have convinced her that the new methods we are supplying her with are what we really want. She has known us to change our mind many times before. Furthermore, she perceives the motives that you hide from yourself. She even sees that though you aren't sincere, you think you are. The whole business of the technique which Freud introduced first (and all applied psychologists since have followed the technique) is the reaction of the subconscious, giving her new images to follow. The whole business of the Church ritual, prayer, or hymn is to provide images for the subconscious.

All physical forms are made out of the same stuff. The occultist says that our subconscious can connect us with every other body in the Universe if you know how to utilize her. All people's thoughts and feelings are made out of the same stuff. All of these that we are attuned to affect us. Fortunately, we do not have to respond to the feelings and thoughts of people we are not attuned to. If we did, we would be at everybody's mercy. The highest would then be at the mercy of the lowest, because the lowest would be dominant. Occultists and mystics say that we automatically and inevitably respond to all the vibrations that we are attuned to at the moment.

This would be very difficult to appreciate if it were not for the radio. We know even if we are not very bright that vibrations are constantly flowing through space and are sent out by other things and people in the form of sound. If it weren't for the radio we could not make these people believe that; while the reasonable person says that if sound also has vibrations there is no reason why thought and feeling should not also have vibrations. We are constantly projecting out from our thoughts and feelings.

Lastly, we come to a power possessed by the Cosmic subconscious alone. All the rest she shares with the personal subconscious; *the power of uniting all opposites together.* The intellectual subconscious has the power of uniting all similar things together.

Occultism teaches that all people are constantly giving out concentric rays of vibration in the same way the Sun is doing. If we have good thoughts and feelings we shall tune in with good thoughts and feelings. We have retuned our radio to catch all the good thoughts and feelings of other people. If we have bad thoughts and feelings we shall tune in with them. We often set our radio to catch all the bad thoughts and feelings of other people. The choice is ours!

This is one way in which THE HIGH PRIESTESS stands for Peace and Strife. Your subconscious can unite you not only with all the present, but with all the past. Nature keeps a record of the entire past, which is imperishable, and which anybody can be in touch with if he knows how to utilize it. It is a sort of photograph stamped on one of the four planes (physical, mental, emotional, and spiritual), a motion picture of everything that has ever happened. By making connection with this through the subconscious, a man finds out not only about his own past lives but also about the past lives of any other person he is liable to contact. *IT IS THE SEEING OF THE PAST WHICH WAS CARRIED IN THE WALLET OF THE FOOL.*

SYMBOLISM

THE HIGH PRIESTESS is represented by this card as if in a portico of a temple, and she is looking towards its shrine. The shrine or the sanctuary which she looks towards is the Pineal Gland, and the occupant of that shrine is the Higher Self, or the earthly representative of the Spirit. She is the Pituitary Body. In her occult function she is termed "The Gate of the Sanctuary," and the sanctuary is the Pineal Gland. There is one physical function which the occultist gives it. SHE IS THE ORGAN OF COMMUNICATION BETWEEN THE THINKING CELLS OF THE BRAIN, IN WHICH THE SELF-CONSCIOUS FUNCTIONS,

AND SHE IS, HERSELF, THE COSMIC SUBCONSCIOUS. It is the connection, or communication, between the front lobe of the brain and the back lobe of the brain. She sends down messages from the front lobe of the brain to the subconscious control, which is situated at the root of the tongue, where the VENUS CENTER is. The Moon Center transfers to the Venus Center the messages of the thinking lobe of the brain, and the Venus Center sends them to the other Centers below her.

THE HIGH PRIESTESS is wearing a SILVER CROWN. Silver is the metal of the Moon. The crown shows the crescents of the Moon, waxing and waning, with the Full Moon orb in between. This is symbolic of the feminine principle which is at the root of all things.

For instance, you raise a finger and you make an image of that. The Pituitary sends that image down to the Venus Center, but as it does not concern her she sends it below to the Solar Plexus that it does concern, and it sees that the message is carried out, all in the flash of a thought. So the Moon Center, or the Pituitary Body, is the channel of communication between the thinking lobe of the brain and the rest of the body. It is the means of communication between the self-conscious and the subconscious. She passes down these messages, for she has no selective faculty. So you see how good a "camel" it is. The camel is one that carries messages. The camel among desert tribes is the vehicle of commerce or war, either one or the other. The pair of combined opposites that the letter stands for is Peace and Strife.

The WHITE CUBE on which The High Priestess sits is the Physical Plane. She sits between the Black Pillar and the White Pillar, holding the balance between them. The office of the subconscious in the body is to keep you in balance. She is at your mercy, and if you give her a wrong message she does as well as she can to keep you in balance. If we give her wrong directives she can't do the job.

The TWO PILLARS represent all the positive and negative forces of the Universe. She is not bound to either, but sits at perfect peace between them, using the one or the other as suits her purpose. "B," the letter on the Black Pillar, is the Intellect. "J," on the White Pillar , is the Spirit (Boaz and Jakin). Spirit and Intellect oppose each other. The High Priestess brings them into union. Intellect wants one thing, Spirit wants another.

That is what we are bid to do. We are supposed to impersonate THE HIGH PRIESTESS. Do not allow moods to control you or utilize you, but utilize them. That is, unless they are moods which uplift you.

If they are moods which cast you down say to yourself, "What is this about?" Then change your mood. *There is in us an all-knowing power in the subconscious which, if we allow her, will keep us in balance*—perfect poise. She keeps herself in perfect poise except in those minor activities where we interfere with her. What a birthright poise is. It would have been our birthright if we had been born an animal. That is to say, if we were utilizing instinct we would be in perfect poise. Why do we, in the self-conscious, lose the poise that from instinct governs the animal and keeps it in poise? We began to manifest Mind in the way that Mind is always initially manifesting and we often unknowingly backslide.

We did that in early childhood when all we were concerned with was the gratification of our appetites. No animal in the wild state ever overeats or over-gratifies its senses. Instinct forbids it. How different it is with our children. If you give them apples to eat they often eat too much. This tendency is noticeable with domestic animals. When animals are domesticated they begin to acquire the gluttony of the human being, and will overeat. It is perfectly right and natural for your child to be a little animal, but since instinct no longer rules the human animal appetite, he must switch from the use of instinct to mind and to reason. He makes it up first by being subject to others' reason until he can build up one of his own. So you see at the very outset of his career as a man, the man-animal must make itself, must improve itself. That is expected. He must be educated out of the stage of human animal, and control that desire to over-gratify his appetites. He must be educated out of that stage by his parents first, and then by society.

The child is expected to accommodate himself to external restriction and to other people's rights, and gradually, in time, build up that balanced restraint we call Reason to take the place of the discarded instinct. As he does this unwillingly, he represses or suppresses protestingly his natural desire. Freud has shown us that this result is indeed equally unfortunate, and his unrepressed nature often leads to what contemporary psychologists call neuroses and complexes.

Through the family and society we have grown up with phases of the subconscious which become poorly balanced before we reach the age of reason. That subconscious has to be reeducated in all of us now that we have developed our reason. Freud set the whole world to fearing the subconscious, whereas she is often our best friend. She can be reeducated to be our best friend, but whether she is our enemy or our best friend, she is also a despot and we have to follow her. She

from instinct to mind
from mind to reason

must be a tyrant. Now what kind of a tyrant shall she be? A bad one or a good one? It is all up to you which she shall be. It depends upon the messages and images you furnish her by the thoughts you habitually think.

In THE HIGH PRIESTESS card you have the subconscious of the Cosmos, the subconscious as the recipient of the messages furnished her by the Creator. If we direct our subconscious wisely we will not be at the mercy of undesirable moods, because she is not subject to that mode. Our moods don't condition her and they won't condition us.

Wisdom is the Cosmic Mind, and understanding is as much of the Cosmic Mind as we can grasp and build through the medium of our body, our personal subconscious.

The tops of the Pillars are shaped like bells with long handles, the lower part being the long handle. The bell cannot fulfill its function unless its bowl has a clapper. The bowl of the bell is useless without the clapper, and likewise the clapper is useless without the bowl. It takes both to make the sound. The clapper represents an image; this image represents the Will, or the self-conscious. The bowl represents the subconscious. The Pillar is also made in that shape to remind us of the Goblet on the Table of THE MAGICIAN. If you will look at the Goblet, you will align downward into the Cosmic Mind-Stuff.

This is the same way we do our own creating. We plunge down our image into the bowl of the subconscious, which forms our image for us, which gives it a body. The same thing is pictured on the Robe of THE HIGH PRIESTESS. The White Cross of the Spirit, which symbolizes Spiritual Will, comes over the concentric five Leaves with four diamonds. These are the ten aspects of the Life Force corresponding to the ten ornaments of THE FOOL. Here there are five on each pillar, or if you count around the pillar, there are ten on each pillar. Ten aspects of the Life Force on the positive side, and ten aspects on the negative side.

Immediately behind THE HIGH PRIESTESS is a VEIL. The first Veil is the curtain of illusion which hides reality. You see it is made very thin, the idea being that it can be seen through. All science is an attempt to see through the Veil. All mysticism is an attempt to see through the Veil. All religion is an attempt to see through the Veil. The mystic and occultist assert that if one works upon his own organism, he fashions an instrument of his own body which will enable him to penetrate that Veil. The occultist tells us that if we develop powers of the subconscious we can see through the Veil as far as it is given man to see through at the present.

On this Veil there are two designs. These two designs are arranged in a pattern and the pattern is partly obscured here by the figure of THE HIGH PRIESTESS. She is blotting out some of the parts of the design. The design in itself, in its entirety, is what the Hebrews call the Tree of Life, on which there are Ten Fruits. You do not see ten here. They are partly hidden by THE HIGH PRIESTESS and the Cube. It is the Tree of Life which you soon have to study as you go on with this work.

YELLOW in the two designs represents the Masculine, the color of THE MAGICIAN, the self-conscious mind. GREEN represents the Feminine, or the subconscious mind. Let us take one of the symbols, the PALM LEAF. It is a universal feminine symbol. It is Green, the color of the personal subconscious of the next card, THE EMPRESS. You have the universal feminine symbol colored with the symbolism of the feminine color. In the center of it is the lobe of Yellow, so the symbolism of this figure is the masculine in the feminine. The self-conscious principle within the subconscious principle. The other symbol is not a leaf, but the formed fruit; that is to say, it is much nearer completion than the leaf. This symbol is the POMEGRANATE embodied within a Yellow Rind. The Pomegranate is a universal feminine symbol because of its numerous seeds. It is embodied in YELLOW. This design indicates the subconscious within the conscious, just the other way around. The above design is a leaf and this design is a fruit.

It is the business of the subconscious to make fruitful the image of the self-conscious. It is the masculine in the feminine and the feminine in the masculine.

Note the FLOOR of the portico is LIGHT YELLOW, the color that goes with ALEPH, and which forms the background of THE MAGICIAN card. When you get to the card TETH, which depicts the final birth of the personal subconscious, you will see that this background is a deeper yellow, the color assigned to the self-conscious. THE COLOR OF THE BACKGROUND IN THE CARDS OF THE TAROT DENOTES THE FIRST STATE OF CONSCIOUSNESS, WHICH IS CHIEFLY INSTRUMENTAL IN PRODUCING THE STATE DEPICTED IN THAT CARD. The background of the card TETH depicts the purification of the present self-conscious and deepens the force set in motion by the self-conscious. The deeper yellow is the shade employed in all the rest of THE HIGH PRIESTESS card—in the fruit, leaves and the Veil, and in the Crescent at her feet. The Crescent at her feet symbolizes the intellectual subconscious.

The Robe of THE HIGH PRIESTESS is made to suggest water, and it is flowing through the Crescent to symbolize that it is cleansing it. The Cosmic Mind-Stuff is always referred to esoterically as water. This is for two reasons: (1) that it visibly vibrates in waves and (2) that it cleanses, since it is entirely untainted. Everywhere in the Universe is this Cosmic Mind-Stuff—not worked up into forms. Of course there are forms also. This Cosmic Mind-Stuff, which is not worked up into forms, is consequently pure and untainted by any human contact. All forms in the world are untainted until they have contacted humanity. Humanity is the only thing which is willful and which has transgressed Nature's Laws.

The immediate parents of the Christ-Child are the Pituitary and the Pineal Glands. Of this mystic union it is the divine offspring.

The Pituitary Gland is analogous to the Virgin Mary of the Gospel narrative, who was with child by the Spirit. "Mary" comes from the word "sea," or "mare." This word use exists in all languages, not merely in Latin. It is simply another way of saying that the Virgin Mind-Stuff is the Great Sea of Substance out of which the universal form was made.

Water is not the only natural object associated with the Holy Ghost; "Milk" is also. In the Old Testament, Canaan was a "land flowing with milk and honey." Canaan symbolizes the Purified Intellect in the purified body. The children of Israel crossed over into it after 40 years of wandering in the desert, and during those 40 years every soul in that vast multitude perished, including the three leaders: Moses, Aaron, and Miriam.

Moses symbolizes the Intuition,

Aaron symbolizes the Intellect, and

Miriam symbolizes the Intellectual Subconscious (the Venus, or THE EMPRESS of the next card).

The Purified Intellect flows with milk and honey—that is, the emanations of the Pituitary and the Pineal Glands. You will note that the Robe of THE HIGH PRIESTESS in this card shades off into milky blue. In another way THE HIGH PRIESTESS is analogous to the Virgin Mary of Catholic theology. Catholic theology, much to the disapproval of the Protestant sect, says that the Virgin Mary is the go-between, the intercessor, between man and God. Recall that the esoteric teaching is that the Pituitary (or Holy Ghost) adapts the

White Light of the Spirit to the use of the Intellect of Man, the self-conscious. It is the go-between connecting the Spirit, which stands for God, and the self-conscious, which stands for his use of cleaning the personal subconscious.

NOTES

EVE – The female sex force
The universal cosmic energy

The intellectual subconscious has the power of uniting all similar things together.

"Change your thinking change your future."

Subconscious
Collective
subconscious

The Intellectual
subconscious

Deductive Reasoning
Mental Analysis

The Union of the M/F energy.

THE EMPRESS.

What is the desire, that transforms the Thinking !!

The method to cultivate attention.

Upon what have you concentrated ?

The subconscious mind conditions every state of the self-conscious mind...but the

Self-conscious mind focuses the subconscious mind on the subjects that will condition it.

4th Hebrew Letter	**DALETH**
Symbol for	**Pair of Opposites—**
	(Wisdom and Folly)
Color	**Emerald Green**
Numerical Value	**4**
Syllables	**DLTh**
Sound	**F-Sharp**
Planet	**Venus**
Translation	**Door**

/ reeducated "

"The subconscious can be retrained

The subconscious is being transformed

The subconscious is represented as a "Wife" who is as her Husband makes her.

The subconscious is controlled by your conscious will – which actively tells it what to concentrate on.

NOTES

THE EMPRESS

ד **DALETH,** spelled in Hebrew DLTh, means "Door." It is the fourth Hebrew letter and the third DOUBLE LETTER. It stands for the pair of opposites, WISDOM and FOLLY (or knowledge and ignorance), for the direction EAST, for the LUMINOUS INTELLIGENCE, for the planet VENUS, color GREEN, and the note F-SHARP. The numerical value is 4.

Cards 0, 1, 2, 3 are to be understood in the Cosmic sense as well as in the personal sense. They describe not only our body of manifestation but the way God (the Logos) made His body of manifestation, which is the solar system. They also describe how you can set about making a better body for yourself to manifest in and how you have made the one you have at present.

Now, let us look at that for a moment on the Cosmic side. In the Cosmic sense you have had the One Will and the Universal Substance—the duality in which the One Energy has to divide itself into two in order to objectify itself. When it is divided into two, the Will works upon the Substance to proceed. The Will works upon the Substance to produce forces, and then forms. The Will depicts images and projects images. These ideas come down into the Sea of Substance of the Cosmic Mind-Stuff, and out of the union of the image devised in the Sea of Substance is produced first force and then forms.

That process is pictured in the middle ground of this card, the WATERFALL IN THE WATERFALL, where the above meets the below. You have seen that the Will is called the superior and the Substance the Inferior, though both are equal. The word *Superior* translates into "Above" and the word *Inferior* translates into "Below." The WATERFALL occurs three times in Tarot Trumps, and always it is a sex symbol—sex union of the masculine and feminine principles. The masculine principle being the Superior, the Idea, the Will; and the feminine the Inferior, the Substance. Remember that *both are really equal* and you must have the meeting of these two, the union of these two, in order to get a product, to find the expression in a product. The products indicate in the Cosmic by the manifested solar system: all made out of ideas of God coming into the Substance of Nature.

Gimel and Daleth are two aspects of the same thing. Gimel is the Cosmic subconscious; Daleth is that Cosmic subconscious made active in bringing forth the image.

53

The Pituitary in you does not carry out your suggestions or your Torah (Law) herself. She merely passes them on to the Venus Center at the root of the tongue. It is the Venus who carries them out or passes them on further where they belong. When a man has reached a certain evolution, his outer, or long-spoiled subconscious, the personal subconscious, and the Cosmic subconscious are at loggerheads. They are opposed to each other. It is the same meaning in mythology, where Venus and Diana are enemies. That is the reason for the Crown that THE HIGH PRIESTESS wears with the crescents facing away from each other. *It is your business to turn these crescents around and make a perfect sphere of them, as in a crown.* In this card, THE EMPRESS, are opposing crescents with the sphere in the middle. The business of self-education is to make these crescents harmonious instead of opposing. You have the same idea in the crescent at the foot of THE HIGH PRIESTESS. Her garment is flowing through that crescent. So the color is tinged, which shows the changing personal subconscious. You include the personal subconscious with the Cosmic subconscious in order to bring it into the Pituitary Gland.

When you take Daleth in her personal significance she is the subconscious. Beth means "Mind," and we have wrongfully educated her in the processes which we call growing up—the growing up of the race. We outgrow the animal nature we were born with by thinking and by coming under the influence of parents, education, law, or society. We had to come under the influence of these four whether we were strong or whether we were weak characters. The words *strong* and *weak* are used without any reference to what we call "moral considerations." The strong character is one who, for good or for evil, fructifies his own subconscious. The weak character is one who, by acting in an entirely neutral manner, allows the fructification to be done by something outside of his own self-conscious—by his appetites which are subconscious, by his passions which are subconscious, and by the influence of people's thoughts without having first made those thoughts his own. That is the difference between a strong and a weak character.

The masculine principle in us (the Mind) is the personal, objective, and conscious mind (the Intellect). It is voluntary and active, as distinct from the subconscious mind in us which follows the lead of the conscious, which is passive and involuntary. When you project your active mind (your Will) into your passive one, the passive mind (subconscious) begins to act and becomes very active indeed, but acts only on the image you have given her to work out. She initiates no action of her own; she is very active, but only with your affairs. She immediately begins to act then upon the image you plant in her.

The majority of persons employ their active mind very little. They are content to live in their own appetites, according to the thoughts or ideas of their generation, or of some masterful people in their immediate environment, people who want to manage. The phenomena of telepathic suggestion, hypnotism, mental healing, Christian Science and the like are merely examples of a masculine principle of one person being projected into the feminine principle of another person. *The strong man or woman does not live upon the impressions made on their minds by others. They energize their own subconscious with their own mental images, whether they are strong or whether they are for good or for evil.* When people are strong they not only energize their own subconscious, but project as much as they can of their self-conscious, their masculine principle, onto those who they come in contact with.

It is very important that you understand this principle, this principle of "gender." You cannot understand the principle of mental or spiritual creation until you understand the principle of gender. Nothing can happen until the masculine fructifies the feminine, until the self-conscious fructifies the subconscious. That self-conscious may be of another person or it may be your Higher Self or it may be of a Master.

What happens is indicated by the Waterfall. The mental stage is stamped from the self-conscious on what it falls into. The fruit which springs up in the picture is wheat. It could be wheat or it could be tares as the case may be. It may be spurious and bad wheat, and that applies to the tares as well. This is the true meaning of the rather ambiguous and unfortunate phrase "as a man thinketh, so is he." That leaves room for interpretation. It ought to be "as a man *images*, so he becomes." YOU ARE WHAT YOUR CHERISHED AND EMOTIONAL IMAGES ARE. The thoughts that you most cherish so make your body. The meaning of THE EMPRESS is "She who sets the house in order." The meaning of THE EMPEROR is "He who sets the Mind in order."

Your house is your body. Venus, or Daleth, remolds your subconscious according to what you desire, and your image is what you desire. The image is nothing in the world but the emotional picture or the thought of a desire. So you see it depends upon your image whether your house is set in order for good or for evil. In either case she sets it in order and she brings out the product that you desire.

The trouble with most of us is that such desires proceed directly from the subconscious without the medium of the self-conscious at all; that is to say, we desire what pleases our body.

The letter Daleth means "door." The physiological center she stands for is at the base of the tongue, the second relay station between the self-conscious (as expressed in your thinking brain cells in the front lobe of your brain) and the subconscious, which is emphasized by your body. That physiological center is the Phyrangeal Plexus. The Phyrangeal Plexus has a special influence upon the thymus and the thyroid gland functions. It has a special influence on the entire chemistry of your body.

It is taught that this plexus receives the patterns or images which your Mercury, your self-conscious, sends first to the Pituitary and then down the Venus Center. She does not carry out your sugges-tions, your "Tora," herself; she sends them down to the Venus Center to carry them out. So the subconscious of your body is represented by the Venus Center and not by the Pituitary. You see, she really is the Door to the lower part of the house. The brain has to use that door to send down messages to the lower part of the house or the rest of the body which the brain uses. She is also the door coming up from the lower part of the body into the skull, and that lower part of the body, when it wants to send messages, has to send them through her.

There are two reasons why she is called Door. She is a door going down to the body and a door coming up. Now we see that the Pituitary Body, the Center, receives communications from the external world by telepathy. The Venus Center and the Moon Center receive those from the external world, but the Venus Center does not send them out. In this respect she might be called the "Door which opens only one way." Both the Moon Center and the Venus Center receive the telepathic messages from the outside, but the Venus Center only receives; she cannot send out.

Here are the important things: she receives according to the attunement you have given her by your habitual images; she receives either wisdom or folly. If your messages are wise she receives wise telepathic images from the outside. If you think foolish thoughts, if your conclusions about the outside world are based upon superficial attention, and you don't think at all but confine your mental activity to daydreams and sensual pictures by recombining the material you find on the recording cells of the brain, then you are tuned in to the whole world of Ignorance and Folly.

If you take the time to pay attention and amend your reason and arrive at reasonable conclusions based on accurate attention in these premises, then you tune in to the general warehouse of the wisdom of the race. You tune in not only to past wisdom, but to the source of present wisdom. You tune in to the plane the occultist calls the superman, the Master. Or, if you are ripe for it, you can receive personal instruction through your telepathy by the messages that enter your body through the Venus Center. Also it is through the Venus Center that you receive messages from the Higher Self.

Instruction, then, either from the Masters or from the Higher Self, is sent to you telepathically through the Venus Center. She relays it up to the Moon Center, sends it on to the thinking cells of the brain where it is received as an intuition; or the Moon Center may send it into the recording lobe of the brain, into the hearing area. Any vibration that enters the hearing area registers there as sound, and this sound is like an actual voice. The natural vibration of this hearing center registers on our conscious mind as a voice. There are apparently very few people in the world who have not fancied that they have heard, at one time or another, a voice speaking to them when there was no voice. That is the functioning of the Venus Center sending the message up to the Pituitary Body. Instead of sending it to the thinking lobe of the brain, she sends it to the hearing area where it sounds like a voice, and it registers there as a sound. They come in as vibration and go out as sound. Mystics and many other people know that there is this voice and that it is a mental vibration. It comes into your body through the functioning of the "door" of the Venus Center.

This is one of the ways you receive inner instruction from the Higher Self or from outside sources. They are either good or bad depending upon how you have tuned yourself. The bad voices are becoming more frequent. You constantly read in the newspapers how murderers say they heard this cry "kill." It is probably true that they did hear a voice crying "kill." There are those who wish to use our bodies as the vehicles of violent deeds, but there is nothing to this if you do not allow it. This should be a grave warning. No one can gain entrance to your body and do you harm if you have not deliberately prepared the way, whose visitation you have not long courted. As on the radio, you get what you tune in for.

Most patients in insane asylums are not insane. They simply open their self-conscious and their body to astral and etheric vibrations, which causes them to act in some way doctors cannot understand.

There is no need for anyone to be alarmed at this state of affairs because no one can enter your body, be he good or bad, for whom you have not deliberately prepared the way.

The mystic and the occultist are always asserting their ideas, which is one explanation for the number of chemists in the world. They say that in the future the development will unfold in the same way that the past has unfolded. They say that for all civilization man has been trying to tame the animal in himself, and that the future, no matter how far distant, can only be a continuation of the same process of controlling the animal in man. Evolution is the same process of controlling the animal in man. Evolution in Nature is only man unfolding the new powers in Nature. Mystics and occultists also say that evolution in man can only mean the unfolding of new powers in him. Evolution itself will, in time, unfold these new powers to the race. Tarot speaks of 12 new powers, 12 extensions of consciousness. The 12 extensions of consciousness are what the 12 SIMPLE LETTERS of the sacred Hebrew alphabet stand for.

The occultist says that the individual can anticipate natural evolution by intensive work upon the animal in him. It is the same kind of work that man has been doing on Nature. Man has given to the plant and animal new powers by training. Can man become the Raphael, the Kant, the Shakespeare merely by training? No, as we look back upon the evolution of man and what we call civilization, we see that what has transformed him from what he was to what he is at present is his faculty of making images—his image-making faculty. Our attention made us see what we needed. We saw what we needed and we imaged ways to satisfy those good things. That is why we are what we are today. *We can, by our images, so transform our bodies that we can extend our present senses, and we have the Tarot cards for that extension of our present senses.*

It is a matter of common knowledge that a man can purify or debase his character by the images he indulges in, and the body is much more responsive to your mind than some would have us believe. Just as a God or a Logos imaged into existence a new universe, so you can image into existence a new universe, so you can image into existence a new body with new powers yet undreamed of by most people. We say that science believes in evolution and that the Mendelian future of evolution is the most satisfactory one yet arrived at (by Mendel).

What is Mendelian theory? Mendelian theory asserts that all the possibilities of evolution in plants existed in the original germ of those plants. It was there all the time. Evolution is only the process of throwing off one by one the inhibiting factors which kept this germ from entirely expressing itself.

If that is true of plants it must be true of man, says the occultist, and he calls the attention of the religious people to the fact that the Bible says the same thing. The Bible says that man is made to be a co-partner with God. God evolved the world out of Himself. If man is made to be co-partner with God, he is made to go on evolving the world out of himself, just as God did. History certainly shows that man is able to hasten the evolution of Nature as well as his own evolution. By an adaptation of Nature man helps to evolve Nature and give her powers she did not possess in the first place, except of course latently.

So you see, if the Bible and the Mendelian theory are true, man can evolve Godship out of himself by recognition of his Godhood and by throwing off the factors which inhibit his kinship. They will be thrown off anyway in the course of time, but he can hasten it by intensive work on himself—by his understanding of who he really is.

Now the one tool that God used and the tool that man has used to evolve Nature and to evolve himself is the image-making faculty. If we are going to work upon our bodies, change our bodies into bodies with new powers, we do it by making images and having faith in those images. The self-conscious makes the image and instructs the subconscious to carry it out.

God evolved the world out of Himself in four stages of creation and man creates in the same way. These four stages are the four tools on the Magician's table.

The Wand (Fire): *Idea*	It stands for Light and the Abstract Idea, unlocalized.
The Cup (Water): *Idea given emotion and an image of Completion*	Stands for concrete pattern. The Abstract Idea brought down, narrowed, given form in your mind as a concrete thing.
The Sword (Air): *organized and manage plan of resources For construction*	The process by which you carve out that concrete Idea.
The Pentacle (Earth): *organized & managed work executed according to Construction plan & TiME cycles*	Physical plane product, the end product of the other three stages.

Mind-Stuff is changed into physical stuff in those four stages, by the executor of the image. The executor is Venus, THE EMPRESS.

The card which carries out the Idea is THE EMPRESS. This symbolizes her carrying out the image which has been transplanted into her by the self-conscious. Card 11, JUSTICE, is the picture of THE EMPRESS in another aspect. It is a picture of THE EMPRESS at work carrying out that image. You will see that she carries it out with the sword in one hand and with the scales (balance) in the other, constantly changing the body. At the same time she is constantly keeping the balance with the scales.

Venus is always spoken of as the Imagination, but she does not make the image. It is made by Mercury, the self-conscious. The mental image is a picture of a thing or of an aspect, a mental likeness of something. Mercury makes the images and Venus carries them out.

The suffix "ation" means a thing that is produced by the action denoted of the root word. The root word of imagination is "image." The word means the production of the thing imaged. That is precisely what this does—produces the thing imaged.

It is the teaching of occultism that the emotions, in the life before this one, created this present body, and had we cultivated different thoughts and moods we should have inherited for ourselves a different body in this life. "As a man thinketh," says an occult doctrine with St. Paul, "so he will become." In each life our mood determines the physical body, with certain physical moods inherited from our parents. Our mental and emotional natures we inherit from ourselves. Even the physical body, in its major characteristics (which we inherit from our parents), has been made by our thoughts and moods in the eons of time—for we have always been. What we inherit from our parents is only the basis of our physical body. The three bodies—the Physical, Emotional, and Mental natures—make up our personality. All this is our subconscious. We inherit the subconscious thoughts tainted by wrong methods of thinking and feeling, and we must try to cleanse it by acquiring right methods. Most of these methods simmer down to one thing: PAYING ADEQUATE ATTENTION TO WHAT IS GOING ON OUTSIDE AND INSIDE OURSELVES. Education, either social or intellectual, seems to decrease rather than increase attention. That is because we are not educated rightly. Education is mostly a matter of memory with us. The animal had to pay attention to many other animals who were trying to gobble him up. People who live close to Nature pay attention to her moods.

We should be able to analyze our thoughts and our moods. Most important of all, we should be able to perceive our motives and our behavior. Instead, we all parade before ourselves motives that we do not possess. Why? In order to blind our eyes to the motives we do possess. Now this is the self-conscious mind. The subconscious is never deficient in attention nor does she ever consciously or unconsciously jolly herself. She attends to her business perfectly. Not only does she do her business thoroughly while we are very slipshod about ours, but she has been at it an infinitely longer time. The self-conscious is a very late comer to Nature. Our self-consciousness becomes marked only when man appears on the scene.

As to the shape of the Hebrew letters, every one means something and has some connection with the mystic truths which they bear. So you see this letter is the basis of the next letter, Heh, and this letter is the basis of the eighth Hebrew letter CHETh. Just exactly what that means we will have to defer until we get to them.

SYMBOLISM

In this card, the horizontal line of the BENCH THE EMPRESS sits on, together with the shield, roughly outlines the form of the letter Daleth. You see it presents so far as it can do so and carries out other ideas; at the same time it represents the corner of the square. The ORANGE PILLOW behind her is also a square. Its sides are curved to represent vibratory motion, and it is decorated with little squares. Remember the instrument of building is the square, the carpenter's square or right angle with which he adjusts every piece of material to see that it is true. If one piece is not set straight, the subsequent pieces which depend on it become crooked also. This square which is indispensable to good building is your image. The perfection of your house, your body, depends on whether your image be good or not.

On the HEART-SHAPED SHIELD is the astrological symbol of Venus, the circle above the cross. The circle is colored GREEN, which is the color of Venus. What does the circle stand for in the signs of the Planets and Zodiac? The circle stands for the superconscious. The cross stands for the self-conscious and the crescent stands for the subconscious.

The GOLDEN SCEPTER she bears in her uplifted hand is a modification of the same symbol. There are two arms in the lower portion of the Scepter. The handle of the Scepter, which is the arm of the cross, swings the arm of the cross vertically from horizontal. This is so that it is parallel to the other vertical arm.

What are images of your desires.

Then she has a CROWN on her head as insignia of her power. This Crown has 12 stars and they symbolize the 12 signs of the Zodiac. The 12 signs of the Zodiac symbolize, among other things, the 12 major states of consciousness, and extension of those 12 states. The Crown always means control. The Crown means that Venus, who carries out the image, has control of the 12 states of consciousness. Their correct functioning depends upon what image the self-conscious makes, whether it is a good or bad function. Through the stars runs a RED RIBBON. RED stands for the Mars vibration and for action. Venus makes active the images of the self-conscious and thus controls the 12 major states of consciousness.

The SPECK OF RED at her throat marks the Venus Center. That is to say, whether you control your Venus for good or bad, she controls you. You are her slave though she is yours. Is that a hard thought? How does she control them? By controlling the images that you make, whatever you set in motion has got to work out in her. *You are a slave to whatever you set in motion! You can set in motion what you please.* In short, you are the slave of your past. The future is yours if you change your images. You are a slave to the past because you have made a body which controls you. The future is yours because you can change your body.

So this answers the old question: Is there a free will or not? THERE IS NO FREE WILL AS FAR AS THE PAST IS CONCERNED. YOU CAN MAKE YOUR FUTURE DIFFERENT FROM YOUR PAST BECAUSE YOU HAVE THE RIGHT OF CHOICE IN MAKING OTHER IMAGES.

In any case, she controls the 12 major states of consciousness no matter what you have made her; however, the original control is with you.

At the base of her throat is a little BLOCK OF RED. That means the Venus Center has now become active. These cards depict the highest state, the highest objective of the type of consciousness to which they refer. This card refers to the Venus Center when it has become completely active. As a rule, the Venus Center is the last center in the body to become completely active, so you see it means very complete control of the body. The Venus Center is the source of the Creative Word. This is a power which you develop in your own body where a word becomes creative, just as the Word of the Logos becomes creative.

Her Hair is ORANGE-YELLOW like THE FOOL's. This means

When you look forward to the place you are going, that is the (Power of) Empress.

The Empress   63

radiant Solar Energy and the mental emanations of radiant Solar Energy. Wherever you see the "hair" in the Bible it means the same thing. Generally it means the same thing in your dreams—your mental vibration.

Like THE FOOL she also wears a WREATH OF GREEN LEAVES. This Wreath of green leaves is the nearest thing we have to sunlight. This Wreath of green leaves has both a psychic and a physical meaning. Leaves are transformed sunlight, sunlight nearest to its original state. Some people say that the leaves of vegetables should be our chief diet. The psychic allusion is to the effect that if you look forward with confident expectancy to the fulfillment of your desire you are just so much nearer its fulfillment. The confident expectancy is what does it. A leaf is a promise of harvest, flowers, or fruit. Just as THE FOOL's eyes are on an image, your eyes are on desire.

Around the neck of THE EMPRESS is a NECKLACE OF PEARLS, which is traditionally ascribed to Wisdom. We have the expression *pearls of thought.* Wisdom and Understanding, in their Spiritual significance, are pretty near the same thing; one is looking back to your Source, the other is looking forward to your Source. You describe a circle. You are her and you look back to your Source; that is the memory of THE HIGH PRIESTESS. When you look forward to the place where you are going, that is THE EMPRESS. Spiritually they are the same thing. It is a difference of application. We descended into matter and we shall ascend out of it. Memory and Imagination are needed for Reason.

THE EMPRESS of this card is the woman spoken of in Revelations in the passage which affects people's imagination so much, and yet, nobody knows what it means. "There appeared a great wonder in Heaven, a woman clothed with the Sun and Moon under her feet; and upon her head a crown of 12 stars, and being with child, travailing in birth." Venus is always with child travailing in birth. She is bringing forth, and is in the act of bringing forth, the image which has been implanted in her by the self-conscious. Now the highest image you can implant in the subconscious and bring forth is what the occultist calls your *Solar Body,* or the *Christ-Child.* This card pictures the methods by which the Christ-consciousness is formed in the individual.

Her gown is GRAY, which is the traditional color of Wisdom. The lower tone of Gray is the color of stone. In these cards Gray has two meanings: one is the mineral, which represents the physical meaning, and the other is the union of the personality with The Higher Self.

The Reclaimation of 12 Lunar germs is one method to seek the Solar germ the Christ-consciousness.

THE FOOL's legs are the color of stone and his body would also be if the robe did not cover it. In this card they are present and it is all discolored. Stone color runs through all the Tarot, but this is the first card in which you see it preeminently. In the Tarot it generally means "union of the personality with the Higher Self." It is like Black, which has two significances.

Like most words in the Secret Teaching, "Stone" has the nature of a pun. The permanent union of the personality with the Higher Self is made possible by the fusing of the "sand" of the Pineal Gland into a crystal, which is symbolic of the Philosopher's Stone. The punning on the word goes much further back. In the Old Testament the Hebrew word for Stone is ABN (Aben), and its secret meaning is the union of the Father with the Son and the union of the Soul with the personality. The numerical value of ABN is 8, and the figure 8 is the numerical symbol of the four aspects of the self-conscious with the four aspects of the subconscious.

The whole purpose of Tarot is to teach how this equilibrium may be brought about. The Tarot teaches how to obtain this equilibrium and how we may secure the union of the personality with the Higher Self, so that the two may function as one here on the physical plane. The Lord's prayer says: "Thy will may be done on Earth (Body) as it is in Heaven (Higher Self)."

NO MATTER WHETHER YOUR IMAGES ARE GOOD OR BAD, YOUR EMPESS MUST CARRY THEM OUT, AND SHE CARRIES THEM OUT PERFECTLY. SHE ALWAYS MAKES FRUITFUL IN THE BODY THE IMAGES OF THE INTELLECT.

Now in this card the images are depicted by the GREEN TREES above the Waterfall and by her attitude. THE EMPRESS symbolizes it by holding up her Scepter in command. She commands the trillions of cells in the body to do her bidding. Her bidding is to make images, symbolized by those Green Trees, and to become the golden harvest below the Waterfall at her feet. If the images are good, the harvest is wheat, or Yellow. If the images are bad, the harvest is also Yellow, but is tares and not wheat. In any case you see the harvest is the product of the mind as symbolized by the color Yellow.

The color of the background of a Tarot card always indicates the chief or instigating force that is back of it, the state of consciousness or the result which the card depicts.

This background you see is Yellow like the harvest. Yellow is the color of THE MAGICIAN and the self-conscious. He is the one who plants the images in the subconscious which she brings forth into harvest. *As a man images, so he becomes through her agency.* As a man images, so is his body. As his body is, so is he. So it is up to you whether your harvest be wheat or tares. The work of the subconscious in harvesting the image is just the same in one case or the other. She performs, with exactness, all the necessary labor of bringing it into being, performing the operation.

The DESIGN on the Robe of THE EMPRESS, so plentifully displayed, is in the shape of the same Venus symbol that you see in the circle over the cross. The circle is the sign of the Zodiac and always means the self-conscious. The cross also means the sacrifice of the lower to the higher. The Venus symbol means that man brings the superconscious into his self-conscious in just the same proportion he sacrifices his lower to his higher. He brings the superconscious into his self-conscious in the same proportion that he sacrifices his intellect to his Higher Self.

This is the condition that you would expect from what you see in history. That is what has happened all along in evolution. The lower nature is sacrificed to the higher one in order to bring in the higher thing. You must use the lower as a stepping-stone and then discard the lower. In order to live together in groups, humans had to agree to abandon certain rights and privileges that they had exercised as individuals, and by which they grew. Now that they are growing up together they must abandon these. Each upward step in evolution has meant a successive sacrifice of the lower image in civilization to the higher. The savage lives entirely in his body, and as he grows civilized he sacrifices his body to his emotions. With more civilization he sacrifices his emotions to his intellect and with more civilization he sacrifices his intellect to something higher, i.e., his intuition or the superconscious.

You are going to realize that there is a meaning in the Color Scale and in the corresponding Sound Scale, a meaning which is basic to the whole scheme of Creation.

What is Green? It is the admixture of Blue and Yellow. Yellow shades into Green and Green shades into Blue. Green states, in terms of color, the projection of the image of the Creator (Yellow) into the seas of subjective Mind-Stuff, which is called Blue in color symbology. That image passing through the four stages of manifestation becomes, at last, a physical plane thing.

The Law of color is the same as the Laws of sound. The Laws of sound are the laws by which the manifested universe was built and by which it is maintained.

The symbol of the ROBE of THE EMPRESS is presented to you as a ROSE flowering out of a crescent of GREEN, the two so put together that they make a circle. The CROSS underneath the CIRCLE is represented by a TREFOIL on a stem and is made with two leaves. The Trefoil always signifies a sex symbol, a sex creation. There is a RED ROSE in a GREEN CUP upon the Trefoil stem, which is a very subtle and charming symbolism. The Red Rose (desire or activity) can only proceed from desire and always flowers out of the image. The Green Cup and the flower are over a Cross; thus, the perfect image is always emanating from the self-conscious, from the lower to the higher.

That is the reason the background of the Venus card is YELLOW. It is the attention of the self-conscious mind which dictates what your desires will be. All the changes which she works in your body, whether they be for a better body or for a worse one (they must be for one or the other), come from the image you furnish her to work upon. The chief symbolism of this card consists in seeing how the acme of improvement can be secured. These cards show the highest state in each of the consciousnesses they depict.

Above the Waterfall there is a grove of trees. There is one tree that stands out prominently as being lighter in color. Across the river from this is another tree with a similar trunk. This tree that stands in the foreground is a more vivid Green. It is shaped like a pine cone and is scored in such a fashion as to suggest a brain. This tree symbolizes the vivified, opened Pineal Gland. It is vivified by deliberate imagery. The other tree, of which you can see only the light Green trunk, symbolizes the Pituitary Body and how Venus does her work. It is beyond and across the water from the Pineal Gland. To awaken these two trees and make them act as one is what Hermes refers to as the Mystic Marriage. The Pineal Gland is vivified by deliberate work of Creative Imagination. It systemizes the images of the self-consciousness carried out in a special sort of way by the subconscious. She does the work. He furnishes the impetus. Ladies often say, "Yes, of course it is our sex that does all the work." Well, it certainly is in this case. It is the subconscious that does the work; he only starts the thing.

How does she vivify the Pineal Gland? The mechanism of this work is symbolized by the cushion she rests upon. "Yoga" means some system or method of securing the union of the personality with the Father. That union is symbolized by the word *stone*. Tarot practice with color and sound is a form of Yoga; Tarot practice accompanied by the self-conscious study of the images of the cards.

The color and sound do the mechanical part of the work that changes the etheric body. The mechanical part of the work is greatly helped by concentration on the cards on the part of the self-conscious. The co-ordination of color and sound regulates the rate of vibration of the seven Centers (referred to also as Chakras, stars or planets of the body). The final objective of this quickening is to open to super-conscious awareness the three ports of entry into the body (the Pituitary, the Pineal Gland, and the Transformed Heart). Through these three come the superconscious. "Master, it is good for us to be here," it is said in that little incident called the Transfiguration. "Let us build three temples."

The opening of the Pineal Gland, the awakening of the Human Mind, is what the mystic and the occultist calls the Deep. Then he goes on and transforms his Heart in addition. This is what is called "the Master."

Now to open the Pineal Gland requires a great many things to happen in the body. Among other things it is necessary to use certain chemicals which are being used in the ordinary sex function. These chemicals are needed to construct certain new cells in the brain. Consequently, while you are constructing these new cells you need all these chemicals.

If you are making these new cells in the thinking lobe of the brain, preparing to open the Pineal Gland, you need certain chemicals from the Mars Center of the body to change them on their way to the think-ing cells of the brain. They are changed in the Heart Center. Here they are transformed into nerve force. They go up from the Mars Center to the Heart Center. Now the Mars Center here is symbolized by the RED CUSHION, which is made like a bolster with a drapery. The Mars Center is present everywhere in the body. When it functions as sex it requires the use of these chemicals that are wanted, in order to make these new cells in the brain. The ordinary function of sex should not use up these chemicals. They can be used in another physical form. They have got to be used in a sort of nerve energy form. What sends them up from the Mars Center to the Heart Center is called "prepar-ing the images that the self-conscious mystically makes."

The Heart Center is symbolized by the ORANGE CUSHION. Orange is the color of the superconscious and is associated with the Heart (the Transformed Heart), whose function it is to bring in the

White-Yellow and the White. The Transformed Heart brings in the Orange. Now Red is changed into Orange by Black. When it leaves the Mars Center and goes to the Heart Center it is transformed into a suitable shape to make new brain cells in the thinking lobe of the brain through the Venus Center and the Pituitary. All this is symbolized by the BLACK CUSHION. See the Black Cushion there covered with the little fine symbols in Gold. It is between the Red bolster and the Orange cushion. Red lifted Black into Orange. So lifting this nerve force is accomplished by these practices, and this force, now a merely physical one, is changed into the Nerve Force in the Heart.

If you think that everybody agrees with your views, and are confident if they don't say anything about it, you know what a gorgeous feeling it is. I am quite sure your self-conscious feels the same way and if there is criticism, you need know nothing about it. One of the many frailties of the self-conscious is its lack of humility and its pompous pretentiousness. It thinks it has all the art there is in the world. The subconscious is full of humility and it has far more art than the self-conscious ever thought of having, so you can imagine it is sort of emotional relief in making fun of this menace, in whose control she is and under whom she is helpless.

Another thing about the subconscious is that she never wastes words in her protests. She is very unique, like Shakespeare and most writers who do not use a vast amount of unnecessary words. Most of your dreams, after you begin the work of reconstruction in your body, concern themselves with voicing the alarm and resentment of the various cells in your body at the changes which have just taken place, and all along, the subconscious has been protesting at your mismanagement.

THE EMPEROR.

5th Hebrew Letter	*HEH*
Symbol for	*Sight*
Color	*Scarlet/Red*
Numerical Value	*5*
Syllables	*HH*
Sound	*C-Natural*
Translation	*Window*
Sign in Zodiac	*Aries*

NOTES

THE EMPEROR

HEH, spelled in Hebrew HH, means WINDOW. It is the fifth Hebrew letter and the first SIMPLE LETTER. It stands for the faculty of SIGHT, for the direction NORTHEAST, for the Zodiacal sign ARIES, for the CONSTITUTING INTELLIGENCE, for the color RED, and for the note C-NATURAL. The numerical value is 5. In Roman characters it is usually H, but sometimes E.

The 22 Hebrew letters are classified as MOTHER LETTERS, SIMPLE LETTERS, and DOUBLE LETTERS. There are three Mother Letters, seven Double Letters and 12 Simple Letters. The Mother Letters stand for the three elements Fire, Water, and Air—not these elements as they appear to us here upon the physical plane, but their subtle principles as they appear on the higher plane. It is the sacred Hebrew teaching that the element of Earth is only a physical plane synthesis, a condensation of the three other elements. That is the reason there is no Mother Letter for it in the Hebrew alphabet, although the alphabet devotes four letters to the elucidation of the other three.

In the attributes assigned to the Hebrew letters, there are no directions assigned to the Mother Letters. The planets of modern discovery, Uranus, Neptune, and Vulcan, are assigned to the Mother Letters. We saw that Uranus was assigned to Aleph, THE FOOL, which is the Mother Letter for Air. Neptune, as you may surmise, is given to the Mother Letter for Water, or Mem, and Vulcan to the Mother Letter for Fire. The so-called planets of the ancients are assigned to the seven Double Letters. We have now had three Double Letters and one Mother Letter. The rest are distributed among the remaining letters.

To the 12 Simple Letters are assigned the signs of the Zodiac. As we have seen, colors are assigned to both Mother and Double Letters as well as to the Simple Letters, and for this reason there are color duplicates in the 22 letters. If we lay them out in their order and take out the Mother and Double Letters, we shall find the ascending color scale—red, red-orange, orange, etc., beginning with the letter HEH, THE EMPEROR, Red. We shall also find that each one of the Simple Letters stands for a faculty or function of the body. Not the present physical plane function or faculty, but the occult extensions of the faculty or function upon a higher plane than the physical, which comes as a result of working intensively upon the body in any form of mystic practice. The color and sound practice with the Tarot cards, accompanied with the mental concentration upon them, is one of the eight forms of mystic practice.

THE EMPEROR (HEH) is assigned the occult extension of the faculty of Sight. We have two phrases in our ordinary speech which figuratively present the same idea. We say "the mental vision—the mind's eye." These are only figures of speech with us, but the occultist says that when we have transformed, by changes in our body chemistry, our brain cells and opened the the Pineal Gland, we can actually see what we now can only reason about. Such a person can see them, can see the Laws of Nature and see them in operation; can see that thoughts and emotions are things as actual as physical plane things; can see color where the ordinary eye sees nothing at all. You have an exact analogy for these two kinds of sight, one merely figurative and the other literal, in the use of the term *visualization.* To most people, to visualize a thing means merely calling the thing vividly to memory, remembering it. Some of you know that visualization has another and actual aspect. We can really see the color with an inner eye, not the physical one. When our physical eyes are open, we seem to be seeing this color through them, but we do not see it by means of them. For we can also see it when our eyes are shut. What we are seeing with is our etheric eyes. You will be able to do this after a comparatively short time of assiduous practice with the correlation of color and sound. As a matter of fact, you have done this all along without thinking that you had developed any unusual faculty.

You do actually see in your dreams and can see far more vividly than in your waking moments. What do you see with? Not with your physical eyes, for they are closed. You see with the same eye that gives you your vision in actual visualization—the "etheric eye," the eye of the etheric body. When we really visualize a color or a thing, we make it ourselves in etheric matter. Just as you have etheric eyes in order to see etheric matter, you have astral eyes in order to see astral matter. Therefore, we can develop mental eyes in order to see mental matter. It is with actual mental eyes that THE EMPEROR sees. When you awake your mental vision, meaning your real and literal mental eyes, then you can see thoughts forming in people's minds. You can see the shapes these thoughts take when they leave the mind and go on whatever errand their maker sends them. *You can see that the Universe itself is mental and has only the appearance of being physical. For everything in the Universe is but a thought of its creator. The mental is the real, and the physical is only the appearance.*

To the Simple Letters are assigned the signs of the Zodiac. All the Laws of Nature, the Greeks taught, are parts of our makeup. *We are the Universe in little.* We have already seen that the Tarot teaches that the seven exterior planets exist in our interior world and that the Tarot practice is designed to make them function correctly. The 12 signs of the Zodiac stand for areas of our own bodies as well as for areas of the Cosmos. In old almanacs you will see the figure of a man divided into 12 areas or regions, each one designated a sign of the Zodiac. The Zodiac is a teaching device invented by occult teachers to describe to man how the Laws of the Universe work out in his own body. The ancients knew of the interrelation of all the parts of man's organism, or the microcosm. What was outside was duplicated inside. What was Above was duplicated Below.

Now what is "reason"? It is the mind, the brain in action, drawing conclusions from its observations. It is a synthesis of the three qualities of mind which are presented by cards 1, 2, and 3. It is based on Attention, Memory, and Imagination. It takes the facts of observation, and with a proper regard to what we have experienced and what we wish to experience, draws conclusions from these observations and makes something new out of them. There would be no reason at all without imagination. When what we see satisfies us and when memory of what we have seen is sufficient, we never need our reason. We call in our reason when we desire a change or to get a new result we have not had before. What does reason do? It protects itself in its conclusions by reasoning about the future in terms of the past; but at the same time we desire something which the past does not present. The only occasion we have to use our reason is when we are pushed to it by our desire for something new, something more than the past affords. *Reason is always based on a memory of a physical fact.* We construct something new only on the basis of what is most like it or what we have already.

Most people are conservative because their memory bids them to be so. Their memory tells them, and history tells them, that where one change is for the better, ten changes are for the worse. Whoever makes a change then is more likely than not to leap from the frying pan into the fire. Thus if we were guided by memory alone, we should never make changes. We are fortunately influenced as much by imagination as by memory. We see a need, we image a way to meet it and our reason shows us how to construct it out of the facts of our previous experience. IMAGINATION IS INDISPENSIABLE TO REASON. IT IS IMAGINATION WHICH IS REQUIRED TO STEP OFF "THE KNOWN INTO THE UNKKNOWN."

Curiously enough, the most factual sciences are at the same time the most imaginative. Astroonomy, physics, and mathematics are all distinguished for their use of imagination. All three have imagined not only invisible matter but an invisible matter that responds to other laws of Nature than our own—the laws of Nature of another solar system. There is another reason why the occultist laughs at the pseudo-scientist who denies the Soul and immortality. "Why," says he, "if all the scientists you boast have dealt with invisibles in a world far different from this one, then why should not theology and philosophy?" If it were not for imagination there would be no reason and we would always be moving around in the memory of present observation. If it were not for memory, imagination would be flighty and never alight anywhere.

It is the union of Memory and Imagination that composes Reason, and both of them are based upon previous "attention." Attention, Memory, Imagination, and Reason are the entire human mental equipment until the superconscious steps in and enlarges it.

The twenty-one Tarot Trumps preceded by zero, THE FOOL, which synthesizes them all, are arranged in three rows of seven cards each. This is called the Tarot Tableau. The cards numbered one to seven represent the seven primary principles of consciousness. THE EMPEROR is the middle card of this row. He is the bridge between the self-conscious and the superconscious. He is the point where the self-conscious has gone as far as it can. The superconscious (the self-conscious functioning in the Pineal Gland) then steps in to help it out. The next three cards all represent the superconscious. Thus you see THE EMPEROR is the exact point of balance between. To pay attention, to remember, to image are the indispensable preliminaries to the use of reason. We desire something other than what we see and we image a way to satisfy that desire. With our reason we objectify that image and we create the way we have imaged.

THE EMPEROR is the link between the human equipment and the superhuman. We shall never bring in the superhuman until we have employed our reason as far as it will go. The act of reasoning is basing a *new conclusion upon an old premise*; employing our observation to make something new. That is why the type of Intelligence that goes with this card is the Constituting Intelligence. To constitute is to frame

To pay attention ⎫
To remember ⎬ lead to the use of reason
To image ⎭

Reasoning is the selection of Relating Values   The Emperor   75

something new out of something old. Reason composes. Composition in art means putting things into a foreground and a background. It is a selection of seeing relative values; choosing is the fundamental act in reason.

When all events and all items coming under our observation are of equal worth, there is no need to reason. Observation tells us at once that all things are not of equal worth and only faulty observation thinks so. Reason assures us that of the numerous things we observe, some of them should be put into the foreground and some of them into the background.

All civilized persons put into the foreground two leading items—pleasure and pain. How shall we escape pain and obtain pleasure? Equally, all civilized persons see that immediate pain and immediate pleasure are not always such predictions of ultimate pleasure and ultimate pain. Rather, we often observe the opposite: that immediate pleasure often means ultimate pain, and immediate pain, ultimate pleasure. The need for Reason, to have accurate Attention to base itself upon, is its attempt to regulate the two, pleasure and pain.

It does not take the mature reason long to discover that the satisfaction of material desires is sternly limited; when its maximum is reached, then returns begin to diminish. If it were not for this law of diminishing returns we should rest content to find our pleasure in the satisfaction of material desire. It takes only a very little accurate attention to discern there is such a law. The wise man looks for some other way to satisfy desire, or for some other channel to run his desires into what will not diminish. At once we find that this inexorable law in the world does not apply, or does not apply in the same manner, in the Spiritual world. Therefore, the wise discard the physical set of values, for their reason assure them that if ever they reach the saturation point in the Spiritual set, it will not be for an immeasurably longer time. Thus it is that everybody's reason, as he grows older or more mature, looks beyond physical satisfactions to spiritual ones; and he is willing to forego immediate satisfactions or undergo immediate physical dissatisfactions for the sake of ultimate gains.

This card, THE EMPEROR, like all the Tarot cards, pictures the highest goal in that state of consciousness—shows the Reason active when Father and Son (Soul and Personality) are one; then we use the mind to see with. This is designated by the STONE THRONE upon which THE EMPEROR sits. When we have reached that stage, Intuition and Reason are the same thing, for the Higher Self is functioning in our bodies and in our Reason. Reason is what the thinking cells of the brain do with the material afforded them by the recording cells of the brain—what the distinctly human part of our brain (the front lobe) does with that part we share with the animals (the back lobe), which records our observations proceeding to us through the senses. We need to pay attention to the external world not as animals but as thinking human beings Otherwise, what they record will be faulty and superficial. These records, be they what they may, are our only safe way or basis for reasoning, whether faulty or accurate.

The character for the letter HEH is a combination of the letter Daleth with the letter Yod, which is the flame out of combinations of which all the sacred Hebrew letters are made. This Yod, or Flame, forms the lower left-hand part of the letter as you look at it. The letter Yod stands for the Spirit, and its numerical value of H is 5. Thus the letter name has the value of 10, or the same as Yod. The first H in the letter name stands for the self-conscious, or inductive reasoning; the second H stands for the subconscious, or deductive reasoning. Together they stand for the entire manifestation or YOD when manifest. For you it divided itself into the "Will" and the "Substance," the Father and the Mother, the self-conscious and the subconscious. These two are equal, though manifesting as the second dependent upon the first and taking the shape which the first impresses upon it. The Creator impressed the Substance with the images upon which He meditated, and she (the subconscious) brought forth the world according to his design.

That which God uses to create is the same as we must use to create—the Will working through the image-making power.

This is why it is said that creation of the Universe began with the letter HEH, the Creative Word. There was at that time nothing else in the Universe but the Will and Substance. The Will, having made the image of the sort of world it desired, pronounced the Creative Word which started the Mother (the Substance) into bringing forth the image. Why then, you may ask, does not Heh come before Daleth in the list of letters? Merely because we know nothing of a world unmanifested. It is only when manifestation has begun that we can see the process. As an ancient Scripture says: "No man perceiveth me as Father until, as Mother, I have brought forth Creatures." All this is rather evasive though it is presented in the meaning of the Hebrew letters Daleth and Heh. Daleth is the Door and Heh is the Window. Abstractly, they are interchangeable forms. A door serves the purpose of a window and a window of a door in an Eastern clay hut. Both are square, as these two letters are.

SYMBOLISM

THE EMPEROR sits on a STONE THRONE. This in its highest aspect denotes the union of the Father (the Higher Self) and the Son (the personality). In its lower aspect it denotes the physical world. Reason sits enthroned upon the physical world and on it are four RAM'S HEADS. The Ram, or ARIES in the Zodiacal sign of this letter and the number of this card, is four. The number of the letter HEH is 5, and you will see an extra Ram's head over the shoulder of THE EMPEROR in the center of the VIOLET CAPE.

THE EMPEROR has made his union with the Higher Self. Note the BLACK CRESCENT shadow curving under the seat. Wherever you see the crescent it means the subconscious, the Moon. This really repeats the symbology of the Stone Throne in its lower sense. Reason sits enthroned upon the physical world.

The ROBE of THE EMPEROR is over a BLUE suit of ARMOR. Reason is always primarily based on memory of a physical fact. The same thing could have been expressed by an undergarment of Blue, but here it is an Armor. Reason arms itself with Memory, and it protects itself in its conclusions by reasoning about the future of the past.

His robe is RED. Red means desire, and the result of desire is action. Red also means sex force, and man, when he has opened his Pineal Gland, uses the sex force in the head. We act only because we desire, and what we desire is prescribed to us by our five senses. This is why five is one of the numbers indicating man. It is also because his figure illustrates a pentagram—two arms, two legs, and a head. Since the number of this letter is 5, man's goal is to become a reasonable creature, a creature in which reason takes the place of instinct in the animal as his dominating characteristic, dictating all his desires and their subsequent actions. We use the problems our observation sets before us.

The direction of this card is NORTHEAST. East, as we have seen, is THE EMPRESS, and she is the one who carries out the images of the self-conscious. Now, what is North? North is the direction assigned to the Mars vibration, which is depicted by the color Red. Also, North is the place of least light, while East is attributed to Venus, who represents the dawn.

We solve our problems, if we can solve them without the aid of the superconscious, by the use of our Reason working through our Imagination. This means the right set of new images backed up with the proper past observation. The Mars vibration is called the destructive force. Why should a destructive force be so closely associated with Reason, which we call the constructive force? Merely because you cannot construct without first destroying. A destructive force working in the head is a constructive force. All animals, plants, and minerals must destroy in order to live. When we eat we have first killed something; then we generally break down its chemical form by cooking it. We break down the physical molecule by mastication and convert it into nourishment. "Man is the chief destructive animal; therefore, the chief constructive one," says Paul Case, "he has become so by the use of his reason." Reason destroys only to put something better in its place. Man alone destroys water to make steam, and destroys metals to make electricity. We destroy far more than external things in order to construct.

Every action we make, every muscle we twitch, every emotion or impulse we feel, and every thought we think breaks down a cell and builds one up again. This is why THE EMPEROR has a VIOLET CAPE. Violet is the color of equilibrium, and also signifies the manifestation, the creation of forms. There can be no creation without tearing down and building up again. To create we throw a thing out of equilibrium and then throw it in again.

Destruction is the basis of our life, the means whereby we live. Construction is the purpose of our life, the means by which we progress.

The whole point then is that we build up to replace what we tear down. If we build with Reason guiding us, we always build something better than what preceded. Occult wisdom refers to the danger of painting pictures of the satisfaction of our lower desires, the work of the debased fancy. When we tear down without building up anything of value, a mental, emotional, or physical cell in the brain will find it easier to paint another picture; so it goes on until we have corroded the mind with our daydreams.

Imagination working in conjunction with Reason always builds something better than she has torn down, but tear down we must, either for good or for evil, from the cradle to the grave. We must all constantly use the Mars force. The Mars in your makeup is what gives you physical and mental force. All personal activity of any kind breaks down cell structure in order to liberate energy. Form is disintegrated, and with the consequent energy a form is created.

The previous letters, being Double Letters, have each represented a center. THE EMPEROR does not represent a center, although he represents the Mars force functioning constructively. The Mars Center is represented by card 16, THE TOWER.

Your Mars Center is just below and back of the Navel. When it functions well, you have a sense of vitality and possess what is called "personal magnetism." When it functions poorly you have lassitude, and a want of force prevents you from being magnetic. THE EMPEROR represents the Mars vibration functioning in the thinking cells of the brain, as the faculty by which we draw conclusions from premises and destroy previous misconceptions. Reason is always destroying previous conclusions built upon superficial attention. As most people pay only superficial attention, Reason is forever at war with what most people think. THE EMPEROR is associated with THE TOWER because he is always at work to break down the Babel structures of mistaken notions. The more you use your reason the more you break it down; therefore, it must follow that the more often you destroy old forms to make better new ones, the faster you progress. It is this idea which is at the basis of Tarot; it shows you how to destroy old forms and rhythms most rapidly.

The card called DEATH represents a highly specialized way of doing what the occultist has all along been doing—killing off certain refractory cells in his body which refuse to quicken their rate of vibration. He does this by the same means he has been using all along—impressing upon his subconscious the images dictated by Reason. This you will see depicted in the background of THE EMPEROR—Yellow striped with Red. The Mars vibration is functioning in the thinking cells of the brain, the self-conscious. Blue (subconscious) mixed with Yellow (self-conscious) makes Green.

Whenever the Stream of Consciousness, which flows from the Robe of THE HIGH PRIESTESS, appears in the background of these cards, it means that the activity thus depicted is controlled by the self-conscious. The stream falling from above into the below in THE EMPRESS card designates the self-conscious image impregnating the subconscious Mind-Stuff.

In this card there is also a stream flowing at the base of the volcanic mountains in the back. It is the same stream that flows from the Robe of THE HIGH PRIESTESS, but here it is colored Violet. Violet is the color of equilibrium and of the creation of forms. The mountains and the hot, dry desert on which the throne sits depict the same thing.

The stream which was Blue in THE HIGH PRIESTESS card has been altered by THE EMPEROR to the color Violet to build his new forms with. It requires the Imagination (the material the subconscious furnishes to make Reason fruitful) to bring forth the images. If there were vegetation on these rocks and on the land, they would be colored Green. That would give a wrong idea, the idea that Reason is dependent upon the carrying out of the image. Reason is not dependent upon his wife, THE EMPRESS, but rules through his wife THE EMPRESS and his Son.

THE EMPEROR has three symbols of power: his Scepter, his Crown, and the Crystal Sphere in his other hand. The Scepter is the symbol of THE EMPRESS slightly modified—he rules through his wife. There are two ways to make a cross in the Tarot, and the T-Cross is called Tav, or Saturn, cross. Saturn you had in the last Double Letter. He represents the condensing and the limiting power. The T-Cross handle on the Scepter of THE EMPEROR not only means that he rules through his wife, who carries out and makes fruitful his image, but also that he sternly controls those images. He limits them and employs only those that Reason wants to be carried out, exercising supervision over images.

The YELLOW SPHERE in the other hand stands for the Christ-consciousness, which in these cards is represented as the son of Reason. Reason rules through his wife and his son. He must be balanced by these two in order to do fruitful work.

On his head is a YELLOW CROWN. A crown is a symbol of control of dominion. There are five BARS in the top of it and each ends in a segment, a square enclosing a circle. The complete Crown thus has ten bars and ten circles. These typify the ten emanations of the Life Power, over which Reason through his wife has control, and which his son, the Christ-consciousness, can manipulate. Each alternate circle is RED to denote that he can make the ten aspects or emanations active, just as through the 12 stars in the Crown of THE EMPRESS runs a ribbon of Red to denote that she makes active in man's body the 12 signs of the Zodiac.

THE EMPEROR has a youthful face and a long white beard, together with white hair, to indicate that he is eternal and eternally young—the oldest thing in manifestation and at the same time the youngest immemorial age and immemorial youth. THE MAGICIAN has Black hair because of the occult action he is shown performing. He is at his occult work of bringing down the "White Light" of the Spirit. To do so, he has to put on the Belt of Eternity, of timelessness, just as

THE FOOL put on a belt of time and space. THE EMPEROR has white hair to show that his work is all Spiritual.

Reason existed before the image-maker when we are thinking of the Cosmic Creation. When we speak in human terms, our reason is based on our attention and the images we make of the world in which we exist.

The Violet Cape of THE EMPEROR is fashioned ike a wheel showing four concentric circles. This at once suggests the four concentric circles of wheels in the JUPITER card, which is one of the seven Centers. The four circles there represent a great variety of things, but one of them is the four stages of an idea as it works out from the image of the Creator through the three other planes into the physical world of manifestation. These four stages are symbolized by the four (4) implements on THE MAGICIAN's table: the archetypal or Spiritual, the Creative, the Formative, and the Physical.

The wheel in the Jupiter card and Jackal-headed boy, who symbolizes the present state of evolution of man—with the body made but the mind still in the making—are Orange. Orange is the color of the volcanic rocks and the desert in THE EMPEROR card. Orange is merely the blending of Red and Yellow. Orange is also the color of the superconscious; it designates the reason of the Creator in making active the images of the Creator. This is accomplished by dividing itself into the two minds (indicated by the two H's in the letter HEH) who impressed the images of the first mind upon the second, who, thereupon, brought them forth.

In the symbolism of THE EMPEROR it remains only to speak of the fingers. One is differentiated for a special use and constitutes another reason why "five" is one of the numbers designating "man." The upward evolution of the animal in regard to mind is indicated by the flexibility of its paws and their differentiation into fingers. Science says that all the wonderful skills of man are made possible by the position of his thumb; and note that both hands of THE EMPEROR make his thumb very apparent. The thumb is to the other fingers what the eye is to the other senses. The thumb and the eye controls, guides, and increases the efficiency of all the rest.

Man's career as maker and architect was made possible by the thumb. So Reason, to which the Hebrew wisdom assigns the function of Sight when its perceptions are occultly opened, makes it possible for man to use all his senses correctly and puts their results at his disposal. So the thumb is an important symbol for Reason.

Reason includes all the cards we have had so far. Also, ageless wisdom states that creation began with the letter Heh. The concealed value of the letter Heh is 14. The outer value is the one generally assigned to the letter; but in addition to that, the letter carried another teaching device. Its inner value arises from the constituents of which it is composed. Heh is composed of Daleth, 4, and Yod, 10, equaling 14. You are now in a position to see what the 14 rays of the white Sun in THE FOOL card means. It was the work of Reason creating the world. Note that they all stream downward. They designate how creation began by the pouring down of the mental images of the Spirit after He had arrived at them in meditation, by the employment of Reason, into the Yellow mental sea of Mind-Stuff. The sea into which the 14 rays come is the Mind.

Fourteen is the number of cards in each Tarot suit. Thus the Tarot suits tell how the Spirit through four different stages of an idea (Fire, Water, Air, and Earth) reached itself down to man on the physical plane in 14 forms each (56 in all). Fourteen is also the number of several Hebrew words which characterize this process. One is ID, Almighty Hand; another is HDH, to stretch the hand out and down—"As above, so below." The Spirit stretched out its hand to us (its Reason). *We can stretch our hand to it—our Reason, the godlike thing in us, that quality which we share with it.* Thus, this word, to show us that the Above is like the Below, means also "to lay hold on."

The Old Testament and the New Testament constantly imply that God made the world in love; and the Constituting Intelligence is Love. The proof of this is that 14 is also the number of the word in Hebrew, DVD; David, meaning Love, "the Beloved." There is an ancient proverb which says "Reason is Love." So here is proof of it in the word "David," which numbers 14 and means Beloved.

Astrology means "to write a Bible in the heavens so that people might know the Laws of their own bodies and minds, and know how God co-created them in accordance with the Laws of the Universe."

SUBCONSCIOUS IS MERELY MIND-STUFF, AND MIND-STUFF IS THE SUBSTANCE WHICH GIVES BODY TO THE MENTAL IMAGE AND MAKES IT BECOME A FORM.

THE HIEROPHANT

6th Hebrew Letter	*VAV or* *VAU in English*
Symbol for	*Hearing*
Color	*Red-Orange*
Numerical Value	*6*
Syllables	*VV*
Sound	*C-Sharp*
Translation	*Nail*
Sign in Zodiac	*Taurus*

NOTES

THE HIEROPHANT

VAV, spelled in Hebrew VV, means NAIL. It is the sixth Hebrew letter and the second SIMPLE LETTER. It stands for the faculty of HEARING, direction SOUTHEAST, for the TRIUMPHANT AND ETERNAL INTELLIGENCE, Zodiacal sign TAURUS, the Bull. The color is RED-ORANGE, note C-SHARP, and the numerical value is 6. In Roman characters it is V.

The letter, which is written VAU in English, is pronounced VAV in Hebrew. When it is intoned it is pronounced WAW. It is intoned constantly because it occurs in the Hebrew word Jehovah, which is spelled Yod Heh Vav Heh, and when it is intoned it is spelled Yod Heh Waw Heh. This is the name of the Hebrew God *jawget.* You note at once that the Heh occurs twice. The Double "h" in the letter name Heh means the inductive reasoning of the subconscious.

In us there is both the self-conscious of God and the subconscious of God, or Nature. In the word Yod Heh Vav Heh you see at once that the Vav connects the two words that stand for Reason (Heh). The Vav connects the two Heh's. Yod stands for the Spirit, or Will. When the Will goes out into manifestation it divides itself into the self-conscious Reason, or Will, and the Substance, which is subconscious, or Deductive Reasoning. The link between this Reason or Will is Vav, or the Higher Self.

The esoteric meaning of the letter Vav is very confusing because its application depends on the letters that are in between it. It stands for any link or anything that connects to other things. Sometimes it designates the Higher Self because the Higher Self is the link between the Spirit and the Personality. Sometimes it stands for the self-conscious, as in RVCh (Ruach), which means Life Breath. "R" (the Sun) and "Ch" (the Moon) in us are united by the self-conscious. Sometimes it stands for the body. The body is our link with the Higher Self. It communicates with us through the body.

The two meanings that this card particularly call attention to are the Higher Self and the body. The Higher Self is the link of the human with his Spirit, and the body is the link between the Higher Self and the self-conscious.

In the Hebrew letters the shape of Vav tells you how closely it is connected with Yod. The flame represents the Spirit. The Secret Wisdom of the Hebrew says that the upper point of Yod, which you will note is

85

very prominent and represents the Will, is the Small Point of our beginning. It comes forth in Its own Nature by pouring itself out and down and manifesting a Universe. It pours out its Will, or Reason, upon man, the product of Nature. The agent by which it pours out Wisdom on man is his body. The agent by which it pours out its Wisdom on the rest of the world is any form which the Cosmic Mind-Stuff takes in response to the image impressed upon it by the Will. All forms in Nature are an expression of the Wisdom of the Will, for man is the first form in Nature which possesses self-conscious Reason. All the rest of the forms possess only subconscious Reason, or the Wisdom of Nature. The Flame represents the Spirit and the Spirit is extended downward by a vertical line. You are at the end of that vertical line.

You will note that the form of the downward vertical extension in this letter is the letter "I" in English. The letter "I" is the most important letter of any alphabet. At its lower level it stands for sheer animal egotism. There are several words in the Bible meaning sin. One of them translates into "too much I." All the same, it is only through selfishness that one progresses, selfishness on its lower level or selfishness on its higher level.

A man begins his spiritual progress and takes his first step in it when he identifies another person with himself. When he identifies another's personal interest with his own (and that progress increases more and more with the number of persons you identify with yourself), he ultimately will be able to identify the whole world with himself. The Christ identifies the whole world with himself. The thing that we all have to do is to identify our personality with our Higher Self, THE HIEROPHANT. So it is with this identification with things outside of yourself with yourself that you take the Spiritual Road. Whether it is taken at its lowest or its highest level, the letter "I" is responsible for all the evolution in the human kingdom. We have evolved through desire. In the beginning it is selfish; at the end it is altruistic.

First we progress by mere animal selfishness; then we identify other people and their interests with ours. The literal meaning of the Hindu word *Yoga* is "union with the Higher Self." Yoga is a system of practice whereby one may so make over this body and gain intuitive perception of the eternal principles of the Universe by identifying himself with the Higher Self, who sees what these general principles of the Universe are. When we gain this intuitive perception we bring down, into the human plane, the knowledge of these principles on which the Universe is founded, and seek to improve our acts and thoughts in accordance with them. We seek to apply them to our problems. Hence the name of the type of Intelligence that goes with this card. We solve our problems by applying to them the eternal principles and the eternal intelligence.

ı The real meaning of the word *self-sacrifice* is to give up a smaller interest for a larger one, to sacrifice the lower for the higher. On this paradox all religions are founded. Any self-sacrifice is before you and is yet to be made. You feel it is a real sacrifice of self. When it is behind you, when it has been made, you see that what you did was to extend yourself rather than sacrifice yourself.

The letter Vav corresponds astrologically to the sign TAURUS, the Bull. This leads us to the two meanings of the word *Bull*, which is the lower body as well as the higher body. THE HIEROPHANT is called the higher body who is another aspect of THE FOOL (Aleph), who was called the Ox, which is similar to the Bull. THE HIEROPHANT depicts the Life Principle at its personal work of instructing the body, and through it, the inmate of that body, the self-conscious.

The goal of the self-conscious is to find union with the Higher Self and to perform the union of the lower body with the higher body. That is done with apparent self-sacrifice, and when it is done, you find you have infinitely extended yourself.

Taurus is an Earth sign and its activity is confined to the human plane. The Higher Self functions elsewhere than on the Human Plane, but we know nothing about it. He has His own activities on His own plane, and all we know of Him is when He functions in us. In the Old and New Testament of the Bible, the word *earth* means the body, not merely the physical part of it. It means the etheric, the entire personality, the threefold body—not merely the physical, but emotional and the mental as well—the refined body, the physical, emotional and mental nature. The emotions and thoughts are also the "earth," though they are higher parts of the earth than the physical part.

The words in the church liturgy, "The Lord is in His holy temple: let all the earth keep silence before Him," refers to the activity which you see in this card—the Higher Self teaching. The Holy Temple is not the church edifice, *it is your skull.* You are the Temple, says the Scriptures. "You are the Temple of the Living God." The Lord is in your skull. Keep still and listen to Him. Let all your earth keep silence before Him. The earth is your mental body, your emotional body and your physical body, your ambitions, your emotions, your appetites and your instincts. Now all of them keep buzzing all of the time, particularly your emotional body, so that you cannot hear the Voice of the Lord in your skull. You must be able to still all three bodies to be able to hear Him.

The astrological symbol of Taurus is a half-circle over a whole circle and both of those apply to the subconscious. They have nothing to do with the self-conscious, of which the astrological symbol is the cross. The Taurus symbol really looks like the head of the Bull with two horns. What this means is that you have no control over getting any intuition. It comes through the Will of the Higher Self. You may seek and seek to get your guidance, but sometimes it does not come for all your seeking. At other times the door is open to you. You have no control over getting intuition. All you can do is to perform the preliminary, conscious, mental steps; but the ability to hear the Inner Voice is secured through practice of some form. You just don't wake up and find that you have this ability. It will not come of itself unless you have assiduously cultivated it in a previous life and brought it over with you, as was the case of Joan of Arc. Generally in each life, by some form of Yoga, you have to recapture it by some form of working on yourself. STILL YOUR MIND AND LISTEN. QUIET YOUR THREEFOLD EARTH AND LISTEN.

When you study this card, take this affirmation along with it: "*I listen for the word of the inner voice.*"

The message received from this card is from the Higher Self and it is called Intuition, the inner teaching. I want particularly to warn you against thinking of Inner Teaching as teaching to the self-conscious alone. The teaching may be directed to the subconscious alone, and that is what it is doing in this card. The teaching deals with telling the two forms of the subconscious in you all that is necessary to bring about the physical changes which they must work in the body in order for you to become truly spiritual, in the mystic sense of the word.

The teaching of the Higher Self is destined to reach the self-conscious ultimately. It comes through the Venus Center at the throat and is passed up the Pituitary Gland, where she sends it into the thinking lobe of the brain, where it registers as a voice.

VAV means *nail* in Hebrew. It is the thing which binds the personality to the Spirit and the Spirit to the personality. VAV is the link to everything—the instrumentality of all constructive power. This is the thing that VAV stands for. A nail is the means by which two things are linked together. You cannot build a house without nails or pegs, which serve the purpose of nails. Even when you dovetail boards together it is on the principle of a nail. So VAV is closely connected with the necessary means of building everything.

All enlightened masters have said, "of themselves, they did nothing, the Father in them did the work, issued His commands, and they obeyed them." Jesus said, "The Father in me doeth the work."

The instrument of the Soul on the physical plane is personality. He works in you willy-nilly. You can let him work in you or you can, as you think, frustrate his work. You have the free choice to Will to His Will, or to frustrate, as you think, His Will. What do you do when you frustrate His Will? You cater to your appetites, emotions, and ambitions through the choice of the body. So here you stand between two Wills—the Will of the Soul and the choice of the body. You can Will to his Will, or you can allow the body to do your Willing for you. If you Will to His Will, he accomplishes His Will easily. If you Will to the Will of the body it means pain in the end. He teaches you by that pain. It is up to you which it shall be.

Between the Higher Self and the body stands the thinking cells of the brain, your Mercury. Mercury can choose to link up with the one or the other. If he links up with the Higher Self, the Higher Self teaches you by the short and easy route. If he links up with the body, the Higher Self teaches you by the long and more painful route; but always he is teaching you. It is he that holds together your body, and he coaxes it or whips it into doing his Will. He trains you just as you train a dog to obey.

With the astrological sign of the Bull goes the idea of worldly possessions. In the horoscope, Taurus is called The House of Worldly Possessions. The reason the Bull is used for that is that in the old days before land property, when the patriarch or head of the family roamed the world at will seeking pasture for his flocks and herds, wealth was reckoned in cattle. "He was a man of so many head of cattle." We still have the word "pecuniary," which comes from a Latin word meaning cattle. If it was a pecuniary matter, it was a matter of cattle. *Your primary earthly possessions are your thoughts, your emotions, and your physical body.* It is really astonishing to read in the Bible of material promise, promises of prosperity to those who dedicate themselves to the Lord. It is this ideal which the Christian Scientist has seized hold of and emphasized so strongly. Surely it must be obvious to everyone that prosperity is used (if this be true) in some different sense from the way we use it. Most of the people that are exalted in the Scriptures were poor and had no sandals.

The two founders of Christianity were Jesus and Paul, and neither of them demonstrated prosperity. Jesus was forever saying, "It is easier for a camel to enter the eye of a needle than for a rich man to enter the Kindom of Heaven." Consequently, promises of riches are all lies, or there is a great discrepancy here. It is quite possible that we have attributed the wrong meaning to the words *riches* and *prosperity*. Maybe they are code words or technical words which have another meaning.

The meaning the Tarot gives to them is, Whatever is needful. You are rich, you are prosperous, if you have what is needful. If you translate the expression in that way, then the promises of prosperity become reasonable. True religion, which is following the voice of the Higher Self, should show us a practical method, and someone there tells you what to do. It is only reasonable to suppose that the Higher Self tells you the things that are needful to do. If you do that, you are spiritually rich, and if you do the one thing that is needful, you are never impoverished.

We live in a world whose primary eternal principle is the Law of Karma. We must reap in this life what we have sown in preceding lives, and also as we have sown in this one if it is feasible. We incarnate in the kind of physical bodies which we have earned, and we inherit the emotional and mental bodies which we have made. The satisfaction of our desires depends upon Karma, the Karma which we have accumulated for ourselves. Granting that this must be so, we can be sure that all things we really need to work out, destiny will give to us.

The trouble is that we think we should be the judges of what is needful, but the only one who can really interpret what is really needful is the Higher Self, not the self-conscious and not the personality. The Higher Self knows our Karma, we do not. He knows our future, we do not. We are ignorant of His plans for us, what He wants us to achieve in this life and in the lives to come. He may be laying the foundation in this life for something that is going to be demonstrated three thousand years from now. How do we know these things?

So you see He is the judge of what is needful and not ourselves. You hear people constantly say in this world of modern science, modern religion, and modern thought that if a person does not demonstrate success either in health or in material affairs he must be a failure, he must be doing something wrong. Such a remark is based upon an abysmal ignorance of the Law of Karma and of the fact that it is the Higher Self, not the personality, which judges one. You have just exactly what you need if you have poverty or if you have illness. A person may be as poor as Job's turkey in this life at this particular moment, yet be doing precisely what the Higher Self wants him to do, which his Karma brings into manifestation because of his thoughts and images. So you see, it would be better to say the Bull is not worldly possessions but worldly requirements.

Whenever you see a Bull in these cards, it does not refer to the Higher Self, but to the astrological meaning of the Bull—that is, the earth, the body. The Bull occurs in the two cards of your daily practice—THE WHEEL OF FORTUNE and THE WORLD. Both of these cards refer to earthly conditions. The Bull, under the name of "ox," also means the Higher Self (THE HIEROPHANT).

The double meaning of the word *Bull* is shown in the teachings of all religions that the lower life of the body must be purified for the higher life of the Soul. This is, of course, the teaching of Christian religion. Christianity is called the Piscean teaching because it is the teaching of the Zodiacal Age represented by the sign Pisces. The previous religious teaching was represented by the sign of the Bull, the age before the Piscean Age. The teaching of the Zodiacal sign of the Bull was the religion of Asia and Europe. It was the greatest rival of Christianity, and Christianity finally suppressed it in Rome about the beginning of the fourth century. It wasn't very difficult to suppress it because it had already absorbed most of Christianity, and many of its liturgies and teachings were precisely the same as those of Christianity.

This religion was Mithraism. It was ushered in by Mithra, a mythical founder who in most respects tallied with the founder of Christianity. He was a Persian god who had been guided by the Supreme Being in a marvelous way and had arisen to be coequal with Him. This is just the way the Christians represented their Jesus Christ, who was the son of God, who by his own efforts had arisen to be coequal with God. Many of the Church's designations of Christ were taken over from Mithraism, where they were applied to Mithra, who was called the "Sun of Righteousness," "The Day Spring from High," "The Light," and "The Almighty," just as Jesus is called in the vocabulary of Christianity. Mithra suffered for the good of mankind, and his death was said to be sacrificial, just as the Christians said of Jesus. Jesus was called the Lamb; Mithra was called the Bull.

The chief incident in the life of Jesus was the crucifixion in which He was said to have sacrificed himself for the sake of the world. The chief incident in the life of Mithra was his struggle with a symbolical bull which he overpowered and sacrificed. In some mysterious way, when he sacrificed the bull he was said to have also sacrificed himself. So you see in the person of Mithra you have the two meanings of the Bull.

THE HIEROPHANT's (the Higher Self) object is to get into your mind and get you to sacrifice the body of the lower self, which is also called the bull. (The bull with a small "b" is sacrificed to the capital Bull with a capital "B.") In the card THE WHEEL OF FORTUNE, you will find the Bull is the body that is reading out of the White Book. That means the earth that composes your body is now acting in accordance with the Spirit and getting His instructions. Your body has now become tamed and ceases to be an obstruction and sets in accordance with the Spirit. In the card THE WORLD, you will find a picture of a very meek bull indeed. He has been entirely tamed. He is now entirely subdued in accordance with the demands of the Higher Life of the body. In studying the Tarot you must keep these two opposite and contrary ideas of the Bull in your mind at the same time, the Bull on the higher level standing for the body. It is the object of the Higher Self here to enter your mind fundamentally, tame the body, and sacrifice the lower bull to the higher one. Remember that the word *sacrifice* is really a joke. It means to give up the smaller interest for the sake of a larger one. It looks to be a sacrifice when it is before you, but when it is behind you, it is a stepping-stone.

You must have been struck by the fact that the Bull and the Ox are very much the same thing. The Ox is the Bull when the Bull is deprived of willfulness or selfishness. THE FOOL and THE HIEROPHANT are one and the same. THE FOOL is the Soul on his way down into manifestation. THE HIEROPHANT is the Soul, thought of as being connected with the manifested body of the physical plane and instructing it. In this card he is teaching his body only the two forms of the subconscious. We will go into that later in THE CHARIOT card, where the Soul is in the body and animating it.

The number of this card is 5. There are only ten numbers. The number is the middle digit between 1 and 9. There is Zero and the series of figures from 1 to 9. Number 5 is the middle digit between 1 and 9. It is the bridge between the first 4 and the second 4. It is called the number of Meditation, the middle number. It is the number of man—not present-day man, but man as he will be when he has co-created and perfected his body. Then it will possess the 15 extensions of his present powers. When he has done this, he has left the kingdom of nature he was born in, the human kingdom, and entered the kingdom of the superhuman.

When you arrange the Tarot cards in a row of seven, the number 4 was the middle card of the first row; 3 on one side and 3 on the other. Number 4 was the bridge between the human equipment of man and the superhuman equipment of man. *Reason is the bridge between the first three and the second three.*

Science says there are four kingdoms of Nature: mineral, plant, animal, and human. The occultist says there are five kingdoms of Nature: mineral, plant, animal, human, and superhuman. The superhuman kingdom is really where man belongs, and he is on his way to it. When he arrives, he will have dominion over the four lower kingdoms and will assist them to evolve themselves into the highest. So the Sage symbolizes man by the five-pointed star, the pentagram. That does not mean present-day man. Man will not become a five-pointed star until he has perfected himself, until he has entered into the superhuman kingdom. The occultist says that man will enter the superhuman kingdom in just the same way as he entered the human kingdom. He left the lesser kingdom by self-disciplining himself. Now, says the mystic, "He will enter the superhuman kingdom by dint of his own exertions. He works upon his own body and so changes it that he enters the superhuman kingdom."

The numbers end in 9. Zero to 9. You would naturally expect that in the scheme of the Universe there are four kingdoms lower than perfected man and four kingdoms higher. This is the teaching of the mystic. Throughout the Universe the same harmony of numbers prevail. There are nine ranks of beings and man is in the fourth and fifth ranks. His object is to get out of the fourth. There are nine ranks of Angelic Beings as well as of form. There are nine stages of consciousness in man, and the stage depicted in this card is the Mediator between the first four and the second four stages. The next card, THE LOVERS, depicts the first of this second four. THE LOVERS means the proper union of the self-conscious with the subconscious, the proper union of the masculine and feminine in every individual. Your accomplishment of the subsequent stages of consciousness depends on how far you succeed in equilibrating, in your own nature, your self-conscious and your subconscious. Your accomplishment of the stage depicted in THE LOVERS depends upon how far you have been successful in listening to the inner voice. Success with THE HIEROPHANT card depends upon how far you have been successful in governing your thoughts and emotions and acts. The perfection of each attainment in each card depends upon the perfection of the previous attainment.

THE HIEROPHANT in this card is imparting to the two kneeling at his feet (they are the two forms of the subconscious in you—the Cosmic subconscious, or THE HIGH PRIESTESS, and the personal subconscious, or THE EMPRESS) how to work physical changes in the body, which depends upon the equilibrium of the self-conscious and the subconscious. This equilibrium is physical matter, not merely mental and emotional equilibrium. The mental and emotional are very important. It is the effort at mental and emotional equilibrium, the effort of the self-conscious, which is the next preliminary of the physical changes worked by the subconscious. As exemplified in the Gospel story of John the Baptist: "The intellect must prepare the way of the Lord and make them straight." *It is the effort of the self-conscious which prepares the way for the changes worked in the subconscious.*

The equilibrium of your self-conscious and your subconscious in your own nature has been typified in the two preceding cards by THE EMPRESS and THE HIGH PRIESTESS. THE EMPRESS is a part of the Cosmic subconscious that you get from THE HIGH PRIESTESS. THE EMPRESS is represented by your personal subconscious, which is respondent to your own self-conscious images.

This card shows the masculine principle, of which your self-conscious is the physical plane representative, impressing the feminine principles, which build your present body, with the knowledge of how to construct a new body—a knowledge you do not possess yourself. This card emphasizes the idea of gender, the masculine principle impressing the feminine one. It has more symbols of gender than any other card.

The sign of this card, TAURUS, is ruled by Venus and it has a great many meanings, one being the Voice. The instruction of the Higher Self is heard through the instrumentality, through the agency of Venus, and she sends it on to the Pituitary. In philosophical terms, this means that you will not have Intuition about anything until you have used your Imagination on it, or until you have done as much thinking about it as you can. This exposes a very silly mistake that was made about Intuition by unthinking people who have absorbed superficially. They say that Intuition comes out of the blue—it goes through no preliminary stages, but comes out of an open sky. That idea is so absurd! You will never find anybody having an Intuition about a matter about which he has not given much previous thought. An artist, for instance, has Intuition only about art, and a scientist only about his particular science.

Intuition is not and cannot be a substitute for all the previous orderly mental steps. What are they? ATTENTION, MEMORY, IMAGINATION, and REASON. Great Intuition comes only after profound intellectualization in all these four stages. Some people think that Intuition is a matter of temperament. It is not that at all. Some people confuse Intuition with those sudden imperative emotions we call "hunches." Now it is true, a hunch is something we cannot explain, and it is sometimes amazingly accurate, but it is not intuition. Why not? Because hunches come from a part of us that is not from the mental part of us. The experience called "intuition" is from the mental part, from the Mental Sphere. The Higher Self has sent it down to that part of us which corresponds to Him, "the Mind." There are four mental steps we use preparatory to Intuition. When you have used them as far as they will go, the Higher Self steps in. If you will still the personality and listen to Him, He will help you out, but not unless it is necessary. Otherwise, how could you ever develop your Attention, your Memory, your Imagination and your Reason? It must necessarily follow, then, that an Intuition goes against Reason. This is very important! It seems untrue, but the moment you anticipate it, you see that it must be true. What is the need of Intuition if Reason will bring you to the same conclusion? There is then no need of an Intuition. Intuition goes farther than Reason can. You temporarily discard your Reason in order to get Intuition. It is always something you would not have arrived at by your Reason, and you employ Reason to carry it out. If you did not resume Reason to carry it out, you would never develop Reason. Many temples of ancient Greece were called "Temples of Divine Intuition and Reason."

This is precisely the same thing you do when you read or when you listen to anybody. You temporarily discard your personality and take up theirs, but if you keep your personality going you hear wrongly what they say. After you have heard what they say, you then use your personality in order to listen or read accurately. Otherwise everything that the other person says you hear through your own emotions and emotional associations.

In order to listen or to read, you have got to discard your personality temporarily. When you think, take it back again and measure what you have heard or read by the light of your personality—that is, by the measuring stick of your personality. So for that reason you must temporarily discard it to get Intuition. After you have got it you must use your Reason to carry it out.

William Blake said: "The greatest enemy of man is his reason. Reason impedes his Divine Rights, His Divine perceptions." He also said, "Nothing counts but intuition." In this respect he is right. Nothing does count but Intuition, if you are fortunate enough to have it. Until you have it, your Reason is what counts. Intuition would not come at all until you had used your Reason to the utmost, and used the three previous steps on which Reason is based. When you receive your Intuition you will always find it contrary to what your Reason has told you, or would have told you. If Reason was sufficient there would be no need for Intuition.

Blake's statement is one of the most interesting illustrations of how in one life we correct certain leading characteristics into which we have gone too far in another life. Blake always said that he had been Socrates. Socrates taught that Reason is the highest faculty of man, and that man could arrive at the same results by Reason as by Intuition. In that respect Socrates was wrong. As Socrates, Blake exalted Reason too much. He was too much for trimming back, too much for going against Reason. That is what always happens to us. When we try to correct a fault we overcorrect it and have to trim back. As it always happens, it appears to be intended. That appears to be the way to correct a fault, by overcorrecting and then trimming back.

There are many thinkers today who believe that the Intuition of William Blake was among the most important things in the nineteenth century. We know he had no Intuition except in those realms to which he had given profound study and thought. You have got to use whatever mind you have, as much as you can, before you get any Intuition.

In Tarot, the direction assigned to this letter VAV and the color of THE HIEROPHANT's robe both tell you the two important parts that Reason plays in the process of getting an Intuition and in carrying it out afterwards. The direction of HEH is Northeast, and the direction of VAV is Southeast. East, you see, is common to both. Wherever you see East it always presupposes THE EMPEROR, because THE EMPEROR always impresses THE EMPRESS (East).

Northeast is a combination of North (Reason) and East (Imagination). THE HIEROPHANT's color is RED-ORANGE, and Red is the color of Reason mixed with Yellow to make Red-orange. North is the sex-power in the head. When it wakes in the head it is called Reason, and East is THE EMPRESS after she has been impressed by her husband, THE EMPEROR. So when you say Northeast, you mean THE EMPRESS having been impressed by Reason, THE EMPEROR.

Now the Robe of THE HIEROPHANT is Red-orange. Red is the color of THE EMPEROR's robe, and Red is the color of the sex-power Reason, the sex-power functioning in the head.

The symbol of Taurus is a half-circle over a full circle. These symbols have a great many meanings. One of the meanings is this: the full circle is the circle of your entire past experience. You have that same thing when you speak your affirmations about THE EMPRESS:

> "I am the luminous intelligence enlightening all experiences
> with the wisdom of the ages."

The other is the Pattern on the Trestle board and refers to the Waterfall in THE EMPRESS card:

> "I am guided moment by moment along the path of liberation,
> filled with the understanding of its perfect Law."

Liberation from what? The imperfect body to which you have condemned THE EMPRESS. Liberation into what? The body which can function on all four planes, which possesses the 15 extensions of consciousness depicted by the TIARA of THE HIEROPHANT.

The sign Taurus rules the ears and the throat. The throat is the link between the head and the body. In astrology, Taurus is ruled by Venus, and the Moon is exalted in Taurus, meaning that the Moon comes to her highest activity in Taurus. *Your body is governed by your mental images.* The highest use of the memory in us is "recollection of the state from which we came, and back to which we are going." This recollection is what is meant by Intuition. *The highest capacity of the memory is reached in Intuition.* We remember something that we think we have forgotten and the Higher Self reminds us of it.

Occultism teaches us that what we call discoveries are really "recoveries," Intuitions that state to us facts which we or the world knew long ago. That is the teaching of Plato in regard to "ideas." "Ideas," he said, "are really the things that we see on a higher plane if we have the Spiritual perception." So when we have mental recollection down here of things we once saw on the higher planes, we have a memory, an idea. It is the same which is expressed in the Bible: "what is to be has been already." The creative powers search out what is past. In other words, people invent by reason of their memories, by reason of their Intuitions.

The occultist knows that even with the tremendous increase in scientific discovery in the last hundred years, we have not, as yet, come abreast of scientific perfection that we enjoyed in the past, in the Atlantean Age, for instance. We have forgotten all about them. We shall come abreast of those discoveries, and then we will go on a little further; that is to say, we will remember still further back.

SYMBOLISM

You have an Enthroned Figure like the Pope sitting between two pillars and giving instructions to two tonsured monks. The PILLARS are alike and they are made of stone. They stand for the union of the personality with the Higher Self, the body with the soul. The two Pillars bear the symbol of the principle of gender, two opposite forces working harmoniously and creatively together. That is the design of the two Pillars that we call, in architecture, "the bell and the clapper" design. This design illustrates the action of a nail when it is driven down into some other body. The Higher Self cannot work alone to this extent and we cannot work alone without the Higher Self. The bowl of the bell is useless without the clapper and the clapper is useless without the bowl. They must work together in order to make sound. A nail is useless unless you have something to drive it into. Unless a nail be driven into wood or a board, it cannot be attached to whatever you want to attach it to.

The two designs on the Pillars are set in deep semicircles, again representing the two forms of the subconscious in you. One semicircle is for the one listener, and the other semicircle is for the other listener. Who are these listeners? They are not the self-conscious and subconscious as you would naturally suppose. Their robes tell you who they are. Who is the one with the Roses? Who is the one with the Lilies? The one with the Roses is your intellectual subconscious, your body with your five senses. The one with the Lilies is your Cosmic subconscious kneeling at the feet of THE HIEROPHANT, who is instructing them. They have tonsured heads and Yokes of Yellow to show they are like monks, entirely abandoned and dedicated to the Higher Self, the source of all Intuitions. The YELLOW YOKES show the yoke of the Higher Self. One of them has Black Dots on it. It can be impressed by the mind. The other cannot be impressed by your mind (the Cosmic subconscious, the Holy Ghost in you), it can only be impressed by His Mind, the Mind of the Higher Self.

The YOKE of the Blue Figure should be LIGHT YELLOW, and it indicates the Cosmic subconscious of the personality. The Yoke of the figure with the Red Roses should be deepest yellow. The two yellows indicate different thoughts. The LIGHT YELLOW indicates the Mind of the Higher Self. The DEEP YELLOW indicates the mind of the lower self in these two phases, that of the self-conscious and that of the sub-conscious. The Blue Figure represents THE HIGH PRIESTESS. The self-conscious of the personality cannot impress her with his images. Only THE HIEROPHANT can do this, but the self-conscious of the personality can impress THE EMPRESS, the intellectual subconscious, which is the other figure.

Let us think on the teaching of the Higher Self. We are going later to transfer it to the self-conscious. The teaching is both the concrete and the abstract; it concerns the Eternal Principles. They are abstract. It shows your application of the Eternal Principles to your own troubles; that is, the concrete.

THE HIEROPHANT is enthroned on a PINK CARPET. Pink is Red-on-White. Red means the Mars force and White means the Spirit. Red-on-White, which is Pink, means the divine use of the Mars force, the Mars vibration.

The name given to a certain use of the Mars vibration is KUNDA-LINI. The next card is based on Kundalini. It is a certain nerve force which you generate in your body, an electrical force which you generate from Meditation. You probably are beginning to generate this force even though you have practiced only a short time with your cards. *It is through the agency of the Kundalini that we are enabled to hear the voice of the Higher Self.* Occasionally when some accident, great excitement, stress, grief, or joy has raised our vibration, we can hear the voice of the Higher Self. Generally and normally it is only by working on ourselves that we raise our vibration, rather than by some external means. Normally it is the rise of the Kundalini in our bodies which enables us to hear the Higher Self.

There are four (4) BLACK AND WHITE STRIPES upon this carpet. They are the Four Keys of the four planes. They are Black and White because they represent the opposing masculine and feminine, as did the two pillars of the HIGH PRIESTESS. When we speak of them as the emotions we see they represent the pleasant emotions and the unpleasant ones. One of the secrets THE HIEROPHANT is teaching these two is how to control their emotions so that their emotions will no longer control them.

THE WHOLE SECRET OF THE LIFE OF THE MYSTIC IS THE CONTROL OF EMOTION.

The two (2) Golden Keys have handles made like the Venus symbol, with the cross turned in. A key suggests a door, and Venus *is* the door. They are the Keys to unlock the Venus Center. The wards of these Keys are noticeably square, and the sign of the Venus Center is a carpenter's square. They are gold, so they represent the use of the energy of the Sun, the use of the Light Force. These three things taken together show that the Keys mean a certain use of the Solar Energy by which we unlock the power of the Venus vibration in the Throat Center. The Keys are the symbols of the unlocked power of the Venus vibration in the Throat Center.

In general, the last thing to demonstrate is the Throat Center, the place where you speak your Creative Word. This secret is like the other. THE HIGH PRIESTESS tells the subconscious the secret, and the subconscious relays it on to the self-conscious.

We now come to the costume of THE HIEROPHANT. He has a Red-orange robe on over a White one. The Blue robe is intermediary between the White and the Red-orange robes, between the innermost robe and the outside robe. Blue, the subconscious, is the vehicle by which the Spirit, the White, expresses itself to the Reason of man. When the Reason acts in accordance with the superconscious, it is Red-orange. The Red is Reason and the Orange is superconscious.

Two WHITE TABS hang down from the crown of THE HIEROPHANT and there are two more hanging down from his throat at the collar. Throat and ears are ruled by Taurus, consequently by Venus. It is the quickened activity of the Throat Center which sends up the message of the Higher Self to the Pituitary, who sends it to the hearing region of the back lobe of the brain. This is symbolic of the two tabs which fall from the ears and the two which fall from the throat. The tabs are four in number to show the functioning of Abstract Thought on all the four planes.

His sleeves are White because he is carrying out the designs of the Higher Self, whose agent he is. We do most of our work with the forearm and with the wrist, and that is why his sleeves are White.

The shoes are White for the same reason. He executes the demands of the Spirit, then carries out the efforts of the Spirit.

He is yoked with the Spirit. He has a White Yoke on. Just as the two beneath him are yoked with a Yellow "Y," he is yoked with a White "Y." Note that the White "Y" goes down in the many concentric folds of his robe, just as the White cross does on the robe of THE HIGH PRIESTESS.

THE HIGH PRIEST (HIEROPHANT) AND THE HIGH PRIESTESS EXIST ONLY TO CARRY OUT THE WILL OF THE SPIRIT. SHE, AS THE SUBCONSCIOUS MIND-STUFF, AND HE, AS THE SELF-CONSCIOUS AGENT OF THE SPIRIT.

Every concept of occultism and every principle is of both genders: masculine and feminine. It is now the one, and now the other. It is feminine in respect to all that is above it, and masculine in respect to all that is below it. Let us see how that works out. The highest member of man's Trinity is feminine to the Creator, but it is sternly masculine to all that is below it. The Higher Self is immediately below it. The Higher Self is feminine to it but sternly masculine to all that is below. What is immediately below it is the man, the human being. The human being is masculine and feminine, but the human being is always feminine to the Higher Self. The human being should be sternly masculine to his body and his body should be feminine to him.

Your subconscious, your Empress, who is feminine to your self-conscious, should rule all the rest of the body with a rod of iron and be sternly masculine to it. She rules each organ in the body. Each organ in the body, while it is feminine, should be sternly masculine to all the cells which compose it to all the areas which it feeds or tends. There is a long procession: masculine, feminine, masculine, feminine, all the way down. The thing is now one, now the other. It is the feminine if you look above, and it is masculine as you look below.

Now in this long procession, the only one who is ever derelict to his duty is the self-conscious of the man. Aren't you ashamed of yourself? He may, and also generally does, cater to his body. He may, and also generally does, refuse to be feminine to the Higher Self. So the self-conscious is the only rebel in the long procession. He lets his body rule him when he should rule the body. He refuses to obey the dictates of the Higher Self when he should be feminine to the Higher Self.

Now we come to something very intricate, and you must be very patient.

The imposing CROWN on the head of THE HIEROPHANT has hanging from it TWO TABS OF YELLOW-DEEP YELLOW, which represent the self-conscious mind and the subconscious mind. He controls both the self-conscious and the subconscious mind. He communicates only through the subconscious mind. His Tiara represents the dominion over Nature. He extends down into the self-conscious and the subconscious, and stretches down into them his possession of the 15 emanations of consciousness and his functioning in the four planes. There will come a time when we have his 15 extensions of consciousness and we can function on the four planes also. It is because of him that we can do this.

If you will look closely you will see that these tabs are not pale Yellow, the pale Yellow of THE FOOL, but the darker Yellow of THE MAGICIAN. If you turn to THE HIGH PRIESTESS card you will see that the portico in which she is sitting is pale Yellow, not the darker Yellow of THE MAGICIAN. She is sitting in the gateway of the Temple and the Temple is the opened Pineal Gland. The opened Pineal Gland means that the personality is functioning and is inspiring the activity of the body.

This Tiara on the head of THE HIEROPHANT is made in the shape of the Pineal Gland, made in the shape of a pine cone. It is made to designate the opened Pineal Gland, which is the Temple in the body in which the Soul functions and from which it directs the personality. The Crown and the Scepter also mean dominion. The Crown of THE EMPRESS means that she has dominion over the 12 signs of the Zodiac in the Body.

What has THE HIEROPHANT dominion over? His Scepter indicates that he has dominion over the four planes. The Archetypal Plane is indicated by the knob at the top, and the three lower planes are indicated by the three cross pieces: The Creative, Formative, and Physical planes. The Tiara indicates the same thing, but in a far more detailed and complicated way. There are three circlets in the Tiara to correspond to the three cross pieces. They are surrounded by three nails meaning "Three in One," and they are the three same things as the circular little knob on the top of the Scepter.

What are these three? They are the self-conscious, the superconscious, and the subconscious, and they comprise the ALL of existence. In the Archetypal World these three exist as one. To come down into the matter of the three lower planes they must split up and become three separate things. These circles in the Tiara you may regard as the self-conscious, subconscious, and superconscious.

The smallest and highest circlet is that of the Crown, where it is constructed with three trefoils with little clover leaves. The three trefoils, in the smallest circlet, represent these three kinds of consciousness when they exist separately, and they also represent matter as well as consciousness. When they represent matter they represent the three qualities of matter. By the manipulation of these three qualities of matter all creation is accomplished. The three qualities of matter are called by the Hindus, *Satva*, *Tamas*, and *Rajas*.

Satva is the tendency of matter to collect into form.

Tamas is the tendency of matter to remain in that form or to be stable.

Rajas is the tendency of matter to disintegrate after the form has served its purpose.

So you can think of these three trefoils as matter when they represent the three qualities of matter, or as consciousness. When we think of them as consciousness, they represent the superconscious, the subconscious, and the self-conscious. There are no separate entities corresponding to these names. They are merely the three ways the One Energy transcends itself. Christianity makes them into the three separate entities because it is the need of the human mind to make ideas personalized. Christianity calls them Father, Son, and Holy Ghost. Theology insists that these are separate, and yet they exist together at the same time as a Trinity.

The next circlet is wider and has five trefoils. What do these five trefoils represent? They represent the fivefold activity of the formative world. This, the formative world, and its activity, is fivefold and is in the formative world the subtle principles of the five centers of sense. These are not the faculties that we have now in the physical body, but are their subtle principles as they appear on the higher plane: hearing, sight, taste, touch, and smell. It is the extension of these five senses into their subtle principles, so that we can perceive them upon higher planes, that we seek to accomplish by our practice with the Tarot cards. These subtle principles correspond to the five elements which, in forms other than ours, exist on all planes.

(1) Ether corresponding to Hearing,
(2) Fire corresponding to Sight,
(3) Water corresponding to Taste,
(4) Air corresponding to Touch, and
(5) Earth corresponding to Smell.

These subtle principles correspond to the five elements.

Now you come to the last circlet. There are seven trefoils. They represent the seven forces of the physical plane. The Hebrew God "Jehovah" was the synthesis of these seven forces. He was called the *Seven Elohim*, or *He of the Seven Elohim*. They are beautifully symbolized in Judaism by the seven branched candlesticks. Seven branches, but one flame. The branches are the seven differentiations of the One Flame. The New Testament calls them the Seven Spirits before the Throne. In the solar system we have seven sacred planets. In our bodies there are seven interior stars, or Centers (chakras), whose vibration we seek to quicken by color and sound practice. This Tiara may well be large and elaborate, as it sums up everything there is in the Universe. The One becomes the Three becomes the Five becomes the Seven by dividing itself, whether you call it on the one side consciousness or on the other side, matter. The difference between consciousness and matter is only relative. In reality they are the same thing in different aspects. *All matter has consciousness and all consciousness exists in matter.*

The alchemist called the seven forces the seven alchemic metals, and they symbolized control over all manifestation. All this is represented by the Tiara. The larger part of this manifestation is invisible to us. We can increase what is visible a great deal by enlarging our Spiritual perceptions; but always the larger part will be invisible to us while we function in the body.

This is what the partly closed, uplifted hand of THE HIEROPHANT means. His hand says that the world to be contacted by the senses is only a small part of the story. That is just the point. The rest of the hand is closed up, which means you cannot contact as long as you are using the physical sense, however sharpened by practice. The major part of the world will always elude you as long as you are in these bodies. The Higher Self can see it all.

REMEMBER: *The message received in this card is from the Higher Self and is called Intuition (THE INNER TEACHING).* He wants to warn you particularly against thinking of the INNER TEACHING as teaching the self-conscious alone. That is what it is doing in this card. The teaching deals with telling the two forms of the subconscious in you all that is necessary to bring about the physical changes, which they must work in the body in order for you to become truly spiritual in the occult sense of the word. The teaching of the Higher Self is destined to reach the self-conscious ultimately. It comes through the Venus Center in the throat and is passed up to the Pituitary Gland, where she sends it into the thinking lobe of the brain as a thought, or into the hearing area, where it registers as a voice.

When you impersonate THE HIEROPHANT you will remember what you are to do in your affirmations—talking to the two forms of your subconscious: your Empress and your High Priestess. Remember, while you are impersonating them, performing all the acts they perform, *you must still all your emotional associations, compose all your emotions and impulses, and listen to the word of the inner voice.* It might come to you at any time.

NOTES

THE LOVERS.

7th Hebrew Letter	*ZAIN*
Symbol for	*Smell*
Color	*Orange*
Numerical Value	*7*
Syllables	*ZIN*
Sound	*D-Natural*
Planets	*Mercury and Venus*
Translation	*Sword*
Sign in Zodiac	*Gemini*

NOTES

THE LOVERS

ZAIN, spelled ZIN, means SWORD. It is the seventh Hebrew letter and the third SIMPLE LETTER. It stands for the occult extension of the faculty of SMELL (smell on the mental plane), for the direction EAST-ABOVE. It is a combination therefore of MERCURY and VENUS, standing for the Zodiacal sign GEMINI, THE TWINS, for the DISPOSING INTELLIGENCE, the color ORANGE, note D-NATURAL, and the numerical value is 7. The Roman character is written Z.

The letter Zain, appropriate to its meaning "sword," looks like an Eastern scimitar. In three of these cards we have swords. As we have seen, the Hebrew alphabet was created out of the Chaldean alphabet, not merely as other alphabets were made to found a language, but also made to convey secret mystic truths to those persons who had the key. These truths, you see, were conveyed in several ways:

(1)   by the shape of the letters,

(2)   by the things they stand for (natural objects),

(3)   by their numerical value, and lastly,

(4)   by a secret value inside a numeral value. This secret value denoted a closer relationship between two letters, whatever the two were.

Now, the letter ZAIN is an illustration of this last-named device of conveying truth by a secret value, just as Heh conveyed the secret value of 14. The secret value of this letter is 16. It is a combination in the shape of Yod, which is 10, and Vau, which is 6. The concealed value of this is 16. Sixteen is also the concealed value of Gimel, whose outer value is 3. So you would tell by this that the two letters have a close inner relationship. Gimel and Zain have for their secret value 16. Sixteen is very important. It is the number of black and white squares on the chess board, and the chess board is a story of life told in occult terms. You will find 16 stripes in the Headdresses of the Sphinxes in the card THE CHARIOT.

The Uniting Intelligence of Gimel and the Disposing Intelligence of Zain are really two aspects of the same thing, two parts of the same Intelligence.

For the Greek occultist the 12 signs of the Zodiac composed the chief repository of the universal Laws of Nature as they worked out in the external and internal universe (the solar system and his own body). The Hebrew mystics expanded the 12 signs of the Zodiac into the 22 letters of the alphabet. Consequently, the Hebrew mystics could devote particular attention to the different aspects of the Zodiacal signs. They had almost doubled the number, and so devoted two letters to this aspect, one uniting and the other disposing.

The only means the personal self-consciousness has of connecting with the Higher Self is through the subconscious, by considering the subconscious in her two aspects, THE HIGH PRIESTESS and THE EMPRESS. The Higher Self is the link between man's personal self-consciousness and his Spirit (the first member, the Son of our Trinity). Until man has opened his Pineal Gland and prepared his body for the Higher Self to come in and take direct control of it, he hears the Voice of the Higher Self only by means of his twofold consciousness (subconscious). You will see him doing this in the next card, which represents the highest principle of consciousness. Just as in THE HIEROPHANT card you saw the Higher Self teaching these two forms of subconscious, so in this card you see that it is the woman who hears the Angel and is man's means of communion with the Angel. She is the one who gets his message and relays it to the man. She is looking at the Angel. The man appears unconscious of the Angel. He is looking at her. So it is through the subconscious that you hear the voice of the supercon scious. She is our means of communication with the Spirit.

This is a very different subconscious from that which Freud and the psychoanalysts have made the world afraid of—a subconscious who drags us down to the level of beasts. It is true she may do this, but it is not her fault. *She has to do what we direct her to do, THAT SHE MUST DO!* Remake her, direct her otherwise, she will pull us up to the Angel, and through her we can hear the Voice of the Angel.

Reason cannot make you aware of the superconscious. This can be done only by the subconscious, until by your Reason you have con structed a new brain. In that new brain is a special mechanism which allows the superconscious to function there—the transformed Pineal Gland. *It is the subconscious which hears the voice of the Angel, and it is the subconscious which raises us up to the superhuman level;* but it cannot do it unless the self-conscious initiates the process and keeps it going. The subconscious is then enabled to raise us to the Angel.

All activities except those which are needed to keep the body going must begin with the mind. All the subconscious does by herself is that which is necessary to keep the body going. In all the rest, all activities begin with the mind. So you see the function of each is sternly limited, and you see here all the functions of the self-conscious and the subconscious. She cannot initiate the Spiritual process, but he can. He cannot construct the mechanism, but she can. So it is necessary that they work together. Together they must work in concert. It is necessary that they play into each other's hands interdependently. In short, they must be Lovers as this card calls them, or Twins as the Zodiac calls them. Thus the necessity of the equilibrium of the two is what Tarot teaches, and it brings about this equilibrium. Since they must play into each other's hands, they must be balanced, and to teach you how to balance the self and subconscious is the object of Tarot and the object of mysticism: *To make the heart equal the head, and the head equal the heart.*

You see in the human kingdom a strong emphasis laid upon sex that was not laid before, and that precise kind of emphasis will not be made again, not in the higher kingdoms. Science says that animals are not self-conscious. The consciousness of our limitations is what we mean by self-conscious. In the rank above man we find that the emphasis of sex diminishes and finally disappears, becoming gender again. The two sexes becoming one again as it was in the beginning. There must be some reason for this. There must be some reason why in the human species a unique emphasis is placed upon the sexes. Gender must have a unique part to play in the evolution of man from his present estate to a higher one. Its unique part apparently is to afford us a means of making ourselves over so that we can enter into the superhuman kingdom of Nature. We are told by Madame Blavatsky, who wrote at the dictation of a Master, that the next race of men will not make physical use of the organs of procreation.

Let us quickly survey man in relation to sex. As we look back over his biological history or over the recorded social history of man we see two very unenviable distinctions setting man apart from the rest of creation. The first is that he is the only animal that maltreats his body in order to extract sensation from it. The second is that he is the only animal that has "victimized" the female of his species because of her biological function. Woman is just recovering from that now. In several of the lower animals we have the female victimizing the male. No animal in the wild state overeats or is oversexed. Instinct is startingly free from either. Instinct won't permit it. "So far shalt thou go and no further," she seems to say to the animal. No sooner do animals come in contact with man in domestication than along with the good results of that contact we see the bad results. All domesticated animals will overeat, although some are wiser about it than others; namely, the cat is far wiser than the dog. One of the results of dog's domestication has been more success in the good things than with any other animal. One of the bad results of dog's domestication has been to oversex him. We have given the dog the humiliating preoccupation with sex, which he did not have when he was a wolf, and which no other animal has but the monkey race. The occultist says that we are not descended from the ape or from a common ancestor as Darwin claimed. So you see, man, in communicating a little of his mind to the animal kingdom, has communicated his own bad use of the mind; namely, his disregard of the body in seeking sensation, to extract pleasure from it.

When the animal lived under instinct, it never overworked the body in trying to extract satisfaction from it. Until we come under the dominion of Reason, so that it exercises over us just as much of an imperious domination as instinct did over the animal, man will continue to maltreat his body, his subconscious, for his own aims (to extract pleasure from it).

Tarot says that your body is an animal which possesses a mind far better than the misused and unevolved mind we have at present. Even if you used it correctly it is still unevolved; it has a long distance to go before it will have evolved as far as the body has.

. You have a mind which you have degraded by impressing upon it your images of "sense" satisfaction. You have degraded the mind of this animal by painting images of sense satisfaction which it had to follow. *You have to discipline it back into the state it would have been—not with hostility, but with love.* What is the state it would have been in? It is the finest body yet invented by Nature. It would have continued to be so if you had handled it properly. Maltreating the body for the sake of your emotions, your ambitions, and even your aspirations, is just as bad for it as if you maltreated it for the sake of sensation.

Superstition and religion have been the prime offenders in counseling people to belabor their bodies with stern austerities. All that was done, you say, for a good purpose; but it was just as bad as if it had been done for a bad purpose. Occultism says that flagellations, starvation, and privation may be worse than debauchery. See how the religious devotee of austerities throughout history, especially medieval history, has maltreated the body. That may be worse than debauchery, because debauchery always brings its penalty, and the connection of the penalty with the crime is seen. If you have ruined your body by religious austerity, it is not recognized to be such. If you do see it, then you are warned not to do it again. The beautiful Saint Francis spent the last years of his life a helpless, childish melancholiac, because said he, "I brought this body to this pass because I have beaten my brother too hard."

The second inevitable distinction of man as a race is that he is the only animal that has taken advantage of woman's biological handicap. She has to produce her young and put in long servitude to bring up her young to where they can look out for themselves. Human children take a long time to get their growth to where they can support themselves. The offspring of other animals take a much shorter time. During all this time woman is under a handicap. She is at the service of her young. Man has taken advantage of that for his own aggrandizement and to make her inferior.

In this respect, too, the Church has apparently been the willing accomplice of the State to degrade woman. See how the State and the religions misread the allegory of the Garden of Eden in order to justify keeping woman in subjection, because it agreed with temperament to do so.

The ideal relation between the self-conscious and the subconscious is depicted in this card, THE LOVERS. You will see the typical relation which exists under the misuse of the mind depicted in card 15, THE DEVIL. Put the two cards side by side and you will see they have outstanding similarities. The ideal relation between the two is THE LOVERS. The typical relation is in the card THE DEVIL, where this subconscious is abused by the self-conscious.

You see a man in this card, THE DEVIL, whose acquisitive sex demands are constantly inflamed by the torch which The Devil carries. He keeps crying to the woman (his subconscious) Give me! Give me! So here her hands are held in the attitude of reluctant submission. She has her face averted from him, and she has to submit but does not wish to. Both man and woman are depicted with tail, hooves, and horns to indicate that they are living solely in their animal natures. She cannot help that because he makes her do it. Upon her head is the Crescent of the subconscious as it should be. There is one upon his also; however, there should not be. It indicates that while she thinks he is living in the self-conscious, he fosters his whole being in the subconscious. He passes his whole being in search for "subconscious sensations." His only use for thought (if indeed it can be called thought) is how to gratify his desire for sensation. Between the two is the STONE to which both are chained. The Stone, among other things, represents ignorance. It is Black at its lower level. It is a half-cube of Black. They are using a half world—the Black of ignorance. The Devil squats on the Stone while he inflames with one hand the self-conscious with His Torch, and with the other he blesses their union.

In all these respects this card tallies with the Zain card. Here in the Zain card is one who sits above and blesses the pair. The attitude of the pair toward each other is likewise indicated by the hands which say to them, "Take me; all I have is yours." He is looking toward her, and her body is facing him but her eyes look to the Angel. The previous card teaches what this means: *The Higher Self gives instructions to the subconscious when you allow him to do so; she takes it and passes it on to the man.*

In both of these cards the two are naked, for in both they are in a state of Nature. In THE DEVIL they are in a state of lower (animal) nature. In THE LOVERS they are in a state of higher nature (on the lower spiral and on the upper spiral). That is to say, between THE LOVERS there is no artificiality, no compulsion, no pretense, and no concealment. Clothes are the symbol of artificiality (concealment, pretense, and barriers) between the self-conscious and the subconscious.

In the Garden of Eden allegory you will remember that only after the two have committed so-called sin, after they had pandered to the animal desires, did they desire to clothe themselves. They saw that they were naked and they complained to God, and God said, "Who told you that you are naked?" In the card THE LOVERS, the trees (behind the woman with the serpent wound up its trunk) immediately make you think of the story of the Garden of Eden.

Like all the allegories of the Church, the real meaning of this story has been forgotten. Like all allegories, which are taken literally, great harm has been wrought by interpreting as actual what was meant to be allegorical. Now for the explanation, as far as it concerns this card, of the allegory of the Garden of Eden story:

Like all allegories and all dreams, this story has many levels; that is, it has to be looked at in several aspects. All the allegories of the Bible and of Greek mythology are so constructed that in all important points they will hold true at various levels. Your dreams, for instance, are allegories constructed by that supreme artist, your subconscious, and they tell you one story at one level and another story at another. Both are true, and probably both are intended.

The Adam and Eve story has several aspects and levels of interpretation. The two levels we are particularly concerned with relate to gender and to sex. The Church has told us the allegory only at the level of sex. What it has said is simply ridiculous to most people. *Whether you take it at the level of gender or at the level of sex, the Garden of Eden represents the actual body. THE CHURCH DOES NOT TEACH THAT!*

Look at the story of the Garden of Eden. It is one of the strangest stories in the world. You are told that there are four rivers in the Garden. Why is that necessary? The Garden of Eden is an allegory for your body, and the four rivers of the garden are the four fluid systems of the body:

(1)   The cerebrospinal nervous system,
(2)   The sympathetic nervous system,
(3)   The bloodstream, or circulatory system, and,
(4)   The intestinal tract.

We are not concerned with these four rivers at present. We shall be in later cards, and so we speak of them now. The flora and fauna of the Garden (the plant life and the animal life in the Garden) are the actual flora and fauna in your body. How shall you grow plants in your body other than the ones you eat? Growth is now occupying the minds of the scientists a great deal. Intestinal gardening, I think, is an attractive name.

The Garden of Eden, then, with these four rivers, is the human body. It was tenanted by two people, a man and a woman. Many of the strange and incredible contradictions of Church teaching spring from regarding the story of the Garden of Eden solely as relating to sex. It has seemed rather preposterous to critics of the Bible that God should have deliberately created male and female. He cursed them for using their functions of male and female, which He had given them, and turned them out of the Garden. Then He blessed them for using the same function and ordered them to propagate (people the earth) and use it as much as possible. That seems very strange. The absurdity of it is enough to make reasonable people doubt the teaching of the Church, particularly when you look at this story literally. Here they were, originally a pair. They had two children, both male. The older killed the younger, and then there was only one child left in the world. This child went off to another country and married a woman there. From whence did she come?

The story of the Garden of Eden had some actual meaning as far as physical sex is concerned. It referred to a state before human life existed on this planet. A state referred to in the Book of Genesis, where the text says: "And God came to the earth and married with the daughters of men." It also referred to a fact that sex has a most important part to play in the evolution of the human kingdom. The evolution of the race could only come about through sex and through pain; only by lifting the sex force to the head could we accomplish our entrance into the Spiritual Kingdom. What is the important part sex plays? The first important part is that man evolves only by his long servitude to his young and to his mate. Second, there comes a time when he must lift up his sex force to make it serve another purpose, another function. It is what brings us from our present state of civilization to its limit in the human kingdom. It is the means whereby we get from the human kingdom to the superhuman kingdom. That is, the same force which is responsible for our upward evolution in the human kingdom will, when transformed, accomplish our entrance into the next higher kingdom of Nature, the superman.

In order to raise the sex force it is necessary to go through a period of abstinence. The length of that period varies with the person and with his Karmic history, be it shorter or longer, when it it is over it is over. When the sex force has been raised, the physical use of sex may be resumed. The attitude of the mystic toward indicating this period of abstinence and raising the sex force is precisely that of the attitude of the principal religious orders which demand chastity. At first they were all occultists. The Church says that no one should undertake the monastic life who has not discovered within himself the positive urge for it. The occultist says it is by no means necessary for everybody to raise his force. You need not try to do it unless you feel urged to do it, and then it is your duty.

There was a period when the processes of the body had to be learned one by one by the self-conscious. When the self-conscious had thoroughly learned them and they became a habit, they fell below the threshold of the self-conscious. They sank to the level of the subconscious, the automatic. That is just what always occurs. You learn something new by paying your whole conscious attention to it. When you know it well enough for it to become automatic, you no longer pay any attention to it. Your body takes care of it (your subconscious). That is just what happened when you learned to walk, for instance. Walking was a very difficult trick for you to learn. You had to pay your whole attention to it, to learn how to keep your balance when you moved about and put one foot before the other. You thought that you would never learn to do it, and all of a sudden you did it automatically. That is what you do when you learn to play music. In childhood you say, "How can she play and talk at the same time?" You learn to do all those things and they become automatic with you. They sank below the level of the self-conscious and your subconscious attends to them.

The story of the Garden of Eden goes on to say that a curse was pronounced upon Eve for listening to the Serpent, and Eve was made subject to her husband; she is subject to her husband not only for good but for evil too. *We make our subconscious.* It was perfect in the beginning but we have degraded it. In the same way we have degraded it, we can free it by our thoughts.

As mankind divided himself into Will and Substance, the Substance (the female part of him) was subject to the Will (the male part of him) from the moment of our birth. From the moment of the birth of the race and from the moment of the birth of the self-conscious and mind, the self-conscious has been engaged in making the subconscious satisfy us and pander to his desires. We have used what mind we have in trying to extract sensation from the body, and have thus degraded our subconscious. We make the subconscious pander to our desire and all desires find their source in the senses. That is why there are five fruits on the Tree in this card.

The reason why the subconscious is an enemy is because we have made her so. She is no enemy of the mere animal, or of the animal at the level of the human savage. She is our enemy only at the civilized level. Why? Because civilized man, in order to dwell together in groups, gave up the satisfaction of his own self. In order for us to live together you and I must give up this, that, and the other thing. We will make laws against these things. We will penalize those who break the laws; but in spite of the laws, the individual wanted to do those things. So the subconscious became our enemy at the civilized level.

The subconscious knows nothing about the "laws" the self-conscious has made, except as you tell her of them. Most of our time, particularly in childhood, is spent in impressing upon our subconscious how much we have to break those laws (those duties laid upon us) when we try to create. The subconscious is genuinely subservient to her husband and is eager to help him do what he wants. Once she knows that he wants to break them, she naturally helps him to break them. I think that man, as a class, still believes that the ideal wife is the wife who "helps him to his desires," be they what they may. Lady Macbeth was the ideal wife because she helped her husband do what he wanted, though she had to murder a lot of people who stood in the way. That is more or less what the masculine idea of it is today.

The HIGH PRIESTESS is not your intellectual subconscious. She is that part of the Cosmic subconsciousness that you have in you. She was never subservient to the self-conscious of God. If you have developed to the point that she is already active in you, at night she, too, tells you things and passes on to you the Intuitions of the HIGHER SELF.

The subconscious handles her affairs perfectly if you will let her. Fortunately, you cannot interfere with most of her work. She does that as perfectly as is possible with the conditions you have made. Why does she do her work perfectly? Because she has never been deficient in "attention" as we are. Since she is never deficient in attention she never deceives herself intentionally as we do. "I was mistaken," we say. "I didn't see that correctly." Furthermore she never deceives herself intentionally as we do all the time—forever pretending to be better than we are so that we will get along with ourselves.

She sees herself without any deceit, clearly, and so naturally has both dignity and humor. She has a reach for dignity and she can permit herself humor. So it follows that you can neither bully nor coerce the subconscious, you have got to treat her square. Why should she yield to you? She knows herself to be the better and older one of the two. Occultism agrees with Freud that our salvation depends upon the reeducation of our subconscious. That is the teaching of both Freud and mysticism. You cannot compel her by browbeating her in the manner of ignorant ascetics, whether they are of the Church or whether they are ascetics for some other purpose. You cannot reach her by mere mechanical repetition, which, alas, they do very much in the Church.

Rituals such as the Eastern prayer wheel, the rosary, and the Western Church services require your full attention. They are not successful with one-half of your mind on them and the other half of your mind on something else. The church service rituals are merely devices to impress your subconscious. If you enter into them with a whole mind and a whole heart, they are very successful, especially in singing hymns, as they are successful in reaching the subconscious. Prayer is a device for impressing your subconscious. If you pray for spiritual blessings you answer your own prayer. If you pray with your mind as well as with your word and emotions, it is successful.

The Tarot cards were invented by supermen and superwomen in order to reach the subconscious in the liveliest manner. That is to say,

the liveliest method of reaching the subconscious is by images in action. All
these cards portray images in action—images in action connected by
sound and color, to which the subconscious is directly responsive.

There is another way of reaching the subconscious and you can
combine it with all the other ways. You can direct her to pay no attention to you when you give her commands, and when she knows you
are in earnest she will take you at your word. Tell her not to listen to
your commands whether they be good or evil, but instead to listen to
the Voice of the Higher Self and the Angels. When she knows you are
in earnest she will obey you, she will do it to your annoyance. This is
not so startlingly novel as it sounds. *You can really train your subconscious to stop you from doing something or making the wrong kind of image if
you actually impress her with the fact that you don't want to do it.* Say to her
precisely with your whole mind, "My dear, you know what a fool I am.
When you see me doing this, stop me, will you?" She will stop
you.

All this reeducation takes time and endless patience. The subconscious thinks she knows very well that you want what you have
been accustomed to doing all your life. She knows that all your life
you have been in the habit of deceiving yourself. When you tell her
you don't want to do these things, you have got to put your whole
mind to it, and finally you may succeed. You pay the penalty for her
perfect use of attention. She has seen all along that you like to deceive
yourself, that you like to do things that you pretend you don't like to
do, so she makes it easy for you to do them. You pay the penalty for her
perfect use of attention, and the penalty she gives you for your habit of
inattention cannot be overestimated. As long as you are inattentive,
you impress her with two images instead of one, and you will defraud
her because she is obliged to act out these images.

ZAIN means *Sword*. There is a sword on THE MAGICIAN's
table. One of the things it stands for is the instrumentality by which an
idea is carved out of the subconscious Cosmic Mind-Stuff into a
physical plane thing. It is the word of processes. Cosmically speaking,
that is what Zain means.

Let me refresh your memory on the four stages of an idea. First
the idea is Abstract; then it is put into a pattern or cup, and this is symbolized by the cup. The pattern is then carved out by a process and
becomes a concrete thing on the physical plane. That is the way man
works in inventing, painting, or making any plan he carries out in
material substance. As with man, so with God. That is the way God

worked with his plan in forming his universe—it is only the concrete forms of an Abstract Thought of God.

"In the beginning God created the Heaven and the Earth." The word *created* in the Old Testament is wrongfully translated. It should be translated "cut apart." It is with this sword God cut apart the Heaven and the Earth. All manifestation is a process of cutting apart (Heaven is the mind, Earth the substance). God cut himself in part, making himself two—the Will and Substance—in order to manifest. The Will and the Substance on THE MAGICIAN's table are symbolized by the Wand and the Cup. Into the Cup he pours other ideas, which are brought into manifestation by a similar process on the lower plane. The human embryo becomes a complex organism by the same process of subdivision. "In the beginning," reads the Scripture, "God cuts apart the earth from the Heavens."

Personally speaking, the sword in Zain stands for discrimination to cut apart the subconscious from the self-conscious. Cosmically speaking, it cuts apart the Will from the Substance.

There are other swords in the Tarot besides THE MAGICIAN's sword. It is really the same sword, but a different aspect of its use. There is a sword in this card. There is a sword in the card JUSTICE. Justice wielding a sword, still another aspect of THE MAGICIAN. It is useful to call THE MAGICIAN's sword the Sword of Processes. The sword Zain stands for is the Sword of Discrimination. You might call the sword in JUSTICE the Sword of Elimination, of cutting out, but they are all the same sword put to these uses:

(1st)   carving out,

(2nd)   discrimination, and

(3rd)   getting rid of undesirables.

The sword of the letter Zain stands for discrimination. Discrimination between what? Between the self-conscious (the Will) and the subconscious (the Substance). Discrimination between the inductive mind and the deductive mind.

No manifestation can exist with unity. It is only when unity becomes duality that the first step toward manifestation has begun.

The astrological sign of THE LOVERS is the Twins. The name *twins*, more than lovers, emphasizes that the two kinds of consciousness are equals; they only appear to be superior and inferior for the purpose of manifestation. Occultists say that you must learn never to mix them. The important thing with Twins is to use both in equilibrium; they can never be equilibrated as long as you mix them.

The act of perfect discrimination is what is called God consciousness. Discrimination depends upon attention; and attention you will remember, involves seeing not only what a thing is like, but how it differs from what it is like. You hear constantly that you can prove anything by analogies, but that is not true. Analogies are excellent proof, but the trouble is that there are so many bad analogies. The reason why analogies are bad is because people fail to see how a thing is different from what it is like, rather than to see what it is like in the first place. A genius sees similarities where other people see only differences, and differences where other people see only similarities.

In Astrology, Mercury rules Gemini, so in psychological terms that means close attention governs the discrimination. It also means a good many other things besides the psychological thing. The great trouble is that people think as a matter of routine and make the classification based on too little observation. They say something is like something else, belongs to the same class, when it doesn't necessarily belong in the same class at all. It may be somewhat alike in one or two superficial aspects.

SYMBOLISM

A GOLDEN SUN streams out its rays on all beneath. The superconscious is here represented as Raphael, the Angel of the Sun. Raphael means *wholeness*, or *health*—the rounded, complete, unobstructed, whole use of the Life-power. It concerns your breathing. That is a secret which you must grow into. The air you take into your body is the Life-power. You haven't as yet learned how to use it wholly, completely. Until you have equilibrated in you the subconscious and the self-conscious, you are obstructing the passage of the Life-power and you cannot use it.

From the head of this Angel stream forth GREEN FLAMES alternating with FLAMES of RED ON YELLOW. RED ON YELLOW typifies Reason. As we saw on the background of the card THE EMPEROR, the mind issued according to the dictates of Reason. GREEN is the color of THE EMPRESS—the subconscious flames (Imagination). One of the flames is the SELF-CONSCIOUS (RED) and the other is the SUBCONSCIOUS (GREEN). The two flames are working together. The creative force in God, Angel, or man works by the use of Imagination. The business of Reason is to create forms. No form can be created until there is equilibrium in the body.

The WINGS of the Angel are RED, denoting that he is full of aspiration, of DESIRE to be ONE with the Fundamental Cause and Universal Energy. His desire is to do the Will of the Father, to create.

His MANTLE is VIOLET. VIOLET is the color of EQUILIBRIUM and the creation of forms. Like all fabrics in the Tarot this fabric is heavily folded and pleated to suggest that *he creates by manipulating vibratory power.*

He is blessing the twofold persons below, the persons who have learned to communicate with the superconscious by means of the subconscious. They are persons who do not intrude on each other's work, but both work together like the two flames on the Headdress, in perfect harmony. The man says to the woman, "Here I am. I want to use you and I want you to use me as seems best to that Angel to whom you are looking, whom I cannot see and can only hear through you."

In the Hands of the Angel is written the character of Zain. Not the printed character, the written one. There are two of them, held in blessing over the twofold consciousness. This indicates that discrimination is as necessary for the subconscious as it is for the self-conscious if we are to have perfect equilibrium in the body. It is just as necessary for the subconscious to discriminate as it is for the self-conscious, because she has perfect discrimination if you will allow her to use it.

You now have three symbols of equilibrium in the body. The numerical symbol of equilibrium is 8. The geometric symbol is the interlaced equilateral triangle. The third symbol is the Sword of Discrimination and the letter Zain. All three mean equilibrium, to have that which calls up a different and divine aspect of equilibrium.

Between the man and the woman is a MOUNTAIN. Between the man and the woman in THE DEVIL card is a black half-cube stone to which each is chained. In the symbology of Tarot a mountain is indicative of something accomplished or to be accomplished. In THE LOVERS card it is something accomplished or to be accomplished by their union. Since the Mountain is between the two, it is to be accomplished by their working together. In either case it indicates the liberty of the Imagination. Imagination is chained when the sex force is dissipated before it reaches the head to stimulate the action of the Pineal Gland.

This Mountain is RED ON BLUE. It means the desire of the self-conscious working upon the subconscious in external nature. It typifies the ability of the equilibrated person to mold the mineral kingdom.

The first great achievement of the spiritualized man is to impress his subconscious that she (the subconscious) remakes his body into a fit dwelling place for the Higher Self, which is the result depicted in the next card. *This remaking of the body is what is meant by being born again, in Christian terminology.* After she has remade his body the next object is to remake Nature outside his body. It is the subconscious carrying out the desires of the self-conscious. The first work that these two people do between them is to make a new body which is composed of mineral substance. The second work has to do with something outside of themselves.

In THE CHARIOT you see the Higher Self setting about the second great achievement to make magic. He is starting to work to remold and reshape the external world about him. That is what is meant by the destiny of man to be co-worker with God. To rearrange the world according to God's pattern. This is really nothing very new. All civilization has reshaped Nature. We take the materials which Nature has formed and try to make them better; we, thereby, make another world. For instance, we have worked up minerals and metals, not only into useable forms, but into amalgams which do not exist in Nature, thus making them more useable. We take a plow and till the land and work up the land into something else. We produce new plants by combinations. We take the old plants and we make new ones out of them. We take the old animals and we make new ones out of them by domestication. We have turned them into new uses.

Throughout what you call civilization we have always reformed Nature to our own uses. We are quite accustomed to this business of reforming Nature. It is comparatively simple to domesticate animals; that is, to impart to the animal some quality of our minds or natures. It is more difficult to remold plants, although we have had a class of specialists working in that area throughout history. Through the genius of science they have worked conspicuous wonders in that particular area. We have made many new edible plants and many new combinations of metals; one of the many useful being steel, which does not occur in Nature.

Actually to change the atoms of a mineral from one kind of mineral to another is a change that only a Master can accomplish.

In steel we amalgamate the molecules of two different elements, but we do not change the atom. A Master can change the atom, but they do not often occupy themselves with anything so unimportant as the miracle Jesus is said to have worked—that is, changing water into wine, or transferring atoms from one kingdom into another. The occultist says that he can do this though he does not often think it worthwhile. A large part of the work of the Masters is to superintend evolution in the mineral kingdom, to manipulate minerals and to forward their evolution. Most people who believe there are such things as Masters think of them as always absorbed in helping man. They are; however, helping humanity begins in the mineral kingdom, and that is only a small part of his work. To direct evolution in the mineral kingdom is the most difficult of all. Why? Because there you have matter at its densest, and the mind of it is the most submerged. Therefore it is the hardest to change.

So the Red-on-Blue Mountain means mastery over the mineral kingdom; it represents perfect mastery. If you have mastered the mineral kingdom you have mastered all the other kingdoms. That is what you can accomplish with perfect equilibrium. Jesus said to his disciples that if they had faith they could move mountains. Faith means confident expectancy. You cannot confidently expect without the knowledge of which Jesus spoke. He did not expect his disciples to go around moving mountains and juggling geography. In the long course of evolution the geography of the Earth has been changed many times. There will be many more changes, molecular changes as well as atomic changes, as well as changes in space.

Now all those changes, then, really will be worked by the Masters and their Agents under instruction from those still "higher" than themselves. It is the Masters who make continents rise and fall when instructed and when it comes time for them to do so. In that sense there are no such things as miracles. A Master can change one substance into another in a way that science cannot yet follow. These changes of course are not against the Law of Nature. The Masters use a higher Law of Nature to supersede a lower Law. We also manipulate the Law of Nature when we make iron float. Iron will not float, but we can make it float by bending it in a certain way because of the amount of air it has displaced. It has displaced more air than its own weight. So you see we manipulate a lower Law of Nature by taking advantage of the higher one. That is the way Masters make these changes. The mystic says there are no miracles in the sense of going against Nature.

The man and the woman in this picture are standing on a level. That is to say, they are equals. The ground, however, is swelling though it undulates. You will always find this kind of rolling ground in Tarot. It depicts cyclic action. All progress of the individual and of civilization comes in waves. There are times when this cannot be done. Now these times are dictated astrologically. It is not that the stars influence these times. They are also influenced by these waves. Stars do not make them. They respond to them as you do. These times are beyond the stars.

Everything—all forms, everyone—is submerged in the pulsating sea of electromagnetic energy, and everything in this sea responds to the pulsations of the sea according to its gearing. You respond in a way that is dictated by your own makeup. Each one is an absolutely unique combination of matter, never made before and never to be repeated again. Each responds to the same pulsation after his kind. Astrology merely helps one to predict, that is all, by indicating certain combinations of matter in the machine he is inhabiting.

A star is a very large thing. We know how it responds and we apply that to ourselves because we are all born under a certain star. It means that we have a certain kind of makeup which will respond to vibrations in the way that the star responds to vibrations. It is because of your makeup that you can be influenced at that time rather than another time, and if you cannot at this time, you must wait until another time.

This man and woman stand on a CARPET OF GREEN. He and she helped create the Mountain. Green is the color of Imagination, when it is used creatively. Behind the man is a TREE with a BLACK STEM and on it are 12 FLAMES of RED ON YELLOW, like the alternating flames on the head of the Angel. These flames are TRIPLE in form; so they are used creatively and three always means sex activity—Father, Mother, and the Image that passes between them. The Father had to divide himself into duality before he could manifest, and creation began by the action of one part on the other. This idea of the Trinity had been made very abstruse by the Christian Church, but it is a very simple one. *There can be no manifestation with unity. Unity must turn itself into duality before there can be a product of the two.*

As long as you keep a thought to yourself and nobody knows anything about it, you correspond to God, the Father. To express that thought you must use another part of yourself, and the thing you express is the Son. You make that thought known by using another part of yourself. If you write, the product of you, your mind and your activity is what is writing. If you speak, part of your mind and your voice become what you say. You take two parts of yourself to express a third part and that is your trinity. *What do you suppose would become of the Christian Church if they explained it in so simple a way? THERE IS NO MYSTERY!* For example: there are three branches of the U.S. Government and every transaction is concerned with all of them.

Here is a Tree, with these triple flames on it. The fruits of this Tree are the 12 types of consciousness typified by the Zodiac. The Tarot expands that into 22 by individualizing some of their aspects.

The BLACK STEM on this tree indicates mystic or occult practice. It is this practice which unlocks all the 12 types of consciousness and starts them into creative activity.

The TREE behind the woman has a RED TRUNK shaded with BLACK and it has FIVE RED FRUITS in a wealth of GREEN FOLIAGE. The five fruits, of course, are the five desires springing from the five senses. All desires arise from the fact that we sense the outside world in these five different ways. All desires arise from the image-making faculty. When we image a thing we should be sure it is an image of what we really desire. That is why it has Green foliage. This tree is intended to make you think of the Garden of Eden because there is a serpent winding up the tree, and he is whispering into the ear of the woman. The Garden of Eden was thought to speak about sex on its lower level. This Tree represents sex at another level, its higher level. That is first of all indicated by the tree trunk—the occult use of sex, Black-shaded Red. The SERPENT is GREEN and the product of desire. The Serpent of the Garden of Eden allegory said, "If ye eat of the fruit of that tree, ye shall be as gods." Elsewhere in the Bible it says in just so many words that the first appearance of the Redeemer was the Serpent in the Garden of Eden. Yet the Church is ignorant of that text entirely. "This same serpent was the first appearance of the Anointed one," says the Bible in another place.

This Green Serpent represents what we call Serpent Fire in the body. The Serpent Force in the body lies coiled in the Saturn Center at the base of the spine, the sacral center. The Serpent Fire is awakened by some form of mystic practice—that is to say, by your Imagination. It ascends the spine in four loops. You will observe this Serpent has four loops. It vivifies the seven Centers as it ascends. Thus you see the TRUNK of the Tree is the SPINE. It ascends into the head. The FOLIAGE of the Tree is the SKULL. It is the Serpent Fire which brings about a union of the personal consciousness with the superhuman consciousness. It does so by making active the Pineal Gland, and by extending the perception of the five senses so that they can perceive matter on the higher planes.

There are really three streams of this Serpent Fire, or Kundalini, as it is called, but only one is given to carry out the parallel of the Garden of Eden story. The other streams loop around the spine, and the third, the most powerful, rushes up through the center hole of the spine. There is a hole there in the center of the spine for that purpose. The third stream rushes up through the center when the two others have prepared the way for it.

The wand of Mercury of Greek mythology dramatizes this whole business of Kundalini. These two Serpents are the two preparatory streams and your third stream in the staff is in the middle. It is the occult symbol of lifting the sex-power. The WAND, in the symbol around which these two Serpents wind, is the SPINE. They meet in the brain just below the Pineal Gland in the thinking cells of the brain (the front lobe). There they construct new cells to replace the old ones, cells which have greater perception than the old ones. Together with the third stream they fuse the sand in the Pineal Gland into a crystal block. The alchemists of the Middle Ages called this block the Philosopher's stone. The Old Testament calls it Amber. In the Wand of Mercury, above the place where the heads of the Serpent meet, there is a pair of wings. These wings picture the extension of the physical senses so that the mind may soar to other planes, which is allegory in itself.

Those who have seen Wagner's *Parsifal* find another personification of Kundalini in "Kundra," the weird, evil woman who was at first the instrument of the black magician, and who afterwards became changed and helped to lead Parsifal to the Holy Grail.

The sex-force means you. On its lower level, as you are raising it, you have to be very careful with it or it will lead you into black magic. When you raise it on its higher level, it brings you to the Holy Grail. Parsifal, you remember, is called the Fool in God, the man who has his eyes on his vision. What is the vision? *Achieving union with the Higher Self.*

The Christian Church quite forgets its own liturgy:
   "This world not made, but begotten."

NOTES

8th Hebrew Letter	*CHETH*
Symbol for	*Speech*
Color	*Amber or Orange/Yellow*
Numerical Value	*8*
Syllables	*ChITH*
Sound	*D-Sharp*
Translation	*Fenced Field*
Sign in Zodiac	*Cancer*

NOTES

THE CHARIOT

CHETH means FIELD, FENCE, or FENCED FIELD. It is the eighth Hebrew letter and the fourth SIMPLE LETTER. It stands for the occult extension of SPEECH (which means "making magic"), for the direction EAST-BELOW, for the INTELLIGENCE OF HOUSE OF INFLUENCE (which means Intelligence emanating from the Higher Self), for the Zodiacal sign CANCER, the Crab, for the color ORANGE-YELLOW, for the note D-SHARP, and its numerical value is 8. In Roman characters it is written Ch.

The numeral value of CHETH is 8, which is the numerical symbol of equilibrium. This card depicts equilibrium in many ways: the result of equilibrium, what equilibrium can achieve, and the equilibrium of the self-conscious with the subconscious of the mind with the body.

The character of Cheth is similar to that for Heh, but the line at the left does not stop short. It is carried up entirely into the top. Heh is the same as the character for Daleth with a Yod added to it, and this Yod is extended up to the top to make the letter Cheth. Thus the letter Cheth is composed of a Daleth (4) and a Vau (6); and its secret value is therefore 10, or Yod. Yod is the nucleus of the sacred Flame alphabet, the letter which stands for the Spirit. The various ingredients of the letter tell you:

(1) When you use your image-making faculty as God does, you become reasonable, and not until then.

(2) That the proper use of Reason is to establish inner equilibrium. The result is, you become one with the Father.

(3) This fits your body for the descent of the Higher Self who thereupon enters it, takes charge of it, and uses it for His purposes. You and He inhabit it together.

What are His purposes? The symbolism of the card will tell you what these purposes are. It tells you how to establish the equilibrium and tells you what the purposes of the Higher Self are.

In astrology the Moon rules the sign Cancer. Cancer is represented by a crab because the shell of a crab resembles the rib basket. The rib basket symbolizes your body, or your Fenced Field, and fences in the upper part of the trunk, which contains all the vital organs.

The symbol of Cancer is composed of two curved lines and so arranged as to form an almost enclosed circle. Thus the circle of the symbol also shows its affiliation with the idea the Hebrew letter stands for: an enclosed fence, a fenced field, or an enclosed space. These two curved lines, each ending in a nucleus, represent the two nerve systems of the body: the cerebrospinal and the sympathetic. The one, the cerebrospinal, is masculine and self-conscious, proceeding from the nucleus of the thinking lobe of the brain. The other, the sympathetic, is feminine and subconscious, proceeding from the nucleus of the heart.

The sign Cancer, which primarily rules the stomach and the female organs or glands, has to do with nourishment. You will see when we come to the letter Yod, which is the secret value of Cheth, that in its esoteric aspect it is the means of spiritual nourishment.

It is impossible to secure the transformation of the body, which will enable it to become THE CHARIOT of the Higher Self, without conquering your moods and emotions or the phases of the Moon in you. The Moon rules Cancer, and you must rule the Moon in you if you wish to transform the body. *You must conquer your emotions.*

That is why the Charioteer wears epaulets upon his shoulders. EPAULETS represent the two phases of the Moon, the two aspects of EMOTION which can be pleasant or unpleasant. The shoulders in a human being are the indexes of emotion. We square our shoulders, we droop our shoulders, we shrug our shoulders. An epaulet, in a suit of armor, was a protection for the shoulders. The symbolism conveys that the Charioteer is protected from his moods. That is, he is no longer at the mercy of moods—now he controls them.

The letter, the sign, and the card all indicate, very emphatically, the idea of LIMITATION. The fence was the most primitive form of the house. House is the meaning of Beth. This card has many of the characteristics of Beth. In the card THE MAGICIAN, we saw that the mind is the house of the Spirit and the body is the house of the mind.

Cheth is called the House of Influence, or the Emanative Intelligence. The root meaning of *influence* is "something flowing in from above." The thought is that of ourselves we do nothing. All our life and action comes from the Higher Self, whose thoughtform we are. Wise men and the founders of all religions have realized this and taught this. "Of myself," Jesus said, "I can do nothing. The Father in me doeth the work." Consequently our Reason assured us that if this be true, our bad actions are prompted by the Higher Self as well as the good. If He (Higher Self) cannot teach us in one way, He teaches us in another—from pain that comes from our bad action. We can choose which it will be, and that is all we can do of ourselves.

A house is an enclosed space and influence is something poured in. Science is telling us now that every bit of our personal activity is the result of the Stellar Energy—energy which comes to us from the stars flowing into our personal field (our fenced field). Our bodies are houses for influence.

The Higher Self is the representative of the Spirit on the mental plane. Thus His Wand, when he can enter our prepared bodies and function there on the physical plane, is Yellow and Blue—the colors of the mind and the Cosmic Subconscious. He comes there for work, and He works his work as symbolized by the colors of the mind (Yellow) and the Cosmic Subconscious (Blue).

A wand is an implement of magic, and magic works up substance (Blue) by the use of the mind (Yellow) into some new form. The Higher Self exerts no effort to perform His magical work through the agency of the body. He can not enter it to do so until you have, by great effort, made it ready for Him.

You do the work, and the work that you do is the manipulation of the seven stages of consciousness which are depicted in the first row of the Tarot.

This card is the end of the first row of the Tarot Tableau. The Tableau is arranged in three rows of seven cards each, and the whole is preceded by THE FOOL, which synthesizes them all, and for that reason is numbered Zero. The first row represents the seven principles of consciousness, those principles on which all the 22 states of consciousness are based.

This card and letter are inclusive of all that has gone before, fencing in, as it were, all the previous ideas. The six principles of consciousness that have preceded are:

(1)   Attention   -THE MAGICIAN
(2)   Memory   -THE HIGH PRIESTESS
(3)   Imagination   -THE EMPRESS
(4)   Reason   -THE EMPEROR
(5)   Intuition   -THE HIEROPHANT
(6)   Discrimination -THE LOVERS

Three of these are of the self-conscious: THE MAGICIAN, THE EMPEROR, and THE HIEROPHANT. How is THE HIEROPHANT of the self-conscious, when Intuition comes from the subconscious? We have to work to get Intuition, we have to WILL our threefold body to keep still that we may properly listen in order to get it. These three, then, are the willed aspects of the Life-Power represented by THE

FOOL. The other three are the subconscious: THE HIGH PRIESTESS, THE EMPRESS, and THE LOVERS. These three, then, are the three receptive aspects of the Life-Power represented by THE FOOL— three active, three passive, three masculine and three feminine. This is the seventh and last principle of consciousness. It is a combination of the others, and it is called RECEPTIVITY-WILL, the union of both. This represents the perfected body. These two words, Receptivity-Will, seem opposed to the non-occult mind. Receptivity-Will seem to be direct opposites; and to understand they are not so is to grasp one of the fundamental ideas of occultism. This is that every concept, every principle, every state or condition is in turn now masculine and now feminine. When it functions in the right way, it is feminine to all that is above it and masculine to all that is below it. It is receptive to above; it wills or dictates to all that is below.

The occultist means by "Will" something very different from the ordinary conception of the word. The ordinary conception is "refusal to accept rebellion." The occultist means just the opposite: "Will" means *willingness to what you have already received, to do the higher Will.* Occultists say that is all you have—willingness to be led by what you think is good or by what you think is evil. He means by "good will" the willingness to be led by the Higher Self. If you are willing to be led by the Higher Self, in that sense "will power" is free, but only in that sense. "Bad" is willingness to be led by the body.

We may elect to use the energy that flows through us as it flows through the "fenced field" in accordance with the Will of the Higher Self. We may defeat it and ally ourselves with the forces that for a while seem to be working against evolution; but it is only the Higher Self that allows you to do this. He can teach you only in that way.

The Psalmist says that the goal of human life is loyalty, dominion, control over all things. The way to achieve dominion is by Receptivity-Will, being feminine to the Higher Self; and assertive, being masculine to the body, to all that is below us. Receptive to Him and making all things below us behave.

The power flowing through us is SOLAR ENERGY. It is our power while we have it. To be positive is to use this energy, whether we use it for good or for evil. To be negative is to allow others to use it whether they use it for good or for evil; and to be negative is to allow your body to use it instead of using it yourself. Generally, when others use it for us, we seem to be using it for our own purposes ourselves. When others can make us do just as they want, they manipulate our emotions. Though we are using Solar Energy and though we do not always recognize it, the use is theirs, not ours.

Nobody can insinuate a thought into your mind if you are a positive person. The way to be positive is for you, yourself, to use the Solar Energy which flows through your "fenced field." There are people continually trying to exercise a mental influence over you wrongly, both by outer and inner means. There is no need to fear such people. They cannot do so unless you invite them in and by reason of your emotions make yourself negative to them. *You yourself can become negative to yourself if you let your emotions control you.* Then the body has the upper hand, for the emotions are of the body. The mind is above the emotions and should always be masculine to them, not feminine. This is the case whether the emotions are constructive or destructive. *The mind should rule until you transform the heart.* There are destructive emotions which should never be indulged in. We should be on our guard against them all the time, we should analyze ourselves. The chief of these are REMORSE and SELF-PITY. Self-survey, with a concrete evaluation of the evil and the good in your action, is highly desirable. That is one of the finest things about monastic life. It insists upon the exact appraisal of all actions and all thoughts. Nothing good can be said of remorse. It simply corrodes the mind and the heart. The past is past; all you can get out of it now is its lesson, and if you have that, there is no reason to regret the past. The same thing can be said of self-pity. You pity yourself because of your limitations; but your limitations were given to you to learn by and evolve by. If your affliction is rightly used it will accomplish that; you evolve and learn by it. If it accomplishes that, there is certainly no occasion for pity but rather, for rejoicing. Our afflictions come from our limitations.

In astrology the planet which imposes our limitations upon us is Saturn, and he is called by astrologers "The Great Schoolmaster." All we learn in each life we learn by reason of Saturn, who imposes upon us our limitations from which arise our afflictions. We have got to have limitations—no limitation equals no field, no form. A form is something which has boundaries. Master this physical fact: were there no limitations to your field, if you had no form, it would not be yours. It would be everybody's. There would be nothing for the Solar Energy to flow through. Energy would be there, but diffused energy does not work; it must pass through a mechanism which limits and concentrates it, and the highest mechanism for that purpose is the properly used human mechanism.

The only way man can learn to use his mechanism properly is by experiment, by the trial and error method. You are absolutely unique—no one can tell you what to do, and if he could, you would not listen.

Sin, so called, is the only educator of humanity; and that is why the Serpent in the Garden tempted man to sin. He said to Eve: "If you eat of the fruit of the Tree ye shall be as gods." This may be translated thus: "When you derive all the education that comes through sin, and suffering for it afterward, then at least you shall be equal to God Himself." "But what," you may ask, "has sin to do with limitations?" By your actions in past lives, you have produced the precise limitations which you are laboring under in this life. Some limitations you must have in order to focus energy or else you diffuse them. Limitations are also the result of past mistakes in this life. And remember, by "sin" is meant "missing the mark."

One of the two things which dictates your present limitations is what you did in past lives, and the other is just as important but very little thought of, and that is what your Higher Self means for you in the future. Limitations are not only imposed for the past but also for the future. We think the limitations imposed on us are wretched, but they are the precise ones imposed upon us *by ourselves and the one who knows us best in all the world—THE HIGHER SELF.*

We, ourselves, made the kind of temperament we have and the kind of mind we have. Having that kind of temperament and mind, which we ourselves have made, puts us both in the kind of body we are in and in the outward circumstances that confront us. They are the best possible for us, we being what we have made ourselves. If you had His (the Higher Self's) perspective, His survey of what you have done hitherto in your long procession of lives, you would probably agree with Him in His estimate of what you need. *There are some people who have the greatest mission in the next life who are the greatest sufferers here.*

Certainly it is true that we can generally see that limitations are good for other people, and we deplore it when they are deficient. We say "things come too easy for him and he was ruined by success too early in life." We say of money, "easy come, easy go." We say of a person with too many gifts, "he had so many he could not handle them anymore." We have a different kind of arithmetic when we talk about ourselves. Nobody objects to early success in life, or to easy money, or to having all the gifts a fairy godmother can bestow.

YOU HAVE MADE YOUR OWN LIMITATIONS. YOUR LIMITA-
TIONS MAKE YOUR AFFLICTIONS. YOUR AFFLICTIONS ARE
RESPONSIBLE FOR YOUR MOODS. *YOU MUST CONQUER YOUR
MOODS.*

The Higher Self may be regarded as the masculine aspect of THE
HIGH PRIESTESS. This is very plainly seen by calling THE HIERO-
PHANT The High Priest. THE HIGH PRIESTESS sat between the
Black and White Pillar in perfect balance and poise. She swayed the
positive and negative forces as she needed them but was not swayed
by them. So does the High Priest on his own plane when we have prepared our bodies for him to enter and function upon his plane. *You
prepare your body by conquering your emotions and utilizing them—the
negative and positive forces we encounter.*

The sign CANCER is ruled by the MOON. You will note that the
two CRESCENT EPAULETS of the Charioteer are made like the typical Greek masks of tragedy and comedy. The real secret of balance is
to stand between these two, essentially moved by neither. You share
with both—are moved by neither. Comedy and tragedy are the
opposite manifestations of the same thing, the play of human life.
Each is a part of the other depending upon how nearly you are at the
moment involved in the event. Things that amuse you when you are a
spectator seem tragic to you when you are the actor. When we look
back upon our life, comedy and tragedy often change places: "Yes,"
we say, "it seems funny now, but I assure you it was a very tragic thing
then." Or we say, "If I could have looked into the future, I would have
seen that what I thought was so bright was the blackest thing that
could have happened." Anyone who writes or acts knows that a thing
is funny or tragic depending upon the way you handle it. You can handle it as comedy or tragedy. What is true of life at second hand, life
simulated by the artist, is equally true of life at first hand, life while you
are living it. If we are willing to detach ourselves from the life we lead,
and intently make the most of it unswayed by the forces we contact,
forces that can sway us so easily if we let them, then we are masters of
ourselves no matter what befalls us. Then we are not overcome by
afflictions on the one hand or prosperity on the other. It would be nice
if we could all be like Epictetus (a Greek stoic), who was born a slave in
Phrygia. His master delighted in maltreating him because he was his
master. And Epictetus would say, "Master, if you twist my leg you will
break it. There, I told you, you would break it."

THE CHARIOT is STONE COLOR. This, on the lower level,

typifies the physical nature of the body. THE CHARIOT is the body, and on the higher level, the union of the threefold personality (or body) with the Father (the Higher Self). When the personality is in union with the Father, it has become so by its mental images, by controlling its thoughts, reconstructing its body so that the Higher Self can enter it and take control. *You are what you are because of your past habits of thinking. You are a slave to your past habit of thinking, but though you are crippled, the future is yours.* You can begin to try to stop thinking that way. If you make the effort to change your mental attitude in the present, by and by you control the forces. *CONTROL YOUR THOUGHTS AND YOU CONTROL THE FUTURE.* It is no longer dense matter that repels it. It is purified so He can enter into it. Thus the BACKGROUND of the card is the YELLOW OF THE MIND. It is the Mind, depicted in the card, that has reconstructed the body and made this result possible.

The figure of the Higher Self as the Charioteer is a very old one and occurs in the Bhagavad Gita. What allows the Higher Self to drive our Chariot? It is stilling the senses which allows the Higher Self to step into THE CHARIOT of our body and drive it for us.

The TWO SPHINXES represent, at their lower level, the emotions. All emotions arise from the senses, the reports the senses bring us of life. The Sphinxes are BLACK AND WHITE, just as the pillars on each side of THE HIGH PRIESTESS represent opposites. Though you think of them as emotions, they represent the pleasant things and the unpleasant things. Most people are slaves to what their senses report, to the moods which grow out of these reports. Most people think the whole object of life is to escape pain and get pleasure. Such people think that the whole object of life is to eliminate the Black Sphinx which reports ugliness and pain. You have already seen that most of our evolution comes through the pain we suffer from having made mistakes, from so-called *sins*. So if it were possible to eliminate pain, as so many of the new cults teach, we should put an end to our evolution; and none of the grand masters of these new cults have eliminated pain. We should stagnate in empty bliss, but fortunately this is not possible.

When we have graduated past the point where we make the grosser mistakes and have grosser suffering, we begin to make the subtler ones. We shall go on making mistakes until we are supermen. The Masters say that they live in deadly fear of making the subtlest mistake of all, *spiritual pride.* When the occultist takes himself in hand and attempts to speed up his evolution toward mastership, he makes his advance by becoming acquainted with the forces represented by the Black Sphinx, the things that on the surface look adverse. He knows that the worse a thing looks the greater its power to help you when rightly managed. You may know you are progressing when you undergo tests that just seem to drop on you from seemingly nowhere. The worse a matter looks the greater is its power to help you if you manage it rightly.

While we are attempting to prepare the body for the entrance of the Higher Self, we must imitate the pose of the Higher Self in the card. Notice that there is no strain whatever in his attitude. He stands at ease. "What," you cry? "How is it possible to conquer moods, to tame the senses, without the utmost effort?" It is true that you must *choose* to tame the senses, choose not to let moods overcome you, choose not to do what you have been in the habit of doing, because that costs you effort. The effort is by no means as great as you think it is. You cannot tame sense by sheer Will. You are under a wrong impression if you think it requires self-conscious tensity to tame the senses. *It needs only the steady, quiet pressure of your Will in making images.* For it is not you who tames the senses at all, but the personal subconscious, THE EMPRESS.

The Moon is the ruler of all practical work in the body. It is she who makes all the changes in the body, the new rhythms, who grooves the new tracks in our brain. It is the subconscious that the mystic labors ceaselessly to transform out of all the animal images of sense-satisfaction which we stamped her with at a less mature time. Though this work is ceaseless, it is effortless. It requires only a change of attitude and constant vigilance on your part. As St. Paul said: "When you find these things in your mind, think of something else."

This change in the subconscious is done entirely by suggestion. It is only the transformed subconscious that can tame the body, as you will see in the next card. The taming is not performed by any tension on the part of the self-conscious. In fact it is impossible for the self-conscious to tame the body. The reason the saints broke down was because they tried to cow the body. The body is an animal, but an animal that is cowed is not tamed. It seizes the first opportunity to break out again when its master's eyes are taken off it. An animal is only tamed when it loves its master and wishes to be tamed. *It is through the services of THE EMPRESS that your body is tamed.* All you have to do is to keep suggesting images to her, and it should be done by *not* giving her bad images.

There are several things about these two Sphinxes, as well as the easy poise of the Charioteer, which charmingly symbolize that it is no effort to drive them. In the first place, they need no harness, or rather, the harness they have is invisible. *The mind is the harness of the senses.* This harnessing is done not by tension but by suggestion, by suggesting to the subconscious.

They wear Headdresses of striped Black and White as you saw in the four stripes on the carpet of THE HIEROPHANT, which means Equilibrium. The symbolism here stems back to the Black and White Pillars of THE HIGH PRIESTESS. The two alternates are measured one against the other. They are kept in balance. There are 16 White stripes and 16 Black stripes in each headdress. Sixteen is the secret value of GIMEL, THE HIGH PRIESTESS, whose card pictures her as sitting between the Black and White Pillars, chained to neither but using each as occasion demands—not swayed by the forces she sways. Sixteen white squares and 16 black squares compose each opposing side in the chessboard, 64 squares in all; and 16 black pieces and 16 white pieces as adversaries. The chess game, like the Tarot cards, was invented to teach occult truths. Sixty-four is the number of a famous Greek word, *Alethia*, which means "truth." The word is a formula for a great many occult truths. The TRUTH which concerns us here is that life is intended to be made up of pain and pleasure in equal amounts. Artists and writers of fiction are often classified as realists or as idealists. The realists believe that they tell the truth about life when they suppress the white side, and the idealist, when they suppress the black side, which is quite exasperating to the lover of the truth. A Pollyanna is hard to endure.

There is another charming item about the Sphinxes which denotes that they are thoroughly tamed: Their tails are neatly curved around and under their bodies. This shows they no longer have any Will of their own to interfere with the Will of The Charioteer. The tail in an animal is the index of emotions, just as the shoulder is with the human being. The Charioteer is driving THE CHARIOT of your personality with your senses all stilled and at his command. They are not dulled by any manner of means; they are more acute: they are at the service of the occupant and not the body. Your personality is a machine that is geared to achieve a unique result not capable of being achieved by any other personality in the world. This is the Light which passes through your channel, the Energy which passes through your body. The Light takes a particular coloring by reason of the fact that you are you. There is only one of you. It takes the coloring intended only when you have freed the channel of obstructions; and these obstructions are the senses that rule you instead of your ruling them.

Your personality must be all-receptive to the Higher Self, receptive to all that is above, if it is going to have the result intended by your Higher Self; also you must be active to everything that is below your body. *You must be willing to control the emotions which arise from the senses.* The senses must be stilled, but at the command of the Higher Self. When this is so, nothing can interfere with the work He has planned to accomplish through us.

This is typified by the huge, WHITE, armored CUFFS of the Charioteer. The forearm and the wrist are the chief tools of accomplishment. We do our work with them. So the symbolism means the chief essentials to our handiwork—the superconscious, the subconscious, and the personality—are protected for us when we let the Higher Self do the work in us. "We stand aside in the battle," as the Gita says, "to allow the Warrior to fight for us." We occupy the middle position between Him and the body—on the one hand all receptivity to Him, on the other all Will to the body.

SYMBOLISM

In numerous ways the chief idea of the card is a *protection, a house.* There are TWO HOUSES at the back; on the one side, a residence which is a protection from the weather and on the other side, a fortification or protection against foes. These two are enclosed by a WALL (a protection). Outside of that, there are two natural protections— a ROW OF TREES and a MOAT. Over the head of the Charioteer is a CANOPY as a protection from the sun, and a BACK to the Chariot as a protection from the enemy coming up from behind. He has on a BREASTPLATE as a protection. There is a SHIELD for a device in the front of THE CHARIOT, and finally, a Chariot itself is a protection, a house on wheels.

Another idea constantly repeated is the juxtaposition of opposing forces, of opposites. Two of these we have spoken of, the masks of comedy and tragedy on his shoulders, and the color of the Sphinxes, but there are others. The group of houses which portray protection from the weather (the residence) are feminine. *It is the subconscious which constitutes your residence.* The group which is militant portrays the Will of the masculine—your protection against external, human forces. The RED DEVICE on the Shield on the Chariot is called in India the Lingam-yoni, and it indicates the interaction of two opposing forces. Each Sphinx does the same. The Black one has a female head and a male body; the White one has a male head and a female body. This recalls the figures on the Veil of THE HIGH PRIESTESS card, which mean the masculine in the feminine and the feminine in the masculine. This, as you recollect, designates occult equilibrium—the equilibrium necessary to reconstruct the body and to work outer magic.

The two BLUE WINGS on the YELLOW SUN, just above the Lingam-yoni, are the result of reconstruction of the body. You extend your senses and you give wings to the Mind. You occultly extend all the five senses. The Yellow Sun is "Mind." The senses soar to Higher Planes.

The walled city of your personality, which is composed of your subconscious and your self-conscious, is protected by a row of GREEN TREES typifying Imagination. The MOAT of BLUE WATER signifies Memory. Your life is protected by both of these things, Imagination and Memory, and Memory is not sufficient until Imagination steps in. The STREAM also typifies the Cosmic Memory. When one has gained union with the Father, he knows his place in evolution, he knows his past lives, to orient himself. Note that this Stream flows from the outside to the outside. Cosmic Memory is not yours, it is yours only to use as it passes through you. Just as the Solar Energy is not yours, it is yours only to use as it passes through you. Cosmic Memory does not belong to you.

"Your house of Life moves on Wheels of Solar Energy" is another way of stating this; therefore, the WHEELS of THE CHARIOT are YELLOW. The CRESCENTS of the two MASKS are YELLOW, for it is the attitude of the mind which makes comedy and tragedy, makes things pleasant or unpleasant.

The BLUE on the CANOPY suggests the sky, and this suggestion is borne out by its being sprinkled with stars. The symbolism is that the Charioteer (through his mystic knowledge, symbolized by his head being in a triangle of Black) knows the astrological seasons for doing things. This was Agrippa's astrological meaning also. This knowledge is his protection. It is not sufficient that a thing be right, but it must also be done at the right time.

Astrologically there are times when a person can accomplish and a time when he cannot. This is another proof of the fact that there is no such thing as "free will." "We take the current when it serves, or lose our venture," says Shakespeare in *Julius Caesar*.

The BLACK TRIANGLE outlines his crown. *Crown* means "dominion." This means that he is the ruler of the forces behind the outward appearance of the stars—the hidden forces of Nature. Most people are afraid of their stars, and that is their destiny. Properly understood, the stars are your means of achieving in this life what the Higher Self wishes for you; just as we say that Saturn who is supposed to afflict you is the "Schoolmaster." The Charioteer is also backed up by the stars, which is another way of depicting the same thing.

The BACK OF THE CHARIOT is formed by four uprights. They stand for the four planes he contacts. Union with the Father holds good in the four planes. The same thing is told you in the WHITE SQUARE on his breastplate. It means the measurement of the White forces, the Spiritual forces, and the use of them on the four planes. The Greek word for this is *tetragrammaton*, and stands for the Hebrew *Jehovah*. (YOD HEH VAU HEH.)

The Breastplate is brass, and the metal of Venus is shaded deeply with Black, or the Imagination used occultly, and it is set on a BLACK BACKGROUND.

On his upper arms is BLUE ARMOR, indicating he is armed with Cosmic Memory. The WHITE CUFFS have a deep, sevenfold fluting. This refers to the seven Centers of the body all purified and at their highest Spiritual rate of vibration. The Centers are grouped as six and one, just as you will see the stars grouped in card 17, THE STAR. There you will see another star, Yellow and eight-pointed, to indicate that the seven Centers working at their highest rate open the Pineal Gland and Pituitary Body, which is the final product of equilibrium.

The EIGHT-POINTED STAR in this card is his Crown. This Crown is made of gold, the metal of the Sun, and the Star indicates the same thing as the eight-spoked wheel on THE FOOL's robe. The Star in his Crown represents Solar Energy made active, and a crown always indicates having dominion. Like THE FOOL, the Charioteer has GOLDEN HAIR and wears a WREATH OF GREEN LEAVES. The Charioteer is THE FOOL—not in his aspect of descending into matter to become the personality, but now as the tenant of the body which the personality has finally perfected for his occupation. In THE FOOL he wears the belt of the Zodiac, which signifies here the same thing as the canopy of stars. He knows how to make all time and space serve him by choosing the appropriate moment.

His SKIRT has EIGHT pleats. Eight is the peculiar number of

CHETH, for eight indicates equilibrium. It is the equilibrated personality which brings about the union with the Father. The figures on it are geomantic. Geomancy is divination by means of figures and lines. Such divination is perfectly reliable when practiced by anyone capable of practicing it. It means the ability to tell the inner nature of a thing by its outward lines and proportions.

◦In this card you see the mature Christ-consciousness setting about his Father's business, which is to assist in the evolution of matter. The SKIRT of the Charioteer tells you that he is furthering evolution by the magic creation of forms. This is what speech means—"the magic creation occultly." He knows what outlines and proportions to give these forms. If you will look at card 19, THE SUN, you will see the infant Christ-consciousness. There he is wielding the Orange Pennant, infusing into all the forms he encounters the vibrations of the superconscious, thereby raising their own vibrations. He is depicted as not yet able to work magic, to create forms himself. That remains for the mature Christ-consciousness. The Horse of Peace upon which the infant Christ is so gayly mounted now becomes THE CHARIOT, emblematic of warfare. The Son of God goes forth to war against those who seek to deter evolution—Black Magicians want to destroy him. They continually attack him to find some weak place in his armor, to surprise him into losing his grip on the two Sphinxes, who are now so docile. A careless moment of uncontrol would lash senses into a fury—no longer teammates, but emotions run wild. There are many reasons that the mature Christ-consciousness is represented as an armed charioteer. He has enemies, but anything that protects also limits.

Card 19 is like this card in depicting that the Christ-consciousness turns his back upon a WALL. The name of the object which CHETH stands for is FENCED FIELD, and this is often spoken of as the Hedge of Protection. *You must be free from the Hedge of Protection in order to do the works of the Father.* The wall in card 19 has eight layers of masonry, and one of its meanings refers to the fact that the Christ-consciousness, once formed, immediately turns his back upon all forms of Yoga, all formulas which were necessary to produce him. As the New Testament says: "Behold, I make all things new." That which protected while the Christ-consciousness was in the making is now no longer necessary; it is discarded. For instance, the abstinence from the physical use of sex, which was obligatory when the sex-force was being raised to the head, is no longer so.

Turning his back to the Wall of Protection in card 8 has another meaning: A Hedge of Protection is also a Hedge of Limitation. To work the works of the Father there must be no limitation except the Laws of Nature—the limitations He himself has made—not for the purpose of curtailing his power but in order to use his power—for there can be no manifestation without preceding limitation. To work the works of the Father the son must be free from the Hedge of Protection.

In card 20, JUDGEMENT, you will see the breaking down of the last body and the resurrection of the three tenants from their coffins: the subconscious, the self-conscious and the infant Christ-consciousness. There the infant Christ-consciousness is arising also, just as the self-conscious and the subconscious are arising from theirs. Now, he has BLACK hair instead of Yellow to indicate that this is an Initiation he has just taken. The rest of the card shows it is an Initiation upon the Astral Plane. He is now free from all binding limitations, and together with his Father and Mother, he forms the mature Christ-consciousness.

CHETH is the symbol of the "occult extension of Speech." One of the effects of raising the sex-force is to confer the power of "magical speech." This is the power to change internal and external structure by speaking the *Creative Word*. If this power exists it must have an organ to work through. Where is the organ located? Each area in the brain is known by modern science to control certain functions, and each exists in duplicate, one on each side of the brain. The area on the right controls the left-hand muscles of the function in question. The one on the left controls the right-hand muscles of function. The right side of the brain thus corresponds to the left side of the body and vice versa. The sole exception known to this double area of the brain is that area which controls the coordination of language for either written or spoken speech. *This unique fact is certainly significant of something!*

An injury to this area of the left side of the brain causes aphasia; but an injury to the corresponding area on the other side of the brain leaves the coordination of language undisturbed. What, then, is the function of this right-hand area, what does it control? It is not improbable that this, at present, unused area in the brain of the normal man is affected by this action of KUNDALINI, which results in the "occult extension of speech."

The power of "magical speech" is usually thought to refer only to the utterance of the Creative Word in such a way so as to bring about changes in the forms of things, both external and internal. Of that we · shall speak in a moment. Is it not also likely that the extension of the faculty of speech, if it is worked by this unused area on the right side of the brain, contributes certain vibrations to the physical voice which arrest the attention of all hearers and cause them to feel that "this man speaks as never man spoke?" Also, is it not likely that the occult extension of the faculty of speech, made by Kundalini vivifying this area, perfects the ability to speak without the use of words at all—what we call telepathy, the projection of thought?

Now let us analyze the act of "magic," or "magical speech." It is conceded always that there can be no construction without preceding destruction. What happens, then, when you construct something by magical speech? A form must be destroyed in order to be remade. Thus it would seem that the word *aum* is merely a "dissolver." It throws out of equilibrium the previous existent state; thereupon, it crumbles. What is it that, after preliminary disintegration, integrates the desired new form?

God, it is said, began Creation by throwing out of static equilibrium the three qualities of matter, by keeping them vibrating separately until worked into another form—combining them by creating a new form. "Aum" must be uttered in another form to reintegrate it to create a new form. How, then, did these recombine, and according to the impulse of what pattern? It was the mind-image which directed the primitive substance into a form. The word *aum* disintegrates the form already existing, and incidentally, it must be uttered in several different ways according to what state of matter the form to be dissolved exists in. This tone required to dissolve a gas would not dissolve a liquid or solid.

The object having been now reduced to primitive substance by the utterance of the Word, the mind-image behind the Word now throws out the archetype as the pattern around which the substance is to reform to make the new object. The mind-image is projected by the functioning of "the occult extension of the faculty of speech" as telepathy or the throwing out of thought formulated into words.

If what Blavatsky says is true, that in the new race the physical use of sex will be discarded and children will be conceived by the Spoken Word, then we must presume that this also will be the magical creation and an extension of the now existing faculty of speech. Since this extension, or the use of this extension, will then belong to the whole race, we must surmise that by that time the whole race will be able to create magically and will be assisting each other, to his degree, in the evolution of matter.

9th Hebrew Letter	*TETH*
Symbol for	*Taste*
Color	*Greenish Yellow*
Numerical Value	*9*
Syllables	*TITh*
Sound	*E-Natural*
Translation	*Serpent*
Sign in Zodiac	*Leo*

NOTES

STRENGTH

מ **TETH,** spelled in Hebrew TITh, means SERPENT. You remember TH is always one letter. It is the ninth Hebrew Letter, and the fifth SIMPLE LETTER. It is the sign or symbol for the occult extension of the faculty of TASTE, and of the function of DIGESTION. It stands for the direction NORTH-ABOVE, for the INTELLIGENCE OF THE SECRET OF ALL SPIRITUAL ACTIVITIES. (You will see how important this card is.) It is the secret of Spiritual activities of the body. The Zodiacal sign LEO, the Lion, is assigned to the letter TETH. The color is YELLOW, the note E-NATURAL, and the numerical value is 9. In Roman characters it is written T.

The form of the letter in the Hebrew alphabet is a conventionalized Snake. The most important teaching of the Ageless Wisdom is concealed in the Snake symbol. In the Hebrew alphabet there are three Snake symbols, TETH, LAMED, and SAMEKH. All three of these letters correspond to cards which are in this second row of the Tarot Tableau.

The Tarot Tableau, you will remember, is divided into three rows, and Teth begins this second row of the Tarot. Samekh ends it and Lamed is in the middle. Lamed is also the central card of the entire Tarot, which shows you its great importance. We shall see that this second row of the Tarot concerns the major Laws of Consciousness and of the Universe. The Snake symbol, you see, begins these Laws, is the middle, and is the End. These three cards deal primarily with the subconscious and superconscious, or the Snake symbol.

The Serpent in the letter Teth is the same as the Serpent in the card THE LOVERS—the Serpent winding up the tree. In the sacred alphabet the three Serpents are conventionalized in order to retain the pattern of the rest of the letters, particularly in respect to the parallelogram which represents the body or the physical plane.

Get in the habit as soon as you can of arranging the cards in the three rows preceded by zero in the middle; row one, row two, and row three. If you have never done that it will give you a thrill the first time you see these cards together, and the thrill will increase with your knowledge of what the subsequent cards stand for:

The first row represents THE CHIEF PRINCIPLES OF CONSCIOUSNESS.

149

The second row represents THE CHIEF LAWS OF
CONSCIOUSNESS AND OF THE UNIVERSE.
The third row represents THE CONSEQUENCE OF
YOUR USING THOSE LAWS, AND WHAT
YOU HAVE ACCOMPLISHED.

You are reading the message down vertically. For instance, here is a card depicting a Principle of Consciousness. It works by the letter which is directly under it, and that Law working from that letter obtains the result of the third card.

Under this card, for instance, is THE DEVIL, showing that the principle of the agents depicted by THE MAGICIAN works through the Law depicted by Teth, or STRENGTH, and achieves the result depicted in THE DEVIL, which, on its higher spiral is an escape from the dominion of the body and its appetites. On the lower level it means plunged into slavery and the appetites of the body. If you use the power of THE MAGICIAN well, according to the Law, you escape the dominion of the body. If you use it poorly you get more and more enslaved to the body.

The first of these seven letters depicted in this second row, Teth, stands for THE LAW OF SUGGESTION. The Law of the subconscious mind is Suggestion, says the Tarot—Freud, religion, and all the legion of applied psychologists in general. Unfortunately this does not get us very far (no two modern psychologists agree on what the subconscious is, or what constitutes a suggestion to the subconscious) unless we learn something more about the subconscious than you can find in Freud, religion, or psychology in general.

The AGELESS WISDOM defines the subconscious precisely, and also defines precisely what kind of suggestion is necessary in order to reach it. First, what is the subconscious according to the Ageless Wisdom? *The subconscious comprises all those manifestations of life below and back of our present awareness, the awareness of the physical brain.* That means all our past, not only in this life but in all our lives, not only all our human lives but all our lives as animal, vegetable, and mineral— everything in our consciousness—everything back of the waking consciousness of this present moment.

Freud and all the applied psychologists and etheric psychologists differ on the conception of the powers of the subconscious. They are tremendously impressed by the subconscious but they cannot define its powers. They say it is boundless.

In the Tarot, the woman is the subconscious, and as the conscious stretches her, so she bends with him. The Ageless Wisdom also defines what constitutes potent suggestion to the subconscious. It says it must not be anything abstract, it must be concrete; it cannot be anything neutral, it must be emotional. And it cannot be anything passive. It must be active. The Ageless Wisdom says, *"The conscious must continually place before the subconscious an image of itself acting, accomplishing what it wants to accomplish—the definite, concrete thing. The greater your desire to accomplish it, the greater the desire, the sooner the subconscious responds."* That is the greatest Law of Life. It *wants* emotion. It does not think you mean business until you are emotional. That is the reason, says Ageless Wisdom, why religion is so necessary in the development of the world. You accomplish so little individually because prayers are so petty. If we were emotional, the subconscious would transform you. So there it is. From time long past the Ageless Wisdom has defined just what the subconscious is and how to get at her. Also it has defined what she will do for the self-conscious if approached in the right way. This third aspect, what she can accomplish for you if you approach her in the right way, is what modern psychology is vaguest of all about. It does not know what she will do for you, but it hints at unknown achievements. The Ageless Wisdom is precise about that also. It says that if you approach her in the right way, the subconscious will first transform herself. Then she will transform the self-conscious in such a fashion as to remake our body and mind, and equip it with powers it does not at present possess, one of which is to remake your environment.

What do we mean by transformation? We mean receiving new powers. When you transform the body you give it new powers. When it turns around and transforms you, it gives you new powers. What are these powers? You have them in the attributes of this card: an extension of the faculty of TASTE, and an extension of the function of DIGESTION. What do we have in THE LOVERS card? The sense of smell. All the Simple Letters indicate an extension of a sense, faculty, or a function of the body. That is what we mean by transformation. We come into new powers. *By your thoughts and by your images you give her new powers and equip her with the ability to transform you and give you new powers.*

The Bible says that you can have dominion over all things if you find out how to control your body. That is the same thing. You can remake your external world if you know how to remake your internal one.

"All this," says Ageless Wisdom, "is accomplished by the right direction of the self-conscious mind to the subconscious mind working through the Law of Suggestion, i.e., giving the subconscious an image to work by and the self-conscious mind giving right direction to the subconscious mind." This image or pattern we have sent will be good or bad in accordance with the ability of the self-conscious mind to pay attention—attention to what takes place in the external world of form. If the image provided by him is good, the subconscious pulls you up. If it is bad she drags you down. A good image is dependent upon good attention. Bad attention always produces a bad image. Sometimes you think things are good, are desirable, worth trying for, and they are not. A man pictures what he wants, what he sees, and if he sees it clearly, it makes a clear picture. *As a man impresses his subconscious, so he becomes. You are what your most cherished thoughts make of you. As a man impresses his subconscious, so his body becomes in the end.*

So you see the subconscious either helps you or hurts you. It has only one power exhibiting itself in two different ways. These two different ways are presented to you in the story of the two serpents of the wilderness in the Old Testament. One of these serpents destroyed the people and the other saved the people. In the allegory of the Old Testament, the people are the cells, your Serpent. The contrast of the two serpents is presented to you in a more subtle way in the Garden of Eden story where there is a tempting Serpent, which the Book of Genesis calls Satan, the subtlest of the beasts of the field. The name of the Serpent in the Garden of Eden story is NACHASH. It enumerates 358. The word meaning Messiah or Redeemer is NECHESH, and it has the same number, 358. So this means that these two words have the closest kind of affiliation. They are only the opposite manifestation of the same thing. You will remember that the Hebrew alphabet is an alphabet in which the vowels are added to the consonants by dots. The Serpent in the Garden of Eden allegory did not tempt Adam, the self-conscious, but Eve, the subconscious. Adam got into trouble listening to Eve, just as she got into trouble from listening to the Serpent. Both Hebrew Wisdom and Freud say that love and hate are the opposite manifestations of the same thing—powerful attraction.

This number 358 has a story of its own to tell. Any series of numbers in which the third number is the sum of the first two is a secret formula for evolution. It represents the Law of Nature which governs form. Translated, this means that temptation and sin are just as much in the scheme of evolution as redemption is; that the first gets you ready for the second by teaching you its lesson. It means that evolution is accomplished by experimentation, and the experimentation is just as important as the accomplishment. Temptation and sin are as necessary to the scheme of evolution as virtue and triumph over sin, because we don't know what virtue is until we find out that sin is unfortunate—then we want the other thing.

Our attention to "good" is "what is good." Our attention to "bad" is "what is bad." Consequently we don't know until we try it and see. Fortunately we don't always have to try it ourselves. We can take other people's word for it.

It is a very naive idea that an All-knowing and All-powerful Creator should invent a person to oppose Him. That is what Theology did. Why is that? Simply because they didn't dare to let people know that God had created evil as well as good, and that evil is a conception of man, not of God. The Bible, I believe, exhibits or exposes its own contradictions where it leaves out this or transposes that. There are many of what you might call "crime clues" in the Bible that give the whole thing away if you can find them. The Book of Chronicles says that Satan moved David to take the census of Israel, and the Book of Samuel referred to the same census, but it simply says that it was Jehovah who moved David to do so. In one place you are told it was the Devil and in the other place you are told that it was God. That is to say that Satan is just another name of God.

Mrs. Mary Baker Eddy, founder of Christian Science, is very much nearer to us than the founders of the Christian Theology, and she puts us in a similar predicament. She wanted to account for the presence of evil in the world. Her explanation is most ingenious but most confusing. She says evil does not exist except as a delusion of the mortal mind. That is just as childish a version of it as the Christian Theology's.

Ageless Wisdom does not resort to anything of that sort to account for the presence of evil in the world. It comes right out and tells us why there is evil, and it says evil is in the world and it is only the instinct of the animal body. It is merely a misused human body because you misused your body. Man comes to use his body all right only after he has learned the lesson and suffered the penalty of misusing it. You must learn how to use your body right, then you will have "right-use-ness" of the body, or "righteousness." That is what the word "righteousness" means—"right use" of the body. Right-use-ness is a matter of growth and knowledge. You can learn the right use of the body only by using it wrongly and only by experimentation. Sin is only "missing the mark." You learn how to hit the mark by missing.

This is the story told by the secret numeration of the Sacred Alphabet where the number 358 is the figuration of the tempting Serpent and the Redeemer. The formula 358 says that the last digit is the sum of the other two. Three is the subconscious; 5 is Reason; 8 is equilibrium. The body is the subconscious. When you use the body in the way that is dictated by Reason, it becomes perfected—you get equilibrium; you get the right use and there is no more sin. Three is the number that is used here for the subconscious. You might have used 4 because, you remember, GIMEL stands for the subconscious just the same as 4 of DALETH. Why is it 3 and not 4? Because 4 is the subconscious in its pure state, the state in which God created it and in which it is impressed by the images of God. It has nothing bad about it, nothing to get rid of. Three is the subconscious when impressed by man's images. There is impurity only in man; there is no impurity in the animal. The reason there is impurity in man is natural: it is because he has vision, and his failure to live up to his vision and his failure to use his mind correctly is what constitutes impurity. Gratification of the senses without regard for other animals is the means whereby the animal evolves. We have vision, we have mind (they have not), and our mind will not let us do this without being assured in some way of an unworthy use of our mind.

So it is only when your mind steps in, thinking to gratify your appetites at the expense of everything else, that it becomes an impurity. It is by the use of Reason that we get rid of this impurity. When the subconscious is used, according to the dictates of Reason, equilibrium is the result. So you see what a complete story is told by that number. When 3 is used by 5, the result is 8, and that is equilibrium. To ignore evil in ourselves or in others is to increase it.

If evil is what I have said it is, and if we must perceive it in order to get rid of it, you see at once how the Ageless Wisdom condemns Mrs. Eddy, because she said to ignore it. We cannot ignore evil without increasing it. How would a child know he is evil if he misbehaves unless he is told so? If he is told so with a smile only, he will not believe it. Why should he? He just thinks it is another quaint way his mother has of being charming.

So we are here to overcome evil and to help others to overcome it. It cannot be overcome by ignoring it, though it sounds awfully noble when you hear someone say in a most glorified way, "I never speak evil of anybody. If I cannot speak good I do not say anything." This only increases the evil in the world. Of course, as in all things, there is a bad way to speak evil of a man as well as a good way, but to ignore evil is always bad. It is true that in the ultimate sense there is no evil. As you have seen, evil came to man only because he had a mind, and mind was a forward step in evolution. Evil is only the temporary consequence of evolution, and there is ultimately no evil. You cannot evolve except by overcoming your temporary evils one by one, and to pretend while we are evolving that we have finished the process is very silly. Yet this is what several cults teach.

Now there is another false teaching that we have to thank distorted Buddhist theology for: "See no evil, speak no evil, hear no evil." In other words, pretend there is no evil. Don't forget who said that—three little monkeys. The monkeys were pretending there wasn't any evil.

Paul Case said very brilliantly: *"Evil is temporary. So is a green apple, because the apple will one day be soft and ripe. That does not prevent it from being hard and green now."* If you pretend it is ripe you know what happens to you—the same unfortunate consequence ensues when people ignore evil in themselves and in other people. I think we ought to tell people in the right way when they are wrong. Perhaps they don't know it. We allow evil to triumph by doing so.

SYMBOLISM

The main figure on this card is a WOMAN, stooped in front of a CRESCENT. Twice you are told she is the subconscious, yet the BACKGROUND of this card is DARK YELLOW. The color assigned to this card is YELLOW. The note is E-NATURAL. The color and the note, then, belong to THE MAGICIAN. They are assigned to the self-conscious also. The background of THE EMPRESS was Yellow, but her color was Green and her note was F-sharp. Both of these attributes are the same as THE MAGICIAN. In this card STRENGTH, the direction NORTH-ABOVE suggests THE MAGICIAN.

It is not North-below as you might expect, but North-above. That means the Mars vibration is managed by THE MAGICIAN, not managed by itself. It is managed by ABOVE, not by BELOW.

Over the head is a HORIZONTAL FIGURE 8, just as there was over the head of THE MAGICIAN. This designates that this peculiar quality of THE MAGICIAN is now possessed by the woman because he has equipped her with it. He has equipped her with this peculiar quality in his effort to transform her, and it is because she has received this peculiar quality from him that she is now able, in her turn, to transform him. What is this quality of hers and of his that he has given her? It is not attention, because she had that before. In fact, we have seen that she had it in a far greater degree than he did. We saw that the "conscious mind" can be very slipshod indeed in paying attention; not so the subconscious mind. Furthermore, we have seen that the conscious was a master in deceiving itself, in pretending that its motives were better than they were; not so the subconscious. It never deceives itself. While we may disguise from ourselves what we want, the subconscious sees through us, knows exactly what we want because she knows where the emotions are; however, we disguise it from the self-conscious. We can reiterate things over and over again until we really think we want them, but the wise subconscious knows, if there is no emotion in those things, we don't want them. Her ability to be deceived by what often deceives you is what makes all the trouble between you. You think that because you do not commit certain actions that you do not want to commit them. The subconscious knows from your emotional mental picture of such that you do want to commit them, and she forces you to do so, to the extent of her power. She reasons precisely as Jesus did. He said, "Paint a mental picture of yourself committing a deed, and that mental picture of committing that deed is in your heart." The very thing which blurs your attention (emotion) shows her unerringly where your desire lies.

So it is not attention that he has given her because she has more of it than he has. It is not insight, it is not candor. What is it? What is his faculty? Will, selectivity, and initiative. He has equipped her with qualities of his will, with the selectivity and initiative which formerly belonged only to him. Until then she could not select or initiate. She had to take what he gave her and make the best of it, and she could start nothing herself. Now, however, she is able to complete the process which he began. He has transformed her with the extra powers which he has given her, and she is able to set to the task of transforming him. She uses it in several ways, but chiefly in the spine and in the sphere of DIGESTION over which function this letter presides.

The digestive processes are, of course, subconscious. The result of the digestive processes hitherto has depended solely upon the food which the self-conscious selects, and on the attention the self-conscious pays to the operation which begins the activity of digestion (mastication). The doctors are quite right when they say none of us have the habit of mastication sufficiently; we do not lubricate our food enough with saliva.

Now up to this transformation of the subconscious, digestion depends entirely on those two things: the kind of food we supply the subconscious to digest and whether we masticate it sufficiently. Now the transformed subconscious does something else with the food. She extracts certain chemicals from the food which she didn't extract before because they were not needed. You were not making any new powers for the body and these chemicals weren't needed. It is with new chemicals she sets about transforming him. Now you are making these new powers and you want new ingredients which before had passed out of the body as waste. She extracts them from the food wherever they are contained. She knows what ingredients the body needs at certain times, while the self-conscious does not.

You feed yourself with the proper kind of food which supplies these chemicals. It keeps changing with the need of the body, with what powers you are developing at the time. Food, and what is extracted from food, is vital to our work of transformation. Our work of transformation is what the Christians call "regeneration." They don't give you the slightest inkling that this regeneration is anything but an emotional process. It is emotional only in a secondary sense; it is primarily physical. Let us throw some light upon the fact that the Church, the Catholic Church, says gluttony is a deadly sin.

There is nothing that reasonable people deride more than the Church's list of the deadly sins. They naturally surmise that deadly sins are the sins that cause you to go to hell and to lose your soul. The seven deadly sins of the Church, to most people, aren't sins at all. They are only vices. They did not cause you to die—you remained dead.

Let us see how that error arose. It came from the New Testament. In the New Testament the word *death* is used many times as meaning "not awakened, not having the Pineal Gland opened." The people whose Pineal Gland is awakened are alive. The list of the seven deadly sins in the Church very conspicuously omits the three sins which Jesus said were the worst: hypocrisy, malice, and simony (which means the selling of sacred things). Of course, when the Church began selling sacred things, they would have a reticence of speaking of that as one of the deadly sins. The Church says the seven deadly sins are only what you and I call vices.

You understand that those vices are deadly in the sense of keeping you dead, keeping you from opening your Pineal Gland. The Church has not explained to you what it means by "deadly." It allows you to think it means losing your soul and going to hell. This is due to the ignorance on the part of the teachers who are passing down these teachings to you.

What are these sins? Sloth, Anger, Pride, Avarice, Lust, Envy, and Gluttony. You cannot tell a sensible person that their "sloth" is going to send them to eternal damnation. To take it in the other sense, it does keep you from opening the Pineal Gland, because to open the Pineal Gland requires constant, vigilant work upon yourself. You cannot be slothful and do it. You have got to pay Attention, and to be slothful means to be sluggish in Attention.

PRIDE: To open the Pineal Gland requires, as shall be shown in another card, the abandonment of the personal Will and a change in your set of values.

ANGER: We have seen already that your emotions get sharpened as you go on in the mystic life. If you do not control your emotions you will simply be swept off your feet by them. The more violent the emotion, the more it disrupts the work you have already done, and you have to begin to do it all over again.

AVARICE: To open your Pineal Gland requires an abandonment of all the material standards of valuation. You must lose yourself in order to gain yourself. If you gain yourself you lose yourself.

ENVY: As you go on in the mystic life you see that you have no reason to envy anybody else. You are what you are because you have made yourself what you are. Being what you are, the conditions in which you find yourself are the best for you until you get out of that condition and make yourself something else. So the man who has Spiritual Reception sees that there is nothing for him to envy in the state of others. He must accomplish that state himself.

LUST: The man in occult life perceives that the only justification for the use of physical sex is love. Also while he is engaged in the intensive work of opening his Pineal Gland he must abandon any use of sex whatever. This is temporarily, while he is engaged in that work.

GLUTTONY: If the other vices mentioned seem very slight grounds on which to condemn a man to eternal damnation, what should we say of "gluttony"? According to the consensus of most people gluttony is rather an amiable weakness and it certainly hurts no one else. "She has an awful appetite," we will say rather pleasantly, "poor dear."

Now this card and this letter stand for the occult extension of DIGESTION. You cannot open the Pineal Gland without a certain specialized act of digestion. To get it you must feed the body certain foods, not because you like them, but because the body needs them and you hurt that process by overeating. Unregulated, it is deadly to that process, as it keeps you from opening the Pineal Gland. The next card, THE HERMIT, tells you more about this process. It tells you in detail about this new process of Digestion, so it will not be described here at length. We must devote a little time to describing the Serpent Power which the three Serpent Letters of the Sacred Alphabet specialize on and of which this card is the first of the three.

To this letter is assigned the INTELLIGENCE OF THE SECRET OF SPIRITUAL ACTIVITY. You cannot be spiritual unless the Serpent Power is functioning in your body. What is the Serpent Power? *The Serpent Power is the concealed potency which exists inside your body and outside your body—everything in the world.* The potency inside your own body is represented by the Green Snake in the card THE LOVERS. The snake is green because to arouse it is the work of the image-making faculty of the self-conscious, and the image-executing faculty of the subconscious. You arouse it by Imagination (image-making).

Where is this Serpent Power? The Serpent Power lies coiled up at the base of the spine in the Sacral Center, the Saturn Center.

It is called Serpent Power for several reasons:

(1) Because it is coiled up ready to spring upward, ready to uncoil. Only by coiling up does it get its power, like a snake.

(2) Because when it does spring, it springs in spirals, and it moves in a subtle, sinuous way around the spine as it rises.

(3) It is called the Serpent Power because it can be very poisonous; but it is poisonous when it is misused, and only then. There is no cause for alarm in that, for everything is poisonous when misused. There is nothing that can harm you more than the Sun, and yet the Sun is responsible for all that is beneficial in the world. In Nature, the Sun produces sterility as well as fertility.

This Serpent Power in the body we call KUNDALINI. It actually kills off certain cells in you and makes new ones. If it is used improperly it kills off the wrong cells. When it is used properly it kills off only the cells which are moribund, which ought to die, which cover the ground. Now, when the self-conscious interferes with the work of the Kundalini (by indulging in mental sex pictures), it sets Kundalini to act improperly and kills off the more valuable cells and tissues instead of the moribund ones, and damages the tissues of the body, especially of the brain. It is the Kundalini Power which, along with the other powers in the end, opens the Pineal Gland. That is the secret of all Spiritual activities. Then the vivified Pineal Gland and the vivified Pituitary Body come together in union as one, and work together to transform the heart—the structure of the heart. That work is started when the Kundalini starts to rise, but it cannot be finished except by the awakened Pineal Gland and the awakened Pituitary Body acting together. When the heart is changed it brings in outside Kundalini, the Kundalini of space. Kundalini, then, is a *concealed potency* within the body.

The whole business of the practical occultist is to find out how to rouse the concealed potency in Sunlight. The concealed potency is even greater than the potency which appears. We are enabled to wield this concealed potency both in ourselves and in the external world by our subconscious, by our body. It is the woman who does it, not the man.

The secret of all Spiritual activity, then, is that the subconscious has at her disposal (if you equip her to use it) the power to control the concealed potency of Sunlight. When we awaken our subconscious, master our emotions and secure equilibrium, then the forces of Nature are at our disposal through the subconscious. First, you have got to use, through your subconscious, the Cosmic Electricity which is concealed in your body, and that will effect the transformation of your body. Then your subconscious, thus transformed, shows you how to control and manage the Cosmic Electricity which is concealed all around you in the form or appearance of simple things—in the air and in the Sunlight. How to employ these hidden forces of Nature is, of course, not given out. This is the real gist of the secret, but it is not given out. It is given only to the man who has proved that he is freed from personal activities, one in whom the Charioteer is working. He no longer responds to personal ambition and greed. And even then mistakes are made, and many to whom the secret has been told have become Black Magicians rather than White ones. They misused their power.

At least we can talk about the mechanism of this power and what makes it possible. In order to function, everything needs mechanism.

The mechanism by which you wield the ASTRAL LIGHT is the TRANSFORMED HEART. This transformation of heart is an actual fact in physical nature. It is not merely a sentimental way of expressing emotional change. It is a physical change, and by this change the heart becomes capable of accomplishing something that it is not, at present, capable of. Tarot says that it is a change from an involuntary, or feminine, organ to a volitional, or masculine, one. What that means, of course, you and I don't understand. This change is pictured in this card by giving the subconscious the horizontal figure 8 which was worn by THE MAGICIAN as an indication that she now possesses his selectivity, his initiative, the two aspects of Will. It can see things by paying attention, selecting from those things and doing something with those things. It can select and it can initiate.

Now this physical change that takes place in the heart is structural. Its cells are changed and it becomes capable of another function which it did not possess before. Up to the time of this change the heart has merely received the universal energy of the Life Power called by the Hindu, *Prana*. It took from the outside and distributed it through the body. We start to take it in and distribute it until the body dies. After the change it continues to do this—but it can do something else in addition. In addition, the tissues of the heart become striped or ribbed. Biology says that involuntary muscles are never striped—only the voluntary ones.

The awakened Pineal Gland allows the superconscious to take entire control of your mind. The Transformed Heart allows the superconscious to take entire control of your body.

Always the vibrations of the superconscious have been breaking upon your mind. Until you awaken the Pineal Gland you are not aware of those vibrations in your body; they break upon it in vain. Until the Pineal Gland is awakened in the mind these superconscious vibrations have no port of entry. They cannot get in, or, at least having no reliable port of entry, they get in only occasionally when, for some reason, your vibrations become very high.

Until your heart is transformed, they break upon your body without getting in. If you keep on with this study you will find that your body begins to do things, your body begins to register things that you do not know anything about.

The structurally transformed heart establishes now a direct relationship between your body and the Universe, between the superconscious outside and the collective cell-consciousness of your body.

The result is twofold: The first result is the taming of the lower destructive animal nature. That is the lion, the bad lion, the raging lion who devours. The lion in its lower sense—THE DEVIL, the misused body. Second, you are enabled to use the Astral Light which is the Lion in the higher sense. The first lion is the one the Bible speaks about as the raging lion seeking whom he may destroy. The second (of the Astral Light) is the Lion of the Tribe of Judah, the God-Consciousness.

If you haven't controlled the heart before it is transformed, the result is lunacy—the control of the subconscious. If you have the heart controlled after it has been transformed, the result is the highest state known to man—what the alchemists call GOLD, the rule of the super-conscious and not of the self-conscious. One of the chief statements of Alchemy is that this Great Work is performed by means of the Sun and the Moon through the aid of Mercury. The Sun is the Pineal Gland; the Moon is the Pituitary; and Mercury is the thinking lobe of the brain, the Intellect. It is performed, then, partly by the self-conscious and partly by the subconscious, with Mercury steering the ship. It is the thinking lobe of the brain supported by Mercury who, by the steady pressure of his will giving his suggestion to the subconscious, does the indispensable work. Everything is explained back to Mercury and it is he who forms the images.

When the personality is at last united to the Higher Self and when the Son is united to the Father, then he sets out to do the Father's work. In terms of the Bible, he becomes co-partner with God; that is to say, he assists in the evolution of Nature.

How does he assist in the evolution of Nature? By the creation of new forms and by raising the vibration of the matter which exists in the present form. That is what the Spiritual man is supposed to do—to raise the vibrations of everything he encounters and raise it automatically. To do this you must wield the Astral Light until you have perfected your body—the collective subconscious of your body. Anything the Spiritual man meets he has the power of raising the vibration of. You see, it is automatic. You say to another person, "You are wonderful. I don't know why it is, but because you are you." Automatically you raise their vibration because of this attitude.

So you see this little child (card 19) with the enormous banner is raising the vibration of everything he meets in the Sunshine. You cannot wield this Astral Light, this Banner, until the Moon has been perfected in you. The Transformed Heart is even more important than the Transformed Head, because now it takes the lead. When an occultist stops with transforming his head, we call him a Black Magician. He is supposed to go on transforming his Heart, and then he is a White Magician.

The head and the heart were always equals, but the head came first until you transformed the heart; then the heart comes first and the head follows the heart.

This reciprocal action is indicated by the figure 8, where the Above becomes the Below and the Below becomes the Above. Its form seems to keep doing this—first saturate the Below with the Above and then saturate the Above with the Below. The more concrete you make your picture of this, the better, and there is no more concrete way to do it than by making this figure 8 in the air. There is an actual figure 8 form in the human body as an index of this change in the head and heart nature. The electric force which is the sole potency in all external things enters the body at the heart and it goes up to the head and goes down again in two loops, making the figure 8. The upper loop includes the Pineal and the Pituitary, the Glands working as one after each has been transformed. The lower loop circumscribes the etheric heart just behind the physical heart. Now, where would these two loops have their meeting place? At the Venus Center at the base of the tongue. The Pineal Gland and the Pituitary Body act as one pouring their force down, and the heart is pouring its force up. Wherever two opposing forces meet there is creation.

The Throat Center is the seat of the Creative Word, and it is by the power of the Creative Word, the Secret Word, that one is able to make forms, create magic.

The WOMAN IN WHITE in this card is really THE EMPRESS, but she is THE EMPRESS at even a higher stage. This is shown by her DRESS (which is WHITE instead of Gray), by the FIGURE 8, by the WREATH OF ROSES in her hair. THE EMPRESS had a wreath of leaves in her hair. The flower is the fruit of the leaves, the leaf is only the preparation for the fruit. She is nearer her goal than THE EMPRESS.

Gray, too, is the color of Wisdom; White is the color of the Spirit. In card three, THE EMPRESS is performing with perfect Wisdom, the Will of the self-conscious. Here she is performing the Will of the Spirit. It is after THE MAGICIAN has transformed her that she takes the lead. This transformation, as you have here, equips her with his peculiar power of selectivity and of taking the initiative. She can now select and initiate, and she begins the new digestion which changes the body. Then she is able, in addition, to bring in from the outside world the Cosmic Prana Electricity to change the body still more and perform transcendental work.

The pattern of ROSES, PETALS and LEAVES in the dress of THE EMPRESS has now become an actual wreath on the head and garland around the body. This GARLAND around her body takes the form of the Figure 8. On some cards it is not done very clearly. So you see that the Figure 8 is of prominent importance in practical occultism. What does that represent? It represents a Law of Equilibrium, a perfect uniting of the mental energy of the self-conscious and the mental energy of the subconscious, so it can control and direct the self-conscious.

Here it represents the union of the Father and the Son, as 8; only it represents it in an indirect way because it is composed of 5 and 3, which equals 53. Fifty-three reduces to 8, 5 plus 3. The Great Pyramid is a building typifying the union of the Father and the Son, and it is built on a base line numerating 8.

A Wreath of Roses always means control of the desire nature. You see what an important figure that is. "Roses" represent the desire nature. "Wreath" represents putting in order and control. Controlling the nature so as to be sure when you do desire, it is the true basic desire you objectify. Now, there is a Wreath of Roses about her form shaped like a Figure 8. In the Paul Case card the Woman has caught the Lion with one loop of the Figure 8, and the other loop goes around her.

In the control, then, of the desire nature, THE MAGICIAN has finally been able to transform his heart, and then his heart is able to bring in the Astral Light for him to wield. The LION symbolizes the Astral Light. The Lion is licking the hand of the Woman in devotion, and his TAIL is curled under his legs. You know what that means. It no longer has any will of its own, it has placed its will at the disposal of its master. That holds good whether you are the owner of the Lion at its lower level, the body, or the Lion at its higher level, the Astral Light. Its power is now placed at the disposal of the owner of the body and not used as it was before, for itself. If you take it at its lower level it means destruction. The appetites of the body are now changed and become constructive, and the body is tamed because it wants to be tamed. Until the animal wants to be tamed it is never tamed, it is only cowed into subjection.

If you take it at the higher level, the Astral Light, what happens?

That is charmingly portrayed by this LION GRIPPING THE GROUND WITH PAWS AND HIS CLAWS. The ground itself is presented as fluid because it is a fusion of water and land. He is gripping it with his paws as if to try to keep himself still. Cosmic Electricity is always on the move, but it quiets itself long enough for you to use it.

In the back is a BLUE MOUNTAIN, which signifies Cosmic Memory, and that is one of the gifts that comes from being able to manipulate Astral Light—having the memory of other lives, of other states, of our past lives, and even of our planetary states.

The GROUND is partly GREEN, liquifying into BLUE, and it is elaborately outlined with BLACK, which generally means the occult. Her WHITE DRESS is filled with BLACK LINES. The Black Lines on the White Dress are to denote the Spirit used occultly. They also denote that is what you can do; you can see the White Light, shining through the darkness, or the darkness shining through the White Light. You see that beautifully portrayed in the card THE CHARIOT, where the Charioteer seems to have a WHITE DRESS which has BLACK behind it, and the black seems to come though the white. There is such a thing as the White Light which is sparkling, and it can be seen in the darkest night. Behind that White Light there is a Blacker Darkness. The Old Testament says that God is in that thick Darkness. "God," says the Old Testament, "is always concealed in a cloud." Black is the outer robe of White when you are using your transcendental nature. *When you are speaking of the Spirit, the Spirit is the outer robe of you.*

The Lion stands for two things: the destructive nature of the body becoming constructive, and the external Cosmic Electricity now being utilized so that it can be used for your power. This Lion is rather unsatisfactory when it is made to serve two opposite purposes; it is far more satisfactory when it is made to serve only one. That is the reason why the Bible is so queer, because it is written in such a way that you can get several meanings out of it, and none seems to be quite the way.

The card is a good illustration of how that way of making the connection is unsatisfactory. Here is this Lion—from one aspect it seems to be trying to open its mouth, and in the other it seems to be trying to close its mouth. The artist drawing the card had to represent action which may seem to be contrary to another action, depending upon the aspect which you have in your mind at that time. From the lower level she is seeming to close his mouth; on the higher level she is opening his mouth.

So it is with everything in the Bible, especially when applying it to allegory. It may be made to serve two purposes, and consequently, not entirely satisfactory in any one.

10th Hebrew Letter	*YOD*
Symbol for	*Touch and Sex Union*
Color	*Yellowish Green*
Numerical Value	*10*
Syllables	*YUD and Sometimes IVD*
Sound	*F-Natural*
Translation	*Hand*
Sign in Zodiac	*Virgo*

NOTES

THE HERMIT

The motive For Action

❯ **YOD**, spelled in Hebrew IVD. It means HAND. It is the tenth Hebrew letter and the sixth SIMPLE LETTER. It stands for the occult extension of the faculty of TOUCH and of SEX UNION, direction NORTH-BELOW, and its type of consciousness is called the INTELLIGENCE OF WILL. The Zodiacal sign is VIRGO, the Virgin, color YELLOW-GREEN, and the note is F-NATURAL. Its numerical value is 10. In Roman characters it is written as J and I, and sometimes as Y.

The Hebrew character YOD is the conventionalized picture of a Flame of Fire. Each letter in the Sacred Alphabet included a Yod, and for that reason the alphabet is called the FLAME ALPHABET.

The value of the letter is 10, and the number of the card is 9. There are only ten numbers—from 0 to 9—and all of the countless numbers which could be extended infinitely are combinations of 0 to 9. This is the final number of the series. When you think of the card it naturally denotes completion, perfection, and realization. Both 0 and 9 typify the Absolute. Zero is the Absolute as it leaves the Source and enters into manifestation. Nine is the Absolute as the goal of existence, the source to which we return when our evolution is completed, the evolution for which you entered this manifestation in the beginning. Zero is the Absolute before it comes into manifestation; 9 is the Absolute after it has completed manifestation. Zero stands for the Higher Self. From our present human point of view the Higher Self is our Absolute because He is the highest, the most complete, the most perfect thing we can contact.

You will find these two ideas pictured in these two cards: the cards 0 and 9. In 0, THE FOOL is a Youth looking upwards to the morning Light as he descends into manifestation. Nine is a white-bearded Ancient, at night, looking down. One of the strangest things that occurs in mathematics is that the properties of these two numbers, which are at the opposite ends of the scale, are the same. The properties of 0 and 9 are the same. Multiply 9 by any number and it always gives 9. No other number will do this save 0. Substitute 9 for 0 in any complex number and the digits will add up just the same, exactly the same total. This process of adding up the digits of a number is called *reduction*. It is used constantly in occult science. It is one of the methods of giving information by the secret numeration of the Hebrew alphabet, or the secret numeration of the Greek or Egyptian alphabet.

There is a similar secret process of figuring to get secret information which works just the other way. It is called "extension." Extension is the sum of all the numbers contained in a given number. Thus 4 is 3 plus 2 plus 1. So 4 by extension will equal 10: 4 plus 3 plus 2 plus 1. This is the way the Secret Wisdom or Secret Knowledge is imparted. Ten, for instance, is this card YOD, and by extension it equals THE MAGICIAN, THE HIGH PRIESTESS, THE EMPRESS, and THE EMPEROR. These four cards taken together comprise all the activities of the Absolute when it comes out into manifestation. Out of these four activities the boundless Universe was created.

Let us take another illustration of how the Secret Wisdom contained in these letters works, and how it is imparted. The extension of 9 is 45. Forty-five is the number of Adam, the word in the Bible which means "man." The knowledge imparted here was to the Hebrew scribe just as plain as if it were written out in so many words. *THE EXTENSION OF GOD IS MAN.* The extension of 9 is 45. Over and over again the Bible says that the extension of God is man. The number 45 reduces to 9—just as if it were written out in so many words that the destiny of man is to become a God. The extension of 9 is 45, and 45 reduces to 9. So that, whatever way you may take it, 9, like 0, always produces itself in all its final changes and combinations.

Now, since Yod is the base of every other letter, it is hence the most important letter in the Sacred Alphabet. It pictures the seed-thought of all the rest. All the other letters simply illustrate the different kinds of growth that seed out of the Astral growth. It is a seed that has 22 branches, as it were, when it grows up. The letter that it stands for in Roman and English is "I," and it is also the most important in those alphabets. You evolve by the "I," the personal pronoun, by first using it at the lower level of the physical body, then at a somewhat higher level of the emotional body, then at the still higher level of the mental body, then at the very lofty level of the Higher Self, and last of all at the level of the third person of your Trinity, which is represented here by Yod, the Spirit.

The words that mean *sin* in the Bible are all very interesting. One of these words means *too much I,* too much of the personal pronoun. It is when you take "I" at the lower level (the level of the appetites, the emotions, and the ambitions) and sacrifice your body, world, and neighbors to your appetites or your emotions, that this applies. There is no such thing as too much "I" when you have identified yourself with your Soul or your Spirit; there is not too much "I" on the higher level. Felt at its lowest, a genus of "I" (that none of us could stoop to in the lowest state of evolution, still "I") is the means by which you evolve. You would not be what you are now if you had not used "I" to the fullest along the lower stage of evolution. Just as the use of "I" has brought you to where you are now, the use of "I" at the highest level you are capable of attaining now will push you to greater heights, and so on. "I," in short, is always the means whereby you evolve, and evolution is endless.

Why would we give to a beggar (granting that we would do such an unwise thing)? It is because it would make us unhappy if we didn't. If so, that is a selfish motive. How could it be otherwise? The only motive for action is desire, and desire always affects ourselves. We sacrifice for a loved one or we sacrifice for humanity. It makes people happier to do so, or, putting it the other way, it makes people unhappy not to do so. We often do things "for conscience' sake," to be perfectly sincere about it, and that is a lofty motive. We are sorry to do it. Then why do we do it? Because we would be sorrier if we didn't. So we evolve, to put the matter in one word, simply by enlarging ourselves to take in all of humanity, until we take in our Souls; until we take in our Spirit and consider ourselves one with it.

It must follow then that the word *self-sacrifice* is a joke. Our business is to learn to think; so, it certainly is not sacrificing to enrich and enlarge yourself; and when you sacrifice yourself you act toward another person as if he were you. You have enlarged yourself to take him in.

Some people say that it is not sacrificing themselves, that they enjoy self-sacrifice. They go out of their way for it. However, their neighbors say that what they call self-sacrifice is only self-indulgence. Most mothers indulge their children too much because it gives them pleasure. They call it sacrifice but their neighbors call it indulgence. The self-indulgence which may describe itself as self-sacrifice is something we don't like to look in the face. It means a lack of desire or of will to act. That kind of so-called self-sacrifice is only a lack of desire or will to act and is just as bad as "too much I." Indeed, it is too much "I." To willfully ignore other people's rights and possessions is no more "too much I" than to be sluggish in our life and to be poked into actions ourselves. It is nowhere near as bad because *we evolve only by our desires and our will to act*. If we have a lack of desire or a lack of will to act we will then forfeit our evolution. The person whose desires are so feeble, that he believes in peace at any price and gives up his will to anyone who cares to wrangle with him, is a good example. That is not noble at all. It is only feebleness of desire or lack of vitality. *TO DESIRE BADLY IS BETTER THAN NOT TO DESIRE AT ALL.* We should always be willing to fight for what we want! Of course there is a wrong way to fight for a thing. Whether or not we fight for a good thing in a wrong way, it is better to fight than not to; and whether or not we desire a wrong or bad thing, it is better to desire than not to desire at all.

As a good analogy for this, and analogies will always help us in everything: it is better to think wrongfully than not to think at all. That is the great trouble with government and with education. It does not encourage people to think—it does not even encourage wrong thinking. In other words, the great trouble with education and with government is that it thinks conformity is everything. If I had only two names for it—"virtue" and "vice"—I would say it is "vice." It is better to think for yourself and think wrongly than to accept the thinking of the community. It is only by desire that we evolve. It is only by our effort to think that the mind grows. Thus, whether we exercise the mind rightly or wrongly in thinking or in desiring, it is important that we should think.

To Think!

It is the teaching of Ageless Wisdom that when man identifies himself with his Soul or his Higher Self, his Higher Self is not any longer needed as the intermediary between himself and his Spirit. Consequently, his Higher Self disappears. It is only a thoughtform and it disappears. We are only a thoughtform, and when we reach our Spirit we will disappear. When we identify ourselves with our Soul, he disappears; then we set out on a long journey to contact our Spirit, just as truly as we set out on a long road to contact our Soul.

This card marks very graphically that situation. Here is the Spirit at the top of the mountain, at the end of that journey. During all of the journey he has held the Lantern out for us to see the way up to Him. The LIGHT in that Lantern typifies the Higher Self, as we shall find when we study the symbolism of this card. He has projected the Higher Self down so that you can see it and come up to It. When you come up to It, "the Light" is no longer necessary; for then you can envision the Spirit yourself. So the Higher Self is withdrawn.

The figure 9 is a zero with a line stretching down from it. You can see that is another way of picturing the same idea—God with a line stretching down to man. The old form of the figure 9, when it is written, has a curling stem. That curve can be continued indefinitely up and around the 9 and then spiralling ever upward. Thus it becomes a picture of evolution, and the One Life which is 0 (zero) constantly spiralling outward, moving down and out all the time. That then, is a picture of evolution. The opposite of this process is indicated in the figure 6, the figure which represents the "arc of involution," or one life involving itself into matter and then after it is involved it evolves. That which is evolved the most is then involved. The next card explains both of these processes in detail, *involution* and *evolution*. So you see the science of numbers, the Secret Numeration of Hebrew words; the shape of the figures 9 and 6 include 0 and all tell the same story. *THE LIFE-POWER IS THE SUM TOTAL OF EVERYTHING.* To make things it involves itself into matter and then evolves out of matter back to its Source, or itself.

God (or 9) unfolds Himself indefinitely in His created Universe. We, the created Universe, are constantly aspiring back to our Source, the thing out of which we came. These things are the reasons why the old Greek philosophers, who were initiated into the Secret Wisdom of the Egyptians, made mathematics the "Divine Science." All these numbers tell the same thing. The Life-Power is the sum total of everything, and all the creatures it has made are destined to be Gods. The powers of the Spirit are reproduced in man. The only difference between man and God is not one of kind but only of degree of expression. It is on this idea that the Secret Wisdom of the Jews is based, yet in the popular religion of Judaism the idea that man could ever become God was abhorrent. Between the two a great impassable gulf was fixed, and that is why St. Paul, in his mission, never succeeded with his listeners. He did, however, succeed with some Greeks (and after them with some Romans). The Greeks and Romans had as a basic idea in their myths the demi-gods, the sons of gods by a mortal parent, male or female, who partook of the nature of their immortal father or mother. So the Greeks and Romans were quite used to this idea, but in the popular religion of the Jews, this was not so. The Jews were always aware of the truth of their teaching, cognizant of this truth.

We are told in the Bible that man is the only thing in the Universe that in its present form can manifest all the ten powers of God. All the potentialities of Divinity are in humanity just as they are in everything else, and we are to evolve them by our own effort in climbing up to Him. So Divinity has ordered it. If it were not so, evolution would be a wasted gesture. Not until we are human can we exhibit the Ten Powers of the Life-Force. The climb up to Him through evolution we claim not as a race, not as a species, *but as individuals*. The effort is suggested by the MOUNTAIN in this card—the effort of climbing up, of overcoming gravity. For *gravity* let us substitute *instinct*. We must overcome instinct and utilize instinct for other purposes. At the end of the upper climb is "union with our Source cosmically"; meanwhile, after we reach a certain point, "union with our Source temporarily." This letter stands for the occult extension of the sex-union.

THE HERMIT stands at the summit of the Mountain, upon the heights of abstract thought, which represents as much of the Spirit as we are able to recognize in our physical bodies. THE HERMIT represents the SUPREME WILL, and the Supreme Will is the eternal urge to evolve, to change, to exhibit variety.

The thing in us which makes us want to climb back to Him is the Light streaming down from his Lantern. All action comes from Him and He is the motive for our action because He coaxes us or bangs it out of us. The LANTERN symbolizes the Higher Self, or the Soul. The work of the Light of this Lantern in the world of Nature is the Jupiter vibration. This is the subject of the next card, which is devoted to telling you how the Light of that Lantern works in all things, first, and then in man. So you see, all action comes from THE HERMIT. There is no life but His, and He is the motive for our action.

What do we act for anyway? Why do you think people chew gum? In order to feel themselves alive. Chewing gum does not make one attractive. Then why do they do it? Just to know they are doing something, so they can feel aware or feel a sense of themselves. There are better ways to be active and to know that you are alive and aware.

This idea of Life! Jesus is always talking about life. "I am come in order that you may have life, and have it more abundantly." So religious people and mystics are trying to increase their life. You cannot afford, then, to make too much fun of the person whose only way of increasing life is by chewing gum.

An explanation of the language of the mystics, the saints, and the occultists is very impressive and very simple. There are no terms to describe its blissfulness, its ecstasy. So it was not entirely wrong when people were much franker in their speech than they are now—that people should try to communicate it (communicate the uncommunicable) in terms of sex-union. Also, as a matter of fact, they knew just what it was—that the whole world is a sex manifestation. When you have reached this point you are constantly recuperated and stimulated by a sex-union with your Higher Self. In all the teachings of all the Scriptures that have ever been given out (but not as a teaching), we understand that the source of life is sex. In church we constantly hear, in terms which are meaningless to most of us, that "this world was not made but *begotten* and brought out of the body of its Creator."

The state of consciousness designated by this card, THE IN-TELLIGENCE OF WILL, is said to be a state of blissful unity with the Father. This bliss is not open to anyone who has not entirely purified his consciousness. It is not clear to the psychological mind that the mystics should express this type, that were called erotic, as the absolutely pure in heart. To do that was not proving their case. Santayana said, "Psychologists generally are like detectives. They are engaged to find evidence for the side they are on and to ignore the other evidence." This bliss is reserved for those who have given up their personal will and identified their will with that of the Higher Self. We are then pure, free from matter and from the bias of the physical plane. We are then in the state of mind in which Jesus was when he said, "I and my Father are One. He who hath seen me hath seen the Father." So, once more we meet the paradox. Jesus was always expressing, "If we give ourselves up entirely, then only do we own ourselves." He who loseth his life, his lower life, shall gain it—his Higher Self. When Jesus said, "I and my Father are One," he meant his Spirit, because he himself had now become his Soul. When we speak of becoming one with the Father, we mean becoming one with the Soul, as our Higher Self, the representative of the Father. On the lower plane of matter the Soul is just a projection of the Spirit down into this plane, usually too low for him to enter upon. We have to come up to Him and He provides us with the means to come.

The only function of the Soul is to project the Light of the Spirit down to the personality, until the personality has climbed abreast of the soul.

The object of the occultist and the mystic alike is the union with THE HERMIT. This letter Yod stands for the occult extension of sex-union. To many people this idea is not literal but figurative. To those people the idea of literal sex-union with God—and with their Higher Self—will be repugnant. Nevertheless, this union is an actual occurrence. It has been described in all the Scriptures and in the personal narrations of all mystics, and the descriptions are incredibly alike. It is just as one writer said, "there is no other way to describe it than this." The description of this union has employed terms which seem grossly sexual to persons who do not understand it. Apparently the experience cannot be communicated in any other terms. When there are no words for a thing, one must take the nearest words to express it. *It is the melting of the personality into something which takes possession of it.* In it, "all sense of self-consciousness is lost and the personality is fused with the universal consciousness." "So great is this experience," said Carpenter, "that if it happens only once to a man, it changes him for the rest of his life." Even with the saints this experience was unusual, and they spent their lives in seeking to repeat it by fasting, praying, and depriving their bodies. Even Jesus had not by any means a continuous state of this feeling of "union." He constantly had to go up to the Mount to pray in order to renew it. In the Psalms, David is always complaining that his God has retired from him.

To become One with the Father in permanent union cannot be achieved by aspiration or devotion alone. This is the trouble with the Church. It gives us an idea that it can. Of course, "the trouble" is only a relative term. It is only a partial truth. Permanent union cannot be achieved by aspiration or devotion alone. The saints and the mystics who have this experience of occasional union can never sustain it. It came and went in a manner inexplicable to them, and the fact that it went caused them many a heart-burning. It would plunge them into grief, sometimes into despair and into softening of the mind. They could never recover from the fact that their Deity had deserted them. They feared that they had forfeited their right to ascend to that height again.

What really happened was that, for one reason or another, they had raised their vibrations to this point where they could contact the Father, but they could not keep it there, for they did not know how it was done. It was only the result of fortuitous circumstances. They attained it by acutely maltreating the body. The object of the occultist is the same as the mystic. He finds out how he can remove the gross matter from his body; that allows him to raise the vibration of his body. This Union with the Father is made easier by an effort of the will, or is kind of an effort of the will. Thus the occultist finds out that he can keep it raised as long as he desires it. So with the occultist the result is a psycho-physiological process, a process partly of the self-conscious mind and partly of the subconscious mind.

The formula for it is given in the Hebrew spelling of the word *Yod* (IVD): *The body reconstructed by the energies of DALETH (THE EMPRESS) linked (VAU, THE HIEROPHANT) with the Spirit (I).* V means "Links."

The reconstructed body which is part of DALETH (THE EMPRESS) links with the Spirit.

In the early Middle Ages this process of reconstructing the body was called "alchemy." Alchemy had for its primary project an emotional and a physical transformation, and the alchemist himself had his own body for the only laboratory he worked in. The process, of course, had been known long before the Middle Ages. It had been taught from time immemorial by the Secret Teachings, and there are many disguised allegories about it in the Old and New Testaments. The beginning of the process is physical digestion. But you have to get ready for that. It is physical digestion that brings about physical transformation.

Physical changes which finally result in the transmutation of the alchemist begin with the chemistry of food. The place where it occurs is hinted at in the story that Jesus was born in Bethlehem. Bethlehem means "The House of Bread"—which is like saying that Jesus was born in the stomach. As if to make sure that no one who had a clue might overlook the allegory it was said again—Jesus was not only born in Bethlehem but in a manger, which is a trough where cattle feed. Your stomach is the trough where cattle feed.

The people who constructed the Tarot were fundamentally acquainted with alchemy. You remember these cards were put out in the guise of playing cards so that the possession of them would not afford incriminating evidence to the Church. In just the same way alchemy was a blind. The alchemists pretended they were seeking a way to turn lead into gold. In a way this was the truth. They sought to raise certain low vibrations in their bodies they called "lead" to the highest vibration of which the body was capable, which they called "gold." The Laws of Nature are uniform and they work everywhere and in everything; and it is quite true that we can perform the miracle of turning external lead into external gold, if we know how to do it. *Law of Nature*

What they were trying to do was to raise the leaden vibration of the body into the golden vibration. However, the object of the alchemist was to keep the Church and the initiated from guessing what their work was, and everything they said was wrapped up in veiled and fantastic language. For instance, they called alchemy "manual operation." On the face of it, that was a perfectly meaningless expression—because they were trying to find some chemical way to turn lead into gold. What did they mean, then, by saying it was manual operation? This was in reference to the importance of this card, THE *recorded virtualized work experimentation*

HERMIT, and the letter that goes with this card, YOD, which means "hand." The Manual Operation means that the work was performed by the activities that the letter Yod presides over. Alchemy, then, is an operation of the potencies of this letter or card, a "manual operation." When we read a tract of one of the alchemists, we wonder why he should be talking that way unless he has a veiled meaning. If it occurred to you, it never occurred to them or rather did not seem to. The meaning was there and is there for us if we have the clues to it.

So, if we are trying to be "centers of expression for the Primal-Will-To-Good," we must diligently employ our intelligence in ascertaining those meanings. When shall we govern our judgment and action in accordance with Justice? When shall we govern our judgment and action in accordance with Mercy? To be merciful at the right time is Justice, and to be Just at the wrong time is injustice. That is the hardest of all things to learn, and it can be learned really only by guidance. Until we are in a state where we can be guided, we must be sharpening our intelligence all the time. To be just all the time is wrong. To be merciful all the time is wrong. It is worse than wrong because it fosters evil.

The astrological sign which goes with this card is VIRGO, which relates to the whole intestinal tract. The intestinal tract is a coil. It is called the BLACK DRAGON because it is coiled and shut out from the light. No ray of light can enter the intestinal tract.

Where the intestinal tract joins the stomach, at the head of this Dragon, is a milky substance which is called "the liquid that does not wet."

The Greeks called this substance *chyle*—and so do we. The alchemists had a very fantastic and apparently meaningless word for it, but which meant a great deal. They called it THE VIRGIN'S MILK. What is this Virgin's Milk in this coil? It is the essence of our food which has been extracted by the digestive fluids, and from those essences is derived the necessary elements for body building.

The natural body requires only certain essences for its normal functioning. There are other essences in the food which are at present not extracted because the body doesn't need them, and they disappear with the waste of the body. "The highest function of Mercury," said the alchemist and astrologer, "is to be found in Virgo." Mercury rules Virgo. It comes to its highest manifestation in Virgo. What they mean is that the Mind (Mercury), the Intellect (the thinking lobe of the brain), governs the highest manifestations the Mind is capable of making.

These are made in this sign. Consequently, the highest thing that Mercury can do is empower the subconscious to utilize this element in chyle, which is not used in the ordinary body. It is this element which is ever essential to what the Christians call *regeneration*, or to make the body over.

If we properly impress the subconscious, she will attend to this for us. It is not at all necessary for us to begin the process. We begin by hungering and thirsting after righteousness—the right use of the body. It has always been known that there is a very intimate connection between digestion and the state of the conscious mind. We all know that digestion has much to do with the ability to use the mind. Everybody knows that an auto-intoxicated person cannot think. The doctors have always told us that if we worry it can cause indigestion. So you see, this close connection between digestion and the state of conscious mind is only a further connection than that which is at present a common-sense teaching.

Mercury rules Virgo and it comes to its highest manifestation in Virgo: it is the only sign in the Zodiac that is distinct in this way. The planet rules it and it also comes into its highest manifestation in it. It is Mercury that does the work. He starts it, he governs it, and he brings it to completion. The work is the highest thing he can perform; it is the work of the higher digestion.

Again, it is important to know that the state of the conscious mind has much to do with the process of digestion. Medicine tells us that digestion has much to do with the ability to use the mind, and that the state of our minds has much to do with the activity of our digestion—that the two things are closely interrelated. Mercury is the thinking lobe of the brain. The Pineal Gland is part of the thinking lobe of the brain. The transformed or awakened Pineal Gland acquires new powers. In occultism the Pineal Gland, when it is awakened, is called the "Third Eye." One of the new perceptions of this "Third Eye" is the true perception of what kind of food at the present moment is required by the body. What to give it, in short, for its occult development at the moment. Our particular need depends upon our physical condition at the time and by our general constitution as indicated by the aspects of our horoscope. We must consider the planetary positions at the time of our birth and the aspects under which we are at present. All those things dictate just what we need.

That need not sound too complex for us because that is precisely what the doctor means when he says, "I think I will put you on a diet."

The particular needs (the occult needs) our body has are satisfied with the chemicals in food, and those needs constantly change. One of the perceptions of our Third Eye is to see what we lack in food at the moment and to see the food which will best supply that need. What we have to do is constantly keep a certain balance of chemical substances in our body.

If you have not heard this before, it may take your breath away. *The chemicals that we occultly need are 12 in number, and each corresponds to a Zodiacal sign; and it cannot be repeated too often that throughout Nature one general law holds sway, in the Sun as in the animal.* Here we will find chemicals, too. There are 12 leading chemicals. Man is not able to recognize these chemicals and the chemicals that are fitted to his need at the moment. He will recognize them when he has acquired that perception by the new Third Eye, which alchemists call "the perception of First Matter."

A few scientists have arrived at a mathematical theory in connection with the theoretical knowledge of First Matter. Sir Arthur Eddington was one of those scientists. He said that the Universe is composed of a scintillating electrical energy. It is known that it scintillates because it is visible, you can see it. Out of it all things are made, and this is First Matter. Eddington goes so far as to use the very term the occultist uses—this basic fiery vibrant energy he calls *mind-stuff.*

The opened Pineal Gland sees not by psychic vision, or vision that takes place with the eye as a vehicle, yet the mind looks through the eye. The vision of the seeing mind (and that, you remember, THE EMPEROR stands for) is a vision independent of the actual eye, yet you see it through the actual eye. The eye is the instrument, the vehicle, that registers the experience of it.

Perception of the chemicals is a personal matter with us. No alchemist writer ever tells you. Apparently nobody who knows will tell us. Perhaps not anyone knows but yourself, but anyone that pretends to tell us is an imposter. Nor can anyone expedite the precise moment for preparing for this experience. It must be done by our own effort. Its discovery, as I have said, comes about from the awakening of the Third Eye. The Third Eye is awakened as a result of Kundalini and the final lifting of the sex-force to the head. When that is done we see directly the fiery essence hidden within the substance of everything. This does not in the least interfere with our usual sight, though I suppose we have to get accustomed to seeing both things at once. When this happens, we perceive what substance contains the chemicals we need at that particular time to balance our chemistry. Alchemists say all these materials are simple, that they are easily procured.

It is the seven Interior Stars which the alchemists would name when they started to change any rate of vibration. Alchemy has existed for time immemorial, and long before the alchemist of the Middle Ages the Book of Revelation summed up the process. The Book of Revelation opens with a message to what are called the "Seven Churches of Asia." Asia is your body, and the Seven Churches are the seven Interior Stars. The Pineal Gland is the Church of Laodicea, and here is the blessing to the Church called Laodicea:

> *Because thou sayest, I am rich, and increased with goods and have need of nothing; and knowest not that thou art wretched; and miserable, and poor, and blind, and naked; I counsel thee to buy of me gold tried in the fire, that you mayest be rich; and white raiment that thou mayest be clothed, and that shame of thy nakedness do not appear; and anoint thine eyes with salve, that thou mayest see.*

That is the message. Kundalini is the fire that changes the Intellect into Gold by creating other brain cells. You see, THE MAGICIAN is the transformed Intellect bringing down the White Light to clothe himself in the White Raiment. That is to say, to change his body, to purify his body, he finally opens the Pineal Gland, The Third Eye. He anoints his eyes with eye-salve, that they may see the fiery energy which is the basis of all the infinite multitude of forms. Under all this infinite multitude of forms there is one law of proportions that operates the entire Universe. He sees how he can rebuild his body with this one law of proportion.

The alchemist wasted no time on the moral, emotional, or esoteric process, as did the mystics. They set to work to try to make physiological changes in their bodies, to transform the chemistry of those bodies, hence the consciousness of those bodies. There is a proverb which says that a man is what he eats. That proverb is true. We, too, are wasting our time if we seek to acquire merely intellectual knowledge, occult knowledge, or teaching through these cards. *The only thing that counts is to secure the necessary physiological changes in our body.*

Tarot is built for that purpose, to facilitate these physiological and psychic changes. Some of us already see those things taking place, and we have a subjective interior perception of certain colors—colors that we see in our brain-stuff with eyes closed. That is a sign that we are already making progress in the work.

The direction of this card is NORTH-BELOW. What is Below? THE HIGH PRIESTESS is Below. THE MAGICIAN is Above and represents the self-conscious. The self-conscious is Above the threshold, the subconscious is Below the threshold. What is North? North is the Mars vibration. North-Below: This is the epitome of the process of transformation; the Mars vibration is transformed and about to enter her by the subconscious.

The whole process is instigated or controlled by Mercury, but always it is the woman who does the work. The self-conscious contributes the steady unremitting pressure of Attention and Will, which starts the process that could not start without it.

XXX The LAW this card stands for is MUTUAL RESPONSIBILITY. The Law of the last card was SUGGESTION. This card is Mutual Responsibility, the responsibility of the self-conscious to the subconscious. Ideas that hold good in your body and hold good cosmically.

⌐ *It is by the Mutual Responsibility of the personality and the Spirit that we evolve.* We are just as necessary to the Spirit as the Spirit is necessary to us. So don't underestimate yourselves. It is by the Mutual Responsibility of the personality and the Spirit that we climb the Mountain to THE HERMIT. The One Will is continually after us to get the response. If it cannot evoke that response it will provoke it. One poet has embodied this thought in a poem called "The Hound of Heaven," in which the Deity takes the form of a hound always at the heels, always pursuing you. We can never get away from the Light streaming down to us by means of the Higher Self, or Soul. We may refuse to climb to Him, but the desire to do so is never entirely killed out, not even in the most vicious of us. We are told that when it is killed out, when it is no longer possible for us to climb the Mountain, we are cut down lest we cumber the ground, as Jesus says in one of his parables. That is to say, we are dissolved and disintegrated; we are set on a shelf until the next evolution, and got out of place here in this one. We are told that there are such things as incorrigible persons. When they are finally demonstrated incorrigibles, then they are ready to disintegrate.

The object of all Yoga is to obtain sex-union with the Father. Most people find themselves unable to express this union except in sexual terms. Thus we come face-to-face with a strange paradox. The Hebrew letter that stands for sex-union with the Spirit corresponds with the Zodiacal sign Virgo, the Virgin. How can that be explained? "Sex," in

Yoga, means becoming pure, identifying yourself with the Father by getting rid of gross matter. So you see, this is more or less in the nature of a pun, this word "Yoga"—it means purification from matter. The same kind of pun or joke is seen in the fantastic expression of the alchemist for this substance, which they call "Virgin's Milk."

You will find that the Bible, Greek mythology, the Rosicrucian Order, the Tarot cards, and our own dreams are full of such puns having much to do with sex matters, yet they haven't any connection with prurience or bad sex. The Christian Church apparently is entirely responsible for our prurience about sex. When someone remonstrated with Mrs. Pearl Buck for her frankness about sex in her Chinese story, she said, "Why, in China we regard sex just like any other part of the body. I don't understand what you mean." We are prurient about sex until we learn to speak of sex just as we speak of anything else. It is impossible for us to get a good, fine occultism out of religion, really, because in religion sex-union seems to be associated with sex in an unclean or bad way. The Christian Church is responsible for that. The Jesus of their allegory was intended to be the Christ-consciousness born of Virgo, born of the purifed body; instead of which they make Jesus an actual man born of a virgin. You see, there is a great difference. It is associating sin and impurity with the sex function. "All men," said the Christian Church, "are born in sin"—therefore, the Savior of man must be born of a virgin, without sin. This, in spite of the patent fact that if there is any sin connected with the sex function, the Virgin Mary is not immune because the Gospel story itself gives Jesus several brothers and sisters.

So you see, putting the story in this way, it is degrading the business of sex. Along came Paul, and I am sure that the Church put into his mouth things he never uttered or even dreamed. Nevertheless, all we know about Paul comes from the New Testament. Paul said, "It is better to marry than to burn." Marriage was bad enough, but it kept you from Hell, at any rate, Paul was saying.

All these blasphemous ideas about sex, the occultist says, were due to the Christian religion. Instead, had the Church taught that sex was the most sacred of man's acts and that it was profanation to engage in it without love, sex in marriage might be far more profane than sex outside of marriage. Had the Church taught that excess in the physical use of sex robbed all the rest of the body of its share of vitality and that the higher use of sex, the Mental use of sex, was the most important step in the evolution of man, then the task of the occultist in reeducating the world about the real nature of sex would have been much smaller than it is.

That, in a word, is what must be done. The whole world must be reeducated as to the nature of sex. As it is now, you find this a very startling consideration—that until 20, 30, or 40 years ago, almost nowhere did anyone engage in any sane discussion of that most important fact of life. This prurience goes hand-in-hand with the utmost licentiousness everywhere. So we owe to the Church the teaching that the Earth is our enemy and that the only way is to run away from it—from the body, from the world.

All this tremendous and piteous misunderstanding of the nature of sex, the occultist says, came from the fact that to open the Pineal Gland requires temporary abstinence from sex. In Tarot and occultism we were taught that the only way to reach God is through the correct use of our Earth, our body. We are taught that far from there being anything degrading in sex, union with God is a sex-union. The occultist marvels that the Church has made such a blunder or could have perpetrated such a belief, when it says that the whole world is a sex act and is begotten by God and not made.

SYMBOLISM

THE HERMIT, this card YOD, is an Earth letter, the VIRGIN. VIRGO is an Earth sign, yet Yod stands for the Spirit and Virgo stands for sex-union with the Spirit. There are four cards in the Tarot Trumps which stand for the element of Earth: THE HIEROPHANT (Taurus); THE HERMIT (Virgo); THE DEVIL (Capricorn); and THE WORLD (Saturn). THE HIEROPHANT stands for the Soul, and THE HERMIT stands for the Spirit. The most exalted state possible to man is represented by the last card, THE WORLD, a state where man is co-administrator of evolution with God. That leaves one card of the Earth sequence unaccounted for, THE DEVIL. THE DEVIL, says Tarot, is but the misuse of our body, a misuse of our element of Earth. THE DEVIL represents the Earth as it is misused because it is misunderstood, misused because we are content to be misled by its profane expression. We don't pay enough Attention, we think that the reports of the senses are actual.

This card—and all the other cards of this sequence—are very exalted cards. One stands for the Soul, the other stands for the Spirit, and the third stands for the highest state possible to man. Consequently we see that THE DEVIL card must be a very good card also if we know how to use it. That is the object of alchemy, to tell us how to use our body, to teach us the mystery of the forces and forms of Earth in our body. That is what the word *Jesus* means—SELF-EXISTENCE LIBERATES— *A man who is master of the liberating power is a Jesus.* The three liberating forces are represented by THE HIEROPHANT, THE HERMIT, and THE WORLD. We cannot liberate that by running away from our body as the Church has counseled. THE DEVIL represents the natural body. The way to change the natural body into a liberated body (the Spiritual body) is by knowing how to manage the forces represented by these three cards.

Jesus, or the Christ in us, the Transformed Heart, comes from the combined force of these three—Virgo, Taurus, and Capricorn. Jesus, in the Gospel narrative, proclaimed that he came to make all things new. Now that is the subject of the last card in this Earth sequence, THE WORLD. We see the Spiritual body making all things new— performing her acts of magic. So the way to attain it is not as the Church taught, to run away from Earth, but to subdue the Earth and then we will understand its hidden nature and utilize its hidden powers. The Christians taught that the body was to be scorned. The occultist says that the body is our only means of manifestation and of mastery, and when we properly discipline it, it is a great liberator from physical conditions.

The Christian religion taught people to run away from the world and to maltreat the body. It said, "Do not do it unless you feel you have a vocation to do it"; but by all means we must recognize that this highest state of mind is the one they advise us to run away from. The Ageless Wisdom says, "You must use your body, you must attend it, and when you have attended it, your body becomes the highest instrument the Universe is capable of forming." The body of man is the only form in all physical nature that can manifest the Ten Aspects of the Life-Power. So do not run away from it but transform it and utilize it.

The background of THE HERMIT card is DARKNESS, which signifies the Source, the Beginning. All religions have pictured Darkness as the Mother of Light—as coming before the Light. In Genesis it says, "And God said, Let there be Light." He was in Darkness when He said it. In some editions of the Tarot, this card has a background that is blue-violet; but in this card it is not, it is merely a darkish gray tint.

The GRAY-COWLED ROBE of THE HERMIT appears to be an allusion to the fact that He is the source of His own darkness. Darkness came before Light; *Light was born out of Darkness.* Darkness is the Father-Mother Originator; the Light is the Child. This HERMIT is muffled up in a Gray-cowled robe. He is concealed from us until we have anointed our eyes with eye-salve.

He is standing on a SNOWY PEAK to indicate that He awaits us at the summit of our evolution, our Spiritual evolution. The name HERMIT signifies that he is alone—that he has no companion, no equal. The PEAK is SNOWY to indicate the HIGHEST ABSTRACT THOUGHT. These Heights you see also in the card 0, the very last thing THE FOOL left behind him as he went down into matter; therefore, in order to get Above—get where he was before he got down into matter—he must reach again the heights of Abstract Thought.

Cosmically speaking, this Figure is what is called the ABSOLUTE, what the Hebrews call JEHOVAH. Personally speaking, He is our Spirit, the highest member of our Trinity. The teaching of occultism is that the Soul is just the agent of the Spirit, projected by Spirit as a "thoughtform" to function on the lower plane, a lower plane than the Spirit can come down and function in.

For the convenience of the eye in this picture, the SOUL is represented as the LANTERN, which He is holding out to those who are at the foot of the Mountain. This Lantern, or the LIGHT IN IT, represents the SOUL. The Lantern has a top which is made like the crown on THE HIEROPHANT's head, in three tiers with a knob at the top. The tiers are arranged in a DOME. The Dome, of course, represents the subconscious. The THREE BARS on the Lantern taken in connection with the knob on the top represent the fourfold world, the Archetypal, Creative, Formative, and Physical worlds. It is THE HERMIT, of course, who starts this fourfold process of creation. His images are Archetypal before they come down into matter.

They finally become physical planets instead of stars. These four planets the occultists call the Four Subtle Principles. The highest one is FIRE, the next highest is WATER, the third is AIR, and the fourth physical planet is EARTH. The occultist geometrically represents these four elements by four equilateral triangles. It is necessary for us to remember these: the Fiery equilateral triangle stands on its base; the Water is the same triangle standing on its apex; the one for Air stands on its base like the one for Fire, but just above the middle of it, it has a horizontal line drawn through it; and the one for the Earth is like the one for Water, but just about the middle of it, it has a line drawn through it, a horizontal line. If you place one of these triangles upon the other you will see the reason for the horizontal line, because they are interlaced. The interlaced triangle represents geometrically (for the occultist) the perfect union, the harmonious communication of the self-conscious and the subconscious. When you have perfect unity of the conscious and the subconscious, then you have united yourself with your Soul, the Father. The process for bringing about this union is to transform the subconscious by means of these images. When she is transfigured, then she turns around, and by the process of the Higher Digestion, transforms you, the self-conscious.

The Lantern THE HERMIT holds is SIX-SIDED, an allusion to the sign Virgo, which is the sixth Zodiacal sign. In that Lantern there is a SIX-POINTED STAR, and it is that which gives the Light. That Star is the Higher Self. The Soul is represented by this six-pointed Star, because the six-pointed Star is the interlaced triangles, and when the personality has interlaced his two triangles, he has made himself equal to his Higher Self. He becomes permanently united with his Higher Self. He has made his Chariot fit for the Charioteer, in the language of card VII.

The two triangles are those of Fire and Water—the triangle of the head and the triangle of the heart. Until we have achieved union with the head and heart in our personality, we cannot achieve union with the Higher Self. The union of the head and the heart is accomplished by suggestion, the self-conscious constantly making images for the subconscious to follow. *In accordance with his image she transforms him.* In the process of transforming herself she has become gifted with new powers, which allow her to transform him. When he is entirely transformed, then the two triangles of head and heart are interlaced; a perfect union with the Father is accomplished.

THE HERMIT has a Wand, a GOLDEN WAND, in one hand. It is the magical Wand of Creation, the same as THE MAGICIAN has upon his Table. In the symbolism of the Tarot, that which is held in the left hand is automatic, and that which is held in the right hand is the more important, the conscious activity. The function of THE HERMIT in showing the way to his creative influence is more important to him than was their creation in the first place. His Lantern is in his right hand.

Nobody knows why the Absolute wished to create. We have the right to assume that His every act must be prompted by desire. We are told that He brought the elements of His consciousness into creation in order that they gain self-consciousness. In other words, that they might have more abundant life. If this was His object, anybody knows that it can only be obtained by making us climb back up the Mountain. Thus to show us the way back, the object and purpose of His creating us in the first place must naturally be more important than the act of creation itself. The act of creation itself was a means, a means existent only for the end that He has wished to achieve. For this was the purpose—"To give us more abundant life."

The Golden Wand is an implement which the personality can also wield. It is by the use of this instrument and the two others on THE MAGICIAN's table that THE MAGICIAN can carve out the physical plane product of his mental ideas. First he has to use these implements on his own body, and by use of them he so refines the dense matter of his body so that the Higher Self, who was unable to do so on account of the density of the body, can now control it personally.

You saw THE FOOL standing upon a Shelf about to step off, and the Shelf was made of a queer formation suggesting that it could be flaked off. It is THE MAGICIAN who flakes off the density of this shelf by his action on his own body. His action is absurdly simple. It consists merely in making images—in keeping in the forefront of his mind that he must provide the matter of which his body is composed. The Shelf (physical body), as well as all the other forms of the physical world, was made by the Spirit from an archetype of mental matter. By descending into successive lower grades of matter, it finally appears as we see it now, and the process is indicated by the four implements on THE MAGICIAN's table: the Wand, the Cup, the Sword, and the physical plane Pentacle, or end-product.

Completion,
accomplishment,
attainment.

Purpose
Progress,
Advancement,

WHEEL of FORTUNE.

The Entire Process of involution and Evolution — A Cosmic Day

11th Hebrew Letter	*KAPH*
Symbol for	*Pair of Opposites—*
	(Wealth and
	Poverty)
Color	*Violet*
Numerical Value	*20—and Some-*
	times 500
Syllables	*KP*
Sound	*A-Sharp*
Planet	*Jupiter*
Translation	*Grasping Hand*

NOTES

THE WHEEL OF FORTUNE

KAPH, spelled KP, means GRASPING HAND. It is the 11th Hebrew letter and the fourth DOUBLE LETTER. It stands for the sign or symbol of the pair of opposites WEALTH and POVERTY (a good manifestation or a meager manifestation, a good body or a poor body), for the direction WEST, the INTELLIGENCE OF CONCILIATION, or REWARDING INTELLIGENCE OF THOSE WHO SEEK, the planet JUPITER, the color VIOLET, and the note is A-SHARP. In Roman characters it is written K. Its numerical value is 20.

KAPH equals the top of BETH plus a parallelogram slanting off from it. Thus it contains the same elements as Beth—Solar Energy descending into form. Kaph pictures that a man's body, like every other form in the Universe, is the out-flowing of Solar Energy into form. Kaph symbolizes that his body is but condensed Solar Energy. All forms are condensed Solar Energy, or as Eddington said, "Sunlight bottled up." A form holds a little bit of the Sea of Electric Energy with which the Universe is filled.

The Egyptians made this letter like a bowl, and the palm of the hand, when cupped, likewise holds something. In the days when the Hebrew alphabet was formed, a bowl was made on a wheel, by the turning of a wheel. It was shaped by the palm of the hand, cupping itself as the wheel spun the clay. The letter has the same idea of spinning, or rotation, and the Law this letter stands for is ROTATION. Number 1 is the beginning of the whirling, and whirling is the basis of all physical manifestation. All forms are something which are spun and number 1 is the first stage of form.

The circle in the center of the card has eight spokes, the same as on THE FOOL's robe, where it appears ten times. This is the electro-magnetic energy of the Solar Energy, which is in constant vibration. This Energy is nearest Spirit, its source, yet it is the basis of all matter. In this card, you see, Spirit is put at the very core of THE WHEEL OF FORTUNE. It says again what the cards have said before—that matter and Spirit are one. Matter is not an illusion, it is merely different from what it appears to our eyes. The energy contained in an atom is identical with what you call your Spirit. *You do not need to acquire energy, only to control what you have.* It is the same energy which is shot out from the Sun. It is this energy which constructs forms. Form is this energy

191

surrounded with a core of matter. The succession of releases of energy from the destruction of forms sets up a rotation. All action is cyclic; it begins, it grows, works its pattern up to its completion and ends. This is observable in the motion of atoms, of planets, of rungs on the spiral motion which builds organic forms. It is universal and fundamental; it moves by fixed conditions and its action is itself a pattern.

Your least personal action is a specific expression of those wheels within wheels of Natural Law typified by THE WHEEL OF FORTUNE. All personal activity is a series of particular expressions of the Cosmic cycles of Involution and Evolution—the wheel of two arcs, Involution and Evolution.

The Zodiacal sign of this card is JUPITER. The Jupiter Center is the largest of the sympathetic nerve centers. The Jupiter cards are 10, 14, 18, and 7. The dominant physiological center of the Jupiter vibration in the body is the largest center in the sympathetic nervous system, and is called the Solar Plexus because of its radiating fibers. The real Sun Center (in occultism) is the heart, while the Solar Plexus is just behind the stomach in the physical body. Sometimes it is called "the abdominal brain." It takes care of all the body which is below it. The Solar Plexus is the chief delegate of the brain in the body. When the brain wants to tell the body to do anything, it sends the message through the Pituitary, through the Venus Center to the Solar Plexus, and that sends it to the colony of cells which it concerns. The Hindu name for it is "Filled with Jewels." In the Jupiter symbol subconsciousness predominates. The primary function of subconsciousness is memory, and every cell in the body possesses adequate memory of everything that concerns its own organ. The Solar Plexus is the great repository of the records of past experiences. All the experiences of your unfathomable complex organism, the story of your biological inheritance as well as your past lives, are there. All the copies of the intricate chemical formulas which are carried out by the groups of cell-workmen, which we call the "vital organs," are necessary to maintain the vital processes of your body in the Solar Plexus. To this Center, impulses originating in the brain ultimately find their way from the relay stations of the Moon and Venus Centers. From here arise to the upper brain the impulses we call instincts.

The Solar Plexus passes out the patterns the brain has formulated to the cell-workmen, which we call the vital organs. Innumerable functions which are performed with conscious knowledge are also directed by the Solar Plexus to learn their past, to learn the Laws of the Universe and to get a firm intellectual grasp on the Law of Cycles which the Solar Plexus symbolizes. That is one of the meanings that this letter stands for—*THE INTELLIGENCE OF CONCILIATION*— understanding how a thing happens to you as a thing apart. You see what its cause was, and you see that it is still becoming a cause to something in the future.

Here is something that happens to you. You seem not at all responsible for it; you seem to be a victim of it, yet it is the effect of a past circumstance for which you are responsible. In this way the Intelligence of Conciliation reconciles all apparent differences. It is dangerous for anyone who is not a Buddha to meditate upon his Solar Plexus until he has awakened the Heart Center, the real Sun Center. Why is that? This is because the Solar Plexus is the seat of instincts. Now, it is the business of civilization, of self-development and of self-sacrifice, to subdue the instincts, which are animal, to uses of the distinct human life. If you meditate upon the Solar Plexus before you put the heart in control of the emotions, your instinct may get too strong for it and you may not be able to handle them.

The functions of the Solar Plexus are what we call the lower psychic powers; that is to say, psychic powers which belong to people who have no spiritual power. The reason the Solar Plexus attends to those powers is because they were instinctive in the Atlantean Race; that is to say, everybody exerted them then. They belonged to that race. Occult history says that they withdrew from humanity in order that the present Aryan race should cultivate its mind, its Reason. Reason was not necessary when you possessed these psychic instincts, and as long as you possessed them you would not cultivate your Reason. These powers are particularly found among the people we call gypsies, people who are somewhat primitive in intelligence. They can, for instance, sense things for which there is no objective evidence, and they have an animal sense of direction. Some of them have a remarkable ability to recuperate physically after an accident and the ability to stand pain that would be too acute for other people. The Red Indians are nearer to the Atlanteans in their biological inheritance. They may have any of these lower psychic powers to a marked degree. All of these powers were withdrawn from this present race in order that we might cultivate our minds, and it is said we shall resume these after our minds have been cultivated. However, the particular task of this particular race is to specialize in the mind.

There was a time when the now-involuntary, automatic actions were learned; when they became "second nature," the control of them passed from the self-conscious brain to the subconscious brain—the Jupiter Center. Its records concern not only your personal history and biological inheritance, but the history of all organic life (a concise summing up of everything from the formation of the nebula from which our solar system was elaborated).

The patient seeker for occult Wisdom is rewarded during sleep and has perception of higher planes. In his dreams he is rewarded. The knowledge gained by the subtler vehicles is made part of the Corporeal Intelligence by being impressed upon the cells of the brain while sleep inhibits sensation. It is in this way that one so often finds the solution to the problem in his head on awakening. It is not "unconscious cerebration," says science; although occultism says there is brain activity. That activity is not yours except as it records impressions from the higher planes. When you are thoroughly acquainted with the Hebrew letters and their attributes and numbers, your subconscious will utilize them to indicate your weak points and the solutions to your problems.

The direction of Jupiter is WEST, the place of sunset. Do not associate West with sunset but with *completion*. The direction of Venus is EAST, the place of dawn. Jupiter is called the GREATER FORTUNE; Venus is called the LESSER FORTUNE. All the Jupiter cards have direct reference to Venus. The chief feature of this card is THE WHEEL. It is a Venus symbol with the pendant folded in. The card symbolizes, in its Cosmic process, the entire process of INVOLUTION and EVOLUTION— or a Cosmic day. During the first part of the process, vitality flows into it. During the second part of the process, vitality flows out of it. Finally there is no more vitality to flow out of it, and the form is at an end. This in-flowing and out-flowing is the fundamental form of forms. Occultism calls it The Wheel of Involution, Evolution.

Thus the card stands for COMPLETION, ACCOMPLISHMENT, and ATTAINMENT, etc. THE WHEEL itself is a symbol of PROGRESS, of ADVANCEMENT. The card sums up the great Law of Cycles.

Its letter, KAPH, GRASPING HAND, signifies that the right adaptation of life depends upon your grasp of this Law. To look at the card intently influences the Solar Plexus, where is the memory of all things, and leads to the recovery of profound truths. It is from the Jupiter Center that scientists get most of their truths—those perceptions of Cosmic Law usually named "discoveries," but which would be better named "rediscoveries."

"That which hath been IS, and that which is to be hath already been; and the creative powers search out that which is past."

A personal grasp of the Law of Cycles reconciles differences; you see why differences should be—that one is the cause of the other, or the balance of the other. It gives you memory of the past, and that Karma is the result of cause and effect. Hence, the Intelligence of Conciliation.

SYMBOLISM

The SPHINX is BLUE, which means it has memory of all things. It has seen all things which have ever been. It bears in its hand the SWORD OF DISCRIMINATION, and with it carves out the FORMATIVE WORLD, as does the implement on THE MAGICIAN's table, the Sword of Processes, of his ideas.

All the ANIMALS are reading from a WHITE BOOK, getting the knowledge of the Law; and the Animals are all Yellow—the ACTION OF MIND, indicating the mind receiving instruction from the Spirit. Yellow is the color of the Sun.

On the outermost Wheel, alternating with letters IHVH, are the Roman letters ROTA. As THE WHEEL turns, these letters read ROTA TARO ORAT TORA ATOR. This is a bad Latin sentence meaning "The Wheel of Tarot teaches or speaks the Law of Nature." Hathor is an Egyptian goddess corresponding to THE EMPRESS. In Hebrew letters the value of all the eight letters on THE WHEEL equals 697, whose digits add up to 22, the number of letters in the Hebrew alphabet and also the number of Tarot Trumps. Each of the sections between the letters is 45 degrees, and 45 is the number assigned to man. So THE WHEEL says MAN eight times, and eight is the number of dominion and equilibrium—equilibrium of the self and subconscious.

Nature constitutes the ALL; and man has dominion over the All if he can have dominion over himself by self-effort. The conception of man extended infinitely is the only conception we are to form of God, and He, too, has dominion over all.

On the SPOKES of THE WHEEL, in the circle representing the Formative World, are the alchemical symbols of Mercury (above); Sulphur (right); Salt (left); and below is the alchemical symbol of Dissolution, identical with the astrological symbol of Aquarius, the Man or Angel in the upper left corner. Man becomes Angel by dissolution, by remaking his body.

What do these symbols mean? In alchemy, the three ways in which the First Matter presents itself are called the three alchemical principles; the sea of scintillating Mind-Stuff is called First Matter. These three alchemical principles are designated as Sulphur, Mercury, and Salt. These symbolic names are not the physical substances so named, but each has qualities characteristic of the physical substance whose name it bears. As matter and consciousness are the same thing, you can look at these three symbols either as qualities of matter or as qualities of consciousness.

The First Matter is the LIFE-BREATH, the One Substance of all things—veiled in thick darkness but manifesting itself in the three aspects that alchemists call the three principles.

In terms of the qualities of matter, they correspond to the three fundamental qualities of matter which the Hindus call *rajas, sattva,* and *tamas;* or, the tendency of matter to change, the tendency of things to fall into rhythm, the tendency of matter to remain as it is. If matter did not contain these three qualities, things would be static.

In terms of Consciousness (for the One Original Energy is a Conscious Energy), they correspond to the self-consciousness (RAJAS, Sulphur); to superconsciousness (SATTVA-Mercury-Rhythm); and to the subconsciousness (TAMAS-Salt). Sulphur is self-consciousness. The likeness to actual sulphur is the fact that self-consciousness is analytical, that it breaks down form, that it is fiery in its action. Mercury is superconsciousness, and it corresponds to the tendency of things to fall into a rhythm; it is the working of the One Conscious Energy, not through the mind and brain, but through the transformed Pineal Gland, which makes possible this direct knowledge of what is beyond the level of our brain and our waking consciousness which functions there. Mercury is quicksilver (superconsciousness) and makes quick in us the Holy Ghost. Tamas, or Inertia, the tendency of things to remain as they are, stands for subconsciousness— all those phases of the One Energy which are below the level of our self-conscious awareness. These phases include all the involuntary physical functions of the body and all the functions of animal life, plant life, and mineral bodies. The likeness of subconsciousness to Salt is that salt is a preservative and tends to prevent the dissolution of physical forms. This is an essential characteristic of subconsciousness, and it manifests as the Law of self-preservation. It is also the basis of memory. The fourth symbol on the Spokes is that of Dissolution.

Alchemists say, "The Great Work," the work of transforming the body and the Pineal Gland, is accomplished by Dissolution. As change for the worse as well as change for the better is due to the dissolution of form, manifestly, "The Great Work" is accomplished only by the right kind of dissolution. All these three qualities of matter, all these three kinds of consciousness are necessary and desirable, good in their place and bad out of their place. No one is lower or higher than the others; all are Spiritual. *It is necessary to have the three in your life in balanced action in your bodies.* Otherwise you will create badly instead of well. The purpose of Tarot is to teach you how to secure proportionate working in your body. In the Tarot cards you have seven self-conscious cards, seven supercon-scious cards, and seven subconscious cards, preceded by THE FOOL.

At the left of THE WHEEL descends the GOLDEN SERPENT of the One Energy, the mental image of God into the Great Sea of Substance, or Cosmic Mind-Stuff. This represents the Arc of Involution, the involution of the Cosmic Radiant Energy into the conditions of substance and form. It is also the same Energy which THE MAGICIAN draws down from above when he wants to create. From the tip of its tail to its head, 13 points are formed. This Golden Serpent in making these 13 points creates ten loops. The Hebrew Doctrine is that there are ten Emanations or outpourings of the One Energy necessary in order to evolve the Universe we see around us. Thus here you have the mental Gold Serpent of the One Energy, with 13 points and ten loops coming down into the other one-half of the Great Sea of Substance, whose color naturally is BLUE, the color of the subconscious. This descent changes matter by setting into operation its three qualities which had, up to this time, been static in equilibrium. It throws them out of equilibrium and the result is that forms start into being according to the image. Just as on the one side, you see the loops of the Serpent growing ever wider and wider, so these resultant forms once begun keep expanding and expanding, becoming more and more complex. Beginning with the mineral, they pass into the plant, the animal, and the human worlds. This side of THE WHEEL is called involution.

The other side of THE WHEEL represents the present stage of EVOLUTION, or the unfolding after the infolding. It is the teaching of Ageless Wisdom that just half of Evolution has been accomplished, three-quarters of the entire Wheel of Cosmic Day. The human body has been almost perfected but we have just begun to develop the mind, and it has not yet become really human. This card pictures that the mind is still animal. Of course I am speaking of the race. Individuals have developed their minds, have become superhuman. Very few have as yet traveled the second half of the arc of human evolution. Those who have we call the "supermen," or the "masters." As for the rest of us, note two things about the HEAD of this Jackal, which tops the human body. Its EYES are turned in, turned on the vision, turned on a level with the letter "A" (descending God), or ALEPH on THE WHEEL. The wise can just see that the vision of THE FOOL, the destiny of man, is to become as a god—for the next letter, halfway between his head and the arc of evolution, is the letter YOD (the Spirit). He is representative of the higher plane; and up to it, far nearer than the eyes can go, stretch the EARS OF INTUITION.

At the top of THE WHEEL sits the SPHINX, bearing the SWORD OF PROCESSES. His color is BLUE, not only for the chief qualities of the subconscious which he shares (memory of all things which have ever been), but also for quietude—he remains unmoved while THE WHEEL of personalities ceaselessly turns beneath him. He is the synthesis of the four animals in the corners and is presented to you as both male and female, as was the Absolute before He divided Himself into Father and Mother for the purpose of manifestation. In his hand he bears the Sword of the Discrimination of Processes. He carves out personality.

EXPANSION is the keynote of this picture. It is said to be the essential quality of JUPITER. The great pattern of BEING is constant expansion. The Serpent ever-expands in the curves he makes as he descends. The product of his descent into matter (the forms contrived by subconsciousness) contain the growing life which becomes ever more complex as it strives toward the expression of more and more life.

THE WHEEL is made of enlarging concentric circles, and the spokes radiate out from the center. RADIATE OUT FROM THE CENTER! *There is the explanation of the whole matter.*

ALL ENERGY COMES FROM THE ONE SOURCE, AND THE SOURCE FURNISHES THE URGE FOR GROWTH, FOR SELF-EXPRESSION, AND IS NO MERE HUMAN EMOTION. It was active on this planet before the appearance of man. It was active before this planet was created. It formed the nebula, shaped the solar system out of the nebula and organized the kingdoms of Nature below man. It now works through man to make him Superman, and is thus victorious over every form of three-dimensional bondage, achieving rulership over all things, urging civilized man to enter into the next form of Nature—Supermen.

The innermost nature of Being is the eternal tendency of giving. If you have doubt of the nature of your desires, test it for this quality of giving. Will the fulfillment of your desire enable you to give out more life? The Divine Energy came to Earth in order, the Gospel story says, that we might have life and have it more abundantly. This desire to give more abundantly of the Life within you is not only the sole right desire, but is said by those who know to be one that was never disappointing. Here steps in the eternal paradox: *The more you give, the more you have.* On the lower spiral, the more you get, the more you want.

All bodily actions of the mind, emotions, and the physical nature are really a part of the flow of Cosmic Life. The realization of this seems to relinquish all personal desire. That is a colossal joke. It is really a sublimation of personal desire to the nth power. We unite with the Divine Beneficence only when all sense of separateness is blotted out.

Meditation upon the One Self, who sits like the Sphinx at the top of THE WHEEL perfectly motionless in the midst of the flux of Cosmic activity, overcomes the sense of "me"—the personal "me," and puts in its place the sense of the Changeless and Unchangeable I. This is depicted in the card called THE HANGED MAN. Do you not see the joke? You have been thinking of him as a martyr, doubtless. Well, he has substituted for our feeble, intermittent vitality Eternal Oneness with the Eternal One Energy. This attainment is the great reward in which all apparent antagonisms are reconciled. This card is also called the REWARDING INTELLIGENCE OF THOSE WHO SEEK. This Intelligence is the desire to relinquish the petty and to become One with the All. The Intelligence has another name even more specific of the process by which we attain the Intelligence of Desire. It is also called the NATURAL INTELLIGENCE. Jupiter is also called the Intelligence of Desire. The motive of all action is desire, and the function this card stands for is WHIRLING ACTION.

Together with the Wheels are the four sacred animals, who symbolize the four fixed signs of the Zodiac. These are also in the Apocalypse of St. John; but, for an explanation of them in the Spiritual sense, let us rather turn to another allegory, that of the Vault of the Rosicrucians. The Rosicrucian allegory is the inner, or esoteric, meaning of the

Christian allegory of the birth of the Christ-Child, just as there is an inner meaning to the riddle of the Sphinx. It tells you in detail precisely how the Christ-Child, or Christ-consciousness, is born in yourself. It tells you that you must be born again. The Rosicrucian allegory tells you how you can be born again—what you must do to your body in order to be born again.

The floor plan of this Vault is heptagonal. A heptagon, or seven-sided figure, is a figure not to be found in the whole length or breadth of Nature, and not to be worked by any mathematical formula. If you want to divide a circle into seven equal parts preparatory to connecting these parts with straight lines, thus constructing a heptagon, all you can do is to do the best your eye and hand will let you. That is, you can do it only by the trial and error method. You must make it yourself by the dint of your mistakes. That is the reason the heptagon was chosen for this Rosicrucian allegory. So, you must remake your body and mind in life after life, by dint of your own mistakes and the education that comes from them.

It was intended that your desires should at first be dictated by your instincts, and after that by your emotions, after that by your ambitions. All these desires are desires to *Get*—thus you become educated. At length you find these lower desires were not satisfactory, and ultimately you no longer are disillusioned. Then you desire to be, to express, to give, and you cannot arrive at this desire except on the stepping-stones of the lower ones. So in life after life you enlarge your desires. In this work no one can help you and no one can hinder you. The worst that anyone can do is to help you to help yourself. You carve out your own destiny. You yourself can decide whether you make your Vault sooner or later, but for all of us it will one day be made.

The sides of this Vault were all 5 x 8 feet. Thus, there were 40 square feet on a side. Forty is the number of the letter MEM, represented in Tarot by THE HANGED MAN. The Law THE HANGED MAN represents is REVERSAL, the reversal of the desires of the personal self for the desires of the Cosmic Self. The desire to be above THE WHEEL—the reevalution of all things in life.

The line bounding every side is 26, the value of IHVH, so that the seven sides represent the seven aspects of THAT which was, is, and ever shall be—the seven ELOHIM, as the Old Testament calls them; the seven-branched candlestick as the Hebrews call them; and the seven spirits before the throne as the New Testament calls them.

If the walls of the Vault were opened flat, they would make a rectangle whose boundary line is 86, and the number of the word Elohim (the 7 Gods) is 86. In the Vault were pictures painted on the walls of these four mystic, sacred animals, and each was surrounded by a motto. Around the Lion were the words "NOWHERE A VACUUM." The Lion is the same Lion that we see in TETH, meaning the all-pervading Stellar Energy. Whether you think of it as the human body or the Stellar Energy, it is the symbol of the FIERY LIFE-BREATH which the Transformed Heart can put into the body. There is no place where the Stellar Energy is not—it fills all space. It feeds our Sun and the Sun transforming it feeds all the forms in its solar system, and later we, too, can feed the forms.

The BULL symbolizes the Law of Limitation under which all forms must come in order to be forms; they have their limits and they cannot transcend them. The halo of letters around the head of the Bull spells "THE YOKE OF THE LAW." In order for a form to become a form, there must be a limit set; but do not forget that "Yoke" is synonymous with "Yoga," and that "Yoga" means "Union." Do not forget that THE HANGED MAN, the man upside-down, is the only one of us who walks erect; and that Jesus taught, as did all preceding founders of religions, that to lay down your life was the way to find it. In the card THE WHEEL OF FORTUNE, you are to regard the Bull, the body, as coming first. You are to make conquest of the Bull, to recognize and use your limitations. When you recognize and make use of your limitations, you link the Bull up with the OX, the meaning of the letter ALEPH, the LIFE-BREATH, and hence with the Lion on the opposite corner of the card, facing the Bull and fructifying the Bull—the body.

The EAGLE represents the House of Scorpio in its aspect, not of death but of RESURRECTION. You have a double meaning: that which kills as SCORPIO sets free as EAGLE. The force that kills is the same which can be transmuted to the head, and there it exalts. You have the same idea in beating a sword into a ploughshare. Around the Eagle is the motto "THE LIBERTY OF THE GOSPELS," which has the hidden meaning of this transmutation of the reproductive energy typified alike by Scorpio and the Eagle, by means of which death is finally overcome.

The halo around the man's head spells "THE UNTOUCHABLE GLORY OF GOD." "Untouchable" has a hidden meaning which may surprise you. It means "unsmirchable," "cannot be spoiled." That means there is no hell. All men are Angels in the making; nothing can stop man from becoming the Angel. You may fall but you cannot forfeit your divinity; it is "untouchable." The poorest slouch you see on the street is an Angel in the making, and nothing can stop the eventual making, not even the Christian doctrine of an everlasting hell. The Founder of Christianity saw this, whatever his followers have made of his teachings. He condemned nobody but hypocrites. He did not in the least object to keeping what hypocrites called bad company; neither did Buddha. They recognized that in sincere people, be they scoundrels or saints, "The Untouchable Glory of God" appears most distinctly. In the hypocrites it is all smothered and muffled up.

12th Hebrew Letter	*LAMED*
Symbol for	*Work and Action*
Color	*Emerald Green*
Numerical Value	*30*
Syllables	*LMD*
Sound	*F-Sharp*
Translation	*Ox Goad*
Sign in Zodiac	*Libra*

NOTES

JUSTICE

LAMED, spelled in Hebrew LMD, means OX-GOAD. It is the twelfth Hebrew letter and the seventh SIMPLE LETTER. It is the sign or symbol for the function of WORK and ACTION, and for its occult extension; for the direction SOUTHWEST; for the FAITHFUL INTELLIGENCE; for the Zodiacal sign LIBRA, the Scales; for the color GREEN; for the note F-SHARP, and the numerical value is 30. In Roman characters it is written L.

The Hebrew character for LAMED is explained in three ways: as a conventionalized picture of a goad or whip, as a picture of a primitive ploughshare, and as an erect serpent. All of these meanings are intended to be suggested by the form of the letter. It would appear to be particularly the first meaning, since the letter itself stands for OX-GOAD. Naturally we connect the object this letter stands for with the object the letter ALEPH stands for. Aleph, the Life-Breath, is the Ox, and that which incites it to action and directs it in that action is the Ox-Goad.

Until the appearance of man on the Cosmic stage, Nature superintended the cultivation of forms unaided by him; after his appearance on the stage he was given a mind and with that mind he could manipulate Nature. The ploughshare, for example, is an instance of it. So, when man came along, he employed Nature's laws to make adaptations of her, adaptations of the forms she had already produced, adaptations demanded by his needs. As his needs increased, his demands for adaptation increased, his need increased, and hence his adaptations of the forms of Nature. The principle by which Nature works in the production of forms is equilibrium. To make a form of any kind there must be four ingredients, and they must be in equilibrium. Those four are heat and moisture (which are called the male and female principles); then there are two principles called cold and dry (which are called anti-male and anti-female). These four must be used in equilibrium to produce a form. EQUILIBRIUM is the Law for which this card stands.

The Law of Equilibrium is everywhere at work, except in the self-conscious of willful man, and even there it works if we could see it over a sufficient perspective. When a man takes himself in hand, he makes every effort to express the Law of Equilibrium in his self-conscious activities, just as his body expresses it internally in its subconscious activities. He makes every effort to express physical

205

poise, emotional balance, and economic justice; not the tiniest fragment in the field of his activity but can express equilibrium if he will, or lack of balance if he will not. This card pictures man's subconscious at work accommodating herself to the changes wrought in his body by his good images and not his bad ones, though with each her work and her purposes are the same.

This is the 12th Hebrew letter and the 11th Tarot Trump. As you see from the shape of the letter, ALEPH is a synthesis of the succeeding letters; and likewise in the Tarot Trumps the numbering begins with Zero, a card which synthesizes them all. Thus the position of this letter LAMED in the alphabet and of this card JUSTICE in the Tarot Tableau is the same. It begins the second half, so it illustrates equilibrium in itself. Also the sign that goes with this letter and card illustrates equilibrium in itself: LIBRA, the scales. This sign begins the second half of the signs of the Zodiac. The first six are Aries, Taurus, Gemini, Cancer, Leo, and Virgo. The second six are Libra, Scorpio, Sagittarius, Capricorn, Aquarius, and Pisces. Astrologers say that in the circle called Involution-Evolution, the first arc, or the process of the infolding, ends with Virgo and the second arc, or the process of unfolding, begins with Libra. In Tarot the card which comes after Virgo, or Yod, is THE WHEEL OF FORTUNE, and the card which succeeds THE WHEEL OF FORTUNE is JUSTICE, or Libra.

THE WHEEL OF FORTUNE pictures this entire process of Involution-Evolution. The side toward the first six signs of the Zodiac pictures the infolding, the Yellow Serpent coming down into the Blue Sea of Matter. The side toward the second six signs of the Zodiac pictures the unfolding of this Sea of Matter thus impregnated by the Golden Serpent into forms. The forms of Nature are being symbolized by his chief form, man. In the first arc, the down arc, that which we call Nature is worked upon. In the second or upward arc, it is she, Nature, who does the working. She does the working until man comes along to assist her by discovering her laws and utilizing them to adapt these forms for his own purposes. Finally he discovers that he can not only make new forms in Nature but can also make over his own body into a new form, not merely cultivating and refining all its senses, but giving it new functions, new perceptions which Nature unaided could not give it. The ultimate product of the cooperative of man and Nature in this respect is pictured in card 21, the 22nd card of the series.

You have in the Tarot Tableau two series of ten cards each, ending with the 11th card, its summation. In each of these two series and ending each of these two cards which close the series, are the four Sacred Animals. In THE WHEEL OF FORTUNE they are reading their instructions from the White Book of the Spirit so that His Will or images may be carried out on Earth through the forms that they make. In the last card of the series, THE WORLD, this is accomplished. His Will now is done on Earth as it is in Heaven. His Kingdom has come. The summation of Involution is the natural man; the summation of Evolution is the Spiritual man. "Man has sown a natural body; he is reaped a spiritual body," said St. Paul. It is the cultivation (the thing that the ploughshare stands for) of the seed that makes the difference. These cultivations must be done by man himself. Man continues the work of Nature, and now wields the Ox-Goad and steers the ploughshare himself. When he has gained, by his own efforts, the equilibrium which Nature possesses as her birthright, he impresses her with new images and so she makes for him a new body, a body which is capable of making a new world. Toward this completion of herself she has always been looking, if we may believe St. Paul: "All nature groaneth and travaileth for the coming of the Sons of Mind." The "Sons of Mind" are the people who have transformed their hearts. The heart is transformed by influences proceeding from the transformed Pituitary and transformed Pineal Gland. When the heart is transformed, men are entirely governed by Reason. The "Sons of Mind" are the distinctly human beings as different from the human animals, the men who are governed by reason, who have conquered instinct, who express in all their self-conscious activities Equilibrium. When the Law of Nature has become the Law of man, then and not until then, do both Nature and man find their perfect expression. The business of the Transformed Heart (which is the "Son of Mind") is to transform all the rest of the world. We are told that we even can transform the weather.

The number of this card is 11, and 11 reduces to 2. This card, JUSTICE, then, is an aspect of THE HIGH PRIESTESS. The similarities of the two cards are at once apparent. In both, a woman, the sole figure, sits between two pillars with a veil behind her, and the cube she sits upon is the physical world. The contrasts are equally important. THE HIGH PRIESTESS has the poise of acquiescence, and JUSTICE has the poise of confident action. THE HIGH PRIESTESS wears BLUE, the color of MEMORY, while JUSTICE wears RED, the color of DESIRE. All action proceeds from desire. THE HIGH PRIESTESS is doing nothing but holding in her hands the Scroll of the Law, the Will of the

Father. JUSTICE, on the other hand, holds the two implements by which she is working ceaselessly, the Sword and the Scales. Her position itself demands effort and concentration. The Black Veil behind THE HIGH PRIESTESS is embroidered with the symbols of the masculine-in-the-feminine and the feminine-in-the-masculine, the way the two opposing forces typified by the Black and White Pillars are involved in matter to produce the forms commanded by the Scroll of the Law, which she holds in her hands.

When THE HIGH PRIESTESS is at work she becomes THE EMPRESS, cosmically speaking, THE EMPRESS who holds in her hand the scepter which symbolizes the Will, the Image of the TORAH of the Father. In us, THE EMPRESS symbolizes the intellectual sub-conscious, the Will. Thus JUSTICE merely explains the Law by which THE EMPRESS works and the tools she works with. Behind the figure of JUSTICE is a veil of VIOLET-RED. Violet-Red symbolizes the making of better bodies out of previous ones. That is the evolutionary (Cosmic) business of Nature, to make better and better bodies; but it is particularly the business of the subconscious depicted here in this card. Her hair is YELLOW deeply scored with BLACK, and this indicates that the images she receives from the self-conscious, and which she is working to carry out, are occult images.

Anyone who has read Carroll's *Man, the Unknown* has a vivid picture of the incredibly stupendous work of the human subconscious in her tireless adjustments to internal and external changes. What would Caroll have said had he known the vast addition to her normal labors caused by the occultist, who is seeking to create a body eons in advance of normal evolution; a body capable of manifesting a special and high kind of life which is fabulous to most human beings at present? To build such a body, the entire present body must be rebuilt. Subtle chemical and even structural transformations are required in every part of it. In making these changes all the cells of the body are called into action. With every change the scales must be balanced anew and another equilibrium secured by the subconscious—the new diges-tion. New elements must be extracted from the blood, making new elements in the body to transform the bloodstream. New cells must be built in the brain and subtle forces must be extracted from the air outside of the body. Forces as yet unrecognized by chemists, such as new electric currents, must be generated in the body and directed, and color and sound vibrations entirely unused before must be employed. In addition to all this, the subconscious must summon to her aid in the spiritual reconstruction of the body certain outside entities called in telepathically by the Moon Center to help her in this reconstruction—and after every tiny change equilibrium comes.

Do you wonder, then, that the voluminous Red Robe of Action seems almost to blot out the Cube of the physical world upon which she is represented as sitting? For this is the meaning of the curious disposition of her Robe in this picture. The intellectual subconscious, acting under occult instructions from the self-conscious, almost entirely effaces the present physical world of the body and substitutes another world. Of the processes by which she carries out his will, the self-conscious knows only theoretically, if that. He would not know how to manage them, and yet her action in this card is precisely the action of THE MAGICIAN, and illustrates the same equilibrium. One-half of her is active and the other half passive. The hand that brandishes the Sword is as strenuous as his hand that brandishes the Wand. The hand that holds the Scales is as relaxed as his finger from which flows down the White Light that transforms his body. These two active-passive, passive-active processes must work simultaneously—the four of them— in order to create a better Spiritual body. That is one of the meanings of the twin symbols on the Veil of THE HIGH PRIESTESS, the masculine in the feminine and the feminine in the masculine.

The third meaning of the character Lamed is a conventionalized picture of the erect serpent. These occult changes, which in the end construct the Spiritual body, are made possible by the rising of Kundalini, the SERPENT FORCE, from her coiled position at the base of the spine. They are made possible by *the use of sex on the mental plane*, which is the term we employ to characterize the bringing down of the White Light, and the so-called "mystic marriage" of the awakened Pineal and Pituitary Glands. The erect serpent signifying this is somewhat in the nature of a pun, for two serpents performing the sex act stand almost erect.

There are three Serpent Letters in the Hebrew alphabet. In TETH, we saw that the tail of the serpent was above its body on the left side. In SAMEKH, the third Serpent Letter, we shall see that the tail is below its body on the right side. The serpent is represented as swallowing its tail—a symbol of Eternity. In LAMED, the tail is down and almost at the direct opposite of the head.

In these three letters, then, you have pictured the Cosmic process: Teth, of Involution; Samekh, of Evolution; and Lamed, your precise point of standing between the two.

Samekh, you find, pictures the very last stages of the body before it reaches the perfected state, and thus it may well stand for the goal of Evolution. How does Teth stand for Involution? It is the projection into matter of the Stellar Energy transformed by the Sun of our solar system. In the card STRENGTH, the body has become so transmuted that it can itself receive the Stellar Energy and transmit it again, making a miniature involution of its own. These two cards, Teth and Samekh, occupy similar positions as regards Lamed, which stands in the middle of the row. They are hence complementaries and sum up to the middle of the row— 22. Any two cards which sum up to 22 are placed in corresponding positions in the Tarot Tableau, and JUSTICE, or number 11, is the mean, or halfway number, between them. The card with the smaller number represents the active member of the pair which, by the Law of Equilibrium which the center card symbolizes, produces the result indicated in the card with the larger number.

Thus in these three cards the "in-flowing" of the Stellar Energy by means of the Law of Equilibrium results in the mixing of the two psychic streams of Fire and Water in the body; a mixing which is performed in the Solar Plexus, as we saw in studying that card. That card depicted the entire process or cycle of Involution-Evolution.

This card, JUSTICE, is the practical application by you, at this moment, of the Law of Involution-Evolution, or action and reaction. In the measure in which you apply it, you will adjust yourself to your environment, and readjust your environment to your advancement— you utilize it.

You will see the same thing said in the direction of the card, SOUTHWEST. South is the Sun, and West is THE WHEEL. The Christ-Child in you, or the Sun, works out certain specific modes of expression as a result of your mental grasp of the Law of Cause and Consequence typified by THE WHEEL. *JUSTICE is the practical application by you of the Law of Cycles.*

Any unfortunate circumstances you are in are the direct consequence of some action which you once initiated. *You made this circumstance yourself.* How shall you handle it so as to equilibrate that former action and at the same time prevent the cause of a future bad circumstance? That is the reason this card stands for ACTION. Although it chiefly concerns the action of the subconscious, the concrete action of the subconscious is determined by the self-conscious. The body contains many structures of error which, if you want your Mars vibration to break them down, will necessitate a change in your mental pictures or patterns.

As JUSTICE in this card has YELLOW HAIR heavily shaded with BLACK, she indicates the intellectual subconscious of a practical occultist who is seeking by daily technique to reconstruct his body.

SYMBOLISM

The TWO PILLARS that JUSTICE sits between are (like the two pillars of THE HIEROPHANT) the two phases of the subconscious. The side the SWORD is on stands for the Holy Ghost Pillar, for the Sword cuts away, and in this respect agrees with the cleansing function of the Holy Ghost which you see pictured in THE HIGH PRIESTESS card, where her Blue and White Robe flows through the Yellow Crescent. This indicates the intellectual or personal subconscious of the ruler of the body. The other Pillar stands for THE EMPRESS, for the Scales are instruments for weighing and measuring, and according to their findings she makes readjustments by which she secures equilibrium. JUSTICE trims off with the Sword where she weighs off with the Scales. She trims things off until they are in equilibrium.

Her TURRETED CROWN is intended to make you think of Venus, THE EMPRESS. It has in front of it a square, and the four sides of this together with the three turrets give the number seven, which is the number of Venus, and also of THE CHARIOT, the perfected body, made by the perfected action of the Seven Centers. In addition, a crown always indicates dominion, and this one indicates that she rules, in the body, the working of the Seven Interior Stars. The SQUARE in front of it is BLUE, and a square indicates measurement. To reconstruct the body by images requires her to take the measure of the cleansing powers of the Holy Ghost and to summon them to her aid.

The GREEN CAPE also makes you think of Venus. It has TWO TABS. Its two Tabs in front are to carry out the idea of the balance and equilibrium. They are made like serpents to suggest the two streams of Kundalini whose rising in the body quickens the action of the Seven Interior Stars over which she rules.

The BROOCH which fastens the cape is a circle within a square. The square always represents the number 4 and the circle represents the number 22. Twenty-six in all—they stand for IHVH, or the One Energy active in the four worlds. The CIRCLE in the Brooch is RED because it is by the use of Mars vibration that she destroys the structure of error in the body.

The HANDLE of the SWORD and the SCALES are YELLOW to indicate that both are in the service of the mind—to balance and to eliminate requires mental analysis. The BLADE of the huge Sword is BLUE to indicate the Holy Ghost. It is she who directs and makes efficient the elimination which the intellectual subconscious wields in order to reconstruct by the body, although the actual work of destruction is performed by the Mars vibration.

Her POSE, like that of THE MAGICIAN, is a difficult one; but unlike THE MAGICIAN, she did not have to learn it by struggle and failure; it was her birthright. Equilibrium is eternally preserved by Nature, it is the basis of her carrying on. Even with our own limited vision we can see it in certain respects, which are important enough to stand for all the rest. We know, for instance, that day and night are equal if we measure them from the perspective of the entire year. So if we had sufficient perspective we should see that Nature maintains exact equilibrium while all the time spiraling upward. The method of her evolution is exactly expressed in our method of locomotion. We draw the back foot up to the front foot, and always as we are doing it we are out of equilibrium. The process of walking, like the process of evolution, consists in throwing out of equilibrium a previous state in order to get a step further, and then throwing ourselves into equilibrium again, just as in our Cosmic march. We threw the body of the lower animal out of its previous equilibrium when, into the human animal, entered the new factor, the mind. Then we proceeded to get ourselves into equilibrium again. The process demanded, first, that we develop the mind to the place where its control over the body was as absolute as was the old control of the instinct; and second, it demanded that the body, thus infinitely improved by the supervision of the mind, furnish in its turn a better mind. When this second process is completed we are once more in equilibrium. If the evolution is to continue, this equilibrium is only temporary. We must be thrown out of equilibrium again by the power which goads us upward, the LIGHT streaming from the Lantern of THE HERMIT, by the urge implanted in us by the Jupiter vibration. "Man does not hop forward on two feet like the sparrow," Carpenter said brilliantly, "but on one after the other." The sparrow moves solely by the subconscious. Man's progress is both by the subconscious and self-conscious—and both in alternation.

This card is probably the most important in the Tarot Tableau. Some people think that these cards are derived from an ancient Egyptian word: the Law of Equilibrium, or Tarot. I have already shown that its central position makes it perform a unique service—as equilibrator between complementary cards, which are all placed in corresponding opposite positions in regard to card 11. In addition, JUSTICE forms a part of three sequences. It is one of the four cards which represent the Venus vibration, the Saturn vibration, and the element of Air. This prominence is possessed by no other card.

The Venus vibration superintends the whole body chemistry and thus is the basis of all the reactions of the personality—not only physical, but also emotional and mental—for, as is our chemistry so is our personality. The Saturn vibration restricts, binds, limits, and sets problems which we must solve. Physical, emotional, and mental poise and balance are the result of the right understanding and use of limitation. Without limitation there can be nothing but diffusion. You cannot achieve without limitation; so to handle your limitations wisely is to have poise and balance.

The SWORD OF JUSTICE has a TAU HANDLE; Tau is the letter that goes with the last card, THE WORLD, which depicts the Saturn vibration and our state of boundless and joyous activity when we have learned to utilize the Saturn vibration. Limitation is the handle which enables us to grasp and wield the Sword of Action. If it had no handle we would cut ourselves. With that Sword the self-conscious should cut off all that is wasteful and unnecessary, whatever does not contribute to a well-poised, balanced self-expression. That is what your subconscious is doing in the body. Just as the kidneys, ruled by Libra, rids the body of waste which would otherwise poison us, so right action made possible by right knowledge of the Saturn principle of limitation enables us to get rid of self-conscious waste. We do not, fortunately, have to worry about our subconscious not being on the job, not attending to her business; she does it always. She is the one who needs to worry about us and our faithful attention to our job; and the truthful interpretation of our dreams shows us that she does worry. Our self-conscious part is to get rid of the obstacles which we continually place in the way of the subconscious doing her job.

We do that by looking out for our thinking and wishing. Thinking and desiring are bodily activities as much as any other one. If we think and desire wrongly we hamper her. *We, the self-conscious, must cut away every detail which we do not wish to make permanent in our bodies.* If we sow in our bodies the seeds of fear, of doubt, of indecision, of which the New Testament calls "filthy imaginings," these will surely spring up there and bear fruit a thousandfold. These are the "Dragon's Teeth" of the Greek myth, which if sown into the Earth spring up as armed men. Also we must learn not only to use our image-making faculty wisely, but also to use our time, talk, and our money wisely too. Time, talk, and money are the most valuable counters to him who leads a mystic life. They should not be spent frivolously. There is only so much time and it should be husbanded. We cannot follow everything, every course. We must select the course most desirable to us and cut out everything which diverts or retards us from our objective. This by no means cuts out amusement and relaxation; rather these are means to further us on our journey—but it does mean choosing these amusements wisely. You have only to look at your own lives to see how few amusements really relax and amuse. Most of our talk is not only a waste of time but destructive to our ends. What is the sense of our endless, useless discussions of hopes and aims with people who are not actually interested in them? What is the use or sense of having the last word? Particularly should the occultist remember this! He is duty-bound when the right occasion offers to exhibit his wares, but he should not try to force them down people's throats. To do so only puts off the day when their interest shall awaken and make them seek what you now so vainly storm them with. Or, if by any reason of your personal vigor and eloquence you coerce them, you only increase their responsibility and your own.

JUSTICE forms one of the four cards devoted to the element of Air. LIBRA is an Airy sign. THE FOOL and ALEPH represent the LIFE-BREATH, the life principle of the Universe and its localized manifestation in any object. As well as representing the Soul of man, he represents the vital principle in all things. The finest and highest expression of the Life-Breath is THOUGHT. The highest expression of Thought is the ABSTRACT THOUGHT, which comes to us in the act of occult Meditation and which it is the function of our brain to make concrete. Through this Meditation we unveil the truth about Nature, the eternal feminine principle ever at work with Sword and Scales. To perceive the Cosmic Mother as she is, to understand her Laws and live in harmony with them, is the goal of man's thoughts.

In Tarot, work and faith are tied up together, since both are attributed to the letter LAMED. "Faith without works is dead," said St. James, and so is work without faith. What is faith? The blind acceptance of some supposed authority, says religion, says common usage, says the dictionary. St. Paul gave the accurate definition of faith in the occult sense of the term: *Faith is the substance of things unseen. Faith is the image which in time clothes itself in a body of manifestation.* Faith in the occult sense cannot be without works, for every image is bound to work itself out.

JUSTICE stands for NATURE AND THE WAY SHE WORKS. What she is working out are the images of God. Those images are clear, definite, altogether good; and when we have perfected our bodies we shall see in all things great and small "the Beauty of Divine Expression." Faith is the confident expectancy that your image, the image that you make, will finally manifest. *Right Brothers*

More importantly, JUSTICE stands for NATURE SEGREGATED IN OUR BODIES. There she is working out our images as well as she can, considering their variance with the images of God. In so doing she is faithful both to His Laws and to our images. If you don't like the result—imitate God. Make your images clear, definite, and altogether good instead of blurred, vacillating, and based upon the fallacy of so-called self-will. In pursuance of them the Faithful Intelligence will fabricate for you a body capable of manifesting those images—capable in time, of those higher perceptions which will make you *see* that the Law of Equilibrium is the basis of Life.

Meanwhile, let your images find physical expression in external purposeful action. It is a fortunate law of life that if we act upon an assumption, we get the same actual results as when we act upon knowledge, else there could be no progress, no manifestation.

Assume that everywhere in this Universe—except in your own mind deluded by the fallacy of self-will—the Sword and the Scales of Equilibrium are ever at work. See to it that you make every effort to express that Law in your thoughts, emotions, and external activities. Nature will do the rest.

NOTES

THE HANGED MAN.

13th Hebrew Letter	*MEM*
Symbol for	*Stable Intelligence*
Element Attributed to	*Water*
Color	*Deep Blue*
Numerical Value	*40 and Some-times 600*
Syllables	*MIM*
Sound	*G-Sharp*
Planet	*Neptune*
Translation	*Seas or Water*

NOTES

THE HANGED MAN

MEM, spelled MIM, means SEAS or WATER. It is the 13th Hebrew letter and the second MOTHER LETTER. It is the sign or symbol for the element WATER; for the STABLE INTELLIGENCE; for the planet NEPTUNE; for the color BLUE; for the note G-SHARP. In Roman characters it is written M. Its numerical value is 40, except at the end of the words when it sometimes has the value of 600.

This is one of the five letters which take another character when they come at the end of a word. These five are called "finals" exoterically; esoterically, they are called the Letters of Judgement. As you will see from your card, they all extend below the line of writing except in this final MEM.

In this case the numerical value of the letter-name, MIM, points to the same close affiliation with another letter, as you saw that Kaph had with Qoph. The value of the letter is 40, but the value of the letter-name, Mim, is 90; two M's and a Yod, 90 is the value of the letter TZADDI, card 18, THE STAR.

Let us now inspect somewhat carefully and minutely (1) the letter Mem, (2) its similarity to Teth, and (3) the similarity of Final Mem to Samekh.

(1) You will find the component parts of the letter Mem in Gimel and Kaph. One side of the letter is made by the top part of Gimel, and the other side is made by Kaph. The two parts just touch at the top and do not touch at the bottom. As in Gimel, the line which descends from the Yod continues externally. The idea symbolized here in both these letters is the same. The Water of the Holy Ghost (that is the fluid Cosmic Mind-Stuff not yet worked up into form) flows like a stream through the body and out of the body; it is not ours, but only ours to use while it flows through. The parallelogram symbolizing the physical body in Kaph is the same as in Mem. The top part symbolizing the descent of Solar Energy into the body is slightly altered, and in the same fashion the top part of Gimel is slightly altered. The two symbolize the vivified Pituitary and the vivified Pineal. These two not only perform individual functions in the occult body, but when united in the so-called "mystic marriage" have another function to perform—that of transforming the heart and bringing to birth there the Christ-Child. This new function is depicted as the eighth Golden Star in the card TZADDI, THE STAR; while the other seven stars,

219

which are White, depict the seven interior planets, purified. As all true stars are suns, it is this star which is represented in Card 19 as THE SUN. This union of the Pineal and Pituitary is depicted in the letter Mem as increasing in intensity and as making more direct the downpour of the Solar Energy into the body.

(2)   The general outline of the letter Teth and the letter Mem are alike, but in detail there are two important differences. The two Yods no longer touch at the top in Teth, and the parallelogram at the bottom has vertical instead of slanting sides. Final Mem has this same vertical parallelogram, and in Samekh one side is vertical and the other slanting. This one side is the only item in which Samekh differs from Final Mem.

(3)   The confusing similarity in these two is emphasized by the facts that the meaning of Samekh is "prop" or "foundation," and Mem is called THE STABLE INTELLIGENCE. It is the foundation which renders the house stable, and thus the ideas the two letters stand for are the same. In the card SAMEKH, or TEMPERANCE, you will see the Angel of the Sun, or the Higher Self, mixing the two psychic streams of Water and Fire in the body. The Higher Self, or HIEROPHANT, is but the masculine aspect of THE HIGH PRIESTESS, or the Holy Ghost. This fact you will see depicted throughout the Hebrew alphabet, where the line descending from the Yod in Gimel is curved, the Yod being in either case the same. The work done by the Angel in the card TEMPERANCE does not complete the transformation of the body. It would appear that this transformation is depicted as complete in both Teth and Final Mem. The square almost outlined by the Samekh is fully outlined by the Final Mem, the only letter making a square in the Sacred Alphabet. One cannot but recall the lines in the Book of Revelation: "And he showed me that great city, the holy Jerusalem, descending out of the heaven from God, and the city lieth four-square, and the length and the breadth and the height of it are equal."

The aspect of Water represented by THE HIGH PRIESTESS card which we were concerned with earlier was the fact that she unites everything—because she *was* everything in the beginning. Everything was made out of her. Therefore there is a common bond between all creatures or things because they are made out of Cosmic Mind-Stuff, or Substance. The card particularly stresses the fact of taking the image that the Father stamped her with. She has in her hands the SCROLL of the Law, the TORAH, and the White Cross on her breast. She takes the image of the Father in just the same way as you saw in

THE WHEEL OF FORTUNE card, the Water with the Snake going down into it, penetrated down into it by a series of curves. This card tallies also with THE HIGH PRIESTESS.

In the official Hebrew religion, the institutionalized religion of the State, some of the people suppressed the part the feminine principle played in the process of Creation, although the Hebrew sages never did. Just so, it pleased the Catholic Church when it early became the tool of the State to announce that the Trinity consisted of three male members. It was the program of Europe to minimize the position of woman in evolution and contribute to her subjection by man.

We have seen that the true meaning of the Garden of Eden allegory had to do with the feminine principle in man, the subconscious, and not with woman. That it was not woman who was ordained by Jehovah to be subject to her lord, but the subconscious to be subject to the conscious. In the same fashion the allegory of the Virgin Mary was mistranslated by the Church as it began to have dreams of power and to curry favor with the State. All suggestion of a feminine principle was eliminated and they announced that the Holy Ghost was a male proceeding from the Father and the Son. Popular demand then insisted upon the inclusion of a feminine principle personified as a woman. The comforting doctrine of the Virgin Mary came forth in about the third century. She was not admitted as a member of the Trinity but soon became the intercessor for humanity with the three others. The whirligig of time brought in its revenges. Though she was admitted by the back door, as it were, she became practically the mistress of the house. None of the Trinity can rival her importance in the mind of the average uneducated Catholic, nor would the occultist contest that importance. For to him the Trinity as put forward by theology is nonexistent. Jesus, the Christ, is not the only begotten Son of God but a Spiritual attitude we ourselves create within our bodies by a psychical-physical process. The Virgin Mary is the Holy Ghost, and it is she who cleanses our personal subconscious from its acquired taints and unites our will to the Will of the Father.

In the Paul Case card, THE HANGED MAN is suspended between the Spirit and the Intellect and takes the place of THE HIGH PRIESTESS between the White and Black pillar. How is this accomplished? Another item in this card informs you. His head hangs below the surface of the earth in a hollow between the two trees, a hollow which suggests an old watercourse. If the water were flowing through it, it would flow right through his head. THE HIGH PRIESTESS is the untainted Cosmic

Mind-Stuff. When the current of the untainted Cosmic Mind-Stuff flows through the man's head and he has stilled entirely his personal mind, he *is* THE HIGH PRIESTESS. This untainted Cosmic Mind-Stuff the Book of Revelations calls "The Water of Life." It is an apt name, for it is out of this Water that all life was made. Both the mystic Hebrew alphabet and the alchemists called it Water.

The conscious act of letting the Cosmic Mind flow through our heads is called occult Meditation. Meditation is the rigid holding of the brain to one concept, and this concept should be of value in purifying us. St. Paul said, "Be ye transformed by the renewing of your minds, and whatsoever things are lovely and of good report, think on these things." *MEDITATION IS THE COMPLETE SUSPENSION OF THE INTELLECT.*

HANGED MAN also means *suspended mind,* because the words "man" and "mind" are from the same Sanskrit root. When personal consciousness is suspended so that all its activities are stilled, one enters into communication with the absolute consciousness. This stilling of all personal consciousness is a very difficult thing. It has to be learned by the trial and error method. "And let him that is athirst come, and whosoever will, let him take of the water of life freely." Here is the usual double meaning. It should be read "whosoever WILL," for to still the active brain requires the strongest exertion of will, and then practice besides. In the above quotation, Paul has expressed the results of the habit of occult Meditation when firmly established. The mind is made new and the mind then remakes the body. The Book of Revelation thus expresses it: "And I saw a new heaven (meaning the mind) and a new earth (meaning the body), for the first heaven and the first earth were passed away; and there was no more sea." (Sea means the welter of emotion which tosses us about.)

The word "Stable" in the expression Stable Intelligence refers to the fixed, firm, unshakable consciousness typified by this card, once we can acquire it by the habit of occult Meditation. Stable is exactly the reverse of all our ideas of water. We say, "as unstable as water," but we are thinking only of the movement of water. As a matter of fact, water itself is of all the combinations of the elements the most stable, the hardest to disintegrate—only electricity will do it. All religions have taught that water is the original thing, that water is primary. "In the beginning," it is written in Genesis, "the earth was water, without form and void, and darkness was upon the face of the deep, and the Spirit of God moved upon the face of the water."

Occultism explains the process of the Stable Intelligence. The image-making faculty of the One Will devised the archetypes and projected them into this sea of matter. From this sex relationship between masculine and feminine principles, forms were finally created in physical plane matter bearing the shape of the original images in mental matter. The four stages of this process you see symbolized by the four concentric enlarging circles in various cards in the Tarot. The process as a whole is symbolized by the Serpent descending into the sea in card 10. *As in God, so in man.* The four stages by which He created are symbolized by the implements upon THE MAGICIAN's table. Both in God and man the self-conscious Will precedes and the subconscious takes form accordingly. The intelligence of the body must always be kept inferior to the intelligence of mind, although they are in reality equals. The Solar Intelligence must never be put out by the Lunar Intelligence. A perfect picture of this occurs during an eclipse of the Sun by the Moon, and darkness in daytime is spread over the face of the Earth.

The number of this card (12) shows that it particularly relates to the relation that should always exist between the self-conscious and the subconscious. Twelve is a combination in digits of power of THE HIGH PRIESTESS working out through THE MAGICIAN. Since Hebrew numbers were in the first place Hebrew letters, they must be read in a similar fashion, from right to left, the last number occurring first, 2 through 1. *We should never let the subconscious have free play. Even when the heart is transformed and we will to follow the dictates of the heart, we must always use our will in the matter.*

That is one of the grave sins of the Church—to let subconsciousness have free play. The whole aim of religious service is to impress the subconscious properly; yet scarcely any sect would admit that at certain times and seasons it deliberately organizes to work its communicants up into mass hysteria. Revival services, whether in Catholic or in Protestant religions, are nothing but this. Brains are not by chance in the top of the head. They are there because they are the last thing in evolution, and they must never be subject to explosions from below. "He that ruleth his Spirit," says the Bible, "is greater than he who rules armies," and the Spirit which inhabits the body can be ruled only by the waking consciousness. The Light in the brain must never be put out in order that the Fire of the body may blaze more brightly.

Meditation is the suspension of the personal mind. Its continued habit results in an entire reversal of the usual way of thinking, an entire reversal of the mental attitude. The very basis of the occult approach to life is the reversal of the usual way of thinking and doing.

This Jesus was saying all the time. He summed it all up in his famous words: "He that gaineth his life shall lose it and he that loseth his life for my sake shall gain it." In detail, he spoke of many reversals of the ordinary values and estimates. A man demands to know why he should do a thing before he goes ahead and does it. Jesus said: "He that doeth my will, he alone shall know the doctrine." A man thinks he is doing very well if he does not speak or act upon a harmful thought. Jesus taught that *to make an emotional image is as bad as committing the deed.* Ordinary morality extends only as far as refraining from evil.

The occultist teaches (as indeed does Freud) that unless you put the energy to use in doing corresponding good, you might as well have committed the evil. The occultist teaches that passivity is worse than thinking, desiring, and acting badly; that the desire to alone possess is a mistaken desire, and the desire to try to control another's actions is the worst desire in the world. The only wise desire is to do the Will of Him that sent you. To use the personal mind and let it direct your actions is the negative way of using the Law; to surrender your mind to the Universal Mind and let it direct your actions is the positive way. That surrender is shown in the picture of THE MAGICIAN, which seems the very quintessence of personal power, but very clearly he is deriving all his power from a higher Source.

The final stage of the alchemical process is typified by THE HANGED MAN. It is the unfoldment of that stage of consciousness expressed by Jesus when he said: "I and my Father are one." This is the only possible basis for the emancipation of the Will, and only by this means, that of laying down his imaginary personal Will, can a man carve out his future. When he has arrived at the stage depicted by THE HANGED MAN, the conditions of human existence, which seem so hard as flint and unalterable to others, become fluid and easily molded. The preliminary stage to this is the remolding of his own body. This mental consciousness comes about only through structural changes in the physical body—changes depicted in card 18, which are called the Corporeal Intelligence. That card is assigned to Pisces, which governs the feet. This is why the feet of THE HANGED MAN are Yellow like the radiation from his head.

SYMBOLISM

Here is a TREE to which a man is bound. The Tree takes the form of a TAU CROSS. The word *tree* and the word *stable* have the same numerical value in Hebrew. To some extent the words are synonymous in our own minds, for we say "as sturdy as a tree." The Tau Cross has always been regarded as the symbol of Life and Salvation. In ancient times the mark TAU was set upon those who were acquitted by their judges. Military commanders placed it upon those soldiers who came out of battle unharmed. Among the Druids it was a sacred symbol. They looked through the forest until they found a tree which could be stripped of its branches until it assumed the shape of a Tau. They then consecrated it with solemn services and ceremonies and cut the word upon it. Thereafter it became a temple and a sanctuary to anyone fleeing from his enemy. The main idea of this picture we are apt to overlook because of our emotional association with the thought of a man bound upside down upon a tree. If you think he deserves any pity, turn the card upside down and you will receive a very different emotional impression. Then he seems dancing in joyous freedom.

The tree represents Cosmic Law, and the main meaning of the picture is that we are totally dependent upon Cosmic Law. This in itself is a reversal of most people's way of thinking. Most people refuse to admit that they and all their actions are the product of forces larger than themselves. They willfully blind themselves to the fact that our life is absolutely dependent upon the Cosmic system. This Tree is a *living* one. The LEAVES are here not solely to indicate THE EMPRESS but to enforce the fact that the wood is alive and growing. This is also the reason that the wood is colored ORANGE (the Red of Action on the Yellow of Solar Enlightenment), which is the color of the super-conscious.

That which binds the man to the Tree is somewhat blurred in the picture. His ANKLE is bound by a ROPE, and the rope is twisted of a YELLOW AND GREEN STRAND. Yellow is for the mind, the image-making faculty; and Green is for the intellectual subconscious, the image-executing faculty.

He is suspended by his RIGHT FOOT. It is the self-conscious that must do the thinking for him if he is to suspend himself in this position: it must not be prescribed by the appetites, emotions, and ambitions of the body. He is suspended by one foot. This, as so often, is in the nature of a pun: only when we are suspended by *Oneness* are we at rest.

This man is really a pendulum come to rest. The thought intended here is that until the great reversal, until we realize that there is but one Will in the world, we are swung to and fro by our subconscious, by the desires of the body. When we realize the One Will, we come to rest. When we are under the delusion that we have a will of our own, we are tossed to and fro, swayed back and forth by our ever-shifting objectives. Suspend yourself from what you want to *be* and *not* from what you want to *get*. The fulfillment of desire is exactly the opposite of what most people think. Desire only breeds more desire. Said Stevenson: "Whatsoever else a man was put on earth for, it was not his own consciousness to succeed; for he has no sooner attained one thing than he desires something further on; no man ever yet felt himself really to have succeeded." This is true. There is but one thing in the world capable of imparting the feeling of success. That is your personal identification with the One Energy.

This youth hanging to the Tree by one foot has WHITE HAIR. In this he resembles THE EMPEROR and THE HERMIT. His mental vibrations are the same as those of the "Ancient of Days." He now feels himself divine beause for the moment he has gone back to his Source and identified himself with It. His object is to keep that feeling all the time, not merely to get it in the act of meditation.

The SOLAR RADIATION is streaming from his head with the White Hair—which means that his brain is stilled of every personal thought. His FEET have the same YELLOW, they carry out the errands of the impersonal mind. There is no action in the feet themselves, they go where they are propelled. The action is in the legs, as the agent of the thighs whence the action arises. Hence his LEGS and THIGHS are colored RED. They take the form of a cross because they are the legs of a man who has laid down his so-called Personal Will. A cross means both self-consciousness and sacrifice. A sacrifice of the lower life to the higher one, of the lower Will to the higher one, of the body to the real Self which inhabits that body. That sacrifice is performed by the mind. We offer up our lower selves as a sacrifice to our Higher Selves, when in our brain the Solar Light is burning and not the lunar.

The man's DOUBLET is BLUE, the color of the subconscious. It is the subconscious that becomes the superconscious, that is, THE EMPRESS when she has identified herself with THE HIGH PRIESTESS. That which converts the subconscious into the superconscious, THE EMPRESS into THE HIGH PRIESTESS, is just the great reversal which this card 12 stands for.

We now come to the subtlest items in the card: his curious position with the ELBOWS CROOKED and HANDS BEHIND HIS BACK. They are meant to suggest the base line of an equilateral triangle. If you draw imaginary lines to the upper point of his hair, as sides of the triangle, you get an inverted equilateral triangle. If you draw imaginary lines to the upper point of his hair, as sides of the triangle, you get an inverted equilateral triangle. The whole figure now becomes a Water triangle under a cross. Now look at card 10, at the symbol on the Wheel which stands for Sulphur (and Sulphur, you recall, stands for the mind). What is it? A triangle with the point up, a Fire triangle, standing upon a cross. The figure of THE HANGED MAN is just the reverse. He is the Transmuted Mind. The Mind which is not objective but subjective. The Mind which does not break down in analysis, but the Mind which in Meditation grasps the synthesis; the Mind which has lost its own will in identification with the One Will.

The number of this card is 12. Twelve reduces to 3. Thus the number emphasizes the importance of THE EMPRESS. You see the leaves which indicate this sprouting all over the Tree, and you see that the man is bound to it by a rope which is half her color. Meditation perfects you in the control and direction of your image-making power. THE EMPEROR bears in his hand the scepter of THE EMPRESS, of Imagination. This signifies that *rulership comes from the right use of the image-making faculty.* "Man" in Sanskrit means "mind," and mind is the combination of Reason and Imagination. Here is this combination hanging upon the Tree; the cross is 4 and the triangle is 3. The legs compose the cross, or Reason, that this man uses only to carry out his superconscious instructions, only to make objective his subjective thought which he has received from his contact with the Wisdom of THE HIGH PRIESTESS.

Alchemists designate the element of Water by the equilateral triangle standing on its point. The element of Fire, for which there is also a Mother Letter, is designated by the same equilateral triangle standing on its base. Therefore the two elements are the same but manifest differently. Fire and Water are one force but two currents— the one flowing up, the other flowing down. The Will is the Fire, the Substance is the Water. The Life Power for the purpose of manifestation divides itself into the two. *When Will penetrates Substance it brings forth forms.*

The material of our bodies is but Cosmic Mind-Stuff. Its most important forms in our bodies are secreted in our nerves, our veins, and in the lymphatic ducts. All these secretions are fluid. They are directly influenced, shaped, and formed by our mental imagery, through the agency of the two nervous systems, the cerebrospinal and the sympathetic. First our mental imagery modifies the nerve fluid, and thus modified, it affects the vital secretions and so changes the chemistry of the blood and the lymph.

The process of alchemy takes place in and through the human body by means of the blood. It is not safe to begin the mental practice of purifying the mind through the act of occult Meditation until we have to some extent purified the body. When the alchemist uses the term "water" he means the Cosmic Substance worked up into the blood and the nerve matter, and specialized in the blood and nerve currents. The purification of this water must be the first work of the alchemist; the physical side of this purification consists in choosing his food carefully, in regulating his eating, in controlling his sex life, and seeing that his kidney elimination is what it ought to be. The mental side of this purification consists in guarding his thoughts and emotions, and thus by his mental imagery, he imposes truer patterns upon the cells of his body, which gradually reshape themselves to his new attitudes. How is it they can do this? *Because the mind controls the body.* The mental vibrations of the Life-Breath are more rapid than the slower and grosser vibrations of the physical plane. Our minds are of the mental plane, our bodies of the physical plane. Furthermore, the physical vibrations of the human brain (the engine of the mind) are the most powerful of all physical vibrations.

Therefore mental imagery is always the controlling force which modifies physical conditions in your body first, then in externals. Your present physical condition is the outpicturing of your predominant mental imagery as developed in this and other lives. Change the pictures and you will change first your body, then your environment. Not all at once because you have not yet developed skill enough to transform your physical conditions quickly. When one is skilled enough to change them quickly, it is called a miracle. If you will keep certain mental pictures always in the field of your mental vision, they will ultimately materialize. This is what makes Tarot so valuable. It gives you an easy way to keep the right mental pictures always in your physical eye. Man, even at his most undeveloped stage, is the son of the Creator of the Universe which He created by mental imagery; therefore, even when man is at his most personal, he is still a true creator. When he relinquishes the personal altogether as typified by THE HANGED MAN, he becomes the center of the directing Will of the Universe symbolized by THE HERMIT.

The letter-name MEM (M=40; I or YOD=10; M=40) totals 90,

which is the value of the letter TZADDI. Tzaddi has the Zodiacal sign Aquarius. The Aquarian Age has just opened. We are told that the time is at hand when the control of all the subhuman states of existence will be generally understood and practiced; it will be done by Meditation. All humanity will to some degree partake of this knowledge and power. Naturally its highest levels will be reserved for those who have become most proficient in the difficult art of Meditation, the art of suspending the mind so that without the slightest interference of personal thought, communication may be opened with the Absolute Consciousness. If accomplished, we may learn the truth about natural Law. The Zodiacal sign Aquarius, which goes with Tzaddi, means "Man the Angel." There is a way man becomes the Angel, and that way is by suspending the personal mind.

The letter Tzaddi stands for the revelation of the Truth about Nature as perceived in the art of Meditation. The letter Tzaddi means "drawing into your own mind the Cosmic Mind-Stuff," and the letter Mem stands for the Cosmic Mind-Stuff.

NOTES

14th Hebrew Letter	*NUN*
Symbol for	*Motion or Change*
Color	*Blue-Green*
Numerical Value	*50 and Sometimes 700*
Syllables	*NUN-NVN*
Sound	*G-Natural*
Translation	*Fish*
Sign in Zodiac	*Scorpio*

NOTES

DEATH

ﬤ NUN, spelled in Hebrew NVN, means FISH. It is the 14th
Hebrew letter and the eighth SIMPLE LETTER. It stands for
the occult extension of MOTION or CHANGE; for the direction NORTHWEST; for the Zodiacal sign SCORPIO, the Scorpion;
for the color BLUE-GREEN; for the note G-NATURAL. The numerical value is 50, except when it is a final at the end of a word, then the
value is 700, and except at the end of the letter-name NVN, where it
has the value 50. The two N's are 50 each, the V is 6; the value of the
letter-name NVN is 106.

This 106 is the number which relates to the practice of the work
which will eventually make the personality equal to the Father. In the
Bible, Joshua was the son of NUN. Joshua was the first Jesus and Jesus
is a spelling of the same name. The first syllable of Jesus or Joshua is
the first syllable of JEHOVAH, or IHVH. The name Joshua, or Jesus,
means that which liberates the Self, or God in you. This liberation is
accomplished by DISSOLUTION, the willed destruction of cells.

The purpose of the practice of occult Dissolution is to achieve
control of the physical, emotional, and mental in the body. The letter
NUN is almost identical with the letter GIMEL. Between the two is
only the tiniest difference, yet it indicates the greatest difference in the
world. In Gimel the vertical line just touches the side of the parallelogram
which symbolizes the body; in Nun the vertical is carried into the
parallelogram and becomes a part of it. This pictures that the control
which Nature always possesses over her processes has been acquired
by dint of hard effort by the self-conscious also; and the self-conscious
uses this acquisition to transform his body; that is to say, to continue
the work of Nature.

THE HIGH PRIESTESS is depicted as sitting between the Black
and White Pillars, holding the exact balance between them and utilizing
each as she needs them. In this card the place of the Black and White
Pillars is taken by the Black Rider on the White Horse and the White
Rose on the Black Pennant. These two depict the same double interchange
of opposites as is shown on her veil—the masculine in the feminine
and the feminine in the masculine. The object of the occultist is to
make his EMPRESS one with THE HIGH PRIESTESS. This union is
depicted in this card, as in THE EMPRESS card, by the Waterfall. The
union of the two the occultist accomplishes by Dissolution—the

233

dissolution of those things which are ready to die, as the Book of Revelation terms them. You will see the same story told in the tonal scale: G-sharp stands for THE HIGH PRIESTESS; F-sharp for THE EMPRESS; the note that interposes between the two is G, the note of Nun, occult Dissolution.

The physical mechanism is the Seven Interior Stars. How does it happen that you can do all this? By the Seven Stars you raise the rate of vibration—all etheric cells in the neighborhood. They each control certain zones in the body—the seven zones—and all the etheric cells in those zones which cannot raise their rate of vibration, which cannot readjust to the higher vibration either because they are lazy or because they are stubborn. They are shaken loose to be whirled out of their body, and instead new cells which are built stand the new pace. Not having been in the body before, the new cells are not set in their ways and do not insist on working in the old fashion. The etheric body is the pattern of the dense physical body. The denser body must of course change also to the exact response.

In the meantime you are changing the mental and emotional body; the new intellectual cells are making new patterns, so the old and emotional bodies are changing also. Old cells are being eliminated, and your old rhythm, your old motives, are starved to death. All your foolish opinions and prejudices gradually die out because you are building in new mental matter and new emotional matter capable of being worked up into new cells which can stand the higher rate of vibration. It is this deliberate, intentional, willed death in your body which makes possible such a change in your organism and habits. In time, that body in which you live does not die. *It becomes consciously immortal.*

You remake the cells which you have killed off by the occult use of the Mars vibration and by the employment of occult images. The process of "willed cell death" and "willed cell reconstruction" according to a new pattern is what makes possible our change of habits and organism, so that eventually we may become immortal.

The Masters tell us that they were once persons like ourselves. Even Jesus, the Christ, in the Gospel stories, is a person in all respects like ourselves. He had learned emotional control over himself in other lives by the experimental method. It is through control over the secret inner fact of sex that the control over the emotional body is gained. The Masters all built themselves in the end a physical body different from that of the average human being in that it has powers that the average person has not and cannot possess. It sustains vibrations that formally it could not sustain. It cannot die until the Masters wish it to do so; it has new powers, thus it would not deteriorate. We are told that some of the Masters, strangely enough, do not desire a young body, but arrest the body they had when they became Masters. It is this deathless Solar Body which is one of the several things symbolized by the Rising Sun in this card 13. Another thing symbolized by the Rising Sun in the card 19 is the awakened and fully functioning Pineal and Pituitary functioning as One.

Mars is the destructive force which, when well used, destroys in order to create better forms. Astrologers say that Scorpio is the house of Mars by night and that Aries is the house of Mars by day. The esoteric meaning of this statement is that Nun is the ruler of form in the World of Formation, and Heh is the ruler of form in the Archetypal World. Once forms leave the Archetypal World they must constantly change; they must be born, mature, decrease, and die, to be reborn again and continue the same process. In the Archetypal World forms never change. They remain always at maturity in full possession of all their powers. In the physical world we can learn to employ ever-destructive Mars force in such a way as to continually construct better forms until at last our form in the physical world is an identical body, equipped with the 15 extensions of perceptions and faculties which the human form possesses in the Archetypal World. This card depicts how the necessary changes are made in the body. All forms must constantly change and what changes them is your manner of thinking—images that you make!

It is said that the figures in this card refer to certain changes which were to take place midway in the Piscean Age (at which time these cards were given out). The old monarchical idea of government was to go. Thus you see the advancing horse trampling down a king who now lies dead under his feet. Then the power of the Church and Piscean religion was to go. You see the Prelate, wearing the Fish Mitre, begging for his life while he is about to be trampled down.

The Ancient Wisdom has always taught its students the true nature of sex. "I came," said Jesus, "to teach both the quick and the dead." The quick were the esoteric students, and the dead the multitude who must be taught by parables and allegories. Such an allegory is the Christian teaching, though now much corrupted from its original purity. The false modesty, which the Christian Church has been so largely responsible for, must be replaced by a high and reverential attitude for the centers where the Fire of Life is most active in the human body. In each of these centers—the Mars Center, which is distinctly a sex center, the Sacral Center, and the Solar Plexus Center—resides the SERPENT FORCE. By Imagination the Serpent Force in these three centers is lifted to the heart and is changed there into nerve force. This transformation goes into the three higher centers, and through this transformation the Scorpion becomes the Eagle. It is the same sex force. All that is changed is the mode of its expression.

The Bible is always talking about regeneration, and although the Christian Church has not explained the term, it means being generated again. You are generated in the second place just as you were generated in the first place (by the sex force), but by a new use of it. It has nothing to do with the reproductive function of the external sex organism. That is to say, the sex force at its higher use is a nerve force.

It is said that even the multitude will, in the Aquarian Age, be told the nature and the inner facts of sex. The monarchical form of government and the Christian religion must go, as well as the idea that women and children are the chattels of men. This idea the Christian Church has stood for, thus supporting the contention of the State. "Woman," said St. Paul, "should find a voice only in her father or her husband or in her 52 male cousins (52 reduced to 7—NVN, value of Nun) if she had not been able to buy herself a husband." In the Middle Ages no woman could marry who was not able to buy her man. Also the Church upheld the contention of the State that children belonged to their parents and had no jurisdiction over their own lives. These outward and external meanings of this card are not the chief ones— perhaps they are only incidental. Card 13 is said to be the only card of the Tarot which refers to temporal, external changes in the world— the changes about to take place midway in the Piscean Age when these cards were given out.

The chief meaning of these four figures (the woman and the child, the king, and the prelate) prostrate, or about to be trampled down by the White Horse, is internal. The occultist must work certain changes in his body. In the course of them, the old Emperor (or ruler of the body) must go; and he is the first to go when we set out to reconstruct the body. The old facts of sex must go—these are symbolized in the card by the figure with the Mitre. The subconscious must go; this is the woman. Even the infant Christ-Child must go, must undergo the death which means rebirth, symbolized in the Gospel narrative by the crucifixion and the resurrection. It is these inner deaths which constitute the esoteric meaning of this card. These deaths and rebirths the occultist works in himself by his own intensive work upon his body (never, never by maltreating it, always by loving it), by a deliberate killing off of old cells, those which are ready to die because we have changed the nature of our thoughts.

The direction of this card is NORTHWEST, which itself indicates change. THE WHEEL (West) represents the measured, recurring changes of the cycle of the Life-Breath through the various forms of Cosmic change which create and deteriorate forms. North represents the sudden, violent changes depicted in THE TOWER.

One of the mistakes of the Church is its interpretation of the fact of death. The frightful burial service of the Church, largely composed of some passages from St. Paul (where they had a very different meaning) has been one of the several factors encouraged by the Church to make men think of death as something to be feared. Whereas the Church should have taught men that no man dies before his time, and that to live after death is the most ghastly of fates. Carpenter beautifully put it thus:

> *Knowest thou not that but for death thou couldst never overcome death? Since by being slave to the things of sense thou has clothed thyself with a body which thou art not master of, thou wert condemned to a living tomb, if that body could not be destroyed. But through pain and suffering out of that body thou shalt come; and through experience thou shalt build thyself a new and better body. And so on many times until thou hast all powers diabolic and angelic in thy flesh.*

Thanks to the blessed fact of reincarnation there is such a thing as individual evolution, until at last we reach the goal of man, to have all powers diabolic and angelic concentrated in the flesh. These 15 powers are symbolized in the WHITE ROSE on the BLACK PENNANT in the hands of DEATH, the destroyer. It is only by his work that we can finally possess them.

As the individual is, so is the nation. Social change only comes about by the death of old ideas, and old ideas only die when the people who hold them die. The people refuse to change, but they die off in time. So in the individual and in society, the actual fact of death is the instrument of progress.

Thirteen in Hebrew stands for a word which means *Unity* and

Love, and of course for that reason 13 is lucky. It also means the Sun functioning through the 12 signs of the Zodiac. It also stands for another word which means *to take away, to separate, to remove.* This is the misunderstood meaning which superstition has seized upon as unlucky; but death is not unlucky to anyone who knows that death means rebirth and that you do not die until it is time for you to die.

The outer features of this card are all concerned with the letter meaning 13; the esoteric features are all connected with the first meaning. The esoteric significance of the card refers to the rebirths which arise from deaths.

The word NUN as a noun means *fish;* as a verb it means "to sprout, to grow." This reference is to the extraordinary fertility of the fish family. It is said that if the cod did not have enemies, its progeny would squeeze all the water out of the ocean in three years.

The Life-Breath is inexhaustibly fertile, both for good or for apparent evil. It is always recreating. If we would give up thinking of death and substitute the word rebirth, we would evolve much faster. The death of everything is its rebirth, the death of every cell is rebirth and science says the cell dies with every movement you make, every move of your emotional, mental and physical body. It dies and is reborn again. This is not a sentimental remark; it is a statement of science. It is up to us whether the cell into which it is reborn is a better or a worse one. *It all depends upon the image we make.* The Fish is the inexhaustible Life Force that swims in the Sea of the Great Waters, the Sea of Substance. It ever produces forms (the Serpent of card 10), descending into the sea of matter. The next form that it makes in us can be better or worse according to our mental images. Better or worse, the new form comes only from the death of the old one. "Know ye not," said St. Paul, "a seed cannot spring up unless it dies?" The cells in us are continually dying, but if we practice mental control we can make sure that they will be reborn into better cells.

The Fish means the reproductive power on all planes, and as such includes physical sex. Everywhere in religion and in occultism you will find concealed or open sex symbols. *Neither religion nor occultism has anything to do with concrete physical sex between man and woman. IT IS OF THE UTMOST IMPORTANCE TO GET THIS STRAIGHT.* Misapprehension of it has led to all the mistaken notions of current psychology about the sexiness of occultism. The reason there are so many veiled sex symbols in religion is because the process theology vaguely refers to as regeneration is precisely what its name implies—

another use of the same force which is employed in generation. It is a nerve force and it has nothing whatever to do with the sex organs. By a certain method the occultist draws off this force from the nerve center (which energizes the sex glands) and applies it to another kind of work. You do not have to be an occultist or mystic to achieve this. It can be done by religious devotion.

This nerve force builds new brain cells in the thinking lobe of the brain, cells capable of higher functioning. These cells enable us to remember the occasions when we transcend the limitations of the physical body, and operate in one of our more rarefied bodies upon a higher plane than the physical. Hence have come about the visions of the saints, visions which in their general outlines are all alike, and therefore believable. To build these new brain cells is the first step in regeneration, and the saints have rarely gone further than that.

The final steps are to vivify the Pineal Gland and to construct a deathless body. These final steps are symbolized by the SUN which rises at the top of the stream in this card. This, then, is the reason there are so many concealed sex symbols in the Church, and so many open ones in occultism. Everywhere in occultism you will find the Serpent, the Fish, and the Scorpion, which all mean the same thing. These terms refer not only to the transmuted sex force, they refer also to the reproductive power of each cell in your body. Each cell in the body is continually recreating itself. It is up to your mental control to see that it makes a better cell each time, a cell capable of a better rhythm. If you change your mental and emotional rhythms, THE EMPRESS will see to it that each of these recreated cells is a better one. All you (the self-conscious) have to do is to regulate your thoughts and your emotions—weed out the wrong motives, the petty ambitions, the foolish opinions and prejudices, to gain emotional control, *and She will attend to the rest!*

SYMBOLISM

The WATERFALL here represents the same waterfall as in THE EMPRESS card. It depicts the union of the Cosmic Mind-Stuff with the personal subconscious—or perhaps it would be clearer to say the reunion. Persephone has now returned to her mother, cleansed of all the taints which she contracted while she was the bride of Pluto, the earthly intellect, the intellect under the influence of instincts and ambitions. The Waterfall is a picture of the process of the Above falling into the Below. Only in this case it means the Holy Ghost and THE EMPRESS, rather than the male principle impregnating the female principle. This river really represents your body finally purified.

The TOWERS behind which the Sun is rising (in the Tarot) represent the "Known." Beyond them stretches the present "Unknown." These Towers have been pushed farther back in the last 100 years than ever before in recorded history. It is the business of science and Intuition to push back these Towers, and it is also the business of individual Intuition to push back all those Towers.

Make known to everyone that there is life after death through the instrumentality of rebirth. We are told that everybody will receive the factual proof that there is life after death. Everyone will receive factual proof that there is such a thing as a deathless body. The people who are living in these deathless bodies now have constructed them themselves; for Nature went as far as she could go when she produced man. After that man has to work in cooperation with Nature to perfect his body. The Bible says: "All Nature groans and travails for the coming of the son of man"; that is to say, for the minds that should work on Nature and perfect it. By adaptation of Nature, man has become civilized, not only working on his own body, but working on the rest of Nature. He made new animals, new plants. Now with the final work, man will construct his own body, he will construct the deathless body. This is the meaning of the rising Sun behind the Towers of the Known, and that will be done in this century.

The other meaning of this RISING SUN is the awakened Pineal Gland and Pituitary Body, both functioning as one. It is said that everyone will know that. Also in this century and with this awakening will come all those new powers, the 12 extensions of our senses and functions and faculties.

The Rising Sun in this card is at the top of the STREAM. This Stream is the Cosmic Mind-Stuff and it symbolizes your body. That is to say, it is the Cosmic Mind-Stuff localized in you. Your body is changed by this Waterfall—by the Above falling into the Below, by the image which you plant in your body, and the body responding to it—by our self-conscious image changing in the threefold body. Wherever the Waterfall occurs in these cards and in symbols, it designates sex.

In the card THE EMPRESS there is a waterfall (which is the heart). That is sex in the sense of gender, the self-conscious fructifying the subconscious in you. In this card, the Waterfall refers to the sex in the cells of your body. The reproductive power of the etheric cells in your body have the power to reproduce themselves.

The RIVER flows from East to West above the Waterfall, and from South to North below the Waterfall. In a concrete sense the Waterfall itself represents the heart. There is a stiff North wind blowing South, which is indicated by the windswept trees and the sailboat on the River. The Boat is rushing madly up the River in the fall. The BOAT symbolizes a tiny segment of the MARS VIBRATION deflected from its natural destination in the Mars Center and is on its way to be transmuted in the heart in a kind of nerve force which can build the better brain. The Serpent Force does *not* dwell in the Mars Center alone. It is localized in the three lower centers, the Saturn, Mars, and Jupiter, and is transmuted in the Heart Center (the middle center) and by it fed to the three higher centers to nourish and rebuild them.

Science as yet knows nothing about this function of the heart, for it is the etheric heart and not the physical heart. Science has begun to recognize the existence of the etheric body, and also it has begun to see that there must be a fundamental, unifying principle in the body which has escaped their localizing so far.

You will find in your dreams much mention of the roads from East to West and from South to North, and vice versa. Often you will find that the person traveling from North to South is conscious of an impending fate, but also conscious that it is not so bad as it seems to be and that it has often been done before. That shows that this tiny segment of the Mars vibration has a consciousness like your own. This tiny segment of the Mars vibration, here symbolized by the SAILBOAT, is what is called by occultism THE FISH. He is an infinitesimal part of the Great Fish, the reproductive force of the Life-Breath, out of which the Universe was made.

It is the sex force of the Father, combined with the Cosmic substance of the Mother, that produces forms, according to the image with which he impregnated her. In the heart the Fish dies and it is transmuted to the Pineal Gland. The entire force is finally raised by the supervision of the Higher Self.

The SKELETON RIDER, riding from North to South and mowing down forms, is the IMAGINATIVE INTELLIGENCE. The WHITE HORSE is the symbol of the Spirit, the WHITE SUN behind the golden, or physical, Sun. Whether you work with these special high type of images or with the ordinary ones, the form which the rebirth will take when you have killed off the old is always the result of your image.

The character Nun is said to be derived from the picture of a fruit because fruit has seed in it of further fruits. The Imaginative Intelligence expresses itself in mental images, and each mental image is the fruit of the previous image and contains seeds of future images. Each mental image is a fruit in the sense that it is the product of former thinking and contains in itself the seed of the future thinking. Each fruit is temporary and should be temporary. You cannot get at the seed in the fruit until the old fruit is decayed or destroyed. Evolution is an unending series of new fruits with new seeds, each fruit being temporary, subject to development, and then to decay.

This Skeleton Rider is clad in BLACK ARMOR. The Skeleton, of course, refers to the fact that each thing must die in order that life may enter another form. The Black Armor is IRON, the metal of Mars, and he has a Red Tassel and a Red Saddle to indicate the same thing—that he kills by a special use of the Mars vibration. BLACK also indicates that this destruction is deliberate and intended. The RED SHIP also indicates the Mars vibration.

The BLACK RIDER on the WHITE HORSE is tallied by the PENNANT he carries—the WHITE ROSE on the BLACK BACKGROUND. If you will remember that the pillars of THE HIGH PRIESTESS are black and white and indicate all opposites, particularly the sex opposites of masculine and feminine, you will see that these two duplicate the fruits and leaves on her veil, the masculine in the feminine and the feminine in the masculine.

The WHITE ROSE signifies purification of the desire nature, not by any means diminishing or banishing desire (it is much increased) but through purifying it. This is the White Rose opened which THE FOOL carried in his hand, symbolizing the vision he had of man at last who became the Angel. He becomes the Angel through the purification of the desire nature, not through the relinquishment of desire. The White Rose also designates the 15 extensions of perceptions and faculties which man will possess when he becomes the Angel. It means the same thing as the Tiara of THE HIEROPHANT. It stands for the 15 extensions of consciousness which the Skeleton will bring you by killing off the old cells. Twelve go for the Zodiacal signs and three for the Mother Letters. Fifteen petals and sepals arranged in four rows, as were the trefoils in the Tiara. We saw they could be looked at from the viewpoint of Spirit and matter. Looked at from the viewpoint of Spirit, One becomes Three becomes Five. Looked at from the viewpoint of matter it becomes the five subtle principles of sensation manifesting on the physical plane as the five qualities of hearing, sight, taste, touch, and smell.

The BLACK SQUARE means the measurement of the occult forces of Nature. The whole standard thus typifies the purification of desire, which combined with the measurement of the occult forces, secures for us the 15 extensions of the faculties and perceptions which are latent in all men, and which is the purpose of the individual self-evolution to develop. The particular occult forces here referred to are connected with Scorpio. To measure and learn how to master them is to overcome death. This is taught you by secret instruction on the inner plane. The occult proverb is: "When the pupil is ready the Master appears." All we know is that Masters say that is what happens to them. Someone told them how to work the final change. The adepts who made these cards say that the Tarot is the best and safest means of getting ready for that secret instruction. It is the willed extermination of the moribund cells of our physical, etheric, emotional and mental bodies by the Mars vibration in the service of the Spirit which finally brings to us these 15 extensions of our perceptions and faculties. These 15 extensions of consciousness are designated by the three Mother Letters and the 12 Simple Letters.

The two so different manifestations of the Fish, the physical and mental, are expressed by the same Zodiacal sign, Scorpio. It was found to be very confusing. So it was once, and so it will be again, we are told, when man as a race has purified his sex desire and uses it under the direction of the Higher Self. It was when man, with the advent of the mind, began to pander to his sex instinct and to employ it for sensation only that it became expedient (to avoid confusion) to designate the raised sex force by the sign Aquila, the Eagle. The constellation Aquila is not in the Zodiac, but it rises at the same time as Scorpio. The Eagle designates the same productive power of the Life Energy when transmuted. In the four fixed signs of the Zodiac (seen in the four corners of cards 10 and 21) you have the Eagle instead of the Scorpion, but elsewhere in the cards the symbol of the Scorpion is used. The Lion in card 8, for instance, has a Scorpion tail.

The number which is the value of the letter-name NUN relates to the intensive work on the body which eventually unites the Father and the personality; and this work, as the card shows, is achieved by Dissolution.

Thirteen is a lucky number. The Greek word *Jesus Kristos* has 13 letters. So what does 13 mean? It means the human personality becomes a Sun functioning through the 12 areas that correspond to the signs of the Zodiac. The same thing is expressed by Jesus and the 12 disciples, and Abraham and the 12 tribes of Israel. So in you, the Sun, the One Energy, expresses itself through your 12 signs, or in your body, in the zones which correspond to the signs of the Zodiac in space.

The full expression of all the powers of the spirit."

The Law of Verification
" To verify is to certify or establish by testing." --- All things are to *estimate* their accuracy"--- This is a process we can confirm by our own actions.--

The Laws of vibrating Energy." Working through the Fourth (4) dimension...d (4th) Dimensional Consciousness...

15th Hebrew Letter	*SAMEKH*
Symbol for	*Wrath*, intensify, zeal
Color	*Blue*
Numerical Value	*60*
Syllables	*SMK*
Sound	*C-Sharp*
Translation	*Prop or Support*
Sign in Zodiac	*Sagittarius*

"A mode of consciousness"--- it is only by withstanding our *temptations* that acquaints us with our strengths."

245

NOTES

TEMPERANCE

ס **SAMEKH**, spelled SMK, means prop or support. It is the 15th Hebrew letter and the ninth SIMPLE LETTER. It stands for the mental modification WRATH; for the direction WEST-ABOVE; for the INTELLIGENCE OF TEMPTATION or TRIAL; for the Zodiacal sign SAGITTARIUS, The Archer; for the color BLUE; for the note G-SHARP. In Roman characters it is written S and the numerical value is 60.

The Chaldean character is almost precisely like MEM Final; it differs only in the shape of the parallelogram at the base, the letter having both sides vertical instead of one on the slant. Without the base, it is practically CHETH, and the constituent parts seem to be RESH, the SUN, drawn down into the body and then sent back up again by the addition of another vertical line at the other side. This recalls "The Emerald Tablet of Hermes":

> All things are from One, by the meditation of One, and have their birth from the One by adaptation. Its power is integrating if it be turned into earth. It ascends from earth to heaven and descends again to earth and receives the power of the superiors and the inferiors.

The shape of the letter SAMEKH seems to say that the Solar Energy has poured itself down and constructed a body, and now the body has reached upward and at-oned itself with its Source. One aspect of this at-one-ment is the obliteration of time; and timelessness, or eternity, is said to be symbolized by the serpent swallowing its tail. The character Samekh is a modification of the circle. It is said to represent the serpent swallowing its own tail. As we have seen in connection with the two other Serpent Letters, Teth and Lamed, the serpent swallowing its tail has two outstanding meanings. The first is eternity—timelessness. This is the belt which THE MAGICIAN has on. THE FOOL put on the belt of the Zodiac when he came down into time and space. THE MAGICIAN when he seeks to bring down power from above girds his loins for action with the belt of eternity. The meaning of this allegory is that the method of magic is to use the Imagination, to assert that mental pattern as if it were actually present.

In Samekh time has become timeless, and the first and the last are one. This is what Jesus taught and what our own Emerson taught. Emerson said we must learn to look at things in endless perspective, to see the fruit in the flower, the flower in the seed, and the seed in the fruit again. The wise man sees that the present is but the fruit of the past, and the future will be the fruit of the present.

The second outstanding meaning of the serpent swallowing its tail symbolizes the end of a cycle. This card is the end of a series of Laws stated by the second row of the Tarot Tableau. The Laws are Suggestion, Response, Rotation, Equilibration, Reversal, Dissolution, and Verification. Just as in the first row of the Tarot Tableau we had a series of Principles of Consciousness, so the second row gives a series of the major Laws of the macrocosm and the microcosm. In the preceding card (THE CHARIOT) was a synthesis of all the preceding Laws. Receptivity-Will combines all the other principles of consciousness; so the Law this card stands for combines all other Laws. This Law is *Verification*.

To verify is to certify or establish by testing. When we construct a machine we verify each part of it before we build it, and when we have assembled all the parts we test the whole machine to see if it has any weak spots before we set it to the work for which we have constructed it. Just as the subconscious tests the body with her scales after she has used the Sword, so with every change which the self-conscious works in itself to secure equilibrium, the Higher Self tests us to see if we have assimilated that change and if it is time to initiate in us a still greater change. All your life experience, inner and outer, subconscious and self-conscious, is a process of continual readjustment to changed conditions. The inner changes, when they are occult, are for the purpose of making your physical body a better vehicle for the expression of the latent potencies of the Life-Power. The outer changes are for the purpose of giving you the emotional and mental control, which will, in the end through the Laws of Suggestion and Mutual Response, work these internal changes. To the former set of changes the subconscious attends, as you see her doing in card 11, JUSTICE. To the latter set of changes, the Higher Self attends. He attends to several inner changes also, and it is these inner changes which form the subject matter of this card.

Vibration is the root meaning *wrath*, and wrath also means zeal and intensity. We are never so intense as when we express wrath. Righteousness is always expressing wrath. Jesus was constantly fulminating, not at sinners as the Church does, but at hypocrites. Why does not the Church follow the example of Jesus and fulminate only at hypocrites? The answer is obvious—because it is the Church itself which makes and encourages hypocrites. It is constantly overlooked, particularly by the pacifists and the evangels of the gospel of love and beauty, that "wrath" is a state of mind which has the greatest utility when rightly applied. It is obvious that when we are growing up we never know that our actions are blamable. Even the zeal of intolerance, intolerance which the occultist rightly condemns as the worst of sins, is useful when rightly applied.

In connection with the word "wrath" there is one other thing to be said. In our stage of evolution, it is as undesirable as it is impossible that we should like everybody. Do not call yourself to account because you do not like certain people. That is to be expected, and furthermore to be utilized when it occurs. Thoreau says that repulsions are just as God-given as attractions. You are made the way you are made for a purpose, and that purpose is *growth*. You are to utilize your personality to attain that purpose. Good haters have accomplished as much in the world of reform as good lovers, perhaps more. The time will come when you are actuated as Tennyson says, "only by the hate of hate, the scorn of scorn." Such a man was Walt Whitman, who loved everybody, but until the time comes with you, utilize your hates, your scorns. Every way the Life Power expresses itself in you has use and can be employed with benefit if it is intelligently applied.

The letter Samekh means a support, a tent peg. A tent peg is to a tent what a foundation is to a house. The occult meaning of this letter is that this is a mode of consciousness which serves as a foundation for the house of the personality. In other words, the Higher Self should be the foundation for your house—the Higher Self which internally mixes the Fire and Water within you and externally sends you tribulations in order that you may profit by them if you will.

The numerical value of the letter-name is 120, or 10 x 12. You have both these numbers in THE TOWER, where they form the golden rain from the flash of lightning sent by the Higher Self, the flash which destroys. The 10 is on the side of the woman, the 12 on the side of the man. Ten is the number of Emanations from the First Cause, which the Hebrew Wisdom taught formed the basis of all phenomena of manifestation. Twelve is the number of the signs of the Zodiac, and this is on the side of the man, or the self-conscious.

The support of our existence is the Cosmic Life Force. It expresses itself in ten ways, then unfolds that expression through the agency of the 12 basic types of consciousness, or activities which the Kabbalah associates with the 12 signs of the Zodiac.

Astrology says the 12 signs of the Zodiac are in our bodies and are associated with 12 areas of our bodies. Associated with these are the 12 basic functions of the body which the Simple Letters of the Hebrew alphabet stand for. They are: Sight, Hearing, Smell, Speech, Taste, Sex-Union or Touch, Work, Motion (from one place to another), Wrath and Mirth (the two extremes of mental-emotional reaction to outer events), Thought (in its higher phase, Meditation) and Sleep.

This classification includes *first*, the five modes of sensation; *second*, the five chief bodily activities; and *third*, the two emotional extremes of reaction from desire, which is the result of what our senses bring us from without.

There are three ways to arrive at the number 120. First, there is 10 x 12. In this connection, note that 10 plus 12 equals 22, the number of all the letters in the Hebrew alphabet, and of the entire circle of Cosmic forces; and also the number which mathematically represents the circumference of any circle. Then there is another way to get at 120. It is 1 times 2 times 3 times 4 times 5. This represents the multiplication of the forces of the five basic aspects of existence: Ether, Fire, Water, Air, and Earth. Each of the five is a subtle principle of our mode of physical sensation. You may think of your life as the working together of Ether with the four elements. The action and reaction of Ether with the elements is known to us only by our sensations. Lastly, 120 is the sum of all the numbers contained in 15; and 15 is the number of one of the Names of Jehovah—JAH, or IH. Considered so, 120 represents the full expression of all the powers of life. It is for this reason that the Bible gives 120 years as the ideal age of man, the right measure of human existence; but, as with most texts in the Bible, this is carefully worded to have a double meaning: "His *days* shall be a hundred and twenty *years*." This is surely a strange way to put it if it means only what it says. It does not mean to limit his stay on Earth to that number of years, but rather to say that each day of the perfected man's life is as 120, or the full expression of all the powers of the Spirit.

In the days when the Hebrew alphabet was invented, people who did not live in cities dwelt in tents and they roamed from place to place following pasturage for their flocks. The occult meaning of this is that the Higher Self is the foundation of your House of Life, whether you Will or not. The more consciously you recognize this and cooperate with Him, the greater your evolution in any one life. It is He who

Tradition #1, learn to work together to overcome all tasks and obstacles before NO...

sends you the external tribulations and tests in order that you may profit by them if you respond to them rightly. It is He who doses out to you your bad Karma from life to life, proportioned in the amounts He thinks you can stand. Thus it must follow, if in any one life you have made spiritual progress, you let loose upon yourself more of the bad Karma than might have been originally intended. It is the object of the occultist to exhaust his bad Karma as rapidly as possible, so much so that sometimes he even asks his Higher Self to let him reap it. It requires a brave and devoted soul to do so and to bear the adversity and suffering this entails. To those who do not comprehend that they are suffering to adjust wrongs done by them in other lives, such afflictions might seem unjustified and to be sent in anger. For such a man often realizes that he is suffering in excess of his bad Karma, and he cries out at the apparent injustice. This kind of affliction is not for the purpose of paying up for the past, but rather of getting ready for the future, for a loftier mission.

The direction of this card is a combination of the subconscious with conscious, of Jupiter (or the Law of Cycles) with the faculty of Attention. That is why the type of Intelligence is so named. If we see THE WHEEL turn and pay accurate attention to its turning, we can perceive every trial, every testing that fits us (if we use it correctly) for a higher manifestation of our powers. All things are tested to estimate their accuracy, whenever we wish to use them for a higher assumption. We must then test the conclusion the assumption allowed us to reach. We test it by "temptation" or by experiment, to see if we are justified in using it as the first step in a following process of reasoning. Just so, the Higher Self must constantly test us by trial to see if we are fitted for a higher mission, our next step in spiritual evolution. This is a process we can confirm by our own action. We never know our weakness or our strength until we have met temptation. The prayer which says "not to be led into temptation," the so-called Lord's Prayer, contains the mendacity of a cowardly scribe, as psychologically ignorant as he was cowardly, if taken literally. "The strong man rejoices to run a race," says the Bible elsewhere, and it is only withstanding temptation that acquaints us with our strength.

The ANGEL is the actuating force in both the outer and inner work of this card, hence the background is WHITE. The outer work of the Angel in this card is done without our assistance, but his inner work can be done only after we have ourselves prepared the body for it by the amount of transformation, of rebuilding taken place in it because of our images.

SYMBOLISM

There are only three other cards which have the White background. They are:

NUN: This card depicts the work of killing off the old cells and transforming the sex force to the head. It is performed by the Spirit itself, subject to the same conditions as here; that you have fitted the body for it by your own intensive work upon it.

VAU: This card depicts the Higher Self relaying to the twin forms of the subconscious (THE EMPRESS and THE HIGH PRIESTESS) the message of the Spirit. The concentric curves of the robe of THE HIEROPHANT are pierced like the concentric curves of the robe of THE HIGH PRIESTESS with the down thrust of the Spirit.

MEM, THE HANGED MAN, is the third card having a White background, which means temporary union with the Spirit in Meditation.

The Angel in this card is only another aspect of THE HIEROPHANT, as is shown by the fact that 14 reduces to 5. Here he is depicted as male, but in the older cards there is often a female figure. True to the suppression of woman in Hebrew and Catholic theologies, all the Hebraic and Catholic figures are male. When the rash sculptor made some female angels to decorate the facade of the Cathedral of Saint John the Divine, an outraged clergy made him remove them. The Angel really represents your personal connection with the supreme Spirit which is both Father and Mother, and the IHVH on the collar of his robe shows that he stands for the Supreme who is both sexes in one.

The inner work he performs, in the man who has prepared himself for it, is depicted by the set of actions in pouring a DOUBLE STREAM from one GOLDEN GOBLET into the other GOBLET. If this were a motion picture he would reverse his hands and pour the other way when the first Goblet became emptied. Here he is pouring, as the CRESCENT denotes, from the subjective mind into the objective mind. The TWO CUPS are GOLDEN; that is, they are your perfected personality into which the influx of the Spirit is streaming. This card stands just below THE CHARIOT, which depicts the Soul occupying the perfected body.

This is the way he perfects it for higher uses. How? He keeps adapting and modifying the personal streams of psychic energy in the actions and reactions of the self-conscious and subconscious minds. He is doing the adapting and modifying of these opposite streams as if he was mixing two liquors in what we call a cocktail shaker. FIRE stands for the SELF-CONSCIOUS and WATER stands for the SUB-CONSCIOUS. This is where the joke comes in calling this card TEM-PERANCE, for the act of tempering steel is to subject it to these two physical opposites. In the Paul Case card, the Angel is pouring water on a Lion and holding a torch to an Eagle, the Lion representing Fire and the Eagle, Water. To pour water on a Lion and hold fire to an Eagle is to instigate the action of opposites. There is also another meaning. In the last card, NUN, the Fish must be raised from the reproductive center (represented by Scorpio and the Eagle, a Water sign) to the Heart Center (represented by Leo) in order to begin those activities which result in the change of the physical organism. The action of the Angel in sending you external trial and internal modifications of your psychic current tells you that all your experiences in life are a process of continuous readjustment to changed conditions without and within. All events external and internal are parts of the process whereby He, who is representative of the One Life, is tempering your personality so as to make it a better vehicle for the expression of the latent potencies of the Life Force.

The color of this letter is BLUE. Fourteen is 7 x 2. (The 2 in you are the conscious and the subconscious, the Black and White Pillar of THE HIGH PRIESTESS, whose number is 2 and whose color is Blue.) Here you have the working of the power represented in THE CHARIOT, 7, through the agency of THE HIGH PRIESTESS. When your body approximates THE CHARIOT of the Higher Self in His aspect of Moon conqueror, or the "stiller" of emotions, he begins in it the work of the Solar Angel. The Solar Angel's work is to perfect the stream of personal consciousness by properly mingling its elements and continuously alternating them. He is doing the solar work as indicated by the SOLAR SYMBOL ON HIS BROW, the rays streaming from his head, and the ORNAMENT matter with the TRIANGLE of YELLOW FIRE impressed upon it. The BROOCH means the mental measurement of the Spiritual forces. The Brooch of JUSTICE was BLUE, signifying that she takes the measurement of the subconscious forces represented by THE HIGH PRIESTESS. The BROOCH of the Charioteer was WHITE, signifying that he took the measurement of the Spiritual forces.

The Angel stands with ONE FOOT submerged in the water, the

foot on which his weight rests; the other foot barely touches the ground. The BLUE WATER symbolizes the Cosmic Mind and the Stuff of which it is composed. The LAND symbolizes the physical body. Land is masculine to Water and Water represents the Cosmic Mind-Stuff; hence, the subconscious. The Angel being the superconscious can communicate (just as THE HIEROPHANT is communicating only with the twin forms of the subconscious) the word that they later are to convey to the conscious.

At the side of the Angel grows a clump of IRIS, in which there are many SPEARS OF GREEN and only TWO FLOWERS. The GREEN stands for the Creative Imagination, of course. Why are the flowers iris? In Greek mythology, Iris was the messenger of the gods. Note that one of these flowers is above and the other below; and the flower below is YELLOW, too. This is to show that the subconscious (which is the messenger of the gods) flowers only from the Creative Imagination.

On the other side of the Angel is a PATH coming from the Pool and stretching away over the green rolling country into the far distance. It is the Path of Evolution. Evolution proceeds from cultivation, and hence the ground is Green. The pathway constantly rises and falls. All progress is in wave motion, by curves of ups and downs. Yet in spite of downs the path constantly ascends if you look with sufficient perspective. As the upward journey is continued, the point of each succeeding depression is higher than the height of each preceding wave. Between the cultivated land and the end of the path there is a suggestion of a great stretch of BLUE LAND. This Blue signifies the planes of consciousness open to us in sleep, from which come the recollection we may later call discoveries, which help us progress.

At the end of the path are the TWO MOUNTAINS OF WISDOM AND UNDERSTANDING, the twin peaks of the subconscious. Above and between these two is the CROWN OF MASTERY, which comes from personal identification with the Higher Self. When we have identified the lower self with the Higher Self, when we can say with Jesus, "The Father and I are One," we have mastery over all the subconscious forms and forces of Nature. The crown and goal of evolution is to become co-workers with God. No matter how lowly or debased we may be at any moment, at any place on the down and up path of evolution, all of us have within ourselves the potency of the Angel. We shall all demonstrate our potency at the end, in spite of all theological dogmas to the contrary.

The TWO STONES or FISHES in the card seem to be connected

by the foot of the Angel. The foot in symbology is a phallic symbol. One of the meanings of the two fishes here is the awakened Pineal and Pituitary. They signify the same thing, you see, as the two irises above them and they occupy the same relative position. It is the Higher Self which joins the awakened Pineal and the awakened Pituitary and brings them into sex action, into the Mystic Marriage. The result of that union is the Transformed Heart, which is symbolized by the three-leaved YELLOW FLOWER. This seems to grow out of a fissure in the ground through which is thrust an arrow which trails away. The ARROW is the Arrow of Trial which is sent you by the Higher Self. The nearer you approach the final transformation, that of the heart, the more arrows He lets fly at you. This fissure is one of the most significant items in the whole Tarot symbology. Let me repeat the fact that the arrow seems to be thrust right through the land, and from the fissure it makes springs out the flower. "Ere the heart can flower," says the wonderful book *The Light on the Path*, "it must bleed, and the whole life of the man seems to be utterly dissolved. Ere the worm can burst forth a butterfly from the dark cocoon it has made for itself, it must be utterly dissolved and reform." Is it fancy that this three-petalled flower is made like a butterfly?

The flower, still in bud, blossoms out from a V-shaped formation of two leaves. This bud is the same as the butterfly flower you see below, arising from the fissure made by the arrow. As both the arrow and the foot indicate that it is the work of the Angel, so the V-shaped leaves indicate that it is the work of the Higher Self.

In astrology Jupiter rules Sagittarius, the Archer. Therefore, this card is one of the four Jupiter cards. In the body, Sagittarius presides over the thighs and Jupiter over the Solar Plexus. It is a well-known physical fact that zeal and courage are closely related to the function of the Solar Plexus and are expressed in the muscular action of the thighs. Merely to flex the great muscles of the thighs when one has fear tends to supply courage and confidence. We express this mental attitude through an erect, firm-standing posture; and to get this we have to call into play the two great muscles of the thighs. Also to take aim we must flex these muscles; and in order to aim we must assume a firm, straight position. Consequently, these muscles are associated by the subconscious with all activities requiring purpose and concentration. If you flex them intentionally when you are afraid, you suggest to her that you wish her to come to your aid with courage and determination. The Solar Plexus, the seat of the instinct of self-preservation, has control over this muscular activity of the thighs, and this is the outer meaning of the rulership of Jupiter over this sign. Of course there is an inner meaning also. THE WHEEL symbolizes the rotation of cycles, the Wheel within Wheels of simultaneous Involution and Evolution. In order to wear the Crown at the end of the path we must get a clear perception that all our personal activities are merely the particular concrete expressions in us of the interplay of Cosmic Forces and of the operation of eternal Laws. These Cosmic Forces and eternal Laws are ours to manipulate one way or the other, but through us they must continually play. Let us take an illustration. When we call our base instincts (the instincts of the animal), they rise to the consciousness of the Solar Plexus.

Yet Jupiter rules Sagittarius, the card of the Solar Angel who gives us our high aspirations. *There is no difference between an animal desire and a high aspiration except the precise way it is expressed in the personal consciousness.* The energy is the same. This fact cannot be too clearly appreciated—it is the same Cosmic Force playing through us.

What, occultly speaking, are aspirations? Merely recollections, which we long to repeat, of thoughts we once experienced before we descended into matter. Such recollections are recorded, along with everything else that ever happened, in the Solar Plexus. Here, too, are recorded all our desires when we were merely in the animal state. We call that desire a low desire now, but it was all right when we were animals, and it was our means of growth then, and now we have another means of growth. If we gratify that low desire it becomes our means of retrogression, of going back into the animal kingdom mentally. This is one of the most-used Bible words for "sin"—*transgression,* which means "going across a boundary." What boundary? The boundary of the animal kingdom, or the boundary of the regions that pertain to you as man. We must not gratify that Cosmic urge on the animal spiral of low desire, but on the human spiral of aspiration.

At the root of all so-called "sins" is something good, something lofty. *A sin is just a mistaken interpretation of the Cosmic urge for growth, for the eventual return to a higher state.* The man who takes that urge out in crime has merely manipulated it on an animal basis; with you it is the same urge manipulated on a human basis.

Besides being one of the four Jupiter cards, this is one of the four representing the alchemic element of Fire. The essential nature of alchemic Fire is threefold. It is depicted in the threefold shape of the letter Shin, which stands for it. For the present purpose we shall consider that threefold nature (physical, mental, and spiritual) merely from one of its aspects. The physical phase is the process of Digestion. First it begins by the destruction of various forms of food and their gradual volatilization up to the point where the "chyle" or "Virgins' milk" is taken by the lacteals into the small intestine. This is the first part of the process. The alchemic art, says the alchemist, is the volatilization of the fixed and the fixation of the volatile. The alchemists, to keep the Church from knowing what they were doing, always expressed themselves in fantastic and apparently meaningless terms. This is what the first part of that extraordinary statement means: the volatilization of the essences fixed in food. The second part is the fixation of the volatile. This means building into the body the energy after it is assimilated. The two together are the physical side of the process of Alchemy. This physical side we are always performing, whether we are alchemists or not, in the action of ordinary digestion. You remember, the alchemist has achieved a higher kind of digestion explained in the card THE HERMIT, in which he volatilizes certain essences contained in the foods that are not required by the ordinary man and are excreted with the waste of the body.

The volatilization of the fixed and the fixation of the volatile apply also to the mental plane. We break down, that is, analyze, our shifting experiences, the volatile, in order to discover the fixed and eternal Laws behind what effect our outward perception senses. This is done by Attention (THE MAGICIAN). He then synthesizes these Laws and Forces into new combinations, and he makes these impressions to that end, the Creative Imagination (THE EMPRESS). These are the two parts of the process on the mental side. Thirdly, here is this same twofold process on the Spiritual plane. By the employment of mental analysis, he is able so to transmute his own body and his own mind as to become superhuman and have dominion over all things.

The first card of the Fire sequence is THE EMPEROR. It represents the activity of the Fire in the head of man and in the act of vision. Card 8 depicts the entrance of the Stellar Fire, the Astral Light, into the body through the Transformed Heart. Until the heart is transformed, the body cannot receive that Fire, and the heart has been brought to this function by THE MAGICIAN working on the subconscious and transforming her.

Cards 4 and 8 belong to what is called the solar current of the Fire, but the activities of the Angel in card 14 belong to what is called the lunar current of this Fire. These two currents he mixes together in this picture. Alchemic Fire is divided into two specialized currents, one called Fire and the other called Water, *but they are the same Force*. This is shown by the fact that both are symbolized by the equilateral triangle. The Lunar Fire enters through the Pituitary and flows down to the areas governed by Jupiter and Sagittarius. The Solar Fire enters through the Transformed Heart and flows up through the areas governed by Leo and Aries. When you complete the Fire action in your body, you are released from three-dimensional consciousness and can work on all four planes.

In card 20 you see the self-conscious, the subconscious, and the Christ-Child rising from their three coffins, the coffins of three-dimensional consciousness. To be able to work on all four planes is the technical meaning, the occult meaning, of the word *spiritual*.

" Suffering is the Great Educator."
The disciplined body will exalt you, will make an angel out of You."

We become human only by shifting our consciousness entirely
om the physical body to the Universal mind... When we control
Masculine and feminine energies in our body we become as Angels

16th Hebrew Letter	*AYIN*
Symbol for	*Sight*
Color	*Blue-Violet* *or Indigo*
Numerical Value	*70*
Syllables	*OIN*
Sound	*A-Natural*
Translation	*Eye*
Sign in Zodiac	*Capricorn*

The Consequences of your own Actions:

The first Stage of enlightenment **NOTES** we raise ourselves

THE DEVIL

AYIN, spelled in Hebrew OIN. It means the EYE as the instrument of SIGHT. It is the 16th Hebrew letter and the tenth SIMPLE LETTER; it stands for the mental modification MIRTH; the direction WEST-BELOW; the RENEWING INTELLIGENCE; Zodiacal sign CAPRICORN, the Goat or the Sea Goat; Color BLUE-VELVET; Note A-NATURAL; and the numerical value is 70. In Roman characters it is written O, hence the spelling OIN.

This card begins the bottom row of the Tarot Tableau. The first row depicted the Principles of Consciousness; the second, the Laws of the Universe and the Inner Life of Man; the third depicts man's seven stages of Spiritual Unfoldment of Enlightenment. Thus, paradoxically enough, the card which is called THE DEVIL describes the first stage of enlightenment. In one word, it depicts a man misusing his instincts. The lower animal does that. The misuse of the instinct is the first and inevitable consequence of possessing a mind. It is a stage through which the individual man, as a race, must pass in order to learn the correct use of his mind. This card called THE DEVIL could as well be called in the language of St. Paul, "the natural body." "We are born," said Paul, "a natural body, and we are raised a spiritual body." *Are raised!* This is undoubtedly an ecclesiastical rendering to make the words of Paul agree with the growing theology of the Church. The very chapter in which these words occur is twisted by the Church so as to make them refer to physical death and resurrection. They really refer to the process by which we make over the natural body while we are here on earth. Instead of the verb "are raised," let us substitute the verb "raise ourselves."

By our own work upon our bodies we convert them from the natural body into the Spiritual body, through the five intermediate stages of enlightenment. The Tarot and the Ancient Secret Wisdom of the Jews insist that the natural body is the first stage of enlightenment, which means that through the misuse of the body we learn at long last the right use, or to be righteous. Zayin (whose card shows the right use of the body and tallies with this card item for item) is merely Ayin preceded by the Sword—The Sword which cuts off the animal in us and finally carves out equilibrium between the self-conscious and the subconscious.

The man in THE DEVIL is really living entirely in his subconscious sensations, although he imagines he is exercising his mind. The body is dictating to him instead of him dictating to the body.

The direction of this card is WEST-BELOW, and this is in itself a definition of THE DEVIL. WEST refers to your body of manifestation and specifically to the Solar Plexus. The Solar Plexus is the seat of the instincts. When the Solar Plexus is not ruled by the self-conscious as it should be, the body returns to the animal state. The ingenuity of the thinking lobe of the brain, which the animal does not possess, is the lobe which should utilize the instincts for higher and distinctly human purposes. Instead it is used solely to pander to the subconscious appetites. TEMPERANCE, the preceding card, has the direction WEST-ABOVE. In it the body of manifestation is controlled by the mind as the agent of the Higher Self, until it is thereby fitted to come directly under the control of the Angel Himself.

How could God do otherwise than create evil, since He created us with an incomplete state of consciousness? Any thing misapprehended or misapplied constitutes evil. It is well here to insist that all evil, all sin, does not proceed from ignorance. Ignorance was the original cause of it. What the Bible calls "perverseness" continues it and carries it further than "ignorance" ever could. We insist on doing things which will hurt us, even after we have found out that they have hurt us. We prefer the immediate gain, and it blinds us to consequent pain. It is in his definition of the consequent pain that the occultist emphatically differs from the Christian. He calls this pain a *consequence* and not a punishment. *The suffering undergone either in this world or in Hell or purgatory is not a punishment dealt out by an angry God. It is only the consequence of your own acts, brought upon yourself.* You have the sole responsibility of leaving it when you are willing to make the necessary effort and undergo the necessary self-disciplines. God has nothing whatever to do with it. To say that He is angry with you for your so-called sin and that He should regard you with compassion, as the occultist teaches, is one of the greatest of blasphemies. Evil is merely the other side of good; hence the occult proverb: "The devil is God upside-down." The meaning of this pregnant saying is this: If you refuse to learn that good is best in any other way, then you have only one way left—by undergoing the pain that the evil will eventually cause you. Suffering is the great educator. This shows you at once the foolishness and blasphemy of the Christian doctrine of an everlasting hell. If hell is everlasting, what are you being educated for? The occultist says that there is a place of suffering corresponding to the

Catholic purgatory, but you can emerge from it whenever you are willing to purify yourself. It exists only between lives. It does not fit you for heaven, but teaches you to make better use of your next life on earth, through the education of suffering.

This idea that the natural body may finally become the Spiritual and Perfected Body is reiterated in many ways in the Secret Wisdom. First, in the character Ayin itself. The ancient Hebrew character is not the one you see on your card, but a circle with a dot in the center. Thus you see it was very definitely like the eye (Ayin means the Eye as the instrument of sight). The dotted circle is also the astrological symbol of the Sun, so you see when they made the letter like this, it was closely associated with the Sun. Of course the makers of the Hebrew alphabet were all versed in Astrology—and yet this Sun is like THE DEVIL. So here is a hint of the basic fact of the Hebrew teaching that the so-called devil is only God "upside-down." *The thing that debases you to hell will pull you up to heaven.* It is the same thing. You either go to hell or go to heaven according to the way you use what this letter stands for. This thing is the body.

The present character Ayin tells you this same fact in another way. This letter has the formation of two Yods and a Vau. This gives you the secret value of the letter as 26, the number of IHVH, or Jehovah. Thus you are told that what debased you, in the misuse of the body, is equally capable of exalting you. THE DEVIL is undisciplined. The disciplined body will exalt you, will make a god of you.

This story is repeated in the type of Intelligence assigned to AYIN, THE DEVIL—the RENEWING INTELLIGENCE. That which tempts you to use your body wrongly opens the door, when you use it rightly, to True Wisdom.

To return to the devil of the Bible—Lucifer, or Satan: The Archangel Lucifer was cast into Hell for his revolt against God, and there he is the cause of man's sin. At the same time the Bible calls him the brightest and best of the Sons of the Morning. The Secret Wisdom of the Bible says that what caused man's fall will also cause his rise; it must follow, if this story is true, that it is Lucifer who supplies us with the means of our Spiritual evolution. The occult teaching is: *Man brings about his Spiritual evolution by his own efforts.* This effort in disciplining his nature and his mind is responsible for the rising of the Fire of Kundalini in him, which is his only means of changing his natural body into the Spiritual body. Kundalini is the Earth Fire, and is the emanation to us of that mighty Archangel Lucifer, who ensouls this planet. He is the helper of humanity rather than its destroyer, and it was because he interfered with the schemes of trying to hasten our evolution and decrease its blind pain that he was cast out from the mental plane and sent to ensoul this planet. He is the origin of the Greek myth Prometheus, whom Jupiter chained to a rock eternally, with a vulture ever gnawing at his vitals, for bringing fire to man to speed up his evolution.

There are reasons why THE DEVIL stands for MIRTH other than that in the Hebrew Secret Wisdom, for they did not believe there was such a personage. You will see written upon THE DEVIL's upraised paw in this card an old Saturn symbol. SATURN stands for limitation. THE DEVIL is encouraging man, the self-conscious, to extract sensation from the body. The spectacle of people madly engaged in killing off all power of response in their bodies was an ironic one to the believers of the Secret Wisdom. No wonder this devil has a sly smirk upon his donkey face! There is still another irony alluded to in the word *mirth*. The letter AYIN means "the EYE as an instrument of sight," and it also means the visible part of a thing, the outside.

Now REASON, THE EMPEROR, has nothing to do with the eye, but with the FACULTY OF SEEING. This card deals with the eye as the instrument of sight, but THE EMPEROR means sight itself, independent of any other instrument. As your spiritual evolution proceeds you shape finer and finer instruments to see with until at length you need no instrument—you see without eyes. THE EMPEROR sees reality because the illusion of the thing does not stand in its way, but with the mind's eye it sees back of the form to the reality behind it. You use those eyes to see with until at length you need no instrument to see with. You use those eyes at the same time as you use your eyes to distinguish material things. Without eyes you see "Truth" behind them. You are all familiar with the fact that you can see without eyes. You do not see with your physical eyes in your dreams, and yet in your dreams you see things more vividly than with your eyes open. With your eyes closed you see colors, and they are more colorful than when you see them with your physical eyes.

It is the transformed Reason that sees reality. The alchemist taught that when the Pineal Gland was opened you could see First Matter. Every form in the Universe is composed of this First Matter, although on the surface the "stuff" which composes these forms seems to have innumerable differences.

The successful alchemist, one who has transformed his brain, sees through his physical eyes, but not by means of them. What he sees he sees through his eye-socket, but he is not using his physical eyes at all. One of the substances he sees is First Matter. He sees what the rest of us call air, space. First Matter is the vibrating electrical, or rather electromagnetic, Energy of which all things are made. The constantly scintillating essence, a spark of Fire; and it is in this ocean of Fire we are submerged just as fish are submerged in water. This is the present conception of science, but Ageless Wisdom has always taught it. We are made of this First Matter and this First Matter fills all space.

To pass through the successive stages from the natural body to the Spiritual body, as illustrated in the last row of the Tarot Tableau, we must learn how to subdue and utilize the alchemic element of Earth, which includes how to conquer and utilize the Saturn vibration, and how to use the Mars vibration. This card forms a part of all these sequences—alchemic Earth, Saturn, and Mars. The Earth cards are THE HIEROPHANT, THE HERMIT, THE WORLD, and this one, AYIN; so you see THE DEVIL keeps very good company.

THE DEVIL represents the Earth, or the body as it is misunderstood by those who are entirely content with superficial appearances. THE HERMIT has implanted in all forms the same urge for growth which drove the Life Power Itself to self-expression. The human being has more of it than any other earthly form, because he possesses a self-conscious brain, a thinking brain. This urge to unfold our power must begin on the lower level first, and then proceed to the higher. The lower level is the complete expression of the animal instincts. The complete expression is our only means of self-realization when we are at that level, and unless we utilize it we shall always stay at that level. Only so long as we misunderstand the element of Earth does it appear to be our enemy. In it there is *forever working* A POWER which seeks better and better forms to enclose the expanding life, the power which science calls evolution.

By the process of civilization we expand our life so that it shall demand a better form, and each man must civilize himself by subduing his animal instincts.

Occultism teaches that the Earth is our enemy only when it is misunderstood, only when we allow it to dominate us. When we can dominate it, it is our means of rising to Godhood. The Earth is our enemy only when we are content with superficial appearances. The superficial tells us that sensation is all. From the Earth, from the body, comes our means of liberation if we know how to control the body.

The card THE WORLD shows the last stage of that expansion through self-control. It is a state of joyous freedom in which man is the co-worker of God in shaping evolution for the rest of the race, which he has outdistanced. When you have reached it, the body possesses a potency which the self-conscious did not possess, but which only the self-conscious, rightly exercised, can confer upon it. That potency is THE POWER TO MAKE ALL THINGS NEW. Hence to this card is assigned the Renewing Intelligence.

The Renewing Intelligence is shown at its work in the last card, THE WORLD; also it is shown at work in the card THE LOVERS. The card THE DEVIL and THE LOVERS are very similar. A figure with wings, one a devil and the other an angel, blesses a man and a woman standing below. The self-conscious in THE LOVERS is not demanding sensation from the subconscious, but offering itself in service: "Here I am, use me as you think best." The subconscious indicates from the position of her hands the same attitude toward him. She is powerful and vigorous, instead of helpless and deformed. She is looking up to the Angel above her, in order to get His message and transmit it to her partner. That is her ultimate work, together with the work of "making all things new," which means being the instrument of magical creation, but she can be thwarted in it if the self-conscious keeps her at the level of the animal kingdom.

The number of THE DEVIL card is 15, which indicates THE HIEROPHANT, or 5, working through THE MAGICIAN, or 1. This tells the story so often told, that THE HIEROPHANT teaches man through the urges of his body for sensation until man has learned, by subduing his instincts, to listen to THE HIEROPHANT on a higher level than mere sensation. That higher level, at its perfection, is shown in card 6, THE LOVERS, and 1 plus 5 = 6.

The Saturn sequence is 11, 15, 17, 21. Progress consists in learning *how to use* the limitations which Saturn sets upon the form you find yourself in, to utilize that which seems to bind you in, but is in reality your only means of expression. When you have learned how to control your body by equilibrating the self-conscious and the subconscious, and so control your mind that you can gain a true perception of the Universe through Meditation, then you can use your body to make all things new, as the last card in the Saturn sequence depicts.

As for your present body and its set of limitations, the Secret Wisdom teaches that you are what you are because, based on what you have been, your present personality forms your best means of progressing.

It is a machine, given you for the purpose of progressing, and you will achieve its purpose if you learn how to utilize your personality instead of letting it utilize you. You act by means of your Mars vibration, and thus this card THE DEVIL forms a part of the Mars sequence also.

❧ The cards of the Mars vibration are 15, 16, 4, 13. This vibration shall be discussed at length in the next card, THE TOWER. What we must note about it now is that card 4, THE EMPEROR, is also in the Mars vibration. THE EMPEROR stands for sight. AYIN stands for the "eye" only, a very faulty and deficient instrument of sight, until we have transformed the brain and opened the Pineal Gland.

The action of the man in THE DEVIL is devoted solely to gratify his instincts. The TORCH THE DEVIL holds to the man's hand is composed almost entirely of RED and thus indicates by its slight mixture of YELLOW that, though endowed with intelligence, he has an almost mindless desire for sensation. Capricorn in astrology is sometimes called the Sea Goat. The Sea is the subconscious, and the goat gambols on the surface of the Sea, as if the sensations which can be extracted from the body are all of life. *The PROPER USE of the Mars vibration, which we learn slowly through innumerable lives, makes us at last reasonable beings.* When we have learned the right use of the body, we use it to perceive reality instead of appearance, and to make forms by magical means as a co-worker with God, as the cards THE LOVERS and THE WORLD illustrate. Reason, in THE EMPEROR card, wears a mantle which indicates the same thing.

SYMBOLISM

Here is a creature who never could have existed, except as the product of imagination: goat's horns, a human head with donkey ears, wings of a bat, the upper part of the gross human body, the thighs of an animal, the legs of a human, and ending in eagle's claws.

The BAT WINGS are there to carry out the black background. This is to be read as darkness, ignorance.

The HORNS are those of a goat because of the sign Capricorn, yet they are fashioned so as to suggest a backbone. Sin means going back to the animal, whose backbone curves and who cannot stand erect.

The HEAD has donkey ears because the man will not listen to the voice of human experience. In the gratification of his instincts he is as stubborn as a donkey.

The HUMAN PART OF THE BODY is gross and thickset because

sin is always the absence of grace and beauty.

The RAISED HAND blessing the pair is open wide as if to say: "You see, all there is to life is the desire for sensation; there is nothing else."

The THIGHS, as we saw in the last card, are the motor power of all action forward. Here they are not human but animal, indicating that the desire for animal satisfaction is all that drives forward the two below his blessing.

The legs end in EAGLE'S CLAWS. This is a very subtle piece of symbolism. The Eagle is the symbol of the upraised sex force, but there is nothing here of the Eagle but the claws—sex used entirely in the service of sensuality.

On the UPRAISED PAW is an ancient symbol of Saturn. Here it signifies that the pair below, instead of utilizing their limitations, have fallen victim to them.

Over the head of THE DEVIL is a crudely constructed PEN-TAGRAM which is inverted. The five-pointed star symbolizes the perfected man. It should stand on two points, the self-conscious and the subconscious as equals. Here it stands on only one point. Now the question is, what is that point? Is it the self-conscious or the subconscious? It is the subconscious but the man *thinks* it is the self-conscious. The man below is living entirely in his subconscious, although he fatuously thinks he is living in his self-conscious. He is wallowing in sensations which he can, for a very limited time, extract from her. He is using his mind for no other purpose than to sharpen his pleasures.

This fact is also indicated by the BODY of THE DEVIL. His head and his knees both form downward in the form of the Water-triangles, whereas a man should be the interlaced triangle, one Water and one Fire.

He is holding the TORCH of the Mars vibration to inflame the man's acquisitive and sexual desires. To satisfy them the man constantly works his body by pandering to them. You may see in her attitude her unwilling submission and that her face is averted from him. Further-more, he has malformed her, just as he has malformed himself. Note that the left shoulder of the woman is lacking, while the left shoulder of the man is developed all out of proportion. The shoulders are the index of emotion, and his emotions are all centered in subconscious sensation; and to feed this he is exhausting her more and more.

They are both bound by CHAINS to the HALF-CUBE on which THE DEVIL squats; yet note that he could lift off his chain if he wanted to. She cannot because she has no initiative of her own until he gives it to her; but he could do it and then lift off hers.

A cube represents the physical world. The half-cube represents a half-knowledge of reality. As half-knowledge is ignorance, the cube is BLACK.

The man and woman have HORNS, HOOFS and TAIL, to signify that they are living entirely in the animal nature. His tail has the RED of Mars and is shaped like a scorpion, denoting that his principal bestiality is sex. Her tail is a BUNCH OF GRAPES, indicating that it is the business of the subconscious to bring to fruit the desires of the self-conscious. To denote this more graphically, the grapes spring from a GREEN CUP, symbol of the power of imagination.

The DEVIL has a NAVEL, as have the man and the woman. This is one of the most subtle symbolisms of the Tarot. It indicates that all are man-made. They picture man at his most bestial and man at his most perfect form. We must exert effort to go uphill—to slide down and back to the animal is to refuse to make the effort. All the nude figures in these cards have navels; all are created by man. The perfect subconscious is just as much created by man as the deformed subconscious. The perfect self-conscious is just as much created by man as the grasping, selfish, sensual self-conscious. *Spiritual man is just as much created by man as natural man.* The LOVERS, the woman in THE STAR, the Infant Christ-consciousness, the dancing design on the last card are all the result of man's own effort. This card, too, is the result of man's behavior—the lack of effort for not trying to be in rightful place in evolution above the animal. He has gone back to the animal by letting himself slide downhill.

This card, THE DEVIL, begins a series which illustrates the stages of unfoldment of our powers by the continued effort at self-control.

Note that all the LIGHT in this card comes from the TORCH. If not for the torch it would be completely dark. That is to say, there would be no light whatever if it were not for the torch inflaming man's desire. It is an inverted torch which gives the least light and most smoke of which it is capable; yet without it there would be complete darkness; so again we have the occult doctrine that it is better to have low desire than no desire at all—better to go to Hell than to be a Hell-dodger. Even THE DEVIL says occultism is the source of light. If you yield to the temptation of THE DEVIL, that is, of instinct, the suffering you will eventually undergo will be your means of progress. If you do not yield you will cultivate will power, and thus your temptation is your means of progress. The temptations of Jesus in the desert were the means whereby he conquered. They came *after* he had acquired power. The desire to use power for selfish purposes is what we all come up against the moment we get power. That is to be expected, for the desire to use power to advance ourselves is inherent in the possession of power. If you will read the story in the Gospel you will see that it is very carefully phrased. Jesus did not deny the power of THE DEVIL. Instead, he used the expression, "Get ye behind me, Satan," which is a very peculiar expression until it is analyzed in the light of occultism.

No wise man wants to put his enemy behind him, but he wants to keep him in front where he can keep an eye on him and see what he is doing. This expression means that the material power of Jesus, the Solar Energy, was incomplete until it became backed up with the energy of the Earth, his body. The body, when controlled, acquires an energy which the mind does not have, and which it did not have itself until it was properly used by the mind. This power is generated by the mind, or the Solar Energy. Every time we withstand the temptation to slip back to animal instinct, we give the body more power to control, until finally it opens to man the power of the Stellar Energy, as you see depicted in card 8, STRENGTH.

This brings us to the inspection of the card at its higher level, the level of occult practice rather than of ignorance. BLACK in the Tarot is to be read at the level of ignorance and sin and also at the level of occult knowledge and practice.

THE FOOL put on the robe of ignorance in order to descend into matter. In order to ascend out of it he must put on the robe of occult knowledge and practice. The STAFF on which THE FOOL carried the Wallet of the subconscious, and by which he opens its treasures, is occult practice, as is indicated by the black wand tipped with red. Let us see what we make of the symbols of this card when they are read at the higher level. Always remember that when a thing serves more than one purpose, it can not be as satisfactory as the thing made for one purpose only.

Read at the occult level, the BAT WINGS and the HORNS are STONE COLOR. Stone symbolizes the union of the personality with the Father, and it is this union which confers upon the personality the ability to soar into higher planes. In the animal, horns are for the purpose of protection. Union with the Father furnishes the personality with its defense and protection.

There are SIX POINTS, made like nails, on the WINGS, and the letter VAU, the Nail, the Higher Self, is number 6 in the Hebrew alphabet. The two marks above the brows of THE DEVIL are V and V, and VV is the Hebrew spelling of VAV. THE DEVIL *is* the Higher Self when you refuse to listen to his teaching any other way than by the pain which comes to you from the unbridled following of instinct.

The FACE of THE DEVIL is PINK, which signifies the divine use of the Mars vibration, RED-ON-WHITE, the color which forms the foundation for the throne of THE HIEROPHANT. THE DEVIL's head has been transformed by Kundalini, when read at the occult level instead of at the level of sin. Also at the occult level the DONKEY'S EARS become ears of intuition. They are very upstretched, listening to the Voice from above.

The Kundalini has entirely transformed the three centers in the head—the eyes and the ears and the mouth—and they are functioning spiritually.

The HAIRY FACE, which is that of a beast when you look at the card in the other way, now indicates mental vibration both in dreams and in our Bible. The strength of Samson lay in his hair, in his mental vibration.

On his CRESCENT-SHAPED MOUTH, so grim at the lower level, when viewed at the other level is the symbol of ARIES, the EMPEROR, or the Mars vibration in the head.

The EYES, which at the higher reading saw all, now mean that they see the smaller part of life. It is the Sight of Aries which shows you what the larger part of life was.

The Beast THIGHS of THE DEVIL become his greatest vehicles for occult force, carrying out the suggestion in the previous card TEMPERANCE (Sagittarius) that in the thighs were the greatest Spiritual force—and Sagittarius stands for the thighs. The thighs are the great strength of Spiritual man, for the Angel carries down into them the mingled streams of alchemic Fire and Water. The scepter carried in the hand of THE HIEROPHANT rests on his left thigh, and it means control of the four planes. The hand of THE EMPRESS rests upon her left thigh, and THE FOOL wears on his thigh the same curious ornament that he wears upon his heart.

On the LEFT KNEE of THE DEVIL is marked the Serpent of Libra, the serpent standing on his tail, the symbol of equilibrium.

The EAGLE CLAWS depict that THE DEVIL keeps his balance in his difficult and strenuous position only by the clutch of the raised sex force. See how hard it must be to keep your balance sitting as THE

DEVIL is sitting. All others have an easy time. See how hard it is for him to keep his poise. When you become an occultist your emotions may sweep you away unless you keep them in harness. If there were no claws, THE DEVIL would topple over. THE DEVIL has a mindless craving for sensation, and you see that in his torch; yet we must go through that stage.

The TORCH is mostly RED with very little YELLOW in it. Yellow is mind. We must all go through that stage until we feel our own limitations. We suffer from them until we make an effort to change them. The "Pollyanna" state of mind is not one to be recommended. Everything is not all right, and this state of mind keeps you from feeling. I beg of you, do not make the best of a bad thing. See how bad it is and try to change it. Socrates said, "No man starts out to be wise until he sees what it costs him to be a fool." He also said that the perception of ignorance is the first stage of knowledge. The progress of the world has come in the same way. Some way has got to be found to overcome obstacles that confront us. The progress of the individual has come from the recognition that some way must be found to overcome obstacles or limitations. Only the painful perception can set our feet on the Path of Liberation. It is the search for sensation which prevents us from seeing it.

There is no other power that can do this for us but the power of the so-called devil, or the suffering in which we have involved ourselves. We cannot have good desires until we have learned by painful experience that bad desires bring pain. So-called evil is necessary because we evolve by transmuting it. This shows us the mad folly of the Church and State in setting up prohibitions against the indulgence of the natural appetites, particularly the folly of the State in calling such indulgence crimes. If prohibitions were successful they would deprive people of their only means of growth. Fortunately, they have never been successful, though they have enabled the Church and State to indulge in all sorts of cruelties by punishing such people. Most of the activities of the institutionalized Church have, distressingly enough, been just interference with the free expression of people's desires.

In the long course of human history there has been no person who found God without having first learned the way by going to THE DEVIL. He had to learn the right way via the wrong way. Sin is just missing the mark, which in the end teaches you how to aim right. "All we like sheep have gone astray." All we includes Himself, and in another place He said: "I am in all things like as ye are." If this meant anything, it meant having sinned.

The outstanding thing about man is that he has to learn to conquer his animal instincts. The child has to learn not to yield to his instincts. We do not put off the child, St. Paul said, until we become the man. We become the man only by shifting our consciousness entirely from the body to the mind. It was not very flattering to humanity, on the part of Jesus, to call us "sheep" so often. For sheep have no minds of their own. They follow each other pell-mell, the right way or the wrong way, the one as easily as the other. Men are drifters, either to the church or to prison.

Occultists have no militant religion and the Christian religion prides itself on militant religion. The occultist does not seek to convert. He is eagerly on the lookout for signs in people who are ripe to be converted. Now the signs of ripeness are very plain and very simple. If a man finds religion unreasonable and science unsatisfactory, then he is ripe to be told about occultism. If he is still content with religion or science or both he is not ripe, and you only create useless and expensive friction in trying to advocate occultism. You retard the time when he will be ripe.

The occultist teaches that all of these men who are now perfect began by conquering their body, and there was a time when their bodies conquered them. The outstanding thing to learn is to live not in the body but in the mind-nature. As I said, that belongs to the child, and we did not put off the child until we became the man. We become a man by shifting our consciousness from the body to the mind. It is a long process, and the Founder of Christianity was constantly comparing men to sheep. Some people think that Jesus was being satiric when he called men sheep.

Aries is a Ram, and Capricorn a Goat. Both are remarkable for their individuality. Both Jesus and Buddha were chided in their day for consorting with sinners. The sinners they consorted with were individualists, not the drifters. Drifters are people who let themselves slide downhill, back to the animal kingdom. Individualists are those who show some energy of soul and mind.

The more of the Life Power a sanctified man can wield, the more he respects those who use what they have in expression rather than in suppression. We are told that the angels have more joy over the one who returneth than over the 99 who merely conformed to what they heard was virtue.

The number of this card, 15, spells IH, the first half of the name Jehovah (IHVH) which is in itself the divine Name attributed to Wisdom, or the masculine principle of the Universe. The feminine principle of the Universe is the Cosmic Mind, which corresponds to what we call Nature. When we control the Nature in our bodies we become as gods.

The theological devil is only the nature in our bodies which we must no longer use as the animal uses it, but as the human should use it, under the dominion of Reason. When we have completed this dominion we are supermen.

With the third row of the Tarot Tableau enters a new element in the Tarot teaching. By reading downward, the vertical rows give us a new synthesis. The first triad is 1, 8, and 15. We can read it at the level of 15 as "ignorance" or as occult practice. If ignorance, then the direction of number is WEST-BELOW, which means that the personality is controlled by the subconscious in its lower form, when THE EMPRESS is debased by THE MAGICIAN. If we read from the level of occult practice, it means that the personality is controlled by the subconscious in its higher form (the Holy Ghost), THE HIGH PRIESTESS, or that THE EMPRESS and THE HIGH PRIESTESS HAVE BECOME ONE.

The message of the Triad at the lower level is this: The image-making faculty of the self-conscious transforms the subconscious through the Law of Suggestion, who thereupon tames the destructive animal nature and releases us from bondage to it.

The message of the Triad at the occult level is this:

The image-making faculty of the self-conscious equips the subconscious with his own powers of selectivity and initiative. He enables her to draw in (through the Transformed Heart) the power of the Astral Light. Thus it backs up the power of the Earth with the power of the Sun, and the union of the two is the Great Magical Secret.

The second stage of unfoldment.
The fundamental Masculine (The Lighting) principle and the fundamental
minine (Tower) principle — Active Thinking controls Passive Thinking.

THE TOWER.

" You are the result of your mental images "

2 - 9 — 16

11
16
27 = 9

17th Hebrew Letter	*PEH*
Symbol for	*Pair of Opposites (Beauty & Ugliness/Harmony & Discord*
Color	*Scarlet*
Numerical Value	*80 & Sometimes 800*
Syllables	*PH*
Sound	*C-Natural*
Planet	*Mars*
Translation	*Mouth*

275

NOTES

THE TOWER

PEH, spelled PH. The 17th Hebrew letter and the fifth DOUBLE LETTER. It means MOUTH, as in the organ of speech, the vehicle by which you speak. It is the sign or symbol for the pair of opposites, BEAUTY and UGLINESS, or GRACE and SIN, or HARMONY and DISCORD; for the direction NORTH; for the EXCITING INTELLIGENCE (exciting in the sense of inciting); for the planet MARS; for the color RED; for the note C-NATURAL. In Roman characters it is written as P and the numerical value is 80. It is one of the letters which has a final form, in which case its value is 800.

The character PEH, like the character SAMEKH, is the character KAPH with an addition. In Samekh the addition is a line ascending from the parallelogram at the bottom and connecting it with the top. The Parallelogram represents the physical body, and the top is the down-pouring energy which formed it, just as it formed all things of our solar system. The letter thus seems to picture man's body of manifestation after it has achieved reunion with its Source. In addition, in Peh, it does not ascend from the parallelogram (which represents the body) but hangs pendantly from the top, that is, from the Solar Energy itself. It is said that this pendant represents the means whereby the Solar Energy could manifest itself finally as a thing upon the physical plane. It represents the energy of gender, the energy engendered by the meeting of the Solar with the Lunar energy (Will with Ambition) whereby the Substance took the shape that the Solar Energy or Will dictated—and became the countless forms of the manifested Universe.

So this letter PEH is a KAPH with a tongue hanging from the upper part. You see it looks a little like a mouth. Kaph is the WHEEL OF FORTUNE, the Spiritual Law of Cycles made articulate. THE WHEEL symbolizes forms. The last time, we had a letter meaning EYE as the organ of SIGHT. Just so, we have here the MOUTH as the organ of SPEECH. Speech is what letter? THE CHARIOT. It is said that God created the Universe by sounding the word; but Speech in occult parlance means that thing which magically creates—CHETH—that a man may so make his body over that he can create magic with it, make things with it. We saw in the last card, AYIN, THE DEVIL, that that was the natural body. The Spiritual body was able to create, to make things magically. The man who has made over his body so that it becomes a great magical agent dominates the positive and negative forces of the

Universe, the negative and positive operations of the Astral Light.

The Gospel story speaks of that in figurative language; that is what it means by "The Word made Flesh." This eternal body is created last. The Book of Revelation says that the first so created was the body of Christ. He was the first Word made flesh, and the Book of Revelation at the same time calls him "the first-born of many brothers." He was the first to make an imperishable body. Many have followed him, and we scheme to follow his example in time. Long before we can manifest that body we have to learn to suppress all the expression of our personality. The personality interferes with the Will of the Higher Self. We must learn to interpose no personal obstacles of our own to the free passage of the Life-Power through our form. We have not yet made a perfect form, but we can keep from interfering with the passage of the Life-Power through the one we have. The way to do that is to relinquish the idea of a Personal Will. You can do that on faith, or you can do that by your Reason. *Reason tells you that there is no such thing as Personal Will, that only you think so. There is at most merely personal choice, but not Will.*

The human body is merely a vehicle, an instrument, to interrupt the forces that flow through it in such a way as to produce something with them, just as an electrical apparatus interrupts the current in such a way as to produce something. The current process of interrupting the force gives you the illusion that you are doing it yourself. It produces various stresses and strains in your body, and so you think you are doing something. All you are really doing is manifesting a resistance to the power. The power flows around that resistance and something is produced by its flowing around it. We are told by those who claim to know that what we think is evolution is really not evolution. Things happen because you are you, because your form is the kind of form it has. So you can take that by reason or take it on faith. Your reason will supply you with knowledge of any electrical machine; the electrical machine does nothing of itself. It is there simply to convert power into manifestation by dint of offering resistance to the stream of electricity which flows through it. It is the electricity that produces the results— the results which are there merely because of the way the machine is made.

The Kaph card pictures creation as the result of the descent of the Golden Serpent into the blue sea of matter. The sea is the Lunar Energy and the Serpent is the Solar Energy. Both the Bible and the Church liturgy tell us that the coming together of the two is a sex act.

"This world," says the liturgy, "not made but begotten."

We see the same idea expressed in the color symbolism. The two original primary colors are YELLOW and BLUE, and RED is the relationship between them, making three primary colors in all. Out of the union of these three, in varying proportions, are all the rest of the colors made.

All action, cosmically speaking, illustrates the working of sex, or gender. Science declares the same thing, that "all action consists of the interworking of opposites." What *excites* or *incites* the action, which contrives forms in the beginning, equally serves to continue and sustain them. Science teaches that all atoms are similar in construction. Atoms consist of a central nucleus of energy, around which particles of matter are grouped in certain patterns—the precise patterns being dictated by the exact quality of that central energy.

This double formation is the combination of Solar and Lunar energy which created the Universe. The double formations give to each atom sex, or gender. This power of sex or gender gives to each atom the power to destroy and recreate itself. In the working of the Mars energy is an eternal destruction and reconstruction. This sex or gender energy functions in every cell of your body. It functions in each group of cells which we call vital organs, and it is this energy which constitutes your life. Only one form of it is specialized in the procreative power of the organism as an entirety. Each cell has also this procreative power.

The energy which constitutes your life, which makes your body-machine work, you express individually in beauty or in ugliness, in harmony or in discord, in grace or in sin; hence the pair of opposites attributed to this letter. At first you express this life as a self-conscious entity or activity, but after a while your body takes on the impress of your mind, and you express its activity subconsciously also.

Each cell of your body, and hence all its vital organs, generates enough of this sex energy to carry on its own functions. The power station which feeds the body with the energy, the additional energy to carry out the instructions from the brain, is the Mars energy generated in the Mars Center. This is the Prostatic Ganglion, located between the spine and the navel.

Commands or ideas go down from the brain, or Mercury Center, through the Moon Center and the Venus Center to the Jupiter Center; and the Jupiter Center relays them to their final destination.

Of all the body areas, the sex area is the most immediately responsive to the brain, hence the Mars Center seems to have a closer connection with the physical sex of the organism, as a whole, than with anything else. The Mars Center feeds the whole body with energy. The Hindus call it "The Abode of the Self," meaning the personal self.

The Mars Center is the storage battery generating all the energy we exhibit in the act of self-conscious living, or doing what we wish to do. When the Mars Center functions well we have a sense of vitality and possess what we call *magnetism*—a quality which need have nothing to do with our state of physical health. When it functions poorly we have lassitude and are depleted of mental and emotional force.

Card 16, THE TOWER, is one of the four cards representing the various workings of the Mars vibration. The Mars vibration proceeds by destruction. It breaks down the cells involved, and with the energy thus liberated, it performs the requisite action and then builds up the cell again. Card 16 represents the Mars vibration itself. The destruction it exhibits depicts what goes on in every physical, emotional, and mental action. A cell is broken down, the generative principle (both masculine and feminine) is thrown out; then the two must build the cell up again.

Card 4, THE EMPEROR, is the Mars vibration functioning in the brain as the faculty by which we draw conclusions from premises. The premises are what we have learned from our observation of life. *Reason always destroys a previous false conclusion.* Whether the reasoning power be slow or rapid, a structure of error is always destroyed by it. Reason is forever at war with what most people think, or rather, think they think. Most people never have a thought of their own. They have inherited, without investigation, the opinions of others. They do not use their own reason at all.

When they find themselves, at last, in a spot where they must reason, they find that they have no premise on which to base their reason. Having taken over the opinions of others, they give slovenly attention to what is going on around them in life. They find that they will have to pay better attention, observe more carefully, before they can use their own reason—before they can draw correct conclusions from their own experience.

Then it is THE EMPEROR who proceeds to break down the false notions we have inherited, or which we ourselves have rashly assumed from superficial attention.

Card 13 is the Mars vibration functioning to stimulate sex glands;

it particularly refers to the occult use of certain indispensable chemicals which these glands furnish the body. The nerve force which energizes the sex glands contributes to the body chemistry the power and materials required for the vivification and transformation of the Pineal Gland, which the occultist seeks to accomplish, and for building brain cells that will enable us to remember what happens to us when we function in our higher vehicles during sleep.

To construct these and other necessary recording apparatus we must have the power and the special chemical constituents which come from the normal energizing of the sex glands by the Mars Center. Card 16 specializes in a certain kind of flash of mental vision which destroys a preceding erroneous structure of the mind or the personality, but that flash of vision does not come from reason, *but from the Higher Self Himself.*

⚫ *WHAT GIVES YOU POWER TO CARRY OUT YOUR IDEAS, WHETHER THEY CONCERN THE EXTERNAL WORLD OR THE INTERNAL ONE, IS YOUR MARS CENTER.*

Card 4, THE EMPEROR, is the Mars force manifesting in the head, manifesting in the brain. The faculty by which you draw conclusions from your observations, your physical observations or your mental observations, is called *Prana* (energy). If you pay particular attention and make accurate definitions of the life you see going on around you, and you reason logically, then you will draw reasonable conclusions from your observations. Reasonable conclusions on your part always destroy the previous erroneous opinions which you had or which you had accepted from someone else. Whether your reasoning power is slow or rapid, the structure of previous error is always torn down and you build up a better structure.

Most people, as you know, form entirely erroneous conclusions from life. Erroneous conclusions are destroyed when you reason well, or when you observe well. THE EMPEROR is always destroying, just as THE TOWER is always destroying, previous erroneous conclusions to build up better ones.

The word *speech* is a figure also. It stands for the vibrations emanating from the body—not only its word, but its actions and its influences. To the letter Cheth is attributed the faculty of Speech. This faculty meant the power to make magic. Magic is made with the spiritualized body. It is the MOUTH which emits the Speech which the Bible says is the destined utterance of man to help in the work of creation by making all things new. When we remake the Mouth and the Eye, we remake the body—remaking two different aspects of the body. The only two features of the face we can change by the nature of our thoughts and our emotions are the eye and the mouth.

We saw that when we read THE DEVIL card at the level of ignorance, it represented man and his body controlled by animal instincts. When we read it at the level of occult knowledge and practice, it represented man and his body controlling and wielding the powers of instinct—the very powers that used to drive him. That controlled mind and body became THE CHARIOT, and the principal business of the Charioteer is to create originally and magically. The Charioteer is the personal reason made one with the Higher Self.

The card THE TOWER can also be read in two ways: the surface meaning, which represents the personality when it thinks in terms of physical, emotional, and mental sensation only; and when used aright, it becomes, with AYIN, the GREAT MAGICAL AGENT. With Peh it becomes the Temple of the Holy Ghost, from which both the conscious and the subconscious may contact the higher planes.

Cheth is called THE INTELLIGENCE OF THE HOUSE OF INFLUENCE. It refers to the influx of the Spirit from above. When the body is rightly used it becomes a vase into which is poured the Divine Influence, for the body is the house. When wrongly used (as it is depicted at the surface level of THE DEVIL and THE TOWER cards), it is a house of influence in a very different sense. It influences its tenant to gratify its appetites and its ambitions. THE DEVIL card specializes on its appetites and THE TOWER card on its ambitions.

One of the Hebrew words for "sin" is spelled PShO. There is another word in Hebrew meaning "Divine Influence," and it is spelled SHPO. The only difference between these two words, whose meanings are at the extreme poles of opposition, is the position of the letter Peh. Sh, or Shin, is the letter of Cosmic Consciousness, a mental grasp of the meaning of the Sea of Fire in which we are all immersed. The card Judgement pictures an initiation upon the astral which ushers us into this consciousness. It shows the coffins of personal consciousness floating on the Great Deep, and their three occupants who have emerged from them into complete understanding. The word meaning "sin," PShO, puts the coffin of personal consciousness (or the personal use of the Mars vibration) before Sh instead of after it. The personal energy of the threefold body is put first. This means that the individual insists upon determining the action of the Life Power by imposing upon it the forms which his appetites or his ambitions demand. Among these people are more than those who pursue their own pleasures at the expense of everything else. *They are the people who practice false yoga; they who seek to impose their own will on the Cosmic Life, i.e., Christian Science and New Thought.* They seek to impress the Universal Consciousness in such a way as to force it to manifest forms they want. This is black magic, and to those who practice it there comes eventually, as to the ruthless followers of ambitions and sensation, the flash of lightning which dashes to the ground their entire false structure of life.

Those who see the Kingdom of God sincerely seek it for its own sake. Then, they are told, all things needful will be added unto them. It must be sought for its own sake. As long as a person seeks it to get things or to get power, he will miss the Kingdom. In the end he will lose the mess of pottage for which he sold it. When the Kingdom of Heaven is sought for its own sake, the body becomes, in the end, the HOUSE OF INFLUENCE (the body which was once the Tower of False Reason). You must not think this minimizes the personality. Personality is all-important, but we must not pander to its desires. We must control and use them as a vehicle for the individual transformation of the Life Power. Each personality, properly controlled and utilized, has a contribution to make to the evolution which can be made by no other personality. In the word ShPO, the two letters P and O are read at the level of the Spiritual body. In the word PShO they are read at the level of the natural body.

ShPO, three letters, and the cards which spell ShPO are 20, 16, 15. Card 20 is the symbol of the Fourth Dimension. On the card there are three beings emerging from three coffins. These coffins are the coffins of the personal consciousness. The personal consciousness of your self-conscious and the personal consciousness of the Christ-Child—equilibration between the two you are able to manage. In card 20, they are floating on a sea, and that sea being Blue is the sea of Divine Wisdom—The Blue of THE HIGH PRIESTESS. Card 16 shows us the lightning flash destroying THE TOWER of False Reason and False Opinion. Card 15 shows you life when it is interpreted merely as sensation. THE DEVIL says to you that sensation is all.

People try to impose their wills upon events, upon the Cosmic Life, to force the Ocean of Divine Wisdom to disobedience, or try to compel the Cosmic Mind-Stuff to take the form they want. They can get away with it for a while if they know how to do it, but this is what we call black magic. Imposing your will on somebody else or on a form of any sort is black magic. Always there will come a lightning flash which shatters these false structures to the ground. The same way if you build yourself a Tower of any false opinion; whether you know how to work black magic or not, your Higher Self will always jolt you out of it. As you generally have free choice, you can build up your Tower the same way after He has knocked it down. The next time He will give you another kind of dose or jolt.

Again we learn of the nature of Peh from the letter-name ALEPH, which is spelled ALP. *Life* is spelled ALP. A is the fiery Life-Breath; L is Equilibrium; P is the Mars vibration. You have got to keep the Life-Breath in equilibrium if you are going to control it. The spelling of ALP, as does the spelling of all the letter-names, tells us the action of the Intelligence or Force the letter stands for. The fiery Life-Breath, Aleph, continually maintains the equilibrium of the Universe by destroying forms which have ceased to be of use.

The first act of creation was to throw out of equilibrium the three qualities of matter which, as long as they remained in equilibrium, were static. The first act of creation was a destructive act. It was destructive in order to make the creation of forms possible. That is the way Nature creates. The seed of plants and animals must be destroyed in order to make new life. The sprout that grows from a bulb feeds on the bulb and destroys it. That is the way man creates. He builds nothing without previously destroying something. That is also the way Nature localized in our body acts. "All personal activity," says science, "breaks down cell structure and thus liberates energy for action and new construction." Any movement, however small, breaks down the cells of our bodies which are engaged in that movement. Any thought burns up the physical cells in our brains. The only way man can create physically, emotionally, and spiritually is by a preceding destruction of his body, his only concern being to build up something as good as what he has destroyed or better.

The body is the out-picturing of the mind, and hence the work of the practical occultist is the substitution of good images for poor ones, true patterns for false ones. True patterns proceed from accurate attention to life, false patterns from superficial attention.

The word the Hebrew Wisdom applies to the Mars force is *whirling*. The "whirling force," wherever it is manifested, always begins by tearing down one kind of form to build up another, yet you and I can defeat its intention in us by persisting in our false patterns of life, by paying such superficial attention that we do not perceive what the true ones are, or if we do, by being too languid or too greedy to want to follow them. Finally the Higher Self (the God "who will not always strive with man") sends a bolt which destroys our willful Tower. Even then we can refuse to learn our lesson. We can begin to build it again, just as it was before, hoping for better luck this time.

THE TOWER in this card is called the Tower of Separateness. As long as there is any idea of separateness in your personality, you will continue to have your House of Life torn down by external and internal calamity. Sooner or later it comes to all. If you have set foot upon the mystic or occult path it will come sooner. You will continue to have your House of Life torn down until you rebuild it as your Higher Self would have it. The interests of all humanity are inextricably bound up with yours. This is only a small part of the sense of separateness. The interests of all Nature are bound up with yours. The interests of the Creator are bound up with yours. We have to cease feeling that we are one thing and our neighbor is another—our neighbor no matter how geographically distant—that animals, plants and minerals are another, and that God is another. Man is only an expression of the One Life, and God is the One Life out of which all things come. Man is no more an expression of the One Life than the animal, the plant, or the mineral. He is a greater agent, thanks to his ability to wield more of the Mars vibration. Whether he wields it in accordance with what we call "evil," he must wield it in obedience to Cosmic Law.

This card PEH, like the previous card AYIN, depicts the human body when it is laboring under the delusion of a personal will, which can do as it pleases. It is laboring under the delusion that sensation—physical, emotional, or mental—constitutes the whole of the Universe. *There is no personal will but there is personal choice.* We can choose to wield our little portion of the Mars force in accordance with what we call good or in accordance with what we call evil. We can build a bad Tower or a good one. In this respect we are put to the narrowest choices, although the field seems large. We can choose to follow what might be called the instincts of the Higher Self, or to follow the instincts of the body. If you, the self-conscious, do not make your personality the vehicle of the appetites of the body, you must make it (the personality) the vehicle of the Higher Self. How then can you pretend to have free will? It is a delusion by which you flatter yourself and confuse your judgment.

The secret meaning of the allegory of the Tower of Babel concerns the appetites, the emotions, and the ambitions of the body. It was built by people whose actions were dictated solely by their bodies. The allegory quaintly states that this arrogant attempt of man to scale the heavens resulted in a confusion of tongues, the permanent separation of nations. The Tower of Pride in the Old Testament was called the Tower of Babel. The Tower of Separateness of Pride was called the Tower of Babel. That allegory images the separateness of man by saying that he made an arrogant attempt to scale the heavens, and God was so frightened that he might do it that He sent them into a confusion of tongues—permanent separateness. That is a very naive way, on the surface of the matter, to account for the fact that there are different languages in the world. All the people of the world spoke one language until they made this Tower of Babel, and that frightened God that He might be invaded, and so he stopped it by separating languages.

The story goes on to state that as these inhabitants journeyed farther from the East, that is, went farther and farther in consciousness from their simple origin and became more sophisticated, they found a plain in the Land of Shinar and dwelt there. *Shinar* means "emotions." Thus, as the story goes, these people decided to live entirely in their emotions, or in their subconscious sensations, from which their emotions arise. Also their minds had something to do with it. They desired to be distinguished from the common people, so they built their tower to make a "name" for themselves. They did not build it of stone, the material provided by Nature, but of brick which they fashioned themselves. This means that they were not content with natural sensations and emotions, but fabricated artificial ones. Nor were their substitutions wholesome ones, for instead of mortar the bricks were joined together with black slime.

The word *brick* is the same in Hebrew as the word for "moon." The tower they build was built of moonshine—that is, of the ideas entirely based on the subconscious. Thus far all was plain sailing with the allegory. But now occurs a strange item. The Lord said that because this people were one and had the same language, they might in the future unite and do any willful thing they wanted to do. To avoid this danger, he scattered them over the face of the entire Earth and divided them with many languages.

In order to develop the mind it was necessary to withdraw their emotional psychic qualities and immerse them still farther into matter. The occult teaching is that when, on account of this deeper immersion into matter and the withdrawal of their psychic powers, the mind is developed; then gradually these psychic powers will be returned to them on a higher spiral—the level of the mind and not the body. We shall then be as "near heaven" as we inherited the power to be, but in addition, we shall have the mental development which we could not acquire as long as these gifts kept humanity from having the use of the mind.

The Atlanteans could have approached heaven with the psychic gifts, but they preferred to employ them to increase their bodily gratifications even as we, as a race, use our minds to increase our bodily sensation.

In card 16, THE TOWER is built of 22 layers of bricks, and stands for the 22 Hebrew letters. The symbolism here is that the things which are wrongly applied to obtain preeminence over one's fellows are the things which, when rightly applied, will be the means of spiritual development. This is one of the basic ideas of the Tarot, and it particularly occurs in these two cards, AYIN and PEH, since they are meant to be read at two levels—ignorant greed and occult knowledge.

SYMBOLISM

Here you have a TOWER crowning an inaccessible PEAK seemingly made of glass. There is no way to climb up to it. If you could climb up the Peak, there is no door in sight, and the windows are very high up. The two occupants of this Tower have fenced themselves off from the rest of the world. It symbolizes the greatest fallacy of mankind. No sooner do people get possessions than they proceed to build around themselves some sort of wall of distinction. They forget one thing: when people cannot get at you, neither can you get at them. These two are virtually prisoners in the Tower that they have built with such care and pain to be exclusive. The Higher Self sees that the only way to get them out is to hurl them out head first, hoping they will strike on their heads. Their heads are made of bone, so they need a pretty hard jolt in order to give up their ideas of separateness.

Here is the self-conscious that has an entirely erroneous idea of itself. It is impossible to build up exclusiveness and make itself separate from everything else. The Higher Self has to adjust so much of that, that it destroys the Tower. You have further choice—you can attempt to build up your Tower again, after which it is destroyed in the same way.

So this is what these two persons constructed out of their little bit of Cosmic Mind-Stuff. They have become so entrenched in it that the only way the Higher Self could get them out was to dash them out by a bolt of lightning, which sets the Tower on fire. This bolt comes from the Higher Self because it takes the shape of two V's and an arrow. The first united it with the card THE HIEROPHANT, and the second with the card TEMPERANCE. Both of these are different aspects of the Higher Self.

The TWO FIGURES are the chained man and woman in card 15. Note that then they were nude, but now they are clothed. The first thing Adam and Eve did after they had sinned in the Garden was to clothe themselves. The meaning of this symbolism is that they are ashamed. They cannot sustain their old, simple frank relations, which they had when they were animal-humans in card 15. They are destined to regain that simple relation on a higher spiral, as we find in the card THE LOVERS. In the long interval between these two states, these partners hide from each other their intentions.

Their clothes are symbolic in color. The woman is dressed just as she should be, in BLUE. The man also has the feminine robe of Blue, when he should be clad in the masculine robe of YELLOW. All the desire of the self-conscious, typified by the RED MANTLE, is that he might live in the body. This is told again in the fact that the WOMAN wears the CROWN, and not the man. He has willingly abdicated to her. Again, note that the Tower itself is crowned with his Crown. The Tower represents the body.

This Tower may be called "the Tower of False Reason." False reason proceeds from the fact that the body desires are dictating the activity of the mind. The subconscious should never wear the Crown; to let her do so is lunacy. People who live in their subconscious imagine that they are in control, when it is really the body (which is the product of the subconscious) that is in control. The occultist is not likely to live in his subconscious. He is more likely than any other person to build a tower of separateness, to consider himself a man of superior knowledge, set off from other people, so forgetful that "He that is greatest among you let him serve the rest." What made Jesus say this so often is of greatest significance. His disciples, to whom he had imparted a little more knowledge of the Kingdom of Heaven than the multitude, were always squabbling among themselves as to which would be the greatest.

The MAN in the card dwells in the appetites of the mind, that is, more in his ambitions than in his bodily appetites. He has crowned THE TOWER (his body) with the CROWN OF INTELLECT, the

YELLOW of the MIND. It is the same Yellow as the LIGHTNING FLASH. The symbolism would be better if the flash were a pale yellow to associate it with the Higher Self and not mere intellect.

This lightning flash is the same as the power which is drawn down by THE MAGICIAN. It is the same thing as is symbolized by the Scepter of THE EMPEROR and by the Wand of the Charioteer. It is the trampling in the onward march of the horse of DEATH. The lightning flash is the universal, fundamental masculine principle—THE TOWER represents the universal, fundamental feminine principle. In THE MAGICIAN card the Tower is the Garden. In THE EMPEROR, the Tower is represented by the Throne on which he is seated. In THE CHARIOT the Tower is the same as the Chariot. In the WHEEL OF FORTUNE, it is the Wheel itself, it is the manifestation of evolution. In the DEATH card it is all these figures that are trampled down by the White Horse.

The LIGHTNING is striking the TOWER, which bursts into flames as it is struck. The FLAMES are both RED and YELLOW. RED is the MARS energy, the Yellow is the SOLAR energy. On the top of the Tower there is a CROWN. The Crown is Yellow, so it means the Solar Energy as it expresses itself in you through the intellect. Your body is topped, as it were, by your intellect. In this case your intellect is used to express its own will, and not the Will of the Father, not the ONE WILL. Here is this Tower of the personality expressing itself as the false will.

In this card the Figures fall HEAD FIRST. It is intended that they should fall on their heads, because the lightning flash of Intuition always destroys old notions and forms new ones. We are obedient to the heavenly admonition if we make the new vision permanent. Most people soon forget it, and rebuild the same old towers, crawl into them again, and then build up the door after them so that no new idea can enter.

Like the torch in THE DEVIL card, this flash and the flames it causes are the sole source of illumination—but for it, all is blackness of ignorance. Yet though it lasts for a single second, it does not entirely vanish. It leaves behind it a falling rain of 22 Yods, the number of the Hebrew letters. Ten fall on the side of the woman, the body. They represent the Ten Emanations of the Life Power required to construct all human forms. Twelve, the number of the signs of the Zodiac, falls on the side of the man. Twelve means the perfect self-expression of these Ten Emanations. Note that the expression of these Ten Emanations depends not on the woman but upon the man. She only carries out his instructions. A man's body is the result of his mental images, just as God's body (the manifested Universe) is the result of God's mental images. The physical depends upon the metaphysical, upon mental imagery, either of God or man.

The great error is the notion that life rests ultimately upon a physical basis. We should see plainly how great this error is, if we are willing to accept the analogy of the creations of artists and inventors. They were all in the first place mental images. The only difference is that we see these being carved out on the physical plane. We do not see God's images being carved out of the Cosmic Mind-Stuff, because it is done by processes as yet invisible to us. In our present limitations we see only the material results.

Whatever the source of our mental image, the structure we dwell in has always been constructed by it. Our bodies and all their acts, external and internal, are the result of mental images made long ago, and they have now become our dominant ones. Having made it thus, it controls us, and so we are compelled to act upon it. CHANGE YOUR MENTAL IMAGES, AND WHEN BY SO DOING YOU HAVE CONSTRUCTED A NEW MENTAL RHYTHM, YOU WILL ACT UPON THAT AUTOMATICALLY, JUST AS YOU NOW AUTO-MATICALLY ACT UPON THE OLD RACE IMAGES. You change the old by destroying it as far as it is possible. Construction must be preceded by destruction. This is true of the tiniest change. It is even more true of the greatest change of all, the change pictured in card 13, which is also of the Mars vibration: the slow change of the natural body to the Spiritual body.

Before we can build a new body which has new fields of perception into other planes than ours, the destruction indicated in cards 13 and 15 must come. Things within and without disintegrate; trials confront us, we seem uprooted. Health may be affected, and our house of life falls about us in ruins. "This thing cannot be good," we cry out passionately, in order to stifle the inner urge to go on doggedly, if need be in spite of all these catastrophes. "This thing cannot be good or all these evils would not happen" is the fundamental human idea of Christian Science. Even they realized that they must account for the universal human experience of catastrophe. They did so by calling this period "chemicalization" and said that it was a necessary, though brief, preliminary. However brief they try to make the preliminary, their own leader never passed through it, for she remained in it her whole life. True, she demonstrated wealth by the method of all material successes, but health and happiness she never achieved.

Even when its victims have no erroneous beliefs, the period is one which all must go through. Mystics call it "the night of the soul." Occultists call it "proceeding in the face of the thunderbolt." Whatever it is called, it is the inevitable precursor of any considerable reconstruction of heart, mind, or body. If you will accept the testimony of all the sages, mystics, and occultists, you will try to believe that these readjustments are necessary, and hence they are the sign of progress. As long as there is any idea of separateness in your personality, you will continue to have your house of life torn down over your head, until it is rebuilt as your Higher Self would have it, so that HE may occupy it.

The BACKGROUND of this card is BLACK, like that of THE DEVIL card; and like that of THE DEVIL, it has to be thought of at two levels. The first is, of course, the level of Ignorance; the second is the level of Occult Perception and Practice, being able to make use of this hidden force. This is the second stage of unfoldment. The inverted torch in the previous card was the first stage of enlightenment. The Torch, when inverted, gives the least light and the most smoke of which it is capable; but in the last card it was the only means of illumination.

Now here, the only means of illumination is the LIGHTNING FLASH. That lasts only a blinding second, but while it lasts it lights up everything. In this card you see it is not distributed as the lightning flash in Nature. It leaves behind it the falling rain of 22 Yods.

The MAN is thrown out of his Tower by the bolt of lightning, after building it by his mental images. You build either a good Tower or a bad one by your mental images. This is a bad one; he built it by superficial opinions on the subconscious, trying to gratify his body instead of gratifying his mind. This man's opinions, which are so superficial, are not even original because always from the beginning of the world the intellect has sought to fence itself away from other people. It has typical methods of doing so. "To most people," as the philosopher Santayana said, "a foreigner is ridiculous, unless he is stronger than you are, in which case he is odious."

Where did race thought come from? People have manipulated each other to produce it. The reason why people try to make us think so much of our own, and so little of other races, is in order to manipulate us better. The structure we dwell in has always been constructed by your mental image, whether for good or for bad. Often our bodies are the result of our dominant mental image in this life or in other lives. Even your skin! If you have practiced faithfully your Tarot for six months, your skin is different in texture, the quality of your flesh is different. *You are the result of your mental images.* They control you and you have to act on them. Hence the erroneousness of thinking you have free will. YOU HAVE ABSOLUTELY NO WILL AT ALL. In all things relating to the present you are the product of your past, but you have the ability to change your future, to change your body responses, by inaugurating new rhythms, by starting new mental images. After you have constructed new rhythms by getting new images, you automatically get them just as you automatically got the old rhythm that you had constructed. You are partly the slave of your past and partly the master of your future.

Now let us read the card at its higher level. There is nothing which serves two complex purposes that can be as satisfactory as when it is constructed to serve only one. This we particularly see in these two figures, when we turn the card upside-down to get the other meaning.

The WOMAN still wears the CROWN, but it is with the man's full knowledge and consent. It means that in the spiritual life, the heart precedes the intellect, and the intellect only carries out its commands.

The ROBE she is attired in is not the subconscious robe of our animal nature, but the Cosmic Subconscious of the Holy Ghost. The same applies to the man's robe. Both are making active in the flesh the Cosmic Mind. This is the "Word made flesh," which the occultist says first occurred in the person of Christ, of whom Jesus of Nazareth was only an incarnation, an embodiment.

This card is faultily composed, for she should be higher than the man, and should appear to be pouring down upon him the blessing which his raised hand is receiving. And vice versa, in the other meaning of the card—she should be lower than the man, for he never falls as low as his body. There is always some mental admonition in him which makes him ashamed. Now the body is not a vase for the heavenly influx. The two are soaring out of the body even as they do from their coffins in card 20.

The THREE WINDOWS are not at the top now, but at the base. They are the three lower centers of the body from which issue the serpent flame, which in time remakes the body. Note that the FLAME is colored RED and WHITE instead of RED and YELLOW, as are the other flames. RED and WHITE in the Tarot means the Divine use of the Mars force. The five-pointed star represents man. If you join the tips of this five-pointed star with lines, you have a pentagram which has the numeric value of 5 x 13 = 65. Sixty-five is the Divine Name ADNI, or in English, ADONAI. It means the Divine use of the Mars power, the fiery stream which pours out of the Cosmos and transforms one expression of itself into another in a never-ending series of changes. Sixty-five reduces to 11, or JUSTICE, the force which produces all natural transformations and manifests in perfect equilibrium. *As above, so below.*

You have read about the lower flames being different from the upper flames. What are these flames? What are those flames which are Red and Yellow? They are the Mars vibration used according to the Divine Expression. Why should these flames be quite different in color and in formation from the lower ones? When the card is turned upside-down, the Tower becomes a hollow pillar into which is streaming a high influence. It really means the highest influx, which is what Kaph means. You see at once that the highest influence starts operating on the self-conscious and the subconscious. They are no longer kept within the physical body, and they can soar upright into space.

There is an occult magic square of MARS. It is a square having five cells on a line and five lines—that is, 25 cells in the square. These cells are so arranged that no matter which way they are read—vertically, horizontally or diagonally—each line sums up to 65—the Divine Expression of the Mars force.

What is the top card in the second vertical row? THE HIGH PRIESTESS. What is the card under her? THE HERMIT. THE HIGH PRIESTESS working through THE HERMIT produces what is pictured in THE TOWER—the subconscious mind which links all opposites together through the laws of response and transfers to the self-conscious mind the flash of intuition sent by the Higher Self.

NOTES

The Third Stage of Unfoldment — Revelation —
Image-executing power of the subconscious —

The Mystic Marriage — Universal Energy — An individual effort.

18th Hebrew Letter	*TZADDI*
Symbol for	*Thought —*
	Meditation
Color	*Violet*
Numerical Value	*90 and Sometimes*
	900
Syllables	*TzDI*
Sound	*A-Sharp*
Translation	*Fish Hook*
Sign in Zodiac	*Aquarius*

295

NOTES

THE STAR

TZADDI, spelled TzDI, means FISH HOOK. It is the 18th Hebrew letter and the 11th SIMPLE LETTER. It stands for the occult extension of THOUGHT (extension of Thought to its highest degree), that is, MEDITATION; for the direction SOUTH-ABOVE; for the NATURAL INTELLIGENCE (meaning Intelligence about Nature); for the Zodiacal sign AQUARIUS, the Water-bearer; for the color VIOLET; for the note A-SHARP. In Roman characters it is written as Tz. Its numerical value is 90. It is one of the five letters which have a final form. In its final form its value is sometimes 900.

The NATURAL INTELLIGENCE means the Intelligence of Nature. In Meditation we bring down into the objective mind, or the brain, the mind of Nature, the subjective mind of the Holy Ghost, called in occult language WATER. Aquarius, the Water-Bearer, refers to the ability of man to bring this Water into his head. One finds this letter and card has affiliations with the letter and card MEM, which pictures the man through whose head the stream of the Cosmic Mind is flowing. The letter-name Mem, spelled in Hebrew MIM, adds up to 90, which is the value of the single letter TZADDI. Also the single character Mem, whose value is 40, is the same as the secret value of the letter Tzaddi. The character Tzaddi is said to be composed of two Yods coming down into a small Kaph, thus its secret value is two 10's and a 20, or 40.

The Law the letter Mem stands for is REVERSAL. The function of MEDITATION is what brings about those changes in the personal consciousness, which leads to the entire mental reversal referred to by this Law, the reversal of all one's estimates of life and the scale of values. The letter also has an important affiliation with THE HERMIT, since not only are there two Yods in the formation of the letter, there is also a Yod in the spelling of the letter-name TzDI. Why are there two Yods in the character? Because the function of the Holy Ghost, or the subjective mind in us, is to connect the Spirit with our objective brain, to interpret the Voice of the Spirit to the objective brain in terms it can understand, and to turn abstract thought into concrete thought. YOD represents the Spirit which, in order to manifest, divided itself into masculine and feminine, hence the two Yods in the character. Both of these descend into the KAPH, or the body of manifestation, but they do not descend automatically; they must be brought into man's body

297

by the effort of the man himself.

The remaining letter in the letter-name TzDI is DALETH, THE EMPRESS. The woman pictured in this card is THE EMPRESS. She is finally made one with THE HIGH PRIESTESS through the cleansing by THE HIGH PRIESTESS's robe which you see flowing through the YELLOW Crescent, which represents THE EMPRESS in card 2. She is the Waterfall in card 3 and also in card 13, which symbolizes the union of THE HIGH PRIESTESS and THE EMPRESS, or the Cosmic sub-consciousness of Nature joined with the intellectual subconscious of man. It is THE EMPRESS working as the agent of her lord, THE MAGICIAN, who is responsible for the entrance into the body of the Holy Ghost.

Seventeen, the number of this card, is 7 working through 1, and 7 is the number of VENUS. Card 8 pictures the transformed Venus, or EMPRESS, ushering into the body the Stellar sex energy by which the body is enabled to perform magical creation. Seventeen reduces to 8, which stands for the INTELLIGENCE OF ALL SPIRITUAL ACTIVITIES. The act of Meditation prepares us to comprehend the Secret of all Spiritual Activities, and how to utilize it when we become aware of it.

Finally, the direction of this letter, SOUTH-ABOVE, shows that it is a combination of South, the Sun, and Above, THE MAGICIAN. This means that Meditation is the control of the currents of Solar force by an act of self-conscious attention and will. We must will our mind to be still and then pay internal attention.

Seventeen—7 working through 1. Seven, THE CHARIOT, which has the type of consciousness indicated by THE MAGICIAN, is what produces this card. RECEPTIVITY-WILL describes the act of Medita-tion by your Will. You quiet your mind, but unless you make it recep-tive no message comes in. The act of Meditation perfectly portrays receptivity—THE CHARIOT working through THE MAGICIAN—(Receptivity-Will working through Attention).

In a word, then, Meditation is the result of the union of the super-conscious with the self-conscious. That is why you have the two Yods coming down into Kaph. Kaph is you. You are the manifestation of the Law of Cycles, the two Yods come into you, the self-conscious Yod and the subconscious Yod specializing as the superconscious. Subcon-scious and superconscious are the same thing. You differentiate them because of your position in looking at it. *That which is below you is just as that which is above you.* You call it "above" and "below" because of your position.

So you see, you may learn of the nature of Tzaddi through all these cards: KAPH, THE WHEEL OF FORTUNE; MEM, THE HANGED MAN; YOD, THE SUN; BETH, THE MAGICIAN; and CHETH, THE CHARIOT. These cards are inclusive; as you go on, of course, they include more and more of what went before as you infer from all these affiliations.

Science has been trying to tell the world how inaccurate your attention is when only the eye is used, for the eye is very faulty, yet the eye is very important. The occultist says that the truth about Nature cannot be seen by external attention alone. It can only be discovered by a combination of the two, external with internal intelligence, investigation from without and Meditation from within. Newton was asked how he discovered things. He said, "I put my mind on them, I look at them very often until they tell me the truth about themselves."

And finally, the occultist says that what most people call religion is not religion at all, it is theology. What really constitutes religion is a sense of the indwelling Presence, and if you pay attention you will see this Presence, you will hear It, you will encounter It.

Many scientists of the 19th century have very defiantly called themselves atheists, when they were actually really very religious people. Huxley was a very religious person but he did not believe in theology. He asserted with the utmost vigor all his life that theology was opposed to Truth, it was but a mask for life. The occultists laughed at such people when they said they were atheists. They said that the difference was that they worshipped Nature, and anyone worshipping Nature worships God. The Christian theology says there is God in three persons—the Father, Son and Holy Ghost. God, not the Holy Ghost, is Nature, so you are focusing your attention at the second and third persons instead of God, the first—HE IS ALL. Christian theology says the three are the same in different aspects. Many occultists become ironical by saying, "At any rate, Christians should not throw mud at you because you are putting your attention on a perfect unity, and most Christians are putting it on a person who is not a member of the Trinity at all—the devil; or they're putting attention on the Virgin Mary, and the Catholic Church does not claim the Virgin Mary to be a member of the Trinity.

"In fact," says the occultist, "what do you mean by *the Trinity*, Father, Son and Holy Ghost?" All three are males; you say the Holy Ghost proceeds from the Father and the Son and then, what does the

Son proceed from? *How can two masculine principles create a third principle?* What do you mean in your liturgy by saying "the world not made but begotten" if you do not recognize a feminine principle? The word is meaningless unless you have two principles, masculine and feminine.

The old Romans were always saying, "these Christians are very droll, they are constantly changing their doctrines and then they change their Scriptures." Research shows that to be the case. Even the translation of the St. James version shows that.

In astrology Uranus rules Aquarius. In Tarot, Uranus is THE FOOL. The sign Aquarius, as Man the Angel, occupies the upper corner of the cards X (10) and XXI (21). This is the corner upon which THE FOOL's expectant and confident gaze is fixed. The vision of THE FOOL as he came down into matter was Man, the Angel—man when he had developed the mental power to fly, to soar into the higher planes. THE FOOL, or the Life-Breath from the very beginning of its immersion into matter, kept urging man forward to his culmination in the Angel.

How shall man develop all his potencies? By the exercise of his faculty of attention in a twofold way—external attention and internal attention. The human race as a whole has just begun to develop the mind through external attention, but only a few individuals, comparatively speaking, have begun the practice of developing their minds through internal attention. The one is not dependent on the other. People who pay internal attention may scorn learning from their outer life. However, the salvation of the world will not come until the two are combined in every and each individual, for the one is needed to check and verify the other.

Uranus is an Air sign, an Air card; and there are four cards attributed to the element of Air. The four cards of the element Air are THE FOOL, THE LOVERS, JUSTICE, and THE STAR.

THE FOOL's expectant gaze concerns the distant vision of the day when man shall become the Angel; when by having perceived what Nature's Laws are and by living in harmony with them (when he has become "Air-minded"), he has achieved mastery of his body so as to become a co-worker with THE FOOL in the evolution of the sub-human kingdoms of Nature.

How can he do this? How can he fit himself to be a co-worker with the Higher Self? "God has made man," said the Bible, "to have dominion over all things." How do we get dominion over all things? By accomplishing in our body the states of consciousness and the activities depicted in the three cards THE LOVERS, JUSTICE, and THE STAR. By exemplifying in our own body what the three cards stand for. You see how important is the body!

The Church has been in the habit of ignoring Nature, and the occultist says nothing could be more illogical than this habit of ignoring the human body. "Nature," says the occultist, "is all you know about God. It is the manifestation of God. If you ignore Nature, you ignore God, and your body is the only means of manifestation. If you ignore your body, you cripple your mind, and in time you put out your mind."

The body of the One Energy is the Universe. Your physical body is the house of your energy. The physical body of you is the house of that little portion of the One Energy which your spirit represents. In all languages the word *spirit* means "air," that which you breathe. The air that you breathe is the physical plane form of that Force out of which the Universe was created. What the occultist seeks to do is to control that Force as it passes through him.

The word for "spirit" in Hebrew is RVCh (Ruach), and it reduces to 7. The 7th Hebrew letter is ZAIN, and it is the second card of this Air sequence. It is attributed to GEMINI, an Air sign. The Life-Breath manifests in seven ways in a sevenfold manner, and that is the reason there are seven planets in your body—the seven Centers. If you have gained control of the Life-Breath as it goes through your body, you have perfected yourself; you have mastered yourself. The alchemists' definition of it is the mixture of Fire and Water with Fire predominating. All creatures live by letting the air pass through them. What is the Life-Breath whose outward form is air? It is the Thought-Force out of which the Universe is created. The occultist seeks to control this Thought-Force as it passes through him, and to control it as it passes out of him to his environment.

The next card after Zain is JUSTICE, the central card of the entire Tarot Tableau, which shows the method by which you gain control. It is done by the self-conscious and subconscious working simultaneously. The self-conscious does two things. It achieves outward control and starts the subconscious on its achievement of inner control. The subconscious does two things. It achieves inner control and then remakes the self-conscious. How do you start outer equilibrium? By acting in accordance with your present perception of what constitutes equilibrium, no matter what it is. No matter what your notion is of social justice, or economic justice, of mental poise, of emotional poise, act on it and your perception of what really is will keep on increasing and you will make a better conception. Perception keeps increasing as it is acted upon and only as it is acted upon, and the more you act upon it outwardly, the more your subconscious will act on it inwardly. The acting on it inwardly is what changes your body, and that is done in the first instance by your acting on it outwardly. It changes your body into another kind of body, which is what Paul meant when he said, "Put off the mortal for the immortal, the corruptible for the incorruptible." Occultists say it has nothing to do with physical death. That is the willful adulteration of the Church. Paul was not referring to physical death at all, but something far removed from physical death. He was referring to a protracted qui-eternal life in this body—a change that would only take place in external life. If you put off the mortal and assume the immortal, then you can keep your body as long as you want it without dying. Occultists believe there are people now living in their physical bodies who have accomplished this transmutation, who have put off the mortal and put on the immortal, put off the corruptible and put on the incorruptible. They have equipped their bodies to see what you and I must accept as a matter of testimony. They can see that the Universe is maintained in perfect equilibrium. The way to see that is to maintain your little universe in perfect equilibrium, and that is all done by acting in accordance with the belief in social and economic justice and poise, and you carry that down to the utmost detail.

The fourth card of Air is THE STAR. It stands for the occult extension of the function of THOUGHT, the function of Thought raised to its highest degree in what we call Occult Meditation. Everyone knows that you cannot think without keeping your emotions still. Even ordinary thinking is blinded by emotions, and that refers to our prejudices too. That is only half the story. Not only is most people's thinking controlled by their prejudices for and against, but in addition most people think in accordance with their wishes. Some wit has said, "Most people think with their wishbones." They think what they want to think. They do not think in accordance with mental processes but with their emotional processes and desires. It is necessary, then, to quiet the emotions for ordinary thinking. FOR OCCULT MEDITATION, IT IS NOT ONLY NECESSARY TO QUIET THE EMOTIONS BUT TO QUIET ALL THE MIND, THE REST OF THE MIND.

This card is also one of the four Saturn cards: JUSTICE, THE MOON, THE STAR, and THE WORLD.

Astrologers say that Aquarius has two rulers. One is Uranus and the other is Saturn. What is Saturn? It is the limiting power. Speaking in psychological terms, it is necessary to limit action of mind in order to use it at all to the object before it—you cannot do any thinking, and if you're going to use your mind at its highest, it is necessary to limit it most and quiet it most. Thought in its lowest form cannot exist unless you control the mind, unless you keep it from running around everywhere. You cannot pay attention unless you control your eyes. Attention means "to make your eyes behave," and then you have to make your brain behave too. You have to make your mind behave to accept the testimony of the brain. You cannot do the most ordinary thinking without control of the mind and control of the emotions. Saturn is the principle of limitation. This card is not only one of the four Air cards, it is also one of the four Saturn cards. JUSTICE is also an Air card and a Saturn card. Astrologers say that Saturn is exalted in Libra (JUSTICE), which means that the limiting principle comes to its highest manifestation in the card JUSTICE. The principle of limitation finds its highest expression in action. JUSTICE represents equilibrium at work.

The next card of the Saturn sequence is this card THE STAR. It comes in the Saturn sequence because Meditation means the strictest, most strenuous control of the mind. *MEDITATION IS THOUGHT AT ITS HIGHEST SCOPE.* It depends on concentration, and the flow of mental images is ceaseless. Unless you restrain it, it is not concentration. Meditation depends first upon concentration. You must learn to keep your mind to one thing. The mental images are constantly in flux and you have to keep that still. Mental image activity is always on jump; if left alone you can think of 20 dozen things in a few moments. Your mind leaps from one thing to another, until you have traveled thousands of miles away from where you started out.

Meditation is the deliberate limitation of this activity to one selected point of thought. You look at one thought. There is another method of Meditation where you empty your mind entirely. The Hindus call that "contemplation." You empty your mind and just watch the flow as it flows through you. That is how this card happens to be in the Saturn sequence—because it is the limiting principle at its highest in the human being. You are limiting your mind to one thought. ×××

The last Saturn card, the Saturn vibration itself, is called THE WORLD. It depicts man sharing in the Administration of Nature, which the Bible says is his goal. The goal cannot be reached without first having unveiled the truth about Nature. That is to say, it cannot be reached without having become proficient in Meditation.

We all know that the underworld of the subconscious is the result of the investigations of the self-conscious. The method is Occult Meditation, and it is Meditation at its pinnacle when it is pursued by the awakened Pineal Gland, or Hermes, THE MAGICIAN. The letter which stands for it (Tzaddi) is called "the Fish Hook." Naturally it must be connected with the letter called "the fish." The letter Tzaddi is called the Natural Intelligence, and the word "natural" in Hebrew comes from a root which means *to sink, to dive*. We shall get the truth about Nature only when the self-conscious sinks or dives for it below the level of the subconscious, and the subconscious is the Water, or Cosmic Mind-Stuff. The Fish Hook is Meditation, and it gets its name from the particular fact that lifting the Mars vibration to the head is one of the automatic products of Meditation. In the ordinary man it goes out in the form of physical sex.

The reproductive force is utilized by the brain rather than by the physical sex. This, then, is sex on the mental plane rather than upon the physical plane. The transformation of the one kind of existence into the other kind of existence corresponds to a physical death and a resurrection; hence the name DEATH given to the card which depicts it. The fish is said to die when it is changed into another form of existence, just as we are said to die when we are changed into another form of existence. It is this continued ascent of the physical sex force to the mental plane in us that makes man into the Angel at last. Hence the sign Aquarius is also the alchemic sign for Dissolution.

grieve/grief   Dissolution is merely a synonym for death, not a death which is considered as ending a thing, but the death which is considered as the thing's entrance into another form of life. To *dissolve* means to *solve*. You dissolve the problem when you solve it. "The death of anything," says the alchemist, "always solves a problem." A thing dies only when it has served its purpose, or when it has, through the misuse of the image-making power, become crystallized and can no longer readjust to change, then our only possible solution is to be killed off and to get another body. We can always keep our bodies elastic and capable of readjustment to change, if we can get in touch with the Solvent which flows through us, the Cosmic Mind.

It merely flows through us; it cannot be retained in any container. We can seize it as it flows. If we can make connection with it, we can apply it to any condition to help us solve that condition or dissolve it. We make connection with it self-consciously only when we deliberately cease all personal mental activity. Meditation must be preceded by stilling the Waters of the intellect (the personal mind), which are always in motion until we deliberately still them, so that the Waters of the Cosmic Mind can flow through unimpeded; and in those Waters we fish for an idea which will help us solve our problem or help us understand Nature and our position in it.

The purpose here is not to teach the art of Meditation. I doubt if it can be taught. It requires not teaching but practice. One must learn how to exclude all other things from his intellect but the one image or thought he has selected to meditate upon. We cannot in reality exclude all other things from the mind, nor hold steady this one mental picture, but we can approximate it. We can repeat this mental image so often and so rapidly that it seems to be one continuous image, like a motion picture, although it is made up of a quick series of disconnected flashes.

The ibis is called a wader, and it does a great deal of wading in order to catch a fish. This is another bit of humor. One must do a great deal of sterile work before he can successfully meditate. The preparatory work is so tiresome and so sleep-producing. So much practice work must be waded through before you can produce results, which is analogous to having to practice five-finger exercises before you can play a composition on the piano. Only those who have an intense desire persevere enough to go through the preparatory stage. It is fortunate that many drop out, for Meditation is the manipulation of an actual fire which is capable of doing great harm to the body if successful before the body is prepared for it.

There is another occult word meaning, or enumerating, 104 which tells you this. It means "Sodom." Sodom in the Old Testament was a wicked city which was destroyed by fire. This refers to the fact that Meditation actually deals with a fire force which burns out old ways of thinking and doing, but which, unless handled carefully, can burn up valuable physical tissue as well. Nor is Meditation one of those things which is safeguarded by its own difficulty of approach. One may be far from successful in Meditation and still do himself a great deal of damage. The damage comes from losing control of the fire. This is graphically called "whirlpooling of the mind," but the physical part of this is the least of its dangers.

The SEVEN CENTERS in this card are WHITE, which means they must be well on their way to purification before it is safe to meditate. That is why the Tarot is the best approach. We are purifying our etheric bodies in which these centers are located, by the correlation of the Color and Sound method; and at the same time we are practicing the necessary preliminary of Meditation—concentration—without any danger of making our minds a vortex. We are trying to focus attention upon the symbolism of the cards. Work on this concentration, upon your etheric body and upon your self-conscious aspirations and images; and before you know it the result of Meditation will have arrived. The cards will tell you something your brain did not know before. You will find that you have "hooked a fish." Meditation is easy when you have learned the knack of it. The fish does not come as a result of concentration; concentration is the indispensable occasion for it. The fish simply swims up into the concentrated mind.

The result of Meditation in the personality is depicted by two other occult Hebrew words numerating 104. One means a quarrel, a dispute. Meditation brings about a new rhythm, and before the dispute has ended in the reversal of all your old estimates, the old rhythms or thought habits will fight desperately for life. The fight is particularly acute in those habits of thoughts concerning personal possession, which is the meaning of the other word. The result of this dispute, when successful, is represented by a third word which means the relinquishment of self. One learns by Meditation to regard possessions as being his merely to administer as a steward, to administer as the Higher Self directs. In this connection let us remember that the sign of Aquarius presides over the ankles. The ankles direct the feet in the way they should go. When we are directed by Meditation we always go the right way.

There are people who take no step into the unknown without consulting their inner guidance as to where they should next plant their feet. This is exquisitely symbolized in the two wings of Mercury which are affixed to his ankles. The two wings symbolize the extension of perception and the faculty which comes as a result of the practice of Meditation.

SYMBOLISM

The seven WHITE STARS represent the seven purified Centers, and their perfect action, when purified, produces the EIGHTH STAR. This STAR is YELLOW, to show that it is on the mental plane.

It is greater than the others, showing that it is the Pineal and Pituitary combined. It is now functioning as one, although each is still keeping its individual activity. The central YELLOW STAR means the combination of the Pineal and Pituitary in what is called THE MYSTIC MARRIAGE. You cannot have the Mystic Marriage until you have opened them both and purified them and perfected them; then they are joined together in the Mystic Marriage. After they have been perfected they function as one, although each has its own function; and so the two together would make an eighth star.

All the stars are eight-pointed. Eight means the perfect transmutation of the Solar Energy. Solar energy, however imperfectly transmuted, constitutes the life of all things. The eight-pointed stars repeat the same idea as the eight-spoked wheel in THE WHEEL OF FORTUNE, the eight-spoked wheels on the robe of THE FOOL, and the eight-pointed star in the crown of the Charioteer.

This card stands for MEDITATION, and Meditation modifies expression of the Solar Energy into the kind of expression which will best affect ourselves and all that lies within our sphere of influence.

The central Yellow Star is the same thing as the Yellow Sun in card 19, the Pineal-Pituitary functioning as one, and transformation of the heart. Why is it a Star here and a Sun there? Because of the other aspects of the card. A star and a sun are the same thing. Thus we must by no means restrict the Solar Energy to our Sun. Our Sun and all its systems revolves about another Sun, which we call a Star, the Sun of SIRIUS; Sirius, with all its systems including us, revolves about another Sun, and so on.

The Solar Energy the occultist speaks of is the Stellar Energy which pervades all space and is collected by the various suns, or fixed stars, of the Universe, and is used by them in their own sphere of influence. All they do with this energy is to transmute it into the kind of energy most adapted to the forms of its own sphere. The occultist says that you yourself are such a sun, when you have transformed your heart, and that you have your own sphere of influence and must adapt the Solar Energy that passes through you into the kind of energy suitable for everything you contact.

You cannot create magically with this Energy alone, but only by a combination of it with the Stellar Energy, which enters your body by way of the Transformed Heart; this is what Jesus meant when he said, "Let your Light shine." He meant that you should not obstruct the channel by which the Light flows in and out of you. You obstruct the channel by exercising your personal will in a way different from the way your Higher Self intended. You are meant to color the Light which passes through you with your personality. That is where the importance of personality comes in. Personality is a machine which contrives a certain sort of resistance to the Light, and differentiates it from the Light of everyone else. As with an electric machine, if it gives more or less resistance than was intended, it does not work well.

Let's return to the Stars, which are curiously arranged—six in a semicircle, holding a large YELLOW one, and another WHITE one on the woman's right side, outside of the semicircle. The six STARS are the Centers, the ones you were born with. The other two you make yourself. You purify and vivify six, but you actually create the seventh Yellow Star, which represents the awakened Pineal and Pituitary functioning as one. You also create the Transformed Heart, which changes from a feminine to a masculine organ. This is symbolized by putting the Heart Star on her right side instead of her left, where it actually is. *Right* in symbology is *masculine* and *left* is *feminine*. Under this Star, which represents the Transformed Heart, is a PINKISH MOUNTAIN, which is the same mountain that you see in the card THE LOVERS. It is RED-ON-BLUE, and symbolizes the mineral kingdom made active. To work miracles, or to magically create, is the work of the Transformed Heart. The most difficult miracle to work is to cause changes in the mineral kingdom, as the atoms are the densest.

The LAND represents the PERSONALITY, or the threefold body. On the highest part of it is a curious TREE, whose formation shows it to be the BRAIN with its two lobes. The RED BIRD perched on the top of the thinking lobe of the brain is the IBIS, or the fish catcher, and hence the fish hook. It is the thinking lobe of the brain—controlled by the will so that all personal thought in it ceases—that captures the ideas resulting from successful meditation.

The WOMAN who kneels upon the land has YELLOW HAIR, which indicates that she is THE EMPRESS, but she is now at one with THE HIGH PRIESTESS. Meditation consists in restoring to THE EMPRESS the power of her Mother, the Cosmic Mind and Memory. She fructifies the land by pouring water upon it, and under her ministration flowers spring up. The land is stippled, like the land in THE EMPEROR card, to represent a desert. It is she who brings Reason to flower; without her it would be sterile. She is pouring water from TWO JUGS. They are curiously made and look like sponges. A sponge sucks in water and gives it out again. The idea here suggests a pulsating action and reaction, each the consequence of the other.

The other HAND of the woman is pouring into the POOL OF

THE COSMIC MIND-STUFF, and stirring it to new vibratory waves thereby. This means that a human being who has developed the power to do so can directly, by use of his body as the Great Magical Agent, alter the Cosmic Mind-Stuff. He can work it up into new forms and "become a co-worker with God" to forward evolution on the physical plane.

Toward this action the GAZE of the woman is directed, and not toward the fructification of the land. This indicates where her chief interest lies. THE IMPROVEMENT OF THE BODY IS MERELY A MEANS TO AN END. THE END IS TO ASSIST IN THE EVOLUTION OF ALL MATTER. The Bible says: "All nature groaneth and travaileth for the coming of the sons of mind." The sons of mind are the human beings who have transformed their hearts, which is the self-performed work of the mind through its agent the intellectual subconscious.

The Woman is posed in a very peculiar way. One KNEE rests upon the earth and her weight is on this. She depends chiefly upon the body to help her. Her RIGHT FOOT rests upon the surface of the pool. In these two respects she is the opposite of the Angel, or Higher Self in card 14, whose left foot touches the land lightly, while his weight is on his right foot which is submerged in the pool. The masculine principle and the feminine principle, wherever they exist in Nature, work in opposite ways, each by means of the other. If the woman had her foot submerged in the water the picture would not portray the fact that her reliance is upon the land. Also, it would be impossible to indicate that her two knees are exactly balanced.

Furthermore, there is another reason. She keeps her balance by her understanding of her Mother, THE HIGH PRIESTESS. She is "filled with the UNDERSTANDING of her Mother's perfect laws." It is through her Understanding that we are able to meditate and learn the truth about Nature. She lays the Truth on to us. That is why she is depicted as naked in this card. There is no concealment in her. You can see that she is not Nature herself from the piece of symbolism described in THE DEVIL card. She has a navel; she is man-made.

The figure of the WOMAN in THE STAR—in connection with both the six WHITE STARS which form the semicircle above her head and the central huge YELLOW STAR—forms a rough outline of the symbol of the planet NEPTUNE, the planet which the occultists say is the higher octave of Venus. Neptune goes with card 12 (REVERSAL), which describes the operations in our heads of the stream of the Cosmic Mind. Thus it is indicated that the intellectual subconscious is now at one with THE HIGH PRIESTESS. She has both her own powers and the powers of THE HIGH PRIESTESS. She not only fashions in the body the 15 extensions of consciousness and faculties (15 little flowering plants), but she creates forms outside the body.

The Woman is NUDE and typifies Nature. She is a combination of THE EMPRESS and THE HIGH PRIESTESS. One half of her, we might say, is THE HIGH PRIESTESS (the half with the foot on the water) and the other half of her is THE EMPRESS (the half with her foot on the land). That is your intellectual subconscious. She is unlike the picture of THE EMPRESS and THE HIGH PRIESTESS in that here she is unveiled. Nature shows herself to us as she is in Meditation. She unveils herself when we have so transmuted our bodies so as to be fit to receive the truth.

If her physical position could be made accurate, her two KNEES would present two opposite angles of a square. The reference is to DALETH, who is number 4 in the Hebrew alphabet. The allegorical meaning of the square is to take the measurement of the force described, and here the force is the TRUE MEASUREMENT OF THE COSMIC STREAM AS IT FLOWS THROUGH US. The position of the woman in outline is like the swastika, the emblem of good luck. The swastika draws attention to a condition where the self-conscious deliberately works through the subconscious to express the One Will, not his own. The whirling cross (or the swastika) contains 17 cells. This card is 17, and thus the swastika is particularly related to it and to Meditation. All the different kinds of crosses are based on what is called the Magic Square of Mars, or a square containing 25 cells, 5 on a line. The ordinary equal-armed cross, called the Cross of Nature, contains nine of these cells. It is the cross you see upon the pennant of the Angel in card 20.

In this card you see PLANTS springing up all over the land. They illustrate the transmuted MARS energy—the Mars energy which flowers from the Creative Imagination depicted here by the three GREEN LEAVES in each little one.

THE STAR represents the third state of enlightenment, REVELATION. The vertical line reads: THE EMPRESS, THE WHEEL OF FORTUNE and THE STAR. The image-executing power of the subconscious, she who sets the body in order when impressed to do so by the right patterns of the self-conscious, works through the law of rotation in the body (the circulation of the various fluid systems, including the blood and the nerve streams). To vivify and purify the Seven Centers makes an eighth one, transforms the heart, and as a result of this, produces the ability to perform external magic, thus assisting in the evolution of Nature.

It is written that after you have found "The Light on the Path"—when we find the beginning of the way within—then THE STAR of your soul will show its light to light you onward to the perfect day. (The perfect Day, of course, is not Starlight; it is Sunlight—Sunlight that never ceases.)

The next card is THE MOON. THE MOON shines only at night and waxes and wanes, but then withdraws from us. The Perfect Sun is the White Sun which you see in the card THE FOOL, the Sun which is back of the sun. The Sun from which the Spirit of man descended to carve out his evolution. The card THE SUN is not the perfect Sun, the White Sun, because that sun withdraws from us, AND THE WHITE SUN DOES NOT.

NOTES

THE MOON.

19th Hebrew Letter	*QOPH*
Symbol for	*Sleep*
Color	*Violet-Red or*
	Crimson
Numerical Value	*100*
Syllables	*QUP*
Sound	*B-Natural*
Translation	*Back of the Head*
Sign in Zodiac	*Pisces*

NOTES

THE MOON

ק QOPH, spelled QVP, means BACK OF THE HEAD. It is the 19th Hebrew letter and the 12th SIMPLE LETTER. It stands for the occult extension of the function of SLEEP, for the direction SOUTH-BELOW, for the CORPOREAL INTELLIGENCE, for the Zodiacal sign PISCES, the Fishes, for the color VIOLET-RED, and for the note B-NATURAL. Its numerical value is 100.

The character QOPH is a combination of KAPH, which forms the upper part of the letter, and VAU, which is represented by the descending line. Thus its secret value is 26, or IHVH. The letter-name Kaph, KP, adds up to 100, which is the outer value of Qoph. There is as close a connection between Kaph and Qoph as we found between Mem and Tzaddi; in each case the letter-name of the former adds up to the value of the latter Single Letter.

The card for Kaph displays very prominently the word IHVH, which is the secret value of Qoph. That card depicts the entire process of Involution-Evolution, or the making of bodies which shall progressively house the One Energy as it enlarges back around the circle of manifestation to its Source once more. This card depicts this same process in more detail.

The Moon superimposed on the Sun (in card 18) is the counterpart of the Serpent projecting itself into the blue sea. The twin energies, which must act together as two aspects (masculine and feminine) of the same energy, are required to cooperate in a sex-union for the making of any body in the stupendous list of bodies, beginning with the stellar nebulas to the very last perfected one in the cycle of manifestation. The One Energy, which actuates all things, cannot be separated from the body and the action of the tiniest invisible bacterium, from one of the thirty trillion cells which compose the human organism, or from the body and action of the largest star. These are all inseparable from the ONE ENERGY whose body is the UNIVERSE ITSELF! The consciousness of every atom in that Universe, the consciousness of every cell of your body, the consciousness of your entire body as one entity, all are precisely similar to the consciousness on the part of the One Energy of its body, the Universe. Each and every body employs the degree of consciousness suitable to it, and that consciousness has gathered around itself the body in which it functions.

The Single Letter Kaph enumerates 20, and 20 equals the

315

letter-name YOD, spelled IVD. We have seen that the secret value of that body, by its own reconstruction of itself, becomes the perfected body. The former is just as much the expression of the Spirit as the latter. This character Qoph means anybody in the entire series, and its secret value is IHVH also. "The Path of Better Bodies" in this card stretches beyond the farthest stretch of human imagination, but the end of it is no more IHVH than the beginning.

What is the difference between the two? Merely the expanding of consciousness, and it is this which has constructed itself an appropriate body to manifest in. Spirit and body are the aspects of the One Reality. The reason for a body is that the Spirit must have some vehicle for expressing itself. Spirit cannot come out into manifestation unless it has a body. Consequently, the One Energy, in order to manifest, divided itself into equal halves. The second half (which the Christian theology calls the Holy Ghost) provided the body for the first half in which to manifest. It constructed the body, but the first half (which the Christian theology calls God the Father) provided the pattern for that body. The body itself was thus constructed by the union; Christian theology calls it God the Son.

To construct any body requires the utmost employment of two Intelligences—that of the Spirit and that of Matter. The Intelligence of one is no less or no greater than the Intelligence of the other; they merely express themselves differently. The first expresses itself in devising, the second in executing. The first we call Inductive Reason, and the second, Deductive Reason. This is all mapped out for you in the numeration of the Hebrew letters. Yod, the One Energy, equals 10, and 10 equals two 5's. The value of the Single Letter Heh is 5, and the letter-name Heh is spelled in Hebrew HH. You have learned that the two kinds of Reason are equal, and that together they make up God.

The direction of the previous card was South-Above; the direction of this card THE MOON is South-Below.

ABOVE means the self-conscious, to which is assigned INDUCTIVE REASON, and BELOW means the subconscious, to which is assigned DEDUCTIVE REASON.

The previous card concerned a self-conscious act, Meditation, and its results in reconstructing your body and its environment. This card concerns itself with the same result, but from the point of view of the subconscious rather than the self-conscious. It pictures not the expanding consciousness but the EXPANDING BODY. The background of both cards is the same—BLUE. This means that the instigating force is the same: the Holy Ghost.

The Yellow Star in card 17 and the Moon imposed on the Sun in card 18 are in each case the masculine and feminine principle which must work together to form a body. In card 17 they represent the very highest manifestations of the two principles which can exist in the human body—the vivified Pineal and the vivified Pituitary. In card 18, the luminary represents this only when you take the card in the higher aspect, that of representing the Spiritual evolution of your body. At its lower aspect it represents both the natural and the Spiritual evolution; that is the natural evolution in man, growing into the Spiritual evolution. To this luminary, the SUN-MOON, are given 32 rays, half short and half long. Since the card concerns the work of the body rather than that of the mind, the long rays are the subconscious and the short rays the self-conscious. Why 32? This is the number of the Hebrew word LAIB, spelled LB, meaning HEART. In occult teaching the heart stands for the great sympathetic nerve system. This is the special system in the body which responds to the impulses emanating from the Subjective Mind, or the Holy Ghost. The other nerve system, the cerebrospinal, responds to the impulses from the Higher Self through his agent (the self-conscious).

The type of Intelligence which goes with Tzaddi in the previous card is the Natural Intelligence, or the Truth about Nature. The type of Intelligence which goes with this card is THE CORPOREAL INTELLIGENCE, or the Intelligence of the body. The self-conscious has to learn the Truth about Nature; the body is born with it, for the body is itself Nature at work demonstrating her Intelligence.

The Corporeal Intelligence is the mode of consciousness which builds a body suitable for the expression of that consciousness which it is to use as its vehicle. There are four kingdoms which form the normal life of this planet: the mineral, the vegetable, the animal, and the human. The fifth kingdom, the Spiritual, or the Superhuman, can be entered by any person who has established his right to do so, but it still resides in the outward form of the human body. He establishes his right to do so by reconstructing it into what the occultist calls the superhuman body, a body with functions and perceptions extended far beyond the physical.

The Corporeal Intelligence has built all the bodies which conduct the normal life of this planet. It is powerless to build the superhuman body unaided. We ourselves must cooperate with it to build this body. What is the superhuman body? It is the body capable of functioning on the four planes, for which the word IHVH stands. These are the Archetypal, the Creative, the Formative, and the Physical.

\\\ These four planes are the four suits in Tarot: Wands, Cups, Swords, and Pentacles. In each suit you have a card which stands for the body itself. The PAGE OF WANDS stands for the body which functions on the ARCHETYPAL PLANE; the PAGE OF CUPS, for the body which functions on the MENTAL PLANE; the PAGE OF SWORDS, for the body which functions on the ASTRAL PLANE; and the PAGE OF PENTACLES, for the body which functions on the PHYSICAL PLANE.

All the bodies except the superhuman were built by the Corporeal Intelligence, carrying out unaided the pattern given her by the Life Power to execute. Your Corporeal Intelligence is only the localized manifestation of that Corporeal Intelligence which has built all bodies in the Universe: crystals, planets, electrons, and atoms, as well as that of plants, animals, and men.

We have no self-conscious which tells us anything about the complex process by which bodies were built, and by which they are carried on. The Intelligence which built them, renews them, and carries them on is most active in us when we are asleep. This consciousness has been steadily at work building bodies and carrying them on ever since the One Energy divided itself into two for the purpose of manifestation. Beginning with simple cells, it had developed from them all the species of animal and human bodies which have lived on this planet. When Nature shall finally have perfected the human body (still far distant in time), she shall have gone as far as she can go. She can at the present time go no farther with our bodies than she has gone. If we would cross over into the superhuman kingdom we must do it ourselves, though with her indispensable assistance. We and we alone can develop, from the bodies we now have, another species of body freed from the limited perceptions of the physical plane and from its inevitable deterioration. This was all intended from the beginning—that man should work out his own salvation.

What the Tarot calls Corporeal Intelligence is that subconsciousness which builds the form the Life Power wants and in which it desires to express itself. It wants to express itself in a certain way. It impresses the Cosmic Mind-Stuff to build a form in which it can express itself in that manner. Consequently, you see that the Corporeal Intelligence has done all the building that was ever done in the world. It built the Universe. It built the Stars. It built the Planets. *It built this planet.* This planet is inhabited or occupied by bodies: Mineral, Vegetable, Animal and Human. It built all those, *BUT IT CANNOT, UNAIDED, BUILD THE SUPERHUMAN BODY.* The human body is as far as it can go unaided. It is powerless to build alone the Super-human body.

We have now arrived at a point in our individual evolution where we have to take a conscious part in future development. This card refers to the means and mechanics by which bodies are adapted to finer and higher forms of Spirit. We supply the Spirit and Nature supplies the body. She needs, however, no instructions from us. Sub-consciousness knows already what to do, and the same law by which she had built our highly complex organism out of simple cells will also work the further changes.

What then does Nature need, and where is the necessity for our taking a hand? Nature needs but one thing from us: the CREATIVE IMAGINATION. The tools she has, but we must commission her to use them. *It is the visualization of the ardent desire to build a better body which enables Nature to set about getting one.* Unless she is thus stimulated, she will not furnish a better body by the ordinary process of her evolution. To speed her up requires that you cultivate the visual imagination, and visualize the result you wish to be achieved. All the people who have trod this path, which leads up to the super-human body, have left us word that this is the only way it can be procured. They were once where we are now, and they built it only by the aid of the Creative Imagination.

Is that anything new? Throughout the entire evolution of the organic world, organisms have been built only in response to the ardent feeling of need. When you intend your mind toward the manifestation of something beyond your limit, your subconscious at once seeks to provide you the means to do so. It will not start going in that direction until the conscious mind has made considerable progress in picturing expectantly what it desires. The Moon is *reflected* light; it follows the conscious mind. Its light comes, in the first place, from the Sun. The conscious mind stimulates the subconscious mind to begin to build the kind of body that will express the image you have habitually impressed upon it. She has already the tools for doing so, but they need to be quickened by you into a new use.

KUNDALINI is an etheric fire which streams upward from the Saturn Center at the base of the spine and moves through all the etheric centers of the trunk, through the Venus Center in the throat up to the two head centers. As it bathes each center it quickens its rate of vibration. This compels the quickened vibration of the zone of the body which each controls, and all the cells have to respond or be shaken loose. Those which are too firmly embedded and persist in their old rhythms are destroyed by the new use of the Mars vibration. Thus you have at one end of the spine (in etheric matter) the Saturn Center, the Administrative Intelligence, ordering all life's activities within their proper bounds and limits by feeding the etheric centers their appropriate amount of etheric fire from the Earth. At the other end of the spine is the *medulla oblongata*, in physical matter, controlling the distribution of the bloodstream, and stimulating to faster or slower action every vital organ of the physical body.

The Medulla is the principal vasomotor center in the body, and it controls the expansion and contraction of the blood current throughout the entire body, and thus manages the functioning of every vital organ by increasing or decreasing its supply of blood.

The Hebrew letter Qoph is a picture of the Medulla, which is sometimes called the knot at the top of the spine. The ancient Hebrew letter resembles a knot tied in a cord, and the modern Hebrew letter is a picture of the spinal cord entering the brain.

Tarot teaches us that while we are in our physical bodies everything must have a physical basis. This means all our development, even our Spiritual development, must have a physical basis. The Medulla is perhaps the most wonderful organism in our wonderful bodies. It is definitely constructed for the purpose of giving physical form to our mental images. This is the way it works:

The place where you see is in the back of the head. The eyes are only the camera lenses, but the sight center itself is just above the Medulla. Any sight produces a slight vibration in the Medulla, which promptly sends this slight vibration to any cell of the body in which the sight should cause a bodily response.

Doctors tell us that people die because they are too weary to stave off death. If you ardently desire to live, you can survive the disease that threatens your body with extinction. The reason for this is that the 30 trillion cells which compose us cling to life far more than we do. Often we have no love of life whatever. They are far more keen on life preservation, but they must yield, in spite of themselves, to a superior force—the self-conscious, which rules them.

If you can learn, by ceaseless practice, to make sharp, clear outlines of the image of your desire, the Medulla acts upon it, and starts the process whereby the Corporeal Intelligence fashions that body which can express it. That is why occultism is constantly asking you to cultivate your Creative Imagination, which means to make mental images sharp, so that by the agency of the Medulla they will create new rhythms, and even new organs, in your body.

Success in any undertaking is always the result of specializing one's body for that undertaking, constructing one for that purpose. The more aspiration and emotion, the sharper the picture. The highest possible exercise of the Creative Imagination is the construction of a new body, and finally, the construction of the perfect body. This body Nature is powerless to construct. It must be built in your Creative Imagination, working with Nature as your agent.

The message of the three vertical cards tells you how to do this. The vertical line begins with THE EMPEROR. He is variously known as the WINDOW, SIGHT, and REASON. He is pictured to you as ruling through his wife and his child, the Christ-Child, whose birth is pictured in the card called THE SUN. Under THE EMPEROR is a picture of his wife working to achieve his images. LIBRA stands for balanced action. He secures it externally, she secures it internally. JUSTICE works physically, emotionally, and mentally. Libra presides over the kidneys, over elimination. You cannot build a new body until you get the functions of the old in perfect condition by the food you eat and through what becomes of that food in the digestive and intestinal tracts.

Bodies on all planes are made by food, and there is the appropriate food on each of the four planes in which the perfected body can function. The food on the Astral Plane is the Emotions, and the food on the Mental Plane is the Thoughts. You can have no physical body and environment unless you feed your emotional and mental bodies the right kind of emotion and ideas. Otherwise they will create in your physical body those structures of error which it is the function of the new use of the Mars vibration to break down. In Pisces is Venus, and in the card JUSTICE she is pictured at work; in Pisces she is exalted. That is, she comes to her highest expression in the building of the perfect body.

Pisces is ruled by Jupiter (THE WHEEL). Your state of consciousness absolutely depends upon the kind of body you have built for yourself; and this kind of body absolutely depends upon how firmly you have grasped the Law of Cycles and tried to live in harmony with it. THE PATH IN THIS CARD IS THE PATH OF BODY CON-SCIOUSNESS. Imagine a better body, and you will at once begin to have one created for you by THE EMPRESS, working in conjunction with THE HIGH PRIESTESS.

We have no self-consciousness which tells us anything about the stupendously complicated, intricate, and innumerable processes by which our bodies were built. That is to say, we do not, or our self-conscious does not, carry on the work of the body. We are not even aware of how it is done. It is carried on by the subconscious—the subconscious that is most active when the self-conscious is away or when we are asleep. This Corporeal Intelligence has been steadily at work since the One Energy divided itself into two for the purpose of manifestation. It began working at once in order to embody the image of the Will, and it has gone on making more and more complex bodies until it has arrived at our human body. That is as far as one can go on this planet.

We can make better bodies by adapting Nature, by working in unison with it. A body is formed from the manifold impressions which are given the natural body. We are told that this was intended in the scheme of things from the very beginning, that Nature should do the work for man until he reached a certain point. If man wanted to go further than that point he would have to do the work himself. Of course, in the process of time our bodies will get better and better. That is simply because we have become more and more civilized, and the process of civilization is one of uniting with Nature to make a better product. We have to take a conscious part in our future development or wait for the much slower processes of time.

Nature needs no instruction from us on how to make these bodies. In fact, we cannot instruct, for we do not know ourselves. What does Nature need? It needs only that we image a better body (if we desire to build a better body), and it then enables our Corporeal Intelligence to set about getting this result.

If we are always striving for emotional and mental equilibrium, we are enabled to set about building us a better body to manifest it in. Unless she has this equilibrium she will not set about it, for she has not the means to do so. The materials for your better body are all being utilized by her in carrying on the ordinary life of the body, so we have to give her some new materials, or divert some of the old materials from the ordinary life of the body.

SYMBOLISM

REFLECTION is the outstanding note of this card. THE MOON is reflecting the SUN, and she, herself, is reflecting upon the PATH OF

BETTER BODIES (which corresponds to the growing body consciousness); the YODS, or the images, of the Father are made flesh by the Mother. REFLECT UPON YOUR IMAGE, AND YOUR BODY WILL RESPOND TO IT BY REFLECTING ALSO.

St. Paul said that we shall all be changed in the twinkling of an eye. He did not refer to the moment of death, for this moment makes no change whatever in us beyond transferring us from our physical to our astral bodies, a change which every one of us temporarily makes every night in sleep. He referred to the change which takes place at a certain point in the Path of Better Bodies, toward the end of it. It is quite true that there is a moment when all things become new and different to the patient toiler after a better body is made, when his mental vision becomes an actuality and his consciousness of regeneration is suddenly complete.

The thing that remains the same, no matter at which level you take the card, is the TWO TOWERS. These also you have seen before in card 13. These are THE TOWERS OF THE KNOWN. Beyond them lies that which is at present unknown. It is the business of science and of individual Spiritual evolution to keep pushing back those Towers. Behind them lies the achievement of the deathless, superhuman body, which you see in card 13 symbolized by the Rising Sun. What you and I are trying to do is to get on that Path, beyond the Towers of the Known. We are getting beyond the limits known to the outside world. It is probable that all of us have set our foot on that Path before. We must recapture our highest state in the previous life and then go on from that to add a little more to it. The occultist believes confidently that there are people called the Masters who have created a body which can function in the Archetypal World, and all these Masters who have created that body say they were once where we are now. Jesus said the same thing. "We have been through all of this. I am only things such as ye are."

They have built their body to function in the Archetypal World out of such bodies as we have, and they have created it with the Creative Imagination. We are told by the occultists that all the bodies of the organic world have been built in response to desire. There was a time when we had no eyes. We only heard things and felt things. We ardently desired to see what we heard and felt, and we pushed out our brain to the periphery in the form of eyes. When you intend your mind (to use the phrase of Newton) and turn it on the manifestation of something which has been before your mind, your subconscious at once tries to give you the means to do so. If you keep at it long enough and intensely enough, your body produces the means.

Your body cannot start in that direction until your conscious mind images, or makes a sharp, definite outline, of what it wants. This is why the subconscious is called the Moon, because the Moon passes on the light of the Sun. THE SUN IS THE MIND—THE BODY RE-FLECTS THE LIGHT OF THE MIND. The Moon shines by reflected light. All the light comes from the Sun. You are very familiar with the fact that while we are in our physical bodies everything is on a physical basis; consequently, if all this is so, we have an organism in our body definitely constructed for the purpose of giving a physical form to our mental image. This organism is the medulla oblongata.

The other thing that remains the same in this card is the SUN-MOON. Whether it is regarded as the natural evolution or the Spiritual evolution of better bodies, they are alike made by the subconscious carrying out the image formed by the conscious. Finally, if you will look on the PATH between the DOG and the WOLF, you will see two pairs of little STONES, which are intended to be two figure 8's. This means that a body, whether the product of the natural or the Spiritual evolution, is achieved only by the double balanced action of self and subconscious, symbolized by the figure 8. The same idea is pictured by the Path passing midway between Dog and Wolf. Whether it is the natural or the Spiritual evolution, the better body lies exactly between the two parents—self-conscious and subconscious, culture and Nature. Our culture must never take us away from Nature, and Nature must never be followed exclusively, but must be restrained by culture.

Let us now read the card at the level of the natural evolution, leading into the Spiritual. Energy precedes Matter, and a nucleus of energy collects matter around it as its body, the kind of energy dictating the kind of matter as well as the density of the matter.

It is the business of the second expression (the body form of the material selected) of the One Life to work itself up into forms dictated by the images of the Father. This Sea of Cosmic Mind-Stuff is at first shapeless and void, just as Genesis says. Occult science teaches that the One Life expands into 15 main expressions, whether you regard it as consciousness or as matter. Regarded as consciousness, these Yods fall from the Sun; regarded as matter, these Yods fall from the Moon. In this picture, on the side of Matter, there are first the three primary qualities of matter; secondly, the five subtle principles of sensation which on our physical plane become the five qualities of sensation that we perceive through our five physical senses; and lastly, the sevenfold differentiation of the Life-Breath, symbolized by the seven planets in the outer world, and by the seven stars in the inner world of our bodies. Regarded as falling from the Sun, these YELLOW YODS stand for the states of consciousness symbolized by the 12 Zodiacal signs and the three Mother Letters of the Hebrew alphabet.

The POOL out of which the Path proceeds is the same as in THE STAR and in TEMPERANCE, and as the river in the other cards—the Cosmic Mind-Stuff into which melts the robe of THE HIGH PRIESTESS. Out of that Cosmic Mind-Stuff brought down from the Archetypal into the Formative World finally emerges the "dry-land," or what we call physical manifestation. Here science enters and says that the organic life of this planet began in the sea. It proceeds to build body after body. Aeons behind us is the stage when the water animal left the sea for the land. At the shore of the sea in this card is a FRINGE OF MINERAL AND PLANT LIFE. Some of the STONES are colored RED, to show that all minerals and stones are alive.

The EARTH begins at once in CULTIVATED GROUND; thus the fringe on the shore stands for the lengthy period before man began any cultivation of the soil. Evolution indicates that the bodies of men and animals grow better and better in spite of fluctuations, temporary setbacks, and blind alleys. The reason bodies grow better and better is to allow adequate expression for the enlarging life that they are called upon to house, and that life is as indestructible as matter, and like matter, it simply takes another form.

Man cultivated the soil, bringing forth cereals, vegetables, fruits, and better forms of plant life. He also domesticated the animals to serve him. All civilization has proceeded from the combination of man and Nature as illustrated in his cultivation of plants and animals. His improvement upon Nature in the animal world reaches its climax in the elephant, the horse, and the dog. The elephant might be taken as the best demonstration of man's success in communicating his mind to an animal. The horse might be taken as the best demonstration of his success in improving, by cultivation, the physical characteristics of an animal. His supreme success is with the dog—it combines both the mental, physical, and emotional improvement.

The wolf has been traditionally known as man's worst enemy and has, through his cultivation, become man's best friend. What transformation is like this? It is a greater transformation than man has so far made of himself. Maeterlinck, in his beautiful essay on "Our Friend the Dog," calls attention to the fact that the dog is the only animal who has, through his love of us, converted himself into another species. "He has solved, in an admirable and touching manner, the problem we should have to solve, if a divine race came to inhabit our planet." The occultist knows what Maeterlinck here suggests: that a divine race *is* inhabiting our planet, and that we must eventually do what the dog has done—convert ourselves from our original species. Our original species is the higher animal "Man," and we must convert ourselves into the superman with a veritable, actual, *new kind of body.*

Now the cultivated ground leaves off and the UNCULTIVATED GROUND begins. Here, then, the natural evolution ends and the Spiritual begins, with the BLUE GROUND, when we begin to bring into our body the Holy Ghost. Just beyond stand the Towers of the Known. The Blue Ground signifies that it is possible to know this region in the sleep of the body, when we connect with the memory of what we were and whither we are returning.

In each Tower there is only one WINDOW. It is high up for only those who ascend the height, those who are capable and can see what stretches before them in the future. The window is BLACK to indicate the occult vision, and there being only one reminds you of the words of Jesus: "If thine eye be single, then thy whole body is full of light." WINDOW MEANS REASON. The two windows (one in each Tower) indicate the self-conscious and the subconscious, the two Reasons working together to produce a new body, and so to move back to the Towers of the Known. As the self-conscious Tower is moved back by the mental vision, the subconscious creates a better body in which to house that vision. The Window, of course, looks ahead and is actually on the opposite side of the Tower, but there is no way that it could be put there on the card.

At the end of the ever-ascending Path stands THE HERMIT on His mountain peak. Card 18 equals 8 plus 1 equals 9, THE HERMIT. The way to reach him is by 8 working through 1, or the woman, STRENGTH, working through THE MAGICIAN. In the path are the two figure 8's, which you saw hovering over the heads of THE MAGICIAN and the WOMAN.

When this card is read at the level of the Spiritual evolution alone, the chief changes are these: Immediately upon the brink of the POOL there is a fringe of BLACK vegetation (including occult images) and a heap of STONES, some of which are touched with RED. The higher meaning of STONE is Union with the Father, and the RED means the

Mars vibration being put at His service rather than at the service of the personality. Thus the Path becomes from its very start the Path of Better Bodies—bodies deliberately created occultly by the personality as it takes itself in hand. The fish who clambers upon the Path is no longer symbolic of the exodus of the water animal to the land. In this, the CRAYFISH is like the Egyptian scarab, symbolizing the SPIRIT.

The Spirit descended into matter, and now the conscious spirit is beginning to climb out of matter and to get upon the Path, where it is no longer conditioned and trammeled by matter. This goal is reached by building a better body for it to function in.

This Crayfish is RED-VIOLET, the color which symbolizes the making of the better body. The chief means of making a better body is the new digestion. In this sense the Crayfish means CANCER, the Crab, and Cancer stands for nutrition.

The special body the occultist is seeking to build in order to manifest a special and high kind of Life Power is constructed by physical, emotional, and mental mechanics. You acquire the physical before you can get the emotional and mental in their potency.

Bethlehem, where the Christ-Child was born, means the place of bread. He was born in a manger, the trough where the cattle feed. You must start with the New Digestion, secreting other elements from the food. All this reconstruction is the work of THE EMPRESS. It is superintended by the Holy Ghost, with whom THE EMPRESS is becoming more and more at-one, through her cleansing the body of its inherited taints.

The FOREGROUND of the card is GREEN, but the greater changes take place in the BLUE region of the background. Note that on the GREEN GROUND, the stage of Spiritual evolution where THE EMPRESS is still doing the chief work, stand the two animals: the DOG (typifying the self-conscious) and the WOLF (typifying the subconscious). The Dog is ORANGE, and is looking toward the Light from above; the Wolf is STONE COLOR, and is looking toward the dog. This means that the dog, because of striving to realize his heavenly vision, has transformed the subconscious and made her one with the Holy Ghost. She is now trying to transform him; but note that although her eyes are fixed only on him, her ears are decidedly pricked upward, while his ears are down. Here you are told again that it is the subconscious which receives intuition, and that she transfers it on to the self-conscious.

The 15 YODS fall upon the BLUE GROUND, and not on the

green. This means that the body cannot receive what these Yods stand for until you have made your EMPRESS one with the Holy Ghost. The Yods stand for the 15 extensions of consciousness indicated by the 12 Zodiacal signs and the three Mother Letters, and by the 15-petalled rose on the pennant of DEATH. THE HIEROPHANT wears a crown composed of them, which means that he had control of them. THE HIEROPHANT is the masculine expression of THE HIGH PRIESTESS. From the very beginning the Universal Mother has been leading us up to the point where she can rain this influence upon us, patiently longing for the self-conscious to make it possible for Her so to transform the body.

The Hebrew word *corporeal*, in the type of Intelligence which goes with this letter, comes from a verb which means "to rain upon." St. Paul said, "Nature awaits with pain the day when the Son of Mind shall come and, by his own effort, allow her to bestow upon the body the equipment intended for it—the equipment which shall advance her three lower kingdoms." Yet, alas, the general effect of the Christian teaching has been to convince the devout that the body is a weight, a clog, something calculated to keep you out of heaven rather than to get you into it. All exoteric religions have rejected the body as man's inevitable enemy. That is the meaning of the text, although it, too, has other meanings: "The stone that the Builders rejected has become the headstone of the corner." The Builders are the religions. Mrs. Mary Baker Eddy is the only leader of a new religion who has taught the importance of the body, even though she has confused her own teaching with the assertion that there is no such thing as matter.

The letter-name QOPH is QVP, or 186. This enumerates three occult Hebrew words which give very important indications of the meaning of the Corporeal Intelligence. The first is "a stone of stumbling." The body is indeed a stone of stumbling to one who does not understand that it is the business of its tenant to utilize it as the transfer of the One Energy, instead of using it for the purpose of getting out of it all possible sensation. The practical occultist seeks to realize the full potency of the body as the transfer of the One Energy. To do this he must equip it with its latent powers.

Two other words enumerating 186 tell us how this can be done. One means "magistrates." There are seven of these magistrates in the human body, and we know them as the Interior Stars. The other word means "increase." It is by increasing the function of the Interior Stars, and through their agency adding to the body organs which remain rudimentary in the average human being, that we become Spiritual in the occult sense of the word; that is, we equip the body with the 15 extensions of perceptions and functions which enable us to operate on the higher plane.

The Christian religion is dying—and always the cults that increase their activities as an old religion dies are seed-bearing mechanisms of the new religion. The institutionalized religion of any period crystallizes these germs of life, and no religion comes to popular acceptance until it has stifled its inner vitality.

The Capricorn Age, which succeeds the Aquarian, will, toward its end, see in its turn the various occult schools increase their outer activity to signal the departure of the religion of that age which we are now helping to usher in. For them it will be in the same condition in which the Piscean religion is now—all its truth and life shackled by the theology which has perverted the spiritual meaning for personal or organizational ends. Although a few understand the meaning of that theology and what it symbolizes, most take the letter instead of the Spirit. As it gradually ceases to live, the cults from which it started are arising to transmit the life, which the forms originally conveyed, into a new form.

Nothing can flourish without its opposite flourishing too. Hence this precise period is rife with the cults of black magic as well as the white cults. The chief activity of the black magicians during the emergence of a new religion is to oppose it until they see that they can no longer frustrate it, and then their object becomes to seize upon it and pervert its doctrines for their own power. The white magicians gradually retire from the new religion they have ushered in, as it falls more and more into the hands of the black and mercenary magicians who have seized upon it for power. The unhappiest thing that ever happened to the Christian religion is thought by its present clergy to have actually been the best—its adoption by Constantine as the religion of the Roman State. Remember, the disciples recognized in the transfigured body of their Master the companion and teacher called Jesus. The body which enters the kingdom of God is the body which enters the Fourth Dimension, and we ourselves must make it, by our own intelligent use of the WISDOM of the Corporeal Intelligence.

NOTES

THE SUN .

20th Hebrew Letter	*RESH*
Symbol for	*Pair of Opposites—*
	Fruitfulness &
	Sterility
Color	*Orange*
Numerical Value	*200*
Syllables	*RISh*
Sound	*D-Natural*
Translation	*Face or Head*
Sign in Zodiac	*The Sun*

331

NOTES

THE SUN

RESH, spelled RISh, means FACE or HEAD. It is the 20th Hebrew letter and the sixth DOUBLE LETTER. It is the sign or symbol for the pair of opposites FRUITFULNESS and STERILITY; for the direction SOUTH; for the planet SUN; for the COLLECTIVE INTELLIGENCE; for the color ORANGE; for the note D-NATURAL. In Roman characters it is written R. Its numerical value is 200.

The character RESH occurs as a component part of six other letters. The character BETH pictures the Solar Energy being brought down into a parallelogram, symbolizing the physical body. The character KAPH is so like it as to be constantly confused with it. The only difference is that the descending vertical joins with the parallelogram at the corner instead of slightly within it. This difference signifies that anybody is but the physical plane manifestation, the blossoming, of the Solar Energy. Thus Beth signifies that you yourself can bring more of this Energy down into a body which already has been constructed by the Solar Energy.

SAMEKH is the character Kaph plus a vertical line going up to the top again, the ascent of the Energy upwards from the body which it has previously constructed.

The character PEH is a Kaph with a Yod hanging from the top of it, making the whole figure look like a mouth with a tongue in it. This signifies the Mars vibration, or what makes the body articulate and what makes it go—which is what the letter stands for.

Next is the character QOPH, which contains a modified Kaph. We are told that this letter signifies the Solar Energy entering the spinal column.

Last, the character TAU contains Resh with a Yod hanging from the top of it.

There is no horizontal parallelogram, for the Yod itself is the Yod indicating the subconscious—the difference between the Yod which indicates the subconscious and the Yod which indicates the superconscious, as you see in the character Aleph.

In addition to these six letters which have a Resh in them, you will find two others which have a slightly modified Resh—the characters TETH and MEM. These two characters have the horizontal parallelogram into which comes down this slightly modified Resh as well as

Vau. In Mem this Vau comes down into the body by means of the Solar Energy, which it touched at the top. In Teth this Vau comes down into the body on its own account, and it is independent of the Solar Energy except only as the body is in the physical plane manifestation of the Solar Energy. The two mingle in the body.

The direction of RESH, THE SUN, is SOUTH. South appears as a compound direction in four other cards:

SOUTH-WEST —   JUSTICE
SOUTH-EAST —   THE HIEROPHANT
SOUTH-ABOVE —   THE STAR
SOUTH-BELOW —   THE MOON

Combine THE SUN with THE EMPRESS and you get THE HIERO-PHANT. THE HIEROPHANT is the SOLAR ANGEL, the same as the Solar Angel seen in TEMPERANCE, who communicates with the self-conscious by means of THE EMPRESS, and who gives THE HIGH PRIESTESS instructions as to her work in the body—to reconstruct it and equip it with its higher powers.

Combine THE SUN with THE WHEEL and you get SOUTH-WEST, or JUSTICE. THE WHEEL in this aspect is the body. The card depicts THE EMPRESS, at work in the reconstructed body, seeking and maintaining the higher equilibrium. The background of this card is YELLOW, showing that she works by reason of the Solar Energy passed on to her by the self-conscious.

Combine THE SUN with the self-conscious and you have THE STAR, SOUTH-ABOVE. THE STAR depicts the results of Meditation, a self-conscious activity.

Combine THE SUN with the subconscious and you have THE MOON, depicting the making of bodies, SOUTH-BELOW. In Meditation the self-conscious contacts the Solar Energy, and in the making of the body the subconscious embodies the Solar Energy.

The sound "R" is made by the open mouth and throat, completely rounding them. The Egyptian hieroglyph for R is a horizontal ellipse representing the mouth. In the Hebrew alphabet the letter Peh means the MOUTH, the letter which stands for the Mars vibration. Both the Mars vibration and the Sun vibration are described by the same words: "hot, dry, masculine." The description of the Sun vibration bears one more term—"life-giving." It is noticeable that this term is lacking in the description of the Mars vibration. In fact, if we should devise a parallel term for the Mars vibration it would be "life-using" rather than "life-giving." The symbolic color of the Mars vibration is RED, while the symbolic color of the Sun vibration is the next color to it, ORANGE.

All these significant similarities must show a close connection, possibly even an identity, between the two vibrations. Particularly when you recall that the "flash of intuition" in the card which depicts the Mars vibration comes unmistakably from the Solar Angel in the cards TEMPERANCE and THE HIEROPHANT. It would seem, then, that the difference between the two vibrations is primarily a matter of emphasis; their essential nature is the same. Mars begins by destruction, yet there can be no construction without preliminary destruction. The Sun begins in construction, though all construction ends in destruction. The Sun which makes a plant withers it also.

Let us now see what we can glean from the number of this card. Nineteen is 9 working through 1. Nine is THE HERMIT, and in the card we are told that He sheds His light on us by means of a Lantern, which symbolizes THE HIEROPHANT, the Solar Angel, the Higher Self. In card 1 we see THE MAGICIAN working by means of THE HERMIT. THE HERMIT is the force he is bringing down to grow the lilies and the roses in his garden (his body). In card 19 we have the ultimate result of that force, the reconstructed body and the birth of the Christ-Child. Nine plus 1 equals 10, and 10 equals 1. Thus THE MAGICIAN raised to his full potency is the awakened Pineal Gland when united to the awakened Pituitary, in what is called The Mystic Marriage. It is depicted by the Luminary in this card with its double rays, masculine and feminine.

By means of the awakened Pineal Gland we get direct Solar perceptions, and it is those in sex-union with the awakened Pituitary which bring forth the Christ-Child. THE SUN IS ITS FATHER, THE MOON IS ITS MOTHER. THE GREAT WORK IS PERFORMED BY THE OPERATION OF THE SUN AND THE MOON BY THE AID OF MERCURY, OR THE SELF-CONSCIOUS AWARENESS. Thus Mercury is responsible for the awakening of the Pineal Gland and the Pituitary Body, joining the two in the mystic union and bringing to birth the Christ-Child as the product of that union.

What is the Christ-Child? It is a romantic name for the equilibrated consciousness, the consciousness composed equally of the self-conscious and subconscious working as one in complete harmony.

There is a Hebrew letter which does not have a Resh in its composition or South in its compound direction. It is nevertheless associated closely with THE SUN because of its color and the Solar Angel which its card depicts. The letter is ZAIN, THE SWORD, in the card THE LOVERS. We know the Angel is the Solar Angel because he is born from the rays of the Sun and because of the symbol of the Serpent with its tail in its mouth, identifying him with the Solar Angel in the card TEMPERANCE, and hence with THE HIEROPHANT. He is blessing and making fruitful THE LOVERS, who have now learned the right attitude toward each other and how to work together in harmony. He makes active the 12 signs of the Zodiac by her cooperation; she brings to perfection the five senses by his cooperation. Between them is a mountain which symbolizes their new joint creation. It is RED-ON-BLUE, or the Holy Ghost made active in both the self-conscious and the body. The mountain in card 6 and the Christ-Child in card 19 are the same.

The Christ-Child, you see, bears prominently on his body the sign of the Water Triangle. His office is to make us as responsive to the Will of the Father as was the Cosmic Mind-Stuff in the first place. It is only in the subconscious, or the Mother, that the Will of the Father appears. The self-conscious Will of the Universe is known to us in what we call "the Laws of Nature" and what these Laws have produced. We can learn to know Nature, *but we can never LEARN to know God, for God is known only to Himself.*

This is naively expressed in the Book of Exodus, where Moses begs God to show him His Glory, and let him see His Face. And God said, "I will make My goodness to pass before thee, and I will proclaim the Name of the Lord before thee, but there shall no man see Me and live. Yet, behold, there is a place by Me, and thou shalt stand upon a rock; and it shall come to pass, while My Glory passeth by, that I will put thee in a cleft of the Rock and I will cover thee with My hand, while I pass by and then I will take away My hand, and thou shalt see my back parts; *but My face shall not be seen.*"

The rock is the Pineal Gland, with its brain-sand fused into the philosopher's stone by knowledge and practice. In it we contact as much of the Solar Energy as is possible to human beings, but it is merely the glory after it has passed by, and remains only in his works.

The letter ZAIN stands for the SWORD. That Sword does not appear in the card THE LOVERS, but it appears in the card JUSTICE, which depicts the subconscious ceaselessly at work attaining equilibrium in the body by means of cutting away with the Sword. In JUSTICE the Sword is destructive; but the same Sword appears in THE SUN card as the constructive ORANGE PENNANT. Instead of cutting away, it now carves out. When equilibrium has been attained laboriously by the subconscious, the self-conscious maintains it with ease and joy. Contrast the child's attitude and poise with that of the Woman in JUSTICE. It brings to mind the alchemic proverb: "After Mercury has discovered First Matter, the rest is Woman's work and Child's play.

The direction of this card, as I said, is SOUTH, and that is the direction of the Sun's meridian height; North is the place of the Sun's lowest light. The light of the North proceeds from the Sun just as the light of the South does. So all these statements show how closely related the Mars vibration is to the Sun. One thing we can be sure of is that the Sun vibration is the Mars vibration directed by the Mind, the Mind of the Creator—an individual Creator when it is like the original Creator.

In all series of numbers, 9 is the end and 1 is the beginning. The end is constantly expressing itself in each person as a new beginning. We are constantly told in occultism that the words of Jesus are held literally: "Behold, I make all things new." In card 19 we have the ultimate result of the force he is bringing down—the reconstructed body—the Christ-consciousness.

The more you let the Sun manifest through you, the more original you become. You become individual. You are the particular instrument geared for the Sunlight to go through. And when you remove all obstruction and let it go through, you are supposed to contribute something to it that no one else can contribute. It is the obstacles in you that are conventional. It is the obstacles in you that are like everyone else. All selfishness, for instance, is alike; it just manifests itself differently. So the obstacles are alike but you yourself are different; so if you wish to strive for individuality, free yourself of obstacles and let the Sunlight go through.

The number of this letter is 20. Zero working through 2. Zero is THE FOOL, which is just another way of saying THE HERMIT (with THE HERMIT as intermediary); but 2 is your form—is Nature. It is very interesting to see that most of the words spelling 19, in Hebrew and Greek, are words which refer to form, that is, Nature—the Mother Principle. Various Moon goddesses in Greece are 19—they spell 19. "Eve" in Hebrew spells 19. How is that? Nineteen goes with words meaning "form"—"the Mother Principle." THE MOTHER PRINCIPLE IS ONLY WHAT THE FATHER MAKES IT. NATURE REFLECTS THE WILL. You know nothing about the Father—the Will—except as it manifests itself through creation. I know nothing that is going on in your mind unless you manifest it in your creation, by your spoken words or written thought. So you see, the Mother itself is only his material. Any form the Mother takes is dictated by the Father. The self-conscious Will of the Universe only appears in what you call the "Laws of the Universe in Nature—the Laws of Nature."

The Moon shines only with the light of the Sun. In the subconscious (or the Mother) the Will of the Father appears. Perhaps we can get more illumination from comparison of THE MOON, THE STAR, and THE SUN. Both THE STAR and THE MOON show the Solar Energy as the original source of their light. In THE STAR, the Stars are all eight-pointed and the large Star is Yellow. What does this card stand for? The work of Meditation. In Meditation the self-consciousness does the labor. The labor is to still the mind, the brain, and the emotions. This is the hardest kind of work; but in itself it is not productive of the result striven for. All you do is get yourself ready for this work. The result comes as a gift from the superconscious by means of the subconscious. As far as you, the self-conscious, is concerned, the result comes automatically. You do all the work and the rest is automatic. The "Fish" hooks itself on your "Hook."

Now in the next card, THE MOON, the position of the self-conscious and the subconscious are exactly reversed. The self-conscious now has an easy time. All you have to do is supply the new mental image. It requires work and practice to formulate the image, and it requires Will; but it requires no painful effort on your part. To construct the body that is capable of making that image is a long and tedious task, and it is performed by the subconscious. In this card THE SUN, the self-conscious and subconscious are exactly balanced. They both work.

You might call these three cards THE LIGHTS, and they add up to 54. Four is REASON and 5 is THE HIEROPHANT. The Reason executing INTUITION. Five plus 4 equals 9. When Reason carries out Intuition, you have GOD, you have THE HERMIT. THE HERMIT has another Light He carries in His hand—the Lantern which is the Higher Self. In that Lantern you see an interlaced triangle, which symbolizes the union of the head and the heart; the product of that union is God-consciousness, depicted in this card THE SUN. The light of this

Golden Sun is the greatest light we may know on this physical plane.

In this card, 19, the CHILD sits buoyantly upon his HORSE, with both ARMS outstretched. The end for which JUSTICE was forever striving is now in him accomplished. In his left hand he bears the gigantic PENNANT, which gives him no trouble at all to wield. His right hand is solely occupied in keeping his balance as he wields it. This symbology means that he pays no attention to wielding the Orange Pennant, for the subconscious attends to it automatically. The only effort he makes, and from the card this appears to be very little, is to balance the Pennant with his other hand, as he swings it, and so keeps his equilibrium.

This card pictures the result which the Christian Church calls Regeneration, but the Church gives no details of how it can be accomplished except to say it is born of water and of blood. The water, it explains, is baptism, and the blood is the atoning blood of Jesus. This is the same old piteous story of the Church failing to understand its own allegory. Nowhere in the Church today are you told that the water and the blood are not literal. The Church has utilized the ambiguity of the allegory to promulgate doctrines quite at variance with those of the real founders of the Church.

The doctrine of the Atonement in its individual application denies all the doctrines of Jesus and Paul when it affirms that there is such a power on Earth or in heaven that can save a man from the consequences of his acts. Jesus said, "Be not deceived, God is not mocked; whatsoever a man sows, that shall he also reap." The expression "God is not mocked" is a peculiar one. It implies that some are being successfully mocked, but it is not God. Who then is mocked, but the Christians who believe that sins can be wiped out by repenting them.

There is a Cosmic sense in which the doctrine of Atonement is true, but it has nothing to do with individual man, but rather with man as a Race. The word really means *At-one-ment*, although the Church teaches that regeneration is accompanied by assiduous mental and emotional discipline. Thus their distortion of the meaning of the water and the blood is somewhat contradicted, but is not so bad as it might be, for the occultist teaches that this mental and emotional discipline is the beginning and the end, as far as the self-conscious is concerned, of the process of regeneration. The rest is subconscious. Occultism says, "This result is accomplished by water and blood, but the words are used in a symbolic sense."

Water is the Holy Ghost, or the Cosmic Mind-Stuff, and it is brought into the body by reason of physical changes in the body chemistry and structure. This physical change is accomplished by infusing into the bloodstream certain new elements extracted from the food. The at-one-ment achieved by the entire process is the at-one-ment of the body with the mind and the mind at-one with the mind of the Higher Self. These two at-one-ments are achieved by the sacrifice (in each case) of the lower to the higher, and the second at-one-ment can come only after the first has been achieved. These two at-one-ments are brought about by the self-conscious. The first is accompanied by another at-one-ment, which takes place in the sub-conscious, although instigated by the self-conscious. This is the at-one-ment of THE EMPRESS and THE HIGH PRIESTESS.

All three at-one-ments must have come to pass in you before the moment pictured in this card can arrive, when your mental vision becomes actual vision and the consciousness of regeneration becomes complete and instantaneous. Generation means coming into a personality; regeneration means becoming a new personality. What is this new personality? The type of consciousness depicted by this letter is denoted by the word *collective*. The first meaning of this word in Hebrew is that we are collectors of the Solar and Stellar Energies passing through us. We collect it in order to transform it, and pass it out again. The second meaning is that in this Luminary—composed of the Sun and the Moon, the union of the awakened Pineal and the awakened Pituitary—has collected all of the Intelligence there is in the Universe—the Intelligence of the Father and the Intelligence of the Mother. The third meaning is that it is a mode of consciousness which synthesizes all the previous modes and recombines them into a new form, which supersedes the rest but makes use of them all. You arrive at the knowledge of why your unique personality has been given to you; that is how to transform the Light in your own particular way. In the words of Jesus, "to let your Light shine."

That sums up the whole occult teaching. Free your channel from obstructions and let the Light come through, the better and not the worse for its passage. Only you in all the world of men and things can give it that contribution. Where did these obstructions come from? From the false Will, whose seat is the intellect.

This leads us to a consideration of the pair of opposites for which this letter stands, STERILITY and FRUITFULNESS. Man is the highest of animals because he alone possesses the thinking lobe of the brain.

He possesses complete awareness of himself as a being, distinguished from the rest of the world. This awareness is personified in Tarot and classic mythology by the name of MERCURY. It is this awareness which constitutes our intellect, or the mathematical activities of the human self-consciousness. The perfect development of Nature is impossible unless man applies to Nature his intellectual or mathematical activities. Man is the measurer, and he uses his mathematical activities to take the measure of himself and of his relation to Nature, in order to bend her to his purposes.

The occultist is told that the human form is employed by the One Will in order to communicate itself to its creation. MAN WAS, IS, AND EVER SHALL BE (in ever-increasing potency) A TRANSFORMER OF MATTER. It is apparent from history that this is so. It is also apparent that He can, in a way given to no other animal or form, reflect the consciousness within him. Such a unique prerogative bespeaks a unique function and consequently a unique responsibility. Occultism says that since the human countenance can radiate the Life Force flowing through the body, and animals cannot, we raise or lower the vibration of every creature we encounter. Because we are beings with intellect, we are more powerful transformers of the Light that passes through us than are the rest of the creatures of Nature.

The One Light passes through all forms, and in its passage it is transformed and passed on to whatever objects lie within our sphere of influence. Jesus said, "Wist ye not that I should be about my Father's business?" Our Father's business is the betterment of all matter we come in contact with, all that lies within our sphere of influence. As long as our intellects are under the domination of the false, the personal Will, we cannot do this. We only lower the vibration of all we encounter instead of raising it. The personal Will resides in the intellect, and the distinctly human function of the intellect is to curb the animal instincts. These instincts reside in the lower, the abdominal, brain—the Solar Plexus. Unless the intellect curbs them and bends them to his purpose, it cannot get at the business of measuring itself and Nature properly. All it does is to devise new and improved ways of pandering to the animal instincts and desires. "All the achievements of the intellect in this repect," say both the occultists and the religionists, "are barren and sterile, and produce nothing but mischief." Only when the intellect curbs the animal instincts and subdues them to its proper purpose can it get to its Father's business and become fruitful.

The purified Will must be perfectly balanced by a purified body.

The personal will must become the Will of the Higher Self, and the personal subconscious must become the Woman in TETH. She must identify herself with the Holy Ghost. She must rid herself of inherited taints and become as pure as the Cosmic Mind-Stuff out of which she came. In this card, MERCURY (or the intellectual awareness) has identified itself with the superconscious awareness; its mental vision has become SIGHT itself. This does not imply that we are to dispense with the intellect. Why discontinue the highest function of man? On the contrary, we are to use our intellects more than ever. We have made them more potent by removing them from the domination of instinct. Instead of putting the instincts at the service of the Solar Plexus, we are to put them at the service of the Higher Self.

The LIGHT from the union of the Sun and Moon streams down through REASON. Reason is the intellect in action, now in constructive action. The change, says the Gospel allegory, is one from death to life. Man under the domination of the intellect—and that intellect under the dominion of the Solar Plexus—is "dead." When his intellect is under the dominion of the Higher Self (whose seat in the body is the vivified Pineal), he is "quick" or "alive." Then for the first time, from the point of view of "Him who sent him," his works are fruitful.

Astrologers say that the Sun is exalted in ARIES, which means that Sunlight comes to its highest manifestation in REASON; and the reason of man, the measurer, governs Nature. All during his history he has been making Nature better by cultivation, devised by his intellectual-mathematical activity. Astrologers say that the Sun governs Leo. Leo is the Woman in TETH. Man has transformed his own subconscious and finally will identify it with the Cosmic Mind. He has done this by making images for his subconscious to follow. The precise nature of these images has been dictated by his measurement of his own experience. Man, the measurer, has transformed his external world. Because we are able to rearrange our physical, emotional, and mental existence, we can so change our bodies that we can lift them out of the kingdom of Nature in which they were born, just as we have cultivated animals and plants into new species. The higher our bodies go in Nature, the higher our minds go in identification with the One Life, and the more use we have for Reason. The only difference is that now it has ceased to give commands; it carries them out. All the poets have said that IN REASON, MAN IS LIKE A GOD.

THE MAGICIAN shows "reason" raised to its highest degree, a process which has been going on all along—using the mind to change your body. These cards always show the highest objective of the thing you are talking about, so the supreme way to use your mind to change your body is after you have awakened the Pineal Gland. The process which has been going on all along reaches a far greater potency than ever before. When the Pineal Gland is awakened, we can lift our bodies altogether out of the human kingdom of Nature into the Spiritual—out of the 4 into the 5, the superhuman.

What has been done? We have cultivated a new species of body just as we cultivate animals and plants into new species. Science now finds out we can cultivate minerals into new species. That is to say, we need not go on responding to environment and to the influences of the race mind and heredity. When you have awakened your Pineal Gland, it is said that this is exactly what happens. You see the Universe from the point of view of the Sun, of the creator of it. You see the relation of "cause and effect," the revolving wheel of cause and effect.

The Sun rules Leo; it comes to its highest manifestation in Aries. LEO is the HEART, and LEO symbolizes THE LAW OF SUGGESTION. The Sun rules the Law of Suggestion. Nature in you (your subconscious) is ruled by the suggestion coming from your self-conscious; however badly your self-conscious works, however rudimentary it is, it is a miniature Sun. It is a Sun in the making. Those whom the occultists call the Masters are those who have constructed the perfect bodies by the Law of Suggestion. They have told us we are what they once were, and Jesus told you the same thing. It is Jesus whom the Church worships. He told you he was a man in all respects as we are. So it would follow that the reason our bodies are such inadequate affairs is that as a race we do not use our Reason at all. Most men use only their prejudices. As someone cleverly said, "When men think they think, they only feel." From our prejudices come our opinions and yet they are not opinions at all. They are only fears. We base our opinions on our prejudices. Where did prejudices come from? From our bodies, from races. They come from propaganda—propaganda put out by the exploiting class. So the opinions of most of us really are only prejudices, and our prejudices are inspired in us when we think we think. We are really just dancing to the wires that pull us puppets and are jerked by the exploiting class. In wartime men will not go to war without a system pulling at their fear and their hate, a system controlled by those persons who desire war because they will benefit by it. The same thing goes on in peace. Constantly the exploiting class is sending out propaganda to influence the subconsciousness of people.

They always din into their ears that if they seek to change their sacred institutions, ruin will follow. They are afraid to change; we are afraid to use our minds on anything.

We resist a change just because it is a change. Inertia is when nothing is unfolded. The change may be good or bad but we do not like the new rhythm; and in addition to that, if you were not compelled to be moved by that very propaganda to which you respond, then fear would make you stand still and rot in your tracks. This is because people do not use their reason. They only use their prejudices. The only use most people make of reason is to justify their behavior after they have done it. As Benjamin Franklin said so wittily: "What is the use of being a reasonable being unless we can use our minds to justify something we have done?"

SYMBOLISM

In the last card you saw the human-faced Moon, and in this card, the HUMAN-FACED SUN. Both are characterized by perfect serenity. We cannot bring to life in us the MOON and the SUN unless we learn to conquer our emotions.

From the SUN proceed 21 YELLOW RAYS, 11 straight and 10 wavy ones. These are arranged alternately, but the series begins and ends with a straight ray, making the first and last straight rays come together. Between these two there is another ray, which is WAVY and BLACK. Black stands for the occult, and the meaning is that this is not a natural ray, but we must make it so ourselves by occult practice.

If you consider this Ray as straight (which it is not), there would be 12 straight rays in all, and they would then suggest the 12 signs of the Zodiac. If you consider this Ray as feminine (wavy), the other feminine rays, which suggest the Ten Emanations of the Life Power, now become 11, but there are only 10. We must seek another symbolism. The YELLOW RAYS stand for the 21 numbered cards of the Tarot Trumps; the BLACK one stands for THE FOOL, which precedes them, and is numbered Zero. THE FOOL symbolizes the Spirit before it descended into matter, and in that state Spirit was both masculine and feminine, or rather, neither masculine or feminine but containing the potencies of both.

We must, by occult practice, make THE FOOL in us. He is the Christ-Child, or the Transformed Heart. The heart is feminine (this is an involuntary organ) until we transform it, when it becomes a masculine, or voluntary, organ. It is said that in the process its tissues are changed and it becomes striped. You will note the play on words in the text which is generally supposed to refer to the crucified Jesus: "With his stripes we are healed."

It is because the heart becomes a masculine organ that it can now safely become the governor of man, and by it the body comes to its wholeness or health. It can at last exercise to the full its intended function. The Transformed Heart is in perfect equilibrium (as you see from the position of the Child, who symbolizes it), and that is the reason it stands for THE FOOL in us. It is in perfect equilibrium, as was THE FOOL, being both masculine and feminine.

The Black Ray is meant to be both wavy and straight, and should be more definitely drawn as such. In all there are 22 rays proceeding from the Pineal-Pituitary, and the 22 is both masculine and feminine. This androgynous quality you have seen in the first card, THE FOOL, and you will see it again in the last card, THE WORLD. The cards in their numbered order are not arranged as alternately masculine and feminine. For instance, card 1 is BETH and card 2 is GIMEL, but card 3 is feminine instead of masculine and card 4 is masculine instead of feminine. This should not trouble you when you remember that each card has a masculine as well as a feminine role to play. For instance, BETH is masculine to the body and feminine to the Higher Self. All the types of Intelligence there are descend into the body from the Pineal-Pituitary. These 22 types are condensed in the face of the Luminary.

All the senses are collected in the face, and the word *countenance* means "that which holds together or contains the five senses." The face is the sole source of four of the five senses, and the sense of touch is most sensitive there, as you will readily admit when you get the tiniest speck of dust in your eye.

The LUMINARY is upon a BLUE BACKGROUND. That symbolizes that the most active agency in bringing about the Collective Intelligence is the Holy Ghost. It is she who purifies the body; and the intellect is, of course, part of the body, although it is the highest part of the body. "There is a force within us, not ourselves, which makes for right-use-ness," says the Bible. The Holy Ghost is that force, which in the end, after we have brought enough of it into our bodies to cleanse them entirely, allows us to use them as they were intended.

This BACKGROUND OF BLUE grows darker as it goes down. This symbolizes the admixture of the Holy Ghost with the mineral kingdom—our clay, or subconscious. Man has perfected his body when he has made his personal subconscious at-one with the Holy Ghost.

Next there is a WALL WITH SUNFLOWERS peeping over it. The Wall in our card has eight courses of masonry and represents man's development of natural conditions. The layers are eight, which correspond with the eightfold energy of the Sun, which we duplicate in our own activities, tallying with the eight-spoked wheels on the robe of THE FOOL. All that man has done in developing Nature has come about through the reports of his five senses. His improvements were always initiated by the attempt to secure from Nature greater gratifications for his five senses.

You will note that on the UPPERMOST LAYER of the Wall are the letters IHVH, a Divine Name summing up to 30, which in Tarot corresponds to JUSTICE and in the Hebrew letters corresponds to LAMED, or equilibrium—equilibrium for which the figure 8 is the graphic symbol, the above becoming the below and the below becoming the above.

On the NEXT LAYER is the divine Name IH. This Name is particularly attributed to the feminine principle, the other to both the feminine and masculine. These letters on the Wall show that the Wall is also to be taken as the eightfold Path to holiness, or right-use-ness, the way to achieve perfection of mind and body. The special significance of this second interpretation of the Wall will appear in a moment. Whether one or the other, the Wall was erected by man using his Reason, his powers of measurement, to lead him to new conclusions.

The SUNFLOWERS are to be taken at three levels. First they represent the four kingdoms of Nature. It is these which man has improved by the use of his Reason, and which still look to man for further development. The Bible says, "All nature groaneth and travaileth together for the coming of the sons of mind." The hope of Nature lies in perfected man, man who has previously used his Reason to perfect his body and himself. Three of the kingdoms of Nature are grouped together, the fourth by itself. This indicates that man need not be conditioned by his past, but that the seeds he sows may be something entirely new, bringing forth new species not previously found in Nature.

In the Cosmic sense rather than the planetary, the four Sunflowers represent the four planes—the Physical, Formative, Creative, and the Archetypal. In this case the meaning is the same as when they are purely physical, only wider in extent. Not only the physical world, but all the higher ones, look for their final development to man in whom the Christ-consciousness has been born. Particularly in the case of the Archetypal World is man unconditioned by his past. The ideas he may bring down into the physical plane through the other two stages are far beyond present limits.

In the third level the SUNFLOWERS represent REASON, whose card is numbered 4 and whose letter is numbered 5. There are four Sunflowers, or five if you count the Child's head as one of them. It is apparently there for that purpose, and it is composed of RED-ON-YELLOW, as are the other Sunflowers. They flower out of a wealth of GREEN LEAVES scored with occult lines. The CHILD (like THE FOOL) wears a long PLUME OF RED, the Eagle's feather, the bird that can stare into the face of the Sun.

Man is the highest of the animals because he can wield more of the Mars vibration, and the Christ-Child can wield more of the Mars vibration than man. THE EMPEROR is represented as ruling through his wife and his child. The Scepter and the Sphere which he bears in his hands represent them—the Scepter, his wife and the Sphere, his child. Here they are symbolized in the row of Sunflowers. The Sunflower is a mimic Sun, symbolizing that in man which has always been godlike.

The WREATH on the head of the Child is composed, not of green leaves, like that of THE FOOL's wreath, but of little Sun symbols, the circle with the central dot. The Wreath must extend around his head; therefore there are 12 symbols in all. They represent the Zodiac and correspond to the belt of THE FOOL. The Child controls the 12 forms of self-expression. As his Mars vibration is entirely at the service of the enlightened awareness, these 12 forms of consciousness are expressing themselves to perfection. The Child joyously wields the ORANGE PENNANT of the STELLAR ENERGY, which streams into his body through the Transformed Heart. It is colored by his own personality, passing through the heart again to raise the vibrations of all he contacts.

He carries it on an OCCULT STAFF. Where his fist closes on the staff he makes the lower loop of a figure 8; the higher loop is formed by the scoring on a green leaf. It is equilibrium that enables him to wield the giant Pennant. He wields it automatically, for it is in his left hand; his right is employed in keeping his balance. This is the business which demands his conscious attention. If at any time he should fail to keep his balance—should he allow his emotions to get the better of him—he would be destroyed. In the Book of Revelation we read of the "red dragon" always waiting to destroy him—desire which has slipped its leash.

The destructive lion of the body has now become the DOCILE HORSE, the eager carrier of the Christ-Child. It is the goal of the body to become the animal carrier of the Christ-consciousness. His extreme docility is no more obvious than in his pricked-up ears.

A Kabbalist proverb declares that "the Spirit clothed itself to come down into matter." THE FOOL is clothed. It divests Itself, one by one, of the thick garments of matter, as It re-sends to Its Source. The Child allegorically represents the True Self set free from the limitation of matter and circumstance. He turns his back upon the artificial erections of the race consciousness. He even turns his back upon the eight forms of Yoga, which have helped to make him what he is. He joyously sets forth in complete liberation from all barriers. "Behold, I make all things new," says the Gospel of the Christ-consciousness. He will find what he seeks, for he will guide his horse to them, although he is noticeably without saddle or bridle. He is directing his horse, as did the Charioteer his two Sphinxes, by the invisible reins of the mind.

Finally, the last word to say about this picture of the Christ-Child is really the first word. *He is man-made.* THE DEVIL is man-made. ●EVERYTHING IN MAN'S TRANSFORMATION, UP TO THE FINAL STEP, HE MUST BRING ABOUT HIMSELF, BY HIS OWN WORK UPON HIS OWN NATURE. HE TRANSFORMS HIS SUBCON-SCIOUS BY HIS OWN IMAGES. The transformed self-conscious is man-made, for though the change is performed by the subconscious, she cannot do it until he has transformed her. The Christ-consciousness is everywhere in the world, but you cannot possess it until you have struggled to get it. We ourselves, with unflagging mind and unfailing ardor, must bring to birth the Christ-Child in the Etheric Center of the heart.

This card, THE SUN, says that the God-consciousness is born from the Sun streaming down through Reason (depicted here as the Sunflower). Alchemy has given, in a fantastic language, how regeneration was to be accomplished. Regeneration comes only from our-selves when the purified Will and purified body work together as one. Each must be purified. How do you purify the personal Will? MAKE IT THE WILL OF THE HIGHER SELF; GIVE IT UP AND TAKE THE WILL OF THE HIGHER SELF INSTEAD. How do you purify the body? MAKE YOUR INTELLECTUAL SUBCONSCIOUS THE SAME AS THE HIGH PRIESTESS: IDENTIFY YOUR INTELLECTUAL SUBCONSCIOUS WITH THE HOLY GHOST.

You see her in THE HIGH PRIESTESS, her robe flowing through the Crescent, through your intellectual subconsciousness.

The Bible says that the goal of man was to become co-worker with God. He becomes a conscious co-worker only when he has awakened his Pineal Gland, and when he puts this development to its proper use after he has done it. You can always misuse this potency to work against evolution as well as to work for it. Until the God-consciousness is born in you there is no safety for you, for you can use your awakened Pineal Gland to be a black magician instead of a white one.

You are going to find that card 21 indicates the consciousness called "The Fifth Dimension," and the Fifth Dimension is explained as a Consciousness above time and space considerations. It is to this Consciousness that Reason is always looking forward. It does not want to become once more unmanifest, to be reabsorbed into the bosom of the Father. It wants to be above space and time considerations. That is to say, it wants to be CAUSE and EFFECT simultaneously. It wants to see what Emerson calls "the flower in the fruit and the fruit in the seed and the seed in the flower."

NOTES

JUDGEMENT.

Command of Universal Energy at Will.

21st Hebrew Letter	*SHIN*
Symbol for	*Heat*
Element Attributed to	*Fire*
Color	*Red or Orange-Scarlet*
Numerical Value	*300*
Syllables	*ShIN*
Sound	*C-Natural*
Planet	*Vulcan*
Translation	*Tooth or Fang*

NOTES

JUDGEMENT

SHIN, spelled ShIN, means TOOTH or FANG. It is the 21st Hebrew letter and the third MOTHER LETTER. It is the sign or symbol for the element of FIRE; for the PERPETUAL INTEL-LIGENCE; for the planet VULCAN (which is the higher octave of the planet MARS); for the color RED; for the note C-NATURAL. Its numerical value is 300. In Roman characters it is written Sh.

This is the Mother Letter for FIRE. From time immemorial the Deity has been associated with Fire. The earliest sacred books (those of India) call the Fire god Agni. The similarity of Agni to Agnus, or lamb, is evident. It is startling to the Catholic when he finds that the Lamb with notched pennant was brought over without any change from the Hindu to the Christian symbology. As a matter of fact, Christians are fire worshippers, though that is about the last name they would care to call themselves. Twice the Bible uses these words: "Our God is a consuming fire," and many other times in both Testaments He is called a Fire. Fire has always been considered the purifier and the most pure thing in physical matter.

The ancient doctrine of the Fire god is at the basis of the doctrine out of which all religions are fabricated: the Ageless Wisdom. We can see this in the secret meaning of the Hebrew letters forming another Bible underneath the Outer one. We can see it in the secret teaching of the Egyptian and Greek languages. We can see it in the Zodiacal language, a secret language for all peoples. We can see it in the Tarot, in Alchemy, in Rosicrucianism—those secret forms of instruction manufactured by the occultists when the Hebrew and Christian churches became encrusted with false doctrines.

The Fire substance is the original substance from which all things are produced. The first step of this substance called Fire, on the way to manifestation, is to become Water. The Fire or the Water pervades everything. Things are made out of that stage of it called Water, but the Fire is the directive principle, the principle which determines what shape and function the thing shall take when it is made.

The primary idea associated with ShIN is Fire, but it is also a symbol of "breath." In the Hebrew Wisdom it has the same numerical value as RVCh ALHIM, Ruach Elohim, the Life-Breath of the Creative Powers. Throughout both occult and religious teaching this intimate connection between "breath" and "fire" is insisted upon. The Bible says: "He

353

maketh His angels breathe and His ministers a flaming fire." Tarot goes further and combines the two openly. THE FOOL, which represents the Spirit, is the FIERY LIFE-BREATH. It is Fire that we breathe, if we had the vision to see it. Science tells us that the air we breathe burns us up. The slow, orderly burning of our bodies constitutes our life. With every breath we consume the waste in our lungs and thus we maintain our body heat. The occultist says that the Higher Life, as well as the physical life of the body, is also maintained by Fire.

In all systems of Yoga, breathing exercises are practiced in order to arouse the Kundalini fire, which in time awakens the Pineal Gland and fuses its sand into the Philosopher's Stone. Occultism teaches that all personal activity breaks down cell structure by combustion. It says it is due to the various types of resistance which the human organism offers to the fiery Life Force as it flows through us. Our bodies are machines precisely as electric machines are; they are made like electric machines for the purpose of offering types of resistance to the current that runs through them. The incandescence of the wire proceeds from the resistance thus contrived, and as a consequence the electricity is made to manifest light, heat, or power according to the gearing of the machine. We are all immersed, these machines, in a sea of Fire which flows through us. This is what is represented by the Mother Letter ShIN.

The number of this card is 20. It is called the number of the Fourth Dimension. Its constituent parts will give you some idea of what the Fourth Dimension is. Twenty equals 0 operating through 2. In the previous card, THE SUN, we saw that the equilibrated heart corresponded to THE FOOL; thus we may express the Fourth Dimension as the Christ in us working through the Holy Ghost. Twenty reduces to 2; thus, the influence of the Holy Ghost is most important. We saw that the last card, 19, equals 9, THE HERMIT or Spirit, working through the self-conscious awareness, or Mercury. Nineteen reduces to 10, and 10 reduces to 1, which is BETH, THE MAGICIAN, the more important influence. That card depicted a newborn infant; this card depicts a resurrection. To bring to birth the Christ-Child is the end result of a self-conscious undertaking. But the resurrection of the body to a higher form of consciousness, called the Fourth Dimensional consciousness, is the work of the Holy Ghost. It must come from something outside themselves.

This fact is depicted in the card; it is the Trumpet call of the Angel which awakens these three and bursts their coffins asunder.

The type of Intelligence this letter stands for is called the PER-
PETUAL. A thing is perpetual when it has no beginning and no end.
This in geometry is represented by a circle, an endless line. The letter-
name ShIN numerates 360, and there are 360 degrees in a circle. The
word "perpetual" in Hebrew is derived from a verb which means "to
stretch." Anything which can continuously be stretched out has no
end and can be termed perpetual. Thus the word, with charming
naivete, sums up the occult idea of evolution. It is a continuous and
unending process of stretching out from the Spirit which is the source.
This stretching out applies both to consciousness and to forms. A new
and finer consciousness is constantly evolved which demands a new
and finer form to manifest it. The state of consciousness is entirely dependent upon the form it inhabits. At present our consciousness is
limited to three dimensions. This card represents the Fourth Dimension and it depicts the Christ-Child as well as his Father and Mother
coming into this state of consciousness. It is evident, then, that the
Christ was not born into this state of consciousness. It is something
achieved later.

Let us see if the Gospel story can shed any light upon this. The
word translated "Jesus" is wrongly spelled and should be spelled with
a "sh" in the middle—Jehoshua. It means "the god liberates or frees
himself." Jesus was born a God but did not free himself until some-
time later in his life. It is of course very natural to surmise that this time
was signaled by the last act of his mortal career, the crucifixion, at the
end of which he cried as he gave up the ghost: "It is finished." When
we next see him he has been resurrected into another kind of body,
and the resurrection has been attended by an earthquake apparently
caused by the visitation of an angel or angels. Presumably, it was this
visitation which brought about his resurrection.

We saw in the last card that THE LOVERS is almost identical with THE
SUN. Let us then read the following sentence in the most striking way
possible: THE CHRIST-CHILD BY DEATH COMES TO RESURREC-
TION INTO A LARGER LIFE.

The card DEATH, we found, means the willed destruction of
cells, both self-conscious and subconscious. The rider on the White
Horse has already ploughed down the old emperor of the body,
Reason, and the self-conscious awareness will follow, and then the
subconscious and her child. They all must die in order to be resurrected
into the deathless Solar body depicted as the Rising Sun at the top of
the Stream. The lower part of the Stream is the personal subconscious;

the upper part of the Stream is the Holy Ghost, the Cosmic Subconscious. The Above falls into the Below in the central waterfall which depicts the heart.

This idea is also stated in the color of the card and letter, GREEN-BLUE, the merging of the personal with the Cosmic Subconscious. When we finally come to possess a body and brain capable of the extensions of consciousness symbolized by the WHITE ROSE on the BLACK PENNANT of DEATH, what is it we become aware of? We become aware of the original ideas of God symbolized by the 14 rays from the White Sun in THE FOOL, and explained in detail in the 14 cards of the suit of WANDS.

These ideas, in order to become embodied in physical matter, descended through four planes: Fire, Water, Air, and Earth—the Archetypal, the Creative, the Formative, and the Physical.

The WANDS suit symbolizes FIRE,
The CUPS suit symbolizes WATER,
The SWORD suit symbolizes AIR, and
The PENTACLES suit symbolizes EARTH.

As a result of the work done by our willed destruction of the cells depicted in card XIII, we have what is depicted in card XX. The name of the card is JUDGEMENT, but as usual that is a play on words. Judgement is the sentence passed by Justice; that is, it is the final result of the perfect equilibrium of the self-conscious and the subconscious. A judgement is the finish of a trial, the decision which is the outcome of it. Also, just as card XV was a jocular allusion to the Christian idea of the Devil, so this card is a jocular allusion to the Christian teaching of the day of the Last Judgement. The New Testament expression is the separation of the quick and the dead. The occult meaning of the text is not the division between the saved and the damned, the sheep and the goats, but the separation of the quick and the dead in us. The dead drops away and we flame into an incandescent consciousness of immortality. Our scale of values, which has been changing ever since we entered upon the occult or mystic path, now undergoes its final change. Then at last comes the bursting of the three-dimensional bonds, which card XX depicts as a resurrection. When it comes it obliterates no consciousness which we have already. We keep all our present perceptions and sensations, otherwise it would be very inconvenient to live among three-dimensional people. We have added new meanings to them, Fourth-Dimensional meanings.

What is the Fourth-Dimensional meaning of things? That which they had before they were brought down into time and space, while they were still Archetypes, Ideas of God. Then only are they unchangeable and unchanging. When they descend into the three lower planes, they come under the law of perpetual change.

Astrologers say that Scorpio, or Nun, is ruled by Mars at night and by Aries, or THE EMPEROR (Reason), by day. Tarot translates this in this way: DEATH, or Change, is the ruler of form and of the World of Formation, while THE EMPEROR is the ruler of the Creative World. The Archetypes are unchanging, but when they descend into the three lower planes, upon each one of which they exist as forms appropriate to that plane, they must undergo constant change. In the end that change is what we call death. Death is but the cessation of one form for its transition to another. HE WHO PERCEIVES THE ARCHETYPE PERCEIVES THE ESSENCE OF THE FORM, WHICH IS NOT SUBJECT TO CHANGE AND WHICH IS THEREFORE ALWAYS IN PERFECTION.

Let us now inspect the character ShIN, which is the only character possessing three Yods. All the Yods in the Hebrew alphabet descend except in Aleph, Peh, and Tau, where there is an ascending Yod of different shape from the others. The discussion of this different-shaped ascending Yod we will omit for the present. This leaves Aleph, a one-Yod letter, and the other one-Yod letters are Gimel, Vau, Zain, Teth, Lamed, Mem, and Nun. Of these one-Yod letters Gimel, Zain, Teth, Mem, and Nun all have a wavy descending line and hence depict the descent of the feminine Fire. Aleph, Vau, and Lamed have a straight descending line and hence depict the descent of the masculine Fire. The two-Yod letters are Ayin and Tzaddi, and these have one of each kind, masculine and feminine.

The business of the Sun of our solar system is to collect and pass the Stellar Fire through its body, and transform it into the Solar Fire. Each creature of the Sun in our solar system is made out of its energy, exists by it, passes it through its body and transforms it by the passage. When we become miniature suns and have transformed the heart, then we can receive the Stellar Energy also, pass it through our bodies and transmit it. This is the reason the stellar tongue of flame enters the parallelogram representing the body upon the side of the subconscious. The self-conscious flame enters the body by the Pineal Gland only. From there it is distributed to the body by the Pituitary in a stream modified by both. The subconscious stream enters the body by the Pituitary alone, is mingled with the stellar stream in the Solar Plexus and conducted to the thighs by the Higher Self, whose seat in the body is the awakened Pineal Gland. The body is prepared for all this higher spiritual work by the action of Kundalini, the Earth Fire which exists in etheric matter and not in mental matter like the other two. Thus Kundalini does the preparatory work for the Christ-Child, and is symbolized by John the Baptist in the Gospel allegory. Kundalini baptizes the Seven Centers and through them the zones of the body they control, and by quickening their vibration makes possible their spiritual development.

The letter ShIN means TOOTH or FANG—tooth in the sense of that which breaks down form and lets the essence escape for another form; fang in the sense of that which kills or destroys. Now what does ShIN break down and what is the thing it liberates? The occult saying is that ShIN destroys the last body. The last body is the body that brings forth the Christ-Child. This is the perfect body for which all Nature has been striving. It is broken down only in a figurative sense, for it still persists after the initiation on the astral, which sets the consciousness free from its limitations. What is broken down is merely limitation.

The character ShIN is said to be composed of three Yods and a Vau. You may naturally ask, by the way, where is the Vau in this letter. That answer is that a Vau means a connecting link of any kind; and here the body or parallelogram is the connecting link for the three Fires. Three Yods and a Vau make 36, and 36 is the sum of the numbers from 1 to 8. In the Hebrew letters this 8 is CHETH. Cheth is called the HOUSE OF INFLUENCE, or THE FENCED FIELD, and the Charioteer is occupying that house after the initiation described in JUDGEMENT has taken place. That is to say, after the three-dimensional limitation it imposed has been broken down. If you read the number 8 by the cards instead of the letters, it comes to the same thing. The Woman in card 8 is the transformed and equilibrated heart. She is receiving into the body for retransmission the Stellar Energy, symbolized by the Orange Lion.

This letter stands for the planet VULCAN. It is thought to be in the orbit of Mercury, the planet nearest the Sun. Occultists have always known of the existence of this planet and have called it the higher octave of Mars, just as Neptune is called by them the higher octave of Venus. The god Vulcan was the Roman god of Fire. His day was the 23rd of August and this date is significant. It is the last day of Leo and the first day of Virgo. Leo is the Transformed Heart and Virgo, the Spirit. The Christ-consciousness is achieved by Fire in the heart and transformed to the Spirit. On that day the priest Vulcan built a great fire in the area of Rome, which was sacred to him, and blessed those who performed this ceremony. Every head of a family was supposed to buy small fishes freshly caught from the Tiber and throw them alive into this fire. It is impossible to figure out the meaning of such a cult and ceremony. It is easy for those to do so who know that Nun means "fish" and "death," and that the triple fire symbolized by ShIN and Vulcan means the perception of the Changeless in the midst of constant change.

A description of this letter says that "the Perpetual Intelligence regulates the motions of the Sun and Moon in their proper order." The Administrative Intelligence says that "it orders all life's activities within their proper bounds and limits." It would seem, then, that if the two Intelligences are not the same in all respects, at least they overlap in this one. The motions of the Sun and Moon in us are surely part of our life's activities. Both this card and the next depict the body when it is entirely under the control and direction of the Higher Self. In card XIV you saw the Higher Self mixing the two currents of the Sun and the Moon in us. We were told that only He could do this. They are not, strictly speaking, *mixed* as you will see when you inspect the twofold stream in that card carefully. They are just side by side. We typify these two currents when, as children say, we breathe out hot or cold. This we can do at will. When we learn how to do so, we can project either the active or the passive current at will. These two are what the alchemists called the Sun and the Moon. They are but two forms of the same Life-Breath, just as breathing *hot* or *cold* are two forms of the actual breath—forms merely mechanical while the other two differ vitally. They are two forms of the same thing shown by their symbols. This is the equilateral triangle in each case, the one pointing up and the other pointing down. Ability to project these two currents flowing through the body in opposite ways is acquired by occult practice in the Creative Imagination. There is, however, an antagonism between the active and the passive states of the Life-Breath. The alchemists say that the Sun is checked by the Moon and the Moon is checked by the Sun. They must thus be alternated in their proper order, each in its own orbit. Knowledge of how to do this is taught by THE HIEROPHANT only, and He directs you when to do it. He makes it known only to those who have done the preliminary work. The only function of books and teachers is to get us ready for the Inner Teacher.

Alchemy is the science of Fire and also the art of directing it. The completion of the art in your organism releases you from three-dimensional consciousness. Alchemy says that the work is performed by the operation of the Sun and Moon with the aid of Mercury. Mercury is the self-conscious Awareness and Will. The Moon is the Pituitary and its influences. The Sun is the Heart Center through which the Stellar vibrations enter. Mercury is responsible for both Sun and Moon in you.

Though the Christ-Child is born in the Heart Center, its highest manifestation is in the head. Astrologers say that the Sun is exalted in Aries. When this same current expresses itself in the Heart Center it rules Leo, and Leo is depicted as the Woman in STRENGTH. Thus the Sun vibration is depicted in these cards once as a man and once as a woman. The Sun current entering at the heart flows up, while the Lunar current entering through the Pituitary flows down.

Astrologers say that the Moon is exalted in Taurus and rules Cancer. The highest thing the Moon can do is to make you hear; and the highest thing the Sun can do is to make you see. The Moon rules Cancer; that is, unless you are master of your emotions you cannot make your body THE CHARIOT for the Charioteer to enter.

The Lunar current flows down into the Solar Plexus, where it meets the Sun current on its way back from Aries. (Note in this connection that the astrological symbol of Jupiter is both self-conscious and subconscious, with the Moon predominating.) From the Solar Plexus we are told that the two currents are conducted to the thighs, and that the journey is superintended by the Higher Self. In the card SAMEKH he is depicted as an Angel, with the Sun symbol on his brow but testing his weight in the water. This, then, is what is meant by Mercury assisting in managing the two Fires in your body, and he himself is the third Fire, the Fire of mind.

Just as these three Fires correspond to the superconscious, the subconscious, and the self-conscious, so these Fires operate in three ways: physical, mental, and spiritual. The physical phase is the higher digestion and building into the body the new elements after they are assimilated, by the medium of the bloodstream. The mental part also concerns, figuratively speaking, a new kind of digestion and building into the mind what has been assimilated by it. We come to pay more accurate attention to the things that happen to us, and we see that what appeared to be mere chance is only an individual (ourself) working through the Universal Law of Cycles. Third, there is this same process upon the Spiritual, or superconscious, plane. By the employment of our new powers of physical and mental analysis and the consequent transmutation of our bodies and minds, we acquire new perceptions one after the other until at last we can perceive "fourth-dimensionally."

We have fixed the two currents of Fire in our bodies so that we can command them at will; yet at the same time we are no longer confined to our bodies, we can emerge from them at will. The body becomes what the picture of THE TOWER becomes when you turn it upside-down: no longer a coffin which either conditions your consciousness or confines your movements.

This double process going on in the physical, the mental, and the Spiritual life the alchemists termed in their fantastic, purposely misleading language, "the fixation of the volatile and the volatilization of the fixed." In the Spiritual part of it (the part we are concerned with in this card), the practical occultist fixes the volatile (the twin currents of Fire) in the substance of this body. As a consequence he makes volatile the fixed; that is, he can emerge from his body whenever he wishes, and even while he is in it, it is no longer his coffin. It is now his Tower of Strength from which he works to perform his mastery of things. Out of their coffins, soaring aloft, issue the conscious and the subconscious, freed at last, just as they are in this card JUDGEMENT. You have seen how it is that even the Christ-Child may have a coffin to emerge from, a coffin which keeps him from awareness of things as they exist on the Archetypal plane before they come down into any of the three stages of matter. The Christ-consciousness cannot shine forth in its entire splendor in the physical world until that initiation called the COSMIC CONSCIOUSNESS takes place upon the astral. This is symbolized in the Gospel allegory by the resurrection, preceded by the crucifixion, of the Christ.

SYMBOLISM

The three figures in the background repeating the three figures in the foreground are a mistake; they only confuse the meaning of the card. They were probably put there to confuse or mislead the casual observer into thinking that the card pictured the Judgement Day of the Bible when Gabriel shall blow his horn. The Angel is Gabriel, the same Angel who appeared to Daniel to explain a vision, who announced to Zachariah the birth of John the Baptist, and who told Mary that she would bring forth Jesus. In the Book of Enoch he is spoken of as one of the archangels. His task is that of intercession, or going between, and he is "set over all the Powers."

In this card, the ANGEL is pictured as the Angel of the Universal Creative Fire. His HAIR is YELLOW FLAMES as well as RED, meaning he is the Angel of the Solar Fire. Since his ROBE is BLUE, he is an angel of the element of Water also. He thus united himself with both Sun and Moon, as did the angel in SAMEKH. The action of Fire on Water creates Air, the substance of breath. The word *Gabriel* in Hebrew reduces to 2, hence the Water is more important than the Fire.

The chief thing we see about him is that he is blowing a MESSAGE through his TRUMPET. Therefore, the message is from THE HIGH PRIESTESS and is a message of Cosmic Memory. The message causes us to remember what we were before we descended into matter, what we were on the Archetypal plane. Thus you perceive that the card tells us at once that when Jesus was resurrected, new perceptions were given him that were higher than he had ever had before. It is said that after we hear this message we can never have a merely personal point of view again—that we have come into a universal consciousness, a higher kind of knowing and feeling. By this message the human consciousness is awakened to what the Hebrew Wisdom designated LORD, which is translated into English as ADONAI. It means the glowing manifestation of the Life Power which pours forth the Cosmos and endlessly transforms one expression of itself into another by a series of perpetual changes. The Mars vibration does the same thing, says the Tarot, and Adonai is the Mars vibration as it is used by Divinity. PERPETUAL DESTRUCTION PRECEDING PERPETUAL CONSTRUCTION.

Adonai has the value of 65. The Magic Square of Mars has 25 cells, five on each line. These cells each have a number, and the numbers are so apportioned that every vertical, horizontal, and diagonal line in it sums up to 65, the Divine expression of the Mars force. All these endless transformations in the Cosmos are produced in accordance with Law. AS ABOVE, SO BELOW. To manifest his little portion of the Mars force in such a way as to further evolution and not impede it, that is the goal of man. Little as his portion of the Mars force is, in comparison with higher beings, he is able to manifest more of it than any other creature who is on this plane. On all planets it is said that he is the only creature who can manifest all the Ten Emanations of the Life Power.

The BANNER on this card is a WHITE SQUARE, therefore the Angel equips the three below him with the measurement of the Spiritual forces, just as the Angel in SAMEKH is equipped with the measurement of the Higher Self. The Banner (which is on the Trumpet) is the Magic Square of Mars. The RED CROSS covers just nine of the little cells. Nine is the number of THE HERMIT and also the number of completion, the last of the series. The Red Cross may be taken at many levels. Its four arms may stand for the four planes. The Christ-Child has now become IHVH and can create upon the four planes, in which case he uses his sex force, which is indicated by the red color. In its narrowest sense, the Cross also stands for the four Rivers of the Garden of Eden, all of which are now functioning perfectly and proportionately in his body. It stands for the four figures in the card: the Angel, the self-conscious, the subconscious, and the Christ-consciousness.

The SOUND Gabriel is BLOWING from his Trumpet is seven-fold. For each of the seven ways in which the Ten Emanations of the Life Power present themselves, we have a corresponding Center in our bodies. The seven ways make the seven basic sounds, and in our practice we relate a sound to each Center. In order to hear Gabriel's trumpet, the seven Centers of the body must all be working perfectly and in unison. The instrument of this final liberation, we are told, is actual sound. To each of the seven tones of the trumpet the seven interior stars will vibrate on a new and grander scale. This is the culmination of man's effort to quicken the rate of his interior stars. It is the culmination of the preparatory work of John the Baptist (Kundalini), who has been bathing them in the water of the River Jordan ever since he started on his occult, or mystic, career.

Though man's own effort must bring him to this point, the symbolism here indicates that the final triumph comes from something outside himself. Perhaps this is only more dramatic than what has been happening all along on his journey. Ever THE HIEROPHANT has been leading him on, and when he reached a certain development THE HIGH PRIESTESS began to take a hand also. This liberation takes place at an initiation upon the astral plane. This is the reason for the COLOR of the FLESH of the three, though it also indicates that now they are entirely at one with the Father. That, too, is the reason that the man and the woman have changed their relative positions. The liberation takes place upon the astral plane, and there all things are just the reverse of the physical.

You have seen for some time the WOMAN GROWING LARGER THAN THE MAN. In THE DEVIL card she was dwarfed and distorted by his ceaseless demands for sensation. In THE LOVERS she took her rightful place in the lead, though by his consent. This predominance of the female in Spiritual evolution does not mean that man's day is over. Although it is quite true that from the beginning of this Aquarian Age women will take the lead, it is a consummation devoutly to be wished for in the light of the unspeakable mess men have made of ruling.

It merely means that the liberated person is more female than male, since through the entire body the Cosmic mind-stream is running. Letting the subconscious rule in ignorance is folly; letting the subconscious rule in full knowledge is Divine common sense, although in man's estimate it is to play "the fool." Besides, by that time the self-conscious has no illusions as to his place in evolution. He realizes that in reality he does not exist, that he was all along only the manifestation of the relation between the two natures of the Spirit—the superconscious above dense matter and the subconscious immersed in it. He has been but the center point of an hourglass where the sand above drops into the sand below.

The HAIR of the WOMAN in the picture is YELLOW to show that she is both THE EMPRESS and the Woman in STRENGTH. The MAN'S HAIR is BLACK to show that he is THE MAGICIAN; he had transformed her and himself by occult practice. The CHILD'S HAIR is BLACK to show that he is the product of his father and that he works by the same occult practices.

The COFFINS are the discarded limitation of their physical bodies, their three-dimensional knowing. The SEA upon which they float is the SEA OF COSMIC MENTAL ENERGY. It is Divine Understanding of the meaning, mechanics, and the goal of Life. It is rimmed around with the SNOWY PEAKS of Abstract Thought. This formless Thought is given us by the subjective mind, and to which the objective mind of the self-conscious gives a local habitation and a name.

Its first precursors were the Lilies THE MAGICIAN made to grow in his garden. These Peaks were the last thing THE FOOL left behind him in his descent into matter. They have now once again become as continuous as then. Man, though ever assisted by the twin agents of the Spirit (the Higher Self and the Holy Ghost), has, by his own efforts, grown into all this understanding of the eternal principles upon which the Universe is founded.

The INNER PART of the coffins is BLACK to suggest not only that he bursts forth from a state of comparative ignorance (advanced in development as he was), but that he has done so by his own occult practices. Man, the image-maker, first transformed himself by his own images, body, and mind. Now in the next card you will see man the measurer, transforming external nature after transforming his internal nature. Man need have no humility even though he sees the truth about his position in the scale of created things. He is but the transformer, it is true, the mathematical point where the superconscious contacts the subconscious.

How colossal is the work which we and we alone can accomplish! Thomas Carlyle once said that "we are in very deed ghosts, but what ghosts we are! We take to ourselves the form of a body and on heaven's mission appear, we expend our forces and fire to reveal the Divine essence in the flesh. Thus, like a God-created, fire-breathing spirit-host does this mysterious mankind thunder and flame in long-drawn, quick-succeeding grandeur through the unknown Deep, but earth's mountains are levelled and her seas filled up in our passage. Can the earth which is but dead and a vision resist spirits which have reality and are alive? On the hardest adamant some footprints of us is stamped in; the last rear of the host will read traces of the earliest man. But whence? Whither? Sense knows not. Faith knows not. Only that it is through mystery to mystery, from God to God."

Carlyle was of course writing from the Christian background. The occultist knows that the Earth is not dead but just as alive as, and no more a vision than, we ourselves are. The Earth with all its teeming mineral, plant, and animal life is just our "little brother" whom we must bring up.

The Tarot cards tell us the secret of how to do it. BY ATTAINING EQUILIBRIUM. There are 56 cards, four times 14, the hidden value of THE EMPEROR, the foster father of the Christ-Child, which is equilibrium itself. These 56 cards reduce to 11, which is the card JUSTICE, or equilibrium. There are 22 trumps, which reduce to 4, which is the number of Reason in the cards and of Daleth in the letters. The suit cards and the trump cards added together make 78, which reduces to 15, which reduces to 6, and card number 6 is THE LOVERS, the perfect equilibrium between the self-conscious Reason and the subconscious Imagination. To the same number 6 reduces the three 14's that go to make up the Christ-Child at birth.

In the Aquarian Age mankind, as a race, will begin to become Fourth-Dimensionally conscious. This resurrection must also be preceded by a crucifixion. The sign of the Aquarian Age is not by chance the same as the alchemic sign of dissolution. The fringe of Fourth-Dimensional consciousness is even now sweeping over the face of the Earth in the unrest and violence, which are destroying in order to build a new race consciousness.

THE WORLD.

22nd Hebrew Letter	*TAU*
Symbol for	*Pair of Opposites—* *(Dominion or* *Slavery)*
Color	*Indigo*
Numerical Value	*400*
Syllables	*ThU*
Sound	*A-Natural*
Planet	*Saturn*
Translation	*Cross or Signature*

NOTES

THE WORLD

ת TAU is the 22nd Hebrew letter and the seventh DOUBLE LET-TER; spelled in Hebrew ThV. It means CROSS or SIGNA-TURE and is the sign or symbol for the pair of opposites DOMINION or SLAVERY; for the direction WITHIN or CENTER; for the ADMINISTRATIVE INTELLIGENCE; for the planet SATURN; for the color BLUE-VIOLET; for the note A-NATURAL. In Roman characters it is written Th, and the numerical value is 400.

The character for TAU is a combination of the letter RESH with YOD. Its secret value is 210, which is the sum of the numbers from zero to twenty. The secret value of this letter means the full manifestation of the powers of KAPH; hence, the many points of resemblance between the two cards. The full power of the body is the ability to administer Nature. This is the climax toward which the whole Wheel of bodies, or evolution, has been moving.

A physical plane body is the result of the downpouring of the Sun, or RESH. The Spiritual body is the result of the downpouring of the Spirit, or YOD; hence the character is composed of the two letters.

The two other cards with which this card has close affiliation and association are the THE HANGED MAN and THE CHARIOT. The pattern on which THE HANGED MAN's card is constructed is the Cross over the Water triangle, while the pattern on which THE WORLD is constructed is the Fire triangle over the Cross—the pattern is exactly reversed. Also the numbers of the two cards, 12 and 21, are the reverse of each other; 12 is THE HIGH PRIESTESS working through THE MAGICIAN, and 21 is THE MAGICIAN working through THE HIGH PRIESTESS. In THE HANGED MAN, THE HIGH PRIESTESS is giving a perception of the Cosmic forces; in THE WORLD, THE MAGICIAN is manipulating and administering the Cosmic forces in magical creation.

Why is the figure in THE WORLD not presented as a man, as the figure in the other card is? Because the Mind, or the Man, is only the agent or executive. The Administrative Power is really Nature herself, localized in you.

THE CHARIOT card, too, is composed on this pattern of the Fire triangle over the Cross. The Charioteer stands in a square which represents the perfected body, and the Cross is always supposed to be a square in the shape of its diameter. In these two cards the central figure is doing the same thing, performing magical creation. Why in the first card is it a man and in the second card a woman? Merely to represent the double reciprocal action of the two Life Principles you see illustrated on the Veil back of THE HIGH PRIESTESS—the masculine in the feminine and the feminine in the masculine. The Charioteer emphasizes the masculine in the feminine part of the coordination; the figure in THE WORLD emphasizes the feminine in the masculine part of the coordination.

This figure is not entirely that of a woman. She is androgynous (both sexes in one). If you will note the legs carefully you will see that they are the legs of a man. Also in THE CHARIOT you will see in the front part of it a symbol representing the two genders in one. The cards CHETH and TAU really mean the same thing—the superconscious is dictating all the actions of the mind and the body. The emphasis is first placed on the mind part, and the emphasis of the second is placed on the body part. The identity of the two cards is shown in the older version of THE CHARIOT card. That symbol, instead of being the symbol of the perfect interaction of the self-conscious and the subconscious, is the letter Tau, TV. When we studied CHETH we saw that it represented the masculine-feminine idea in its philosophical principle, Receptivity-Will. We saw that it represented the summation and the union of all the ideas of the previous cards from 1 to 6. The number 21 is the summation of all the numbers from 1 to 6; that is, 1 plus 2 plus 3 plus 4 plus 5 plus 6 equals 21. Thus TAU is like CHETH in that it is the summation of all that has gone before.

Twenty cards have gone before in the Tarot Tableau, and this is the 21st. The teaching of the Tarot concerns the self-conscious mind (which is masculine); the subconscious mind (which is feminine); and the superconscious mind (which is represented by both THE HIGH PRIESTESS and the Higher Self). There are seven cards devoted to each. The root of the self-conscious mind is THE MAGICIAN; the root of the subconscious mind is THE EMPRESS. THE MAGICIAN perfected, united with the Higher Self, and THE EMPRESS perfected, united with THE HIGH PRIESTESS, are the two aspects of the superconscious in us.

This card shows the culmination of the powers of THE EMPRESS in us. The number of the card designates this fact. Twenty-one is 7 x 3, or the power of THE EMPRESS manifested seven times by each of the interior stars working in their highest vibration. A description of the

Administrative Intelligence says that it directs all the activities of the seven planets, associates their activities, and guides them all in their proper course.

The Hebrew word for "administer" is NOBD. This is what the word means by the Tarot spelling—DEATH, DEVIL, MAGICIAN, and EMPRESS. In order to fit ourselves to take charge of the Cosmic energies and administer them, we must first kill off all the old cells that cannot take up the higher vibration and make new ones; and second, we must master our bodies and thus perceive the occult use of THE DEVIL. These are the two occult problems: (1) how to form the new body out of the ashes of the old one, and (2) how to use our bodies to forward the evolution of the world. The last two letters of the word NOBD indicate the means whereby we solve these two problems—by the work of THE MAGICIAN and work of THE EMPRESS. The work of THE MAGICIAN is twofold: he attends and he wills. He controls his body in accordance with his powers of attention, both external and internal. The work of THE EMPRESS is simply to develop the images of THE MAGICIAN. It is through her development of his new and better images achieved by more accurate attention that she makes, at last, the perfect body—a body in which the seven planets are all synchronized and working at their highest vibration.

The Administrative Intelligence directs the operation of all seven planets, but it is specifically concerned with Saturn. This means that Saturn governs them all. It governs them all because it is the seat of the Kundalini power, just as in the physical body the medulla oblongata governs all the organs of the body by increasing or diminishing their supply of blood. The Saturn Center, at the other end of the spine and in etheric matter, governs all the other centers by increasing or diminishing their supply of the vivifying Kundalini. The Kundalini power in our bodies is really the power by which the Universe was created and exists. When we control this power we can administer it outside our bodies in creative functions.

The pair of opposites attributed to TAU are DOMINION and SLAVERY. We have already studied how this pair of opposites works out when we studied AYIN, the color attributed to the two letters being the same, BLUE-VIOLET. When we read THE DEVIL card at the level of ignorance, we saw that the man was in bondage to all of his body. The desire to extract sensation from it controlled him. When we read THE DEVIL card at the level of occult perception and practice, we saw that the body became a very different thing; in fact it was his very means of magical creation in the external world. Read at this level, the natural body (the body under the enslavement of its instincts) became the Spiritual body, the body which is the vase of the inpouring Spirit.

This card, THE WORLD, is that body and it is also the body depicted in the card THE TOWER, when we turn it upside-down. That which was once our "stone of stumbling" becomes our stepping-stone to the dominion over all things which the Bible says is the goal of man. This fundamental idea of Tarot is repeated over and over again. *Control what now controls you, and you shall control all things. CONTROL OR BE CONTROLLED.* The card AYIN at its obvious level presents the second part of the alternative. The card TAU represents the first part.

So the original form of the body, the natural body, is illustrated in THE DEVIL card. The final form, the Spiritual body, is depicted in this card. In the first case you signed your name, being illiterate, with a cross. In the second case, you finally come to know how to write your real name, your real signature. The Bible says that the real name of MAN is the ANGEL, the one who has dominion and can soar. There is a word which is tragically misunderstood—the word *resignation*. It really expresses the same thing as the substitution of your actual name for the cross, the substitution for the unknown quality, the quality which you finally found it stood for all the while. The root meaning of the word "resignation" means a "re-signing"—to sign your name over again in the new and knowledgeable way. "Resignation," as we unfortunately use the word, in defiance of its valuable root meaning, signifies a passive acceptance of misfortune. "Too often," said Maeterlinck, "resignation is but a gesture of futility employed when all other gestures have failed, and the only thing we can retrieve from the wreck is to make a virtue of a necessity." To submit when you have found you cannot do anything else, to submit to your afflictions, is one thing— but to conquer THROUGH them is another. To conquer through them is to learn the message they bring you, and to build that message into your consciousness. To see that it could be learned in no other way is to understand that the affliction was really but a small price to pay for it.

To learn how to "re-sign" your name is the same thing as the alchemists meant when they said you must learn to understand the hidden nature of the Earth. The alchemic element "Earth" is not the material of the planet we live on, but rather our threefold body. The Liturgy uses the word in the same sense: "The Lord is in His holy Temple, let all our earth keep silence before Him."

The way of attainment is not to escape from the Earth but to learn to master the forces and forms of the physical plane. The Hebrew Wisdom taught that there are only three elements: Fire, Water, and Air. They taught that Earth is the synthesis and condensation of these three. This, then, tells the whole story. The Earth comprehends all there is in the manifested Universe if we learn to read it aright—to disentangle its secrets. The alchemic symbol for Earth shows that it is a mixture of Fire and Water, with Water predominating. "Earth," says Genesis, "was originally water, and the Spirit of God (or Fire) brooded over the water, which was without form and void, and thus it took shape and became peopled with living creatures." The condensing power, the limiting power, that which makes the void take shape, is symbolized by SATURN.

Thus you have Earth as the condensed form of Fire, Water, and Air, and Saturn the power which condenses them. There are four Earth cards and four Saturn cards in the Tarot. Each sequence tells the same story. At first you see the Earth and Saturn wrongly, and they conquer and use you. In the end you see them correctly, and you conquer and utilize them. In the former case it is slavery; in the latter, dominion—each sequence tells the means of conquest in some detail. They can all be summed up in two words: thought control. Thought control is the difference between dominion and slavery. Only man himself can accomplish the transformation of his Earth. Man himself can transcend his limitations only by learning how to use them correctly. The whole process of attaining the Cosmic Consciousness and cooperating with the administration of the Universe stems back to THE MAGICIAN, the image-maker.

The Saturn cards are 11, 15, 17, 21. They sum up to 64, which reduces to 10, which reduces to 1, THE MAGICIAN.

The Earth cards are 5, 9, 15, 21, which sum up to 50. Fifty is the number of NUN, or the willed destruction of unwanted things in the body. The meaning is inescapable. Man, the image-maker, ascends from SLAVERY to DOMINION, signs his real name instead of the cross, and learns how to utilize Earth and Saturn instead of being their victim, all by the simple concrete process of refusing to indulge in what St. Paul calls "filthy imaginings," and thinking on whatsoever things are good. A task that is simple enough to be within the range of the simplest, and difficult enough to tax the vigilance and patience of the strongest and wisest. "He that controlleth his spirit," says the

Bible, "is fit to sit down with kings." Spirit here means the spirit that is in his Earth, in his body, or the personality that Saturn has imposed upon him.

The teachings of the four Earth cards repeat over and over again the teachings of THE HIEROPHANT and THE HERMIT: that a High Being has implanted the Earth of the physical body with an urge to liberate itself and ascend to its Source. In card 21, the Saturn vibration shows the goal you will reach if you follow that urge of joyous and creative freedom, under obedience to Cosmic Law, as illustrated by the dancing figure with the two wands.

At first thought it may seem that a person who is dancing is not hemmed in—that he is entirely following his whims. But dancing exhibits control in a far more complex way than walking or running, for in dancing you follow a more intricate pattern of steps. Where there is no pattern there is no dance, only uncoordinated movements. In the same way it is only by obedience to the correct perception of the Laws of Nature that we are enabled to control Nature.

The practical teaching of the four cards of the Saturn sequence is summed up in its first card, LIBRA. Saturn comes to its highest expression in Libra. The figure of JUSTICE is wielding the SWORD and the SCALES. The Sword is grasped in her right hand. This means that cutting away is her chief business, and for everything that she cuts away she must achieve a new equilibrium. The letter-name ALEPH tells us that the FIERY LIFE-BREATH is forever using the Mars vibration, achieving and maintaining equilibrium by destroying those things which have outlived their usefulness. In the same way with the subconscious of the person who is trying to achieve and maintain self-conscious poise and balance: he does it by eliminating bad images; she follows his lead by eliminating the structure of error, or bad images in the body. Jesus and Paul reiterated constantly that you must be born again to enter the kingdom of heaven. Unfortunately the Church confines this to the objective effort—that you must think, feel, and behave in another fashion. The occultist, however, says that Jesus and Paul meant the statement for the subconscious also. The whole body must be born again. It is born again through the work of THE EMPRESS, in cutting away old cells in the body that refuse to change their rhythms in accordance with new vision and new rhythms of the self-conscious. The alchemist says that dissolution is the secret of the Great Work, and dissolution refers to the destruction that comes of wielding the Sword. We have already seen this in the Hebrew word for "administer,"

NOBD. The first step in preparing ourselves to create magically, or to administer Nature, is to kill off our old cells and make new ones.

The meaning of the letter-name TAU is the full manifestation of the powers of 20, or the powers of KAPH, which enumerate 20. In the card THE WHEEL are seen the four animals in the corners: the Lion, the Eagle, the Angel, and the Bull. They are called the "four fixed signs of the Zodiac." All are Yellow, and they are all reading from a White Book. They illustrate the action of the Yellow background in the zero card, THE FOOL, which emanates from the White of Spiritual Sun. These four animals studying the instructions of the Spirit are depicted on White Clouds upon a background of Blue. The same four animals are also in the corners of the 21st card—they are no longer studying from the White Books, and they themselves are somewhat different.

The Angel and the Eagle are colored ORANGE and YELLOW, the bull is YELLOW striped with RED, and the Lion is ORANGE. What do all these changes mean? Card 21 presents the perfected body, while card 10 presents our body of manifestation at its present stage of evolution. If we wish to advance our stage of evolution and get a better body, we must try to contact the Spirit with our minds. Note that where Yellow occurs in the Angel, the Eagle, and the Bull in card 21, it is pale Yellow, the Yellow of the Higher Self. It is not the Yellow of THE MAGICIAN, as it is in THE WHEEL OF FORTUNE card. We no longer need to ascend to the Spirit—its agent in the person of the Higher Self has come down to us.

The color of the Bull means that the body is now reconstructed according to the desires of the Higher Self. The orange beak of the Eagle means that the mind dictates the use of the Stellar sex power itself. It is the same Lion whom you saw in card 8 licking the hand of the purified EMPRESS, and he is now placing himself at her disposal. The card THE WORLD presents the last body in the long series of bodies whose making is depicted in THE WHEEL OF FORTUNE. The jackal-headed man has at last arrived at the full use of his mind.

TAU is the final letter of the Hebrew alphabet, and as such represents completeness, the end of manifestation. The letter-name is spelled ThV; and V in Hebrew is not only a letter but is also the conjunction "and." Thus you are told that there is no end. What is depicted by the card is but the end of a cycle, and that evolution itself is not limited by the goal of this solar system.

The idea we receive from the Christian religion, whether justly or not, is of a static heaven where things have reached a state of perfection, remaining so forever and ever. *"Thine be the kingdom and the power and the glory forever and ever."* The Hebrew Wisdom taught a continuous evolution, a continuous unfolding. Just as the musical octave ends only to begin another octave on a higher spiral, so that state of perfection represented by the last letter of the Hebrew alphabet is only the end of one phase of endless life, which forms the beginning of a higher plane.

We are told that the next phase after the human evolution is the superhuman evolution. What the latter means we cannot conjecture; the mind cannot grasp its scope. The problem of human evolution is twofold: to cultivate the mind to its utmost potency, and to use it only in the service of the Spirit. The Jekyll and Hyde story is a great allegory of the animal in man slipping from the control of the mind and finally destroying both body and mind. When we have conquered instinct we find we have another enemy to conquer—the mind itself. We use the very means by which we conquered the first enemy. The Frankenstein story is the great allegory of our second enemy. It pictures the mind man has made and finds unable to control.

The only way to control the mind is through the transformed Heart. The animal in us toilfully creates the mind and at last emerges and takes control. Then the mind in us toilfully creates the Transformed Heart, and in the end it must emerge and take control of the mind. At any point in this long process either the animal or the mind may lose control. Then our work is for the moment undone. We must pause in our work to readjust our mistake and the results of it before we can resume it. When we have finished the process of perfecting ourselves and the matter which composes our bodies, we then set about the task that was assigned to us from the beginning of this solar system: to help Nature perfect all the other matter in this planet. This much we know. After that, on a higher octave, who knows?

SYMBOLISM

The entire BACKGROUND of this card is the Cosmic Mind-Stuff in which the Dancer dances, and which the Dancer helps to manipulate. She manipulates it by the use of her two wands. Each wand is DOUBLE-HEADED. The wand of the Charioteer has only one head and represents the fact that the Solar Force is incomplete until supplemented by the Lunar Force. You are told the same by the allegory of Jesus and the Devil in the wilderness. Having refused to succumb to the temptations of the Devil, Jesus therefore had power over him and commanded him to "get behind" and thus back him up—that is, to unite his force to that of the Spiritual force in order to manipulate the Cosmic Mind-Stuff, or to create magically.

The WAND in the Dancer's RIGHT HAND represents the masculine in the feminine. The WAND in the LEFT HAND represents the feminine in the masculine. This reciprocal interchange of power is depicted by the fruits and leaves on the Veil of THE HIGH PRIESTESS; by the horizontal figure 8 over the head of THE MAGICIAN and the transformed EMPRESS; and by the symbol of Aquarius, the perfected man. The two wavy lines say the Above is like that Below, and the Below is the Above.

The WREATH surrounding this figure is made like an ellipse or zero, the no-thing, which THE FOOL represents. The Wreath is composed of FOUR ROWS OF GREEN LEAVES, the Creative Imagination working in the four planes. These leaves are held together by the Mars vibration, which is the activity of sex and gender; and its form being two 8's, it repeats the idea of the Dancer's two wands, of the two 8's which hover over the heads of THE MAGICIAN and the transformed EMPRESS in cards 1 and 8.

The Dancer's being enclosed in this Wreath symbolizes that there is nothing to limit the free action of the Dancer except the Laws of Nature and the Will of the Higher Self. ALL MAGICIAL CREATION MUST BE OBEDIENT TO THE LAWS OF NATURE. There is nothing supernatural—the so-called miracle only utilizes the Laws of Nature on a higher spiral. The principle of this is one which man is already familiar with and has utilized for himself. Iron and steel will not float, but man can make it float by hollowing it out and utilizing the specific gravity of the air thus enclosed.

Man cannot go contrary to the Laws of Nature but must work with and by means of them, on a lower or higher scale. He can go contrary to the Will of the Higher Self, and this is what the black magician does. The Higher Self allows man to choose, and gives man the rope of his personal will, by which man eventually hangs himself. Even though a man has achieved the equilibrium of the body, permitting him to create magically by means of it, he is as much entitled to his choice to go wrong as the ordinary man who only yields to his animal instincts, or a more evolved man who yields to his ruthless ambitions. Sooner or later all must reckon with the Higher Self, and all must pay the Karma of their acts. The only difference between the black and the white magician is that the white magician never makes magic except in obedience to some higher authority.

The Dancer has YELLOW HAIR to identify her with THE EMPRESS, and the RED FILLET running through it symbolizes the mind and mental plane made active. The SCARF around the figure is VIOLET, the color of KAPH. The FRINGE on the top of the scarf forms the letters of the Hebrew word which in English means "Judah." Judah refers to the Transformed Heart. The Lion of the Tribe of Judah is the lion in the lower corner. The word seems to be written on top, to show that the Transformed Heart takes the place of the head. This idea has already been given to you in the letter RESH, where the letter standing for the equilibrated heart means the head. It is given to you again in this dancing figure.

To the careless observer this seems a wholly feminine figure; but the close observer will see that the lower part of it is as masculine as the upper part is feminine. The idea of the androgyne cannot, of course, be satisfactorily expressed as a picture. The Renaissance painters tried to express it by their fragile, effeminate Christs, but it does not seem that they were at all successful; indeed they were worse than unsuccessful, for they gave the wrong impression of the Christ, making him weak and insipid. This picture tries to symbolize that superconsciousness, as brought into the body of THE EMPRESS, is now directive power, and the self-consciousness is motor power. She directs and he executes.

The "superiors" are the masculine and the feminine principles as exhibited in the higher mental world—that part of the Higher Self and the Cosmic Mind which in us inhabit the awakened Pineal and Pituitary. The "inferiors" are the intellect and the intellectual subconscious. These latter two are both of the personality, yet they are the most rarefied part of our Earth (the body), which is the real Earth in symbolism.

The Transformed Heart is called THE HOLY CITY in chapter 21 of the Book of Revelations, and this card is number 21. "And I saw the Holy City, the new Jerusalem, coming down from God out of heaven, prepared as a bride adorned for her husband. And I heard a great voice out of heaven saying, 'Behold the tabernacle of God is with men, and He will dwell with them, and they shall be His People, and God Himself shall be with them.' "

The figure in this card represents both the husband and the bride. The husband is THE EMPEROR who rules (as that card tells you) through his wife and his child, the intellectual subconscious and the Transformed Heart.

The direction of this card is "no-direction"—CENTER, or THE WITHIN. In the previous card we had, as far as the human being is concerned, the Fourth Dimension. In this card we have the Fifth Dimension, which stands for the point in the middle of the symbol of the Sun. It is the Sun which makes our space and time relations. THE POINT IS ABOVE AND BEYOND ALL RELATIONS OF TIME AND SPACE. EVERYTHING IS "NOW" AND EVERYWHERE IS "HERE."

This is the meaning of the Greek myth in which Saturn kept giving birth to children and then eating them up. The perfected people who possess the type of consciousness that goes with this card are sometimes called "The Lords of the Secret of Saturn." They understand concretely what this myth of Saturn devouring his children means. The Fourth Dimension is ushered into human understanding (as we saw in the previous card) by the Angel trumpeting a sevenfold sound. The sevenfold sound may be called the Word of the Logos of the solar system. The sound which ushers in the Fifth Dimension is said to be uttered by the logos of the previous solar system, Sirius. It is called in occultism *the soundless sound.* The myth of Saturn devouring his children signifies the merging of the subjective and objective modes of consciousness into that higher consciousness where subject and object are one.

The old geometrical expression "squaring the circle" expressed the same idea. The square occultly considered represents the structure made by the two forms of human consciousness, the diameter of which makes the cross. The circle occultly considered represents the superconscious. To square the circle means to bring down the superconscious by the understanding of a human being, limited by his body—that is, into the understanding of the personality. Squaring the circle thus indicates the highest reach of the human mind.

The occultist says that man can become superhuman, and thus to square the circle for the superhuman mind portrays a goal far beyond this. It is what happens when the mind, made superhuman, contacts the previous solar system of Sirius. Just as there are other and greater solar systems behind Sirius, so there are other dimensions of consciousness beyond the fifth. "The human mind," said St. Theresa, "is infinitely perfectible."

This you are told by that most wonderful of all alphabets, the Hebrew alphabet. It contains all for those who learn its meaning, for all who meditate and see beyond the printed form into the life of the letters. TAU is the final letter, and as such represents completeness, the end of manifestation. The letter-name is spelled ThV, and V in Hebrew is not only a letter but also the conjunction *and*. Thus you are told that there is no end, that man may climb from perfection to perfection.

The Tarot cards are the means for climbing from this perfection to perfection. Impersonate each card as you study the card. Veils upon veils will be lifted, until you see with clear Divine Vision the ONE you truly are—and seeing the One, you see and know the ALL. That One is the ANCIENT OF ALL ANCIENTS—beyond time, beyond space, beyond *human* comprehension.

KEYS TO THE KINGDOM

O brave Fool, come ye down from the Golden Plane,
and find what our Father has sent us for.

O Magician, transform us and this world
with our Father's White Light.

O High Priestess, wash us clean
in the Virgin Sea of thy Substance.

O Empress, bring forth from thy womb
the Perfect Christ-Child in us all.

O Emperor, tear down with thy Reason
the Babel towers of our mistakes.

O Hierophant, teach us thy Perfect Balance,
tdhat we migdht not stumble on our journey Home.

O Lovers, bring forth within us
the Love which can never die.

O Chariot, speed us forth into battle,
that we might conquer only ourselves.

O Strength, roar now in our hearts
as you have roared in our bodies.

O Hermit, guide us with thy lantern bright
unto our own Eternal Light.

O Wheel fo Fortune, turn faster in us,
that our circles might be accomplished.

O Justice, cut down our enemies within us,
that we might regain our Balance.

381

O Hanged Man, suspend our selfishness from the Cross of Salvation,
that our wills might never obstruct God's Will.

O Death, destroy all that is unlike the Father in us,
that we might witness the Dawn of Eternal Life.

O Temperance, with our fire and water temper us,
that our vessels might hold the Holy Spirit.

O Devil, teach us through pain and suffering,
when pleasure and fortune lead us astray.

O Tower, topple us from the fabled heights of our folly,
until we build in ourselves the Lord's Tower.

O Star, expand within our hearts,
as we bathe ourselves in the Spirit.

O Moon, reflect in us the Mind of God,
until we reflect His Grand Design.

O Sun, fill us with the Will of God,
until we fill the world with His Light.

O Judgement, awaken us with thy Clarion Call,
that we might arise from all that is dead within us.

O World, thank you for the dark embrace of thy fertil soil,
which brings forth the Christ-Blossom
from the God-Seed in our hearts.

—Todd Steiner

INDEX

STAY IN TOUCH

On the following pages you will find listed, with their current prices, some of the books now available on related subjects. Your book dealer stocks most of these, and will stock new titles in the Llewellyn series as they become available. We urge your patronage.

However, to obtain our full catalog, to keep informed of new titles as they are released and to benefit from informative articles and helpful news, you are invited to write for our bi-monthly news magazine/catalog. A sample copy is free, and it will continue coming to you at no cost as long as you are an active mail customer. Or you may keep it coming for a full year with a donation of just $5.00 in U.S.A. & Canada ($20.00 overseas, first class mail). Many bookstores also have *The Llewellyn New Times* available to their customers. Ask for it.

Stay in touch! In *The Llewellyn New Times'* pages you will find news and reviews of new books, tapes and services, announcements of meetings and seminars, articles helpful to our readers, news of authors, advertising of products and services, special money-making opportunities, and much more.

The Llewellyn New Times
P.O. Box 64383-Dept. 572, St. Paul, MN 55164-0383, U.S.A.
• • •

TO ORDER BOOKS AND TAPES

If your book dealer does not have the books described on the following pages readily available, you may order them direct from the publisher by sending full price in U.S. funds, plus $1.50 for postage and handling for orders *under* $10.00; $3.00 for orders *over* $10.00. There are no postage and handling charges for orders over $50. UPS Delivery: We ship UPS whenever possible. Delivery guaranteed. Provide your street address as UPS does not deliver to P.O. Boxes. UPS to Canada requires a $50 minimum order. Allow 4–6 weeks for delivery. Orders outside the U.S.A. and Canada: Airmail—add retail price of book; add $5 for each non-book item (tapes, etc.); add $1 per item for surface mail.

FOR GROUP STUDY AND PURCHASE

Because there is a great deal of interest in group discussion and study of the subject matter of this book, we feel that we should encourage the adoption and use of this particular book by such groups by offering a special "quantity" price to group leaders or "agents."

Our Special Quantity Price for a minimum order of five copies of *The Rabbi's Tarot* is $38.85 cash-with-order. This price includes postage and handling within the United States. Minnesota residents must add 6.5% sales tax. For additional quantities, please order in multiples of five. For Canadian and foreign orders, add postage and handling charges as above. Credit card (VISA, Master Card, American Express) orders are accepted. Charge card orders only may be phoned free ($15.00 minimum order) within the U.S.A. or Canada by dialing 1-800-THE-MOON. Customer service calls dial 1-612-291-1970. Mail Orders to:

LLEWELLYN PUBLICATIONS
P.O. Box 64383-Dept. 572, St. Paul, MN 55164-0383, U.S.A.

Prices subject to change without notice.

GROWING THE TREE WITHIN:
Patterns of the Unconscious Revealed by the Qabalah
by William Gray

The Qabalah, or Tree of Life, has been the basic genetic pattern of Western esotericism, and it shows us mortals how to make our climb steadily back to Heaven. When we study the Qabalah, open ourselves to it and work with it as an Inner Activity, we gain wisdom that will illuminate our individual paths to perfection. Qabalah means "getting wise" in the broadest possible sense.

Formerly titled *The Talking Tree*, this book presents an exhaustive and systematic analysis of the 22 Paths of the Tree of Life. It includes a detailed and comprehensive study of the symbolism of the Tarot cards in which author William Gray presents a viable yet unorthodox method of allocating the Major Arcana to the Paths. Of particular interest is his attempt at reaching a better understanding of the nature of the English alphabet and its correspondence to the Tree of Life.

Gray contends that the "traditional" Tree is a living spirit that needs to be in a continual state of evolution and improvement. It is the duty of all those who love and work with it to cultivate and develop it with every care. This includes both pruning off dead wood and training new growth in the right directions for future fruiting. *Growing the Tree Within* does precisely that.

0-87542-268-3, 468 pgs., 6 x 9, illus., softcover $14.95

ARCHETYPES ON THE TREE OF LIFE
The Tarot as Pathwork
by Madonna Compton

The "Tree" is the Kabbalistic Tree of Life, the ageless mystical map to the secrets of the Universe. By working with its 10 circular paths and 22 linear ones, you can find answers to life's most profound questions. By mapping archetypes on the Tree, you can trace mythological and religious themes as well as those symbols that stir the psyche on deep inner levels. It can help you bring out your latent powers and develop your full potential.

Archetypes on the Tree of Life symbolically examines the meanings and uses of the 22 paths based upon their correspondences with the Tarot trumps and Hebrew letters. The first half of the book is a scholarly approach to deciphering the archetypal symbols behind the etiology of the Hebrew letters, names and numbers. The second half is designed to enhance creativity and intuition through meditations and exercises that bring the material alive in the reader's subconscious.

Along the way, you will investigate the mystical and allegorical interpretations of the Old and New Testaments and compare these and other mythologies worldwide to the Tarot archetypes.

0-87542-104-0, 336 pgs., 6 x 9, illus., softcover $12.95

ARCHETYPES OF THE ZODIAC
by Kathleen Burt

The horoscope is probably the most unique tool for personal growth you can ever have. This book is intended to help you understand how the energies within your horoscope manifest. Once you are aware of how your chart operates on an instinctual level, you can then work consciously with it to remove any obstacles to your growth.

The technique offered in this book is based upon the incorporation of the esoteric rulers of the signs and the integration of their polar opposites. This technique has been very successful in helping the client or reader modify existing negative energies in a horoscope so as to improve the quality of his or her life and the understanding of his or her psyche.

There is special focus in this huge comprehensive volume on the myths for each sign. Some signs may have as many as four different myths coming from all parts of the world. All are discussed by the author. There is also emphasis on the Jungian Archetypes involved with each sign.

This book has a depth often surprising to the readers of popular astrology books. It has a clarity of expression seldom found in books of the esoteric tradition. It is very easy to understand, even if you know nothing of Jungian philosophy or of mythology. It is intriguing, exciting and very helpful for all levels of astrologers.

0-87542-088-5, 576 pgs., 6 x 9, illus., softcover **$14.95**

GODWIN'S CABALISTIC ENCYCLOPEDIA
A Complete Guide to Cabalistic Magick
by David Godwin

This is the most complete correlation of Hebrew and English ideas ever offered. It is a dictionary of Cabalism arranged, with definitions, alphabetically in Hebrew and numerically. With this book, the practicing Cabalist or student no longer needs access to a large number of books on mysticism, magic and the occult in order to trace down the basic meanings, Hebrew spellings, and enumerations of the hundreds of terms, words, and names that are included in this book.

This book includes: all of the two-letter root words found in Biblical Hebrew, the many names of God, the Planets, the Astrological Signs, Numerous Angels, the Shem ha-Mephorash, the Spirits of the *Goetia*, the correspondences of the 32 Paths, a comparison of the Tarot and the Cabala, a guide to Hebrew Pronunciation, and a complete edition of Aleister Crowley's valuable book *Sepher Sephiroth*.

Here is a book that is a must for the shelf of all Magicians, Cabalists, Astrologers, Tarot students, Thelemites, and those with any interest at all in the spiritual aspects of our universe.

0-87542-292-6, 528 pgs., 6 x 9, softcover **$15.00**

THE ENOCHIAN TAROT
by Gerald and Betty Schueler

The popular deck of cards known as the Tarot has been used for many centuries for divination, fortunetelling and self-initiation through meditation. The Enochian Tarot, an 86-card deck, is the first to utilize the mystery and magical power inherent in Enochian Magic.

The Enochian Tarot explains in detail the meaningful correspondences behind the structure of this deck. It discusses, for example, the difference between the 22 Paths on the Qabalistic Tree of Life, on which traditional Tarot decks are based, and the 30 Aethyrs of Enochian Magick (the Enochian deck has 8 extra cards because there are 8 more Aethyrs than Paths). The book also includes tables and figures for easy comprehension of an otherwise difficult subject, as well as tips for reading the cards for fun or profit.

The unique system of Enochian Magick was revealed to John Dee, court astrologer to Queen Elizabeth I of England, and his partner Edward Kelly by the Enochian Angels who inhabit the Watchtowers and Aethyrs of the subtle regions of the universe. The authors are foremost authorities on this subject and have published a number of books that have made a fascinating magical system accessible to a wide audience.

0-87542-709-X, 352 pgs., 5-1/4 x 8, illus., softcover **$12.95**

THE ENOCHIAN TAROT DECK
Created by Gerald and Betty Schueler
Painted by Sallie Ann Glassman

The Enochian Tarot is a deck of cards which is primarily used to foretell the future. Forecasting the future, however, is only a superficial use of the massive powers of the Enochian Tarot. Here is a powerful tool which allows you to look deep inside your subconscious and "see" the direction your life is taking. The Enochian Tarot is an easy-to-use system of self-discovery which allows you to see your relationship to God and the universe.

The Tarot is your map of life. With it you can choose the road you want to wander. Instead of being an uninformed victim of your subconscious will, you can gather your inner strength and consciously change the path your life is to take. The Tarot is your key to self-determination, and with that key you can open any door.

The Enochian Tarot Deck consists of 86 cards which are divided into 2 main sections: a Major Arcana and a Minor Arcana. The Major Arcana is a set of 30 picture cards which are also called The Greater Arcana, Trumps, Atouts, or Triumphs. These cards are symbolic representations of various cosmic forces such as Doubt, Intuition, Glory, etc. The Minor Arcana contains 56 cards which represent the Four Enochian Watchtowers. The Minor Arcana is divided into 4 "suits" called Earth, Water, Air, and Fire.

0-87542-708-1, boxed set: 86 cards with booklet **$12.95**

THE NEW GOLDEN DAWN RITUAL TAROT
Keys to the Rituals, Symbolism, Magic & Divination
by Chic Cicero & Sandra Tabatha Cicero

This is the indispensable companion to Llewellyn's New Golden Dawn Ritual Tarot Deck. It provides a card-by-card analysis of the deck's intricate symbolism, an introduction to the Qabalah, and a section on the use of the deck for practical rituals, meditations and divination procedures. The Tarot newcomer as well as the advanced magician will benefit from this groundbreaking work.

The highlight of the book is the section on rituals. Instructions are included for: ritual baths, Lesser Banishing Ritual of the Pentagram, Tarot deck consecration ritual, using the Tarot for talismans, scrying with the Tarot, dream work with the Tarot, the Golden Dawn method of Tarot divination, and much, much more.

The Golden Dawn is experiencing a widespread revival among New Agers, Wiccans, mystics and ceremonial magicians. This book and companion deck are just what people are looking for: traditional Golden Dawn knowledge with new rituals written by authors with "magickal credentials."
0-87542-139-3, 256 pgs., 6 x 9, illus.   **$12.95**

THE NEW GOLDEN DAWN RITUAL TAROT DECK
by Sandra Tabatha Cicero

The original Tarot deck of the Hermetic Order of the Golden Dawn has been copied and interpreted many times. While each deck has its own special flair, The New Golden Dawn Ritual Tarot Deck may well be the most important new Tarot deck for the 1990s and beyond.

From its inception 100 years ago, the Golden Dawn continues to be the authority on the initiatory and meditative teachings of the Tarot. The Golden Dawn used certain cards in their initiation rituals. Now, for the first time ever, a deck incorporates not only the traditional Tarot images but also all of the temple symbolism needed for use in the Golden Dawn rituals. This is the first deck that is perfect both for divination and for ritual work. Meditation on the Major Arcana cards can lead to a lightning flash of enlightenment and spiritual understanding in the Western magickal tradition. The New Golden Dawn Ritual Tarot Deck was encouraged by the late Israel Regardie, and it is for anyone who wants a reliable Tarot deck that follows the Western magickal tradition.
0-87542-138-5, boxed set: 79-card deck with booklet   **$19.95**

THE LLEWELLYN PRACTICAL GUIDE TO
THE MAGICK OF THE TAROT
by Denning & Phillips

"To gain understanding, and control, of Your Life"—Can anything be more important? To gain insight into the circumstances of your life–the inner causes, the karmic needs, the hidden factors at work—and then to have the power to change your life in order to fulfill your real desires and True Will: that's what the techniques taught in this book can do.

Discover the Shadows cast ahead by Coming Events. Yes, this is possible, because it is your DEEP MIND—that part of your psyche, normally beyond your conscious awareness, which is in touch with the World Soul and with your own Higher (and Divine) Self—that perceives the astral shadows of coming events and can communicate them to you through the symbols and images of the cards.
0-87542-198-9, 252 pgs., 5-1/4 x 8, illus., softcover   **$8.95**

THE WITCHES TAROT
The Witches Qabala, Book II
by Ellen Cannon Reed

In this book Ellen Cannon Reed has further defined the complex, inner workings of the Qabalistic Tree of Life. She brings together the Major and Minor Arcana cards with the Tree of Life to provide readers with a unique insight on the meaning of the Paths on the Tree. Included is a complete section on divination with the Tarot cards, with several layout patterns and explanations clearly presented.

The Major Arcana cards are also keys to Pathworking astral journeys through the Tree of Life. Reed explains Pathworking and gives several examples. An appendix gives a list of correspondences for each of the Paths including the associated Tarot card, Hebrew letter, colors, astrological attribution, animal, gem, and suggested meditation. This book is a valuable addition to the literature of the Tarot and the Qabala.

0-87542-668-9, 320 pgs., 5-1/4 x 8, illus., softcover **$9.95**

THE WITCHES TAROT DECK
by Ellen Cannon Reed and Martin Cannon

Author Ellen Cannon Reed has created the first Tarot deck specifically for Pagans and Wiccans. Reed, herself a Wiccan High Priestess, developed The Witches Tarot as a way to teach the truths of the Hebrew Kabbalah from a clear and distinctly Pagan point of view. Changes include a Horned One in place of the traditional Devil, a High Priest in place of the old Hierophant, and a Seeker in place of the Hermit. Comes complete with an instruction booklet that tells you what the cards mean and explains how to use the "Celtic Cross" and "Four Seasons" layouts. The gorgeous, detailed paintings by Martin Cannon make this a true combination of new beauty and ancient symbolism. Even many non-pagans have reported excellent results with the cards and appreciate their colorful and timeless beauty.

0-87542-669-7, Boxed set: 78 full-color cards with booklet **$17.95**

THE WHEEL OF DESTINY
The Tarot Reveals Your Master Plan
by Patricia McLaine

Here is an irresistible new tool for self knowledge found nowhere else. *The Wheel of Destiny* delves into the "Master Plan Reading" of the Tarot's Major Arcana and provides detailed information about the individual, much like a reading of an astrological birth chart.

The book explains how to lay out the 22 cards and delineates the meaning of each card in whatever position it falls. The reading provides deep and specific information on divine purpose; strengths and weaknesses; talents; past lives; karmic patterns; relationships; physical, emotional, and spiritual development; and much more.

All the reader needs is this book and a Tarot deck. No previous knowledge of the Tarot is required, yet serious students of the Tarot will find many new truths and profound perspectives. The Master Plan Reading has been field tested by the author on clients the world over, ranging from the person next door to celebrities like Peter Sellers and Susan Strasberg.

0-87542-490-2, 480 pgs., 7 x 10, illus., softcover **$17.95**

TAROT SPELLS
by Janina Renee

This book provides a means of recognizing and affirming one's own personal power through use of the Tarot. With the practical advice and beautiful illustrations in this book, the reader can perform spells for: Influencing dreams, Better health, Legal matters, Better family relations, Beating addiction, Finding a job, Better gardening and more. Thirty-five areas of life are discussed, and spells are provided which address specific issues in these areas.

The reader uses Tarot layouts in combination with affirmations and visualizations to obtain a desired result. Many spells can be used with color, gemstones or magical tools to assist the reader in focusing his or her desire.

Graced with beautiful card illustrations from the Robin Wood Tarot, this book can be used immediately even by those who don't own a Tarot deck. No previous experience with the Tarot is necessary. Those familiar with the Tarot can gain new insights into the symbolism of their own particular deck.

0-87542-670-0, 288 pgs., 6 x 9, illus., softcover   **$12.95**

ROBIN WOOD TAROT DECK
created and illustrated by Robin Wood
Instructions by Robin Wood and Michael Short

Tap into the wisdom of your subconscious with one of the most beautiful Tarot decks on the market today! Reminiscent of the Rider-Waite deck, the Robin Wood Tarot is flavored with nature imagery and luminous energies that will enchant you and the querant. Even the novice reader will find these cards easy and enjoyable to interpret.

Radiant and rich, these cards were illustrated with a unique technique that brings out the resplendent color of the prismacolor pencils. The shining strength of this Tarot deck lies in its depiction of the Minor Arcana. Unlike other Minor Arcana decks, this one springs to pulsating life. The cards are printed in quality card stock and boxed complete with instruction booklet, which provides the upright and reversed meanings of each card, as well as three basic card layouts. Beautiful and brilliant, the Robin Wood Tarot is a must-have deck!

0-87542-894-0, boxed set: 78 cards with booklet   **$19.95**

MODERN MAGICK
Eleven Lessons in the High Magickal Arts
by Donald Michael Kraig

Modern Magick is the most comprehensive step-by-step introduction to the art of ceremonial magic ever offered. The eleven lessons in this book will guide you from the easiest of rituals and the construction of your magickal tools through the highest forms of magick: designing your own rituals and doing pathworking. Along the way you will learn the secrets of the Kabbalah in a clear and easy-to-understand manner. You will discover the true secrets of invocation (channeling) and evocation, and the missing information that will finally make the ancient grimoires, such as the "Keys of Solomon," not only comprehensible, but usable. This book also contains one of the most in-depth chapters on sex magick ever written. *Modern Magick* is designed so anyone can use it, and it is the perfect guidebook for students and classes. It will also help to round out the knowledge of long-time practitioners of the magickal arts.

0-87542-324-8, 592 pgs., 6 x 9, illus., index, softcover   **$14.95**